Research Methods in Psychology
Ideas, Techniques, and Reports

CHRIS SPATZ
Hendrix College

EDWARD P. KARDAS
Southern Arkansas University

Boston   Burr Ridge, IL   Dubuque, IA   Madison, WI   New York   San Francisco   St. Louis
Bangkok   Bogotá   Caracas   Kuala Lumpur   Lisbon   London   Madrid   Mexico City
Milan   Montreal   New Delhi   Santiago   Seoul   Singapore   Sydney   Taipei   Toronto

Higher Education

RESEARCH METHODS IN PSYCHOLOGY
Published by McGraw-Hill, a business unit of The McGraw-Hill Companies, Inc., 1221 Avenue of the Americas, New York, NY, 10020. Copyright © 2008 by The McGraw-Hill Companies, Inc. All rights reserved. No part of this publication may be reproduced or distributed in any form or by any means, or stored in a database or retrieval system, without the prior written consent of The McGraw-Hill Companies, Inc., including, but not limited to, in any network or other electronic storage or transmission, or broadcast for distance learning.
Some ancillaries, including electronic and print components, may not be available to customers outside the United States.

This book is printed on acid-free paper.

1 2 3 4 5 6 7 8 9 0 FGR/FGR 0 9 8 7

ISBN: 978-0-07-253074-2
MHID: 0-07-253074-X

Vice president and Editor-in-chief: *Emily Barrosse*
Publisher: *Beth Mejia*
Executive editor: *Michael J. Sugarman*
Editorial coordinator: *Katherine C. Russillo*
Marketing manager: *Sarah Martin*
Managing editor: *Jean Dal Porto*
Production editor: *Emily Hatteberg/Mel Valentin*
Art director: *Jeanne Schreiber*
Art editor: *Ayelet Arbel*
Illustrator: *Dartmouth Publishing, Inc.*
Design manager: *Laurie Entringer*
Senior photo research coordinator: *Nora Agbayani*
Photo researcher: *Judy Mason*
Production supervisor: *Jason I. Huls/Randy Hurst*
Cover credit: *© age fotostock/SuperStock*
Composition: *10/12 Sabon, by Techbooks*
Printing: *45# New Era Matte, Quebecor Fairfield*

Credits: The credits section for this book begins on page 466 and is considered an extension of the copyright page.

Library of Congress Cataloging-in-Publication Data

Spatz, Chris, 1940–
    Research methods in psychology/Chris Spatz, Edward P. Kardas.
        p. cm.
    Includes bibliographical references and index.
    ISBN–13: 978-0-07-253074-2 (hardcover : alk. paper)
    ISBN–10: 0-07-253074-X (hardcover: alk. paper)   1. Psychology—
Research—Methodology—Textbooks.   I. Kardas, Edward P., 1949–   II.
Title.
BF76.5.S633 2008
150.72—dc22

                                                            2006035088

The Internet addresses listed in the text were accurate at the time of publication. The inclusion of a Web site does not indicate an endorsement by the authors or McGraw-Hill, and McGraw-Hill does not guarantee the accuracy of the information presented at these sites.

www.mhhe.com

. . . to teachers and especially those teachers who bring enthusiasm and their own ideas to class. My family benefited from many such teachers. I especially acknowledge Harriet A. Smith and Mary Duncan Goodloe who taught in one-room schoolhouses and Charles Reid Moose who taught in a two-seat Taylorcraft taildragger.

Chris Spatz

. . . to my Mother

Edward P. Kardas

Brief Contents

Contents

4 MEASUREMENT   93

5 DATA EXPLORATION AND DESCRIPTION   125

6 STATISTICAL TESTS   159

Preface

TO INSTRUCTORS

This book is for psychology and behavioral science majors and minors who are taking their first undergraduate course in research methods. The teaching package consists of:

- Textbook with 12 chapters and 3 appendixes
- McGraw-Hill Online Learning Center Web site maintained by the authors
- Instructor's Manual by the authors
- Electronic Test Bank by the authors

The textbook's organization and particularly its style help it stand out among the texts that are available for this course. Foundational materials on the nature of science, psychological research, ethics, measurement, and statistical methods are covered in the first part of the book. The heart of the text is the chapters on research designs—designs that psychologists and other behavioral scientists use widely today. These chapters focus on between-subjects and within-subjects designs, the identification and control of extraneous variables, ANOVA, and especially on the interpretation of results. The book concludes with an innovative two-chapter sequence that addresses the nuts and bolts of conducting a research project and reporting it.

The chapters in this book can be taught in orders different from the one we present. For courses in which students develop a written prospectus or carry out a data-gathering project and write it up, chapter 11 can be assigned early and referred to throughout the course. A course might begin with chapter 2, Research in Psychology, saving chapter 1, Science, to serve as an overview at the end of the course. Chapter 10, Observational, Qualitative, and Small-*N* Research, which employs designs that seldom use random assignment, can be taught without loss of continuity before chapter 7, Design I: Between-Subjects Designs, which introduces random assignment. Two chapters that should be taught in order are chapters 7 and 8, Design I and Design II.

College and university curricula differ in the sequencing of the research methods (RM) and statistics courses. Traditionally, statistics is taught first. However, some curricula employ a combined RM/statistics course, whereas others teach RM first, followed by statistics. Obviously, no single textbook is appropriate for all three models, but this one accommodates the first two.

Students who have had statistics or are taking it concurrently will find that chapter 5, Data Exploration and Description, and chapter 6, Statistical Tests, provide a welcome review of descriptive and inferential statistics. One-way ANOVA and factorial ANOVA are covered in chapter 9 Complex Designs. For curricula with a combined RM/statistics course, chapters 5 and 6 serve as an introduction to statistics, but will likely need to be supplemented with additional problems and materials. Problems can be taken from our Test Bank.

SUPPLEMENTS FOR INSTRUCTOR

The supplements listed here accompany *Research Methods in Psychology: Ideas, Techniques, and Reports.* Please contact your McGraw-Hill representative for more information.

Online Learning Center for Instructors

This extensive Web site, designed specifically to accompany *Research Methods in Psychology: Ideas, Techniques, and Reports* offers an array of resources for both instructor and student. Among the features included on the password protected Instructor's side of the Web site are online versions of the Instructor's Manual, PowerPoint Slides, and Test Bank, with answers. These resources and more can be found by logging onto the text site at www.mhhe.com/spatz.

Instructor's Manual

Written by Edward P. Kardas, Southern Arkansas University and Chris Spatz, Hendrix College

The Instructor's Manual is organized by chapters and is designed to assist instructors new to the teaching of research methods, as well as more experienced professors. The Instructor's Manual includes learning objectives, glossary terms used in the chapter, an annotated outline, teaching points, background material (books, articles, and Web sites), student activities, and discussion questions. The Instructor's Manual resides on the instructor's side of the Online Learning Center (OLC) at www.mhhe.com/spatz.

Test Bank

Written by Chris Spatz, Hendrix College, and Edward P. Kardas, Southern Arkansas University

This comprehensive Test Bank includes true/false, multiple-choice, fill-in-the-blank, matching, and short-answer questions. The test questions are organized by chapter and are designed to test factual, applied, and conceptual understanding. This important instructor resource is accessible on the instructor's side of the Online Learning Center.

PowerPoint® Presentation Slides

These slides cover the key points of each chapter, serving as a springboard for your lectures. They can be used as is, or you may modify them to meet your specific needs.

PageOut™

PageOut™ is the easiest way to create a Web site for your course. It requires no prior knowledge of HTML coding or graphic design, and is free with every McGraw-Hill textbook. Visit us at www.pageout.net to learn more about PageOut™.

As a full-service publisher of quality educational products, McGraw-Hill does much more than just sell textbooks to your students. We create and publish an extensive array of print, video, and digital supplements to support instruction on your campus. Orders of new (versus used) textbooks help us to defray the cost of developing such supplements, which is substantial. We have a broad range of other supplements in psychology that you may wish to tap into for your course. Ask your local McGraw-Hill representative about the availability of supplements that may help with your course design.

TO STUDENTS

This book is about the scientific methods and scientific thinking that psychologists use to investigate behavior and mental processes. By understanding and applying these methods, and this thinking, you can collect data and arrive at valid conclusions about subjects that pique your interest. In addition, you will be able to make suggestions to others and even detect flaws in research. Some of these flaws are common in popular thinking.

This book has a number of features that are designed to help you accomplish your goals for this course. The first on our list is perhaps the most important.

- We address readers as beginning researchers poised to make discoveries and solve problems, rather than as students whose task is to learn definitions and lists. Indeed, several examples that are used extensively are based on published undergraduate research.
- Chapters begin with a *short summary* and a *list of objectives* to orient you to the chapter; after finishing the chapter, the objectives serve as a review list.
- All *glossary words and phrases* are printed in bold where they are introduced. Their definitions are printed in sidebars on that page and in alphabetical order in the glossary.
- A reference to a table or figure in **boldface type** in the text means to examine the table or figure at that point. The bold type makes it easy to return to your place.
- As the material in a chapter unfolds, *Stop & Think* boxes pose questions. The answers to these questions are in the text that follows. These questions help keep readers engaged by creating a style that alternates between didactic and Socratic.
- *In the Know* boxes let you in on the kind of inside information that a professor might offer in conversations outside the classroom.
- The two kinds of exercises at the end of each chapter, *Chapter Review* and *Thinking Critically About Research,* provide opportunities to recall the chapter material and apply it to new situations. Answers to all exercises are provided.
- The *Know for Sure* terms at the end of the chapter and the pages where they are defined serve to aid review.
- The final two chapters on conducting and reporting research provide a detailed guide for courses or curricula in which a data-gathering project is required.

One caution is in order about our conversational writing style—it is not the style you should use for your report of an empirical study. Our style is designed to be engaging and to be sure that important and difficult points are understood. For example, we are deliberately redundant about some of these points. To write up empirical research, however, we recommend (as many others in psychology recommend) American Psychological Association (APA) style, which has a rigid organization and terse, constrained prose. Of course, the purpose of journal articles is to convey a lot of information in very little space to readers who are quite familiar with background information and with APA style. A textbook, on the other hand, has lots more space to work with and an audience that varies. We hope you like our style, but we don't recommend it (and don't use it ourselves) for journal articles.

FOR STUDENT

Online Learning Center for Students

This extensive Web site, which accompanies *Research Methods in Psychology: Ideas, Techniques, and Reports,* offers an array of resources for students. The student side of the Online Learning Center provides helpful information that includes learning objectives, chapter outlines, multiple-choice questions, true-false questions, essay questions, and Web links for each chapter. These resources and more can be found by logging on to the text site at www.mhhe.com/spatz.

ACKNOWLEDGMENTS

Our partial list of acknowledgments of those who have helped us with this book include:

Charles Brewer, the 1996 American Psychological Association Teacher of the Year who read the entire manuscript and provided reams of helpful comments.

Elena Yakunina, a student at Southern Arkansas University who worked all the problems at the end of the chapters and made suggestions.

Duff Campbell, Hendrix College, who provided statistical output with *Mathematica.*

Our colleagues and students at Hendrix College and Southern Arkansas University who provided references, criticism, corrections, and encouragement during this project.

Our colleagues at Ouachita Baptist University, Loretta McGregor, Randall Wight, and Randy Smith, who provided us with a place halfway between our two institutions where we could meet and work on our manuscript.

Hendrix College and Southern Arkansas University whose support was absolutely necessary for the completion of this book. We are grateful to our respective institutions.

In ways too numerous to mention, our families contributed to this long-running project. They deserve much more than a mention in a preface.

In addition, we wish to acknowledge the helpful reviews of

Kimberley Duff—Cerritos College

Joshua D. Landau—York College of Pennsylvania

Lou Milanesi—University of Wisconsin at Stout

Monica Mori—Concordia College

Lucy J. Troup—Colorado State University

William Wozniak—University of Nebraska at Kearney

One of the big goals of this book and your course is that you will get much better at analyzing conclusions that are based on data. Because there are so much data out there in life as we all know it, we expect that your improved skills will be quite useful in many endeavors, especially those you engage in after your research methods course is finished.

Chris Spatz
Edward P. Kardas

1

Science

OVERVIEW

This chapter describes characteristics of science that separate it from other approaches to knowledge. A history section tells of scientists whose research changed our understanding of the world. Analyses of science by philosophers, the nature of social science theory, and a description of how knowledge of research methods can help you on the job, in graduate school, or at home are all covered.

OBJECTIVES

After studying this chapter and working through the exercises, you should be able to:

1. Define *science*
2. Identify some key scientists and their contributions to science's history
3. Place psychology among the other scientific disciplines
4. Explore the relationship between technology and science
5. Compare the types of theory in different branches of science
6. Contrast four types of social science theory
7. Describe how knowledge of research methods can help you beyond this course

Welcome to the science of psychology. This book is about how psychologists use scientific methods to discover new facts about behavior and cognitive processes and to explain what they mean. Learning about how the science of psychology is practiced and applying its methods can be fun and educational. Even if you never work as a scientist, you will be able to use the things you learn in this course for the rest of your life. As for your authors, we love teaching psychological research methods; it's great fun.

SCIENCE TODAY

Science is everywhere today. In the 500 years since science emerged, it has grown into a large number of scientific specialties. **Table 1.1**[1] shows a list of scientific specialties based on the membership categories of the American Association for the Advancement of Science. As you can see, psychology is among the social sciences. Within each science specialty there are disciplines and subdisciplines. Later in this chapter we list the disciplines and subdisciplines within psychology. The growth and diversification of science reflect its success at understanding nature. Because nature is so vast, no one specialty can describe it all. Instead, each scientific specialty studies its own small part of nature. Psychology's part centers on the behavior and cognitive processes of humans and other animals.

Millions of men and women around the world work as scientists; all of them share a common intellectual heritage called **science.** Since the 1700s, science has become the dominant methodology for discovering

TABLE 1.1	Scientific Disciplines		
Physical science	*Biological sciences*	*Social sciences*	*Computational*
Astronomy	Agriculture	Anthropology	Information, Computer, & Communication
Atmospheric	Biology	Linguistics/Language	Mathematics
Chemistry	Medical	Psychology	Statistics
Geology	Neuroscience	Economics	
Geography	Pharmacological	Geography	
Physics		Political	

Note: Derived from American Association for the Advancement of Science Membership Categories.

science A method of inquiry that uses unbiased empirical observation, public methods, reproducible results, and theory to reveal universal truths about the universe.

---

[1] **Boldfaced** table or figure references indicate that you should examine the item. The boldface makes it easier for you to return to the spot where you were reading. Boldfaced words are defined in the margin and in the Glossary.

new facts. Each scientific specialty created its own collection of knowledge, its own subset of methods for gathering data, and its own theories. Each scientific specialty has its own textbooks (such as this one) designed to teach students how to become members of that specialty. However, science cannot be learned entirely from reading. Ultimately, you learn science by doing science. A central theme of this book is that the best way to learn about the research methods in psychology is to conduct your own research. Most likely you will take your first steps under the supervision of a practicing scientist such as, perhaps, your instructor for this course. Later, many of you will conduct your own independent scientific investigations. Those may take place in other courses, graduate school, or on the job. The essence of doing science is discovering facts about the world. What could be more exciting? Let's get to work.

The chapters that follow represent an early 21st-century snapshot of how psychologists conduct scientific research. Psychologists today conduct research very differently from the way their predecessors did when psychology emerged in the late 19th century. The guidelines and accepted practices for research change in all scientific disciplines, and psychology is no exception. As you progress through this book, we will explain topics for which guidelines have changed (such as ethics) or may be in the process of changing (such as statistical analyses).

CHARACTERISTICS OF SCIENCE

Science is a particular way of asking questions and obtaining answers. Of course, there are other ways to ask questions and get answers. Legal systems are an example. In legal systems that follow common law, juries decide questions of guilt or innocence of defendants after lawyers for the prosecution and lawyers for the defense present their cases. Legal systems are an adversarial method of inquiry. The lawyers for each side are opponents (adversaries). The judge administers the court and makes the lawyers follow its rules so that the facts are presented fairly. Juries decide their verdict based on a number of factors, such as sentencing options and jury personality structure (Devine, Clayton, Dunford, Seying, & Pryce, 2001). Juries do not make their decision by following scientific methods.

The first steps toward becoming a scientist involve learning the rules and methods of science. Scientists not only answer their own questions, they also articulate the methods they use to answer those questions. In science, the methods used and the answers produced are tightly bound to each other. In addition to methods, scientists also follow established ethical practices. We discuss research ethics in chapter 3. For now, suffice it to say that following the ethical rules of science is a major part of being a scientist. Let's now take a closer look at science itself.

Like most complex ideas, science is not easily defined. The four characteristics of science that we examine are: empiricism, the public nature of science, the replication of scientific results, and theory. These four characteristics are included in nearly all definitions of science.

In the Know

As one example of a definition of science we offer Goldstein and Goldstein's (1978) definition of science as an activity characterized by three features: a search for understanding, achieving that understanding by creating general laws or principles, and testing those laws and principles experimentally. In this text, we concentrate on how psychologists achieve understanding about behavior, how they create theories to explain that understanding, and, most important, how they conduct the experimental tests necessary for achieving scientific understanding.

Empiricism

An empirical answer is one that is based on observation. Think of **empiricism** as experiencing things for yourself or as collecting data to answer your questions. The essence of empiricism is that observers attempt to discover facts in an unbiased manner. Much of this text covers methods that yield empirical, or unbiased, results. The important point is that scientific answers come from unbiased observations, not opinions. The importance of empirical observation is illustrated in the history of our understanding about the physical composition of the moon. Scientists have come a long way from early speculations that the moon was made of green cheese. After the invention of the telescope, astronomers made better observations and saw that the moon's surface was anything but smooth. Later, another remote-sensing instrument, the mass spectrometer, revealed much about the mineral composition of the moon's surface. During the first *Apollo* mission in 1969, actual moon rocks were collected and returned to Earth. Today, the physical nature of the moon is no longer a matter of speculation. Using telescopes, spectrometers, and lunar samples, scientists possess a fairly complete picture of the moon's surface (Blewett, Lucey, Hawke, & Jolliff, 1997). The answer to the question of the moon's composition, although not completely known, has been revealed by empirical observations made from Earth and from actual lunar samples.

In a general sense, all science and all psychology depend on observations that are carefully planned and made. Much of what you will

empiricism Philosophical and scientific approach to knowledge that uses unbiased observation to discover truths about the world.

learn in this book relates to becoming a skilled and unbiased observer. Making such observations is one of the first steps toward becoming a scientist. Planning our everyday decisions is probably a good idea. In research, however, planning to collect data is a requirement, not an option.

Public Nature

A second characteristic of science is its public nature.[2] Typically, scientists **publish** their findings in scientific journals (chapters 11 and 12 include details about scientific publication). Journals published by scientific societies and commercial publishers constitute the main repository of scientific data including scientific results, methods, and theories. Some of that publication is now in online journals, making access much easier for you (and other scientists). Regardless of the medium used, published data are a defining characteristic of science. Without publication, scientists could not easily disseminate the answers they find. With publication, however, other scientists can easily access those answers (especially with searchable online databases, a topic we cover in chapter 11). Publication means that once a scientist discovers an answer empirically, others need not repeat the research; they can just look up the answer.

Replication

Sometimes, scientists do wish to repeat the empirical procedures of other scientists to confirm the original findings. This kind of repetition is called **replication,** and it is an important part of science because it creates confidence in scientific conclusions. Scientists are skeptical by training and they want to admit only correct conclusions into the collection of scientific facts. They know that data must be collected properly. So, when they publish their conclusions they also publish the methods they used to obtain those conclusions. In this way, other scientists who wish to replicate (or verify) the original results can use the same methods. When other scientists obtain results similar to those originally published, the original conclusions are confirmed. However, when other scientists fail to replicate, the original conclusions are called into question and additional replications are attempted. If those fail too, the original results and conclusions may be discarded altogether.

publish Recording of scientific results, methods, and theories to create a permanent knowledge base of science.

replication Repeating an experiment with the same procedures or with planned changes in the procedures to confirm the original results.

---

[2]Not all science is public. At times, governments and corporations engage in scientific work but keep the results secret due to factors such as national security or competitive business practices.

In the Know

The characteristic of replication is illustrated by the aftermath of a 1989 press conference announcement by two chemists, Stanley Pons and Martin Fleischmann. They announced that they had discovered cold fusion, a source of energy similar to the sun's, but one that occurs at room temperature. Their key finding was the unexpected and excess energy that they measured in a laboratory experiment. Afterward, other chemists attempted to measure those energies but could not replicate the results. Eventually, the initial surge of enthusiasm about cold fusion and its implications waned, especially after a group of scientists at the Massachusetts Institute of Technology published a scathing review of methodological flaws in the original research. A few scientists are still pursuing cold fusion, but most scientists do not consider it a part of the facts about chemistry because it was not reproducible. (See Voss [1999] for details about the cold fusion controversy.)

Theory

Scientists do more than collect and publish empirical data and the methods they use. They also create **theories** that help explain the data and stimulate ideas for new studies. Theories can be verbal explanations, mathematical formulas, or simply analogies that help scientists understand the phenomena they study. Near the end of this chapter, we discuss theories in more detail and compare theories in physical science, biological science, and social science.

Empiricism, the public nature of science, replication, and theory work together in an interlocking way. New data are collected that confirm or call into question recent theories. Those data are published; other scientists replicate the results. New studies are carried out to flesh out details. Theories are revised and the process continues. Most scientists adopt science as a career because they seek answers to their questions and they believe that science is the best way to answer those questions.

A BRIEF HISTORY OF SCIENCE

theory The cognitive frameworks by which scientists understand the phenomena they study and which guide them toward future research.

Long before science emerged, humans attempted to answer questions about the natural phenomena they observed. But they did not possess the scientific tools or methods necessary to explain the causal mechanisms behind those phenomena. Unlike today's scientists, ancient observers could only pass their observations from generation to generation orally. So even if they discovered some useful and beneficial knowledge (such as medicinal plants), they could not explain why they worked nor could they record their observations for others to see and use. The earliest known antecedents of science are found in Greece starting around the year 600 BCE. Later, Socrates, Plato, Aristotle, and many other Greeks formalized *philosophy,* a system for investigating the world and disseminating the results. Those efforts were a necessary precursor to science. However, science did not arise until about 500 years ago during the Renaissance. The interim between the fall of classic Greco-Roman civilization and the emergence of science was characterized by a retreat from direct study of the world and an embrace of faith-based revealed knowledge. Let's now look more closely at some of the historical milestones that led to science, and eventually, to psychology.

Myth, Magic, and Mystery

Ancient humans used myth, magic, and mystery to explain the phenomena they observed (Roszak, 1975). Myths are stories that explain the world and its people. Unlike scientific explanations, myths are not grounded in observation. Some myths explain the origin of the world. For example, the Greco-Roman myths are stories of gods, titans, nymphs, and humans. In that mythology, the world emerged from chaos when an unnamed god reordered chaos into sky, earth, and sea. Nearly every culture has its own origin myths that attempt to explain the "big" questions of life: Who am I? Why am I here? What is my purpose? Myths provide nonscientific answers to these age-old questions.

Magic consists of rituals, performed by knowledgeable individuals, that purportedly ensure success in hunting, courtship, and other activities. Magic's rituals survive still as in the behavior of brides before they take their marriage vows; many avoid the sight of their grooms on their wedding day until after the marriage ceremony begins. Modern science has dismissed many magical rituals as ineffective, but they persist. For instance, topping a new building with a tree as seen in **Figure 1.1** is a magical ritual that is still practiced. When the construction of a building first reaches its final height, many contractors and owners hold a topping ceremony in which a tree (and/or a flag) is attached to the building for good luck. This tradition continues as do countless others.

Learning about secret rites and hidden knowledge through a process of initiation defines mystery. Primitive cultures introduce members of their tribe to secret knowledge and sacred rites as do modern fraternities and sororities. Early scientists such as Isaac Newton and Rene Descartes demystified knowledge by posing solvable problems instead of treating them as unsolvable mysteries (Horgan, 1996). Cultures that adopted science replaced myth with history, magic with technology, and mystery with reason (Roszak, 1975). Of course, science has not completely replaced

FIGURE 1.1
Topping a building.

older ways of knowing as people still make appeals to authority, harbor superstitions, and consult sacred texts.

The Long Road to Modern Science

The first antecedents of scientific thought emerged in Greece over a three-century period from approximately 600 to 300 BCE. During those years, a succession of thinkers laid foundations for later scientific thinking. Also during this period, other Greek thinkers created disciplines that are now used by scientists, including logic, geometry, and mathematics.

Socrates and Plato   Socrates (470–399 BCE) set out to understand concepts such as truth and beauty (and many others) by searching for their essence in everyday objects or actions. He and his most famous student, Plato (427–347 BCE), examined their own thoughts and ideas and not the world around them. After Socrates' famous death,[3] Plato

---

[3]He was condemned to drink hemlock, a poison, for corruption of the young and neglect of the gods.

founded the Academy of Athens where he taught philosophy in the
Socratic tradition and amplified the ideas of his teacher. He searched
his own mind even more deeply, searching for the ideal or the abstract
form of everyday objects. For example, he articulated the idea of an ideal
chair, but believed it could not be built. It existed only in the philoso-
pher's mind. Real chairs could only approach the ideal chair but
could never achieve it. (Philosophers still love to use chairs as examples.)
However, one of Plato's students—Aristotle—stands out as perhaps the
first scientist.

Aristotle   Aristotle (384–322 BCE) became Plato's student when he was
17 years old and remained at the Academy for 20 years (see **Figure 1.2**).
After Plato died, Aristotle traveled extensively, tutoring along the way. He
tutored Alexander the Great, the son of Phillip of Macedon. Later, Alexander's military conquests helped spread Aristotle's ideas. Eventually,
Aristotle returned to Athens and founded his own school, the Lyceum.
His school, unlike Plato's Academy, studied a variety of topics, including
astronomy, physics, zoology, politics, economics, ethics, poetics, and psychology. Unlike Plato, Aristotle looked out to the world rather than into
his mind for answers to his questions. His emphasis on observation marks
him as an early empiricist.

As an empiricist, Aristotle wrote about many topics, including psychological ones. His book *De Anima* (Latin for "On the Soul" or "On the
Mind") discussed many psychological subjects such as emotions (anger,
joy, pity, hate, and others) and comparative psychology (animal behavior).
In other works, he wrote about memory, sensation, perception, imagination,

FIGURE 1.2
Bust of Aristotle.

and dreaming. Although Aristotle wrote about a wide variety of topics that today are studied by psychologists, he is not considered to be the first psychologist. His methods were primarily observational, not experimental. It was not until 1879 that someone began to study behavior and cognitive processes experimentally. Before we can talk about him, however, we must explain the Middle Ages, a 1,000-year-long detour on the road to science and psychology.

The Middle Ages   The Middle Ages is the historical era that came between the fall of Rome (476 CE) and the beginning of the Renaissance in Italy (about 1450 CE). The disintegration of Roman authority combined with the westward migration of Burgundians, Franks, Huns, Goths, and Vandals led to a Europe characterized by a patchwork of many fiefdoms, each ruled by a warlord. By 1000 CE, however, large nation-states had emerged and nearly all of Europe was Christianized. Christian religious dogma (rigid and unquestioned beliefs) had replaced empirical observation. During the Crusades (1096–1270 CE), Europeans rediscovered the older Greek knowledge from Arabic translations of Plato, Aristotle, and other ancient texts. Once again, scholars studied the classic Greek texts, but the words were regarded as unalterable truths, not as a guide to further empirical investigations. Near the end of the 12th century, universities were established to train clerics. The universities of Bologna, Paris, and Oxford (**Figure 1.3**) are usually recognized as the first

FIGURE 1.3
Oxford University.

European universities. The task of students in the medieval universities was to learn classic Greek texts and the Bible, not to expand knowledge beyond their words.

In the Know

The course of study at medieval universities was much different from today's curriculum. The *trivium,* or introductory curriculum, consisted of three courses: grammar, logic, and rhetoric. The *quadrivium,* or advanced curriculum, consisted of geometry, astronomy, arithmetic, and music. Books were produced by hand and were rare. Relatively few men (and hardly any women) attended universities, and those students came from the clergy (or aspirants to the clergy) and the nobility.

Near the end of the Middle Ages, the urge to expand the horizons of knowledge using empirical methods once again reasserted itself. Reports from explorers such as Marco Polo, the analysis of the sky by Copernicus, and Gutenberg's invention of the printing press created an atmosphere that supported a new approach to knowledge. That approach was science.

Science Emerges

Horgan (1996) contends that large-scale surprises about the universe are science's main contribution to the history of thought. Thus, we examine Galileo's astronomical discoveries, Darwin's theory of evolution, and Einstein's revamping of Newtonian physics as examples of scientific surprises. Naturally, we could have included other examples such as Newton's work on universal gravitation, Wegener's continental drift theory, or Watson and Crick's description of DNA. Their work, and that of many others, are worthy examples of surprises from science that changed the way we live and think.

Although no exact date marks the beginning of science, the astronomy studies of scholars such as Copernicus (1473–1543), Brahe (1546–1601), Kepler (1571–1630), and Galileo (1564–1642) all qualify as early science. Astronomy had long been important to the Church[4] because of the necessity to set the date of Easter, a religious feast whose date can range from March 22 to April 25. The Church's cosmology was based on the work of Ptolemy, a 2nd-century astronomer. In his cosmology, Earth

---

[4]"Church" here refers to the pre-Reformation Roman Catholic and Greek Orthodox churches.

FIGURE 1.4
Galileo.

was the center of the universe and the sun circled Earth, rising in the east and setting in the west. Ptolemy's **geocentric model** (earth centered) of the universe had seven heavenly bodies (Mercury, Venus, Mars, Jupiter, Saturn, the moon, and the sun) that revolved around Earth. The stars were fixed in place equidistantly in the outermost sphere or eighth heaven. In sharp contrast, Copernicus's **heliocentric model** placed the sun at the center, which dramatically challenged the Church's long-held beliefs. Wisely, Copernicus withheld publication of his book *De Revolutionibus Orbium Caelestium (On the Revolutions of the Heavenly Spheres)* until after his death. Eventually, his book and his teachings were condemned by the Church. Science had revealed its first great surprise: Earth was not the center of the universe.

Galileo, the Heavens, and the Church

geocentric model Model of the solar system in which the earth was in the center orbited by the sun, moon, the five planets, and surrounded by the stars.

heliocentric model Model of the solar system in which the sun is the center and the planets orbit the sun.

The life and work of Galileo Galilei **(Figure 1.4)** exemplify the struggle between early science's empiricism and the Church's efforts to maintain a static worldview based on the Bible and the works of Aristotle. Early in his education, Galileo switched from medicine to mathematics. Later, he taught at the University of Pisa where he began to apply mathematics to physical systems (notably pendulums and balls rolling down inclined planes). After hearing of the invention of the telescope, he built one and improved it. Eventually, he decided to turn his telescope skyward.

Through his telescope, Galileo saw things in the sky that no one had ever seen before. The moon had mountains, the Milky Way was composed of stars, and Jupiter had four moons. This last observation branded him a heretic in the eyes of some because Galileo claimed there were 11 heavenly bodies rather than 7. Perhaps more importantly, Galileo also claimed that observations from nature were certain and such certainty should be used to correct the Church's interpretation of scripture. Although Jesuit astronomers at the Roman College confirmed Galileo's observations, they continued to interpret the results according to a geocentric model. In 1616 the Church warned Galileo not to "hold or defend" the Copernican heliocentric model of the universe as fact. He could, however, teach it as an abstract, mathematical hypothesis. Fearing the Inquisition[5] (which had already burned other scientists at the stake), Galileo agreed. However, in 1633 when he was 70 years old, Galileo was again summoned before the Inquisition. A book he had published the year before, *Dialogues Concerning the Two Chief World Systems,* was the cause. In that book, three characters (a scientist, a simpleton, and a fence-sitter) argued the merits of the heliocentric and geocentric models of the universe. Although Galileo presented his book as a fantasy and had received prior permission from the Church to publish it, the furor that ensued caused the Church to suppress both the book and Galileo. The Inquisition perceived the book to be teaching the Copernican model as fact, which violated its earlier injunction. At his trial, Galileo was forced to recant (take back) his teachings. After he recanted, Galileo was placed under house arrest for the remaining 9 years of his life, where he continued to write and publish. During this time he wrote *Discourses Relating to Two New Sciences* which elaborated the foundations of the modern scientific method. The book was published in the Netherlands. In 1992, the Catholic Church formally withdrew its charges against him.

Darwin and Evolution

In 1831, 22-year-old Charles Darwin (1809–1882) **(Figure 1.5)** set sail as the naturalist on the HMS *Beagle,* a British warship, for a 5-year voyage around the world to collect scientific specimens. During the voyage Darwin traveled to Brazil and the Pacific Ocean, visiting the Galapagos Islands, Tahiti, New Zealand, and Australia. At each stop, he collected many plants and animals and began noting their relationships. Back in England, he tried to organize his collections but was unable to infer an organizing principle. Fortunately, he chanced upon Thomas Malthus's book *Essay on the Principle of Population.* Malthus proposed that external events, such as wars and illness, keep human populations in check. Without these checks, humans would reproduce so quickly that the earth's

---

[5]The Inquisition was a mechanism set up by the Church for exposing heretics or people who did not believe the Church's teachings. During Galileo's lifetime, the Inquisition had the power of life or death over people accused of heresy.

FIGURE 1.5
Charles Darwin.

crops and animals would all be consumed. Darwin modified and expanded Malthus's metaphor, applying it to all biological populations.

Today's version of Darwin's idea is that the checks on growth are barriers that all species, plant or animal, must overcome if they are to reproduce. These barriers are environmental (such as shelter, floods, and droughts) and biological (such as predators and competition for mates). Darwin proposed that all organisms are in a daily struggle to overcome these barriers and that only certain ones succeed in reproducing. Darwin was impressed with the variation that occurs in every species. He also saw that some of these variations were more adaptive than others for overcoming barriers. Species with these adaptive characteristics reproduced in spite of the barriers. Darwin called this process **natural selection.** Over eons, the characteristics of a species changed due to the survival and reproduction of individuals with adaptive characteristics. Individuals without these characteristics left no progeny and if there were no other adaptations in the species, it became extinct. In summary, reproduction of adaptive characteristics is evolution by natural selection and dying out is extinction. Being cautious and recognizing the implications of his theory, Darwin was in no hurry to publish his controversial ideas without solid empirical support. He continued to collect data.

In 1858, however, Alfred Russel Wallace, a young biologist working in the East Indies, wrote Darwin about his research and theories on evolution, which were quite similar to Darwin's. Darwin's colleagues feared that Darwin would lose scientific priority to Wallace, so they arranged for

natural selection
Survival and reproduction of living things best suited to particular environments.

papers by Darwin and Wallace to be presented together at the 1858 meeting of the Linnean Society, a forum for biological discussions.[6] Neither paper caused much interest, but Darwin hurriedly completed a manuscript of his book. The publication of Darwin's *Origin of Species by Means of Natural Selection* (1859) caused a revolution. The first print run of 1,250 copies sold out in one day and created a new worldview that still arouses passion and controversy today.

The theory of evolution was a big surprise. It forced people to rethink their relationship with living things. Like Galileo, Darwin opened up a completely new scientific way of looking at the world and the species that inhabit it. Once again, older worldviews were in conflict with newer ones that had been revealed by science's empirical methods.

Einstein and Relativity

In 1905 Albert Einstein (1879–1955) **(Figure 1.6),** an obscure Swiss patent examiner who was also a PhD candidate in physics, surprised the scientific world by publishing three extraordinary papers on physical phenomena. The first paper on the particle nature of light won him the Nobel Prize in 1921. One of the other two papers explained Brownian motion, the previously unexplained movements commonly observed in microscopic systems. Molecules themselves were causing the movement. The third paper eventually made him a worldwide celebrity; its topic was special relativity. In it, he demonstrated that time was a necessary fourth

FIGURE 1.6
Albert Einstein.

[6]The first scientist to make a discovery or create a theory receives the most credit. So, scientists compete to present their results and theories first in order to ensure priority.

dimension to the three dimensions of space and that energy and mass were equivalent ($E = mc^2$). When he extended that paper in 1915 to include gravity (general relativity) and when his theoretical predictions were later empirically confirmed, Einstein became a worldwide celebrity.

Einstein's surprises were startling. His equations showed that time and space were not invariant, but that they changed depending on the motion of the observer. The equations also indicated that gravity warped space itself, a prediction confirmed by Edington's observations of stars during a solar eclipse in 1919. At the atomic level, Einstein's definition of light as quanta (small packets of light energy) led to the development of quantum mechanics, which was yet another scientific surprise. Like Galileo and Darwin before him, Einstein prompted a completely new worldview in which very small or very fast particles followed rules unlike any in the observable world.

Psychology

The idea of applying scientific thinking and methods to phenomena of mind, behavior, and cognition emerged during the 19th century. Much of the early work was in psychophysics, which sought to demonstrate mathematical relationships (laws) between a physical stimulus from the environment and a psychological perception within a person. Ernst Weber (1795-1878) and Gustav Fechner (1801-1887) were the first to discover and publish psychophysical laws. Working independently, they discovered the first lawful relationships between physical stimuli and perceptions of those same stimuli. Others with a more biological orientation, such as the physiologist Hermann Helmholtz (1821-1894), published empirical studies on vision and audition. His analysis of color vision, an extension of earlier work by Thomas Young, became the Young-Helmholtz trichromatic theory of color vision, which is still taught today. Physician Paul Broca (1824-1880) discovered a relationship between the brain and a specific behavior by performing an autopsy on a man who had lost the ability to speak. The autopsy showed a lesion in his left temporal lobe, a part of the brain now named Broca's area. Researchers Georges Romanes (1848-1894) in England and Edward Thorndike (1874-1949) in America studied animal behavior. Romanes explored the evolution of cognition in animals and humans. His work led to the field of comparative psychology. Thorndike, too, studied animals early in his career. His pioneering work in animal learning anticipated behaviorist psychology. However, it was a physiologist turned psychologist, Wilhelm Wundt (1832-1920), who first intentionally established scientific psychology.

Wundt **(Figure 1.7)** began his academic career as a medical doctor, but his appointment as assistant to Johannes Müller, one of the most famous physiologists of his time, turned Wundt toward the principles of science and physiology. Later, when Wundt joined the University of

FIGURE 1.7
Wilhelm Wundt.

Leipzig as a professor of scientific philosophy, the stage was set for the founding of psychology. In 1879, Wundt established the first research laboratory devoted to the scientific study of psychology. Wundt's research was directed primarily toward consciousness. Wundt and his students studied the mind by examining their thoughts while they engaged in controlled, experimental situations. This method is called *introspection*. Wundt's courses at Leipzig were very popular and many students from all over Europe and the United States came to Leipzig to earn PhD degrees in psychology under Wundt. Among the Americans were G. Stanley Hall (1844–1924) and James McKeen Cattell (1860–1944) who were important contributors to the establishment and growth of psychology in the United States. Psychologists eventually abandoned introspection because of its methodological flaws. John B. Watson (1878–1958) introduced a new methodology, *behaviorism,* which replaced introspection and its emphasis on the mind. Behaviorists defined psychology and psychological research in terms of changes in behavior in response to changes in the environment. Behaviorism is still influential in psychology today. Cognitive psychology emerged after World War II using a new metaphor, *computation*. Cognitive psychologists study cognitive processes (perception, memory, learning, and others) scientifically. The "cognitive revolution" spawned by cognitive psychology is another major area of contemporary psychology.

In some ways, psychology also began as a scientific surprise. The mind, it turned out, was subject to scientific study. Today, psychology has grown beyond its early mentalistic approach and psychologists study a wide range of topics. **Table 1.2** lists alphabetically the fields and subfields of psychology as organized by the American Psychological Association (APA). Table 1.2 lists 71 topics. Some of the topics have one or two levels

TABLE 1.2	APA List of Psychological Topics

1 Addictive Behavior

2 Aging

3 AIDS

4 Art/Music/Literature

5 Behavior Analysis

6 Behavioral Neuroscience

7 Child Abuse

8 Clinical/Counseling/Consulting

   8.1 adolescent

   8.2 assessment/diagnosis

   8.3 child clinical/pediatric

   8.4 geriatric

   8.5 interaction/communications

   8.6 process/outcome

   8.7 professional

   8.8 psychopathology

      8.8.1. organic

      8.8.2 personality/behavior disorders

      8.8.3 schizophrenia

   8.9 psychotherapy/treatment—methods

      8.9.1 behavioral/cognitive

      8.9.2 dynamic/psychoanalytic

      8.9.3 existential

      8.9.4 humanistic

   8.10 psychotherapy/treatment—population

      8.10.1 group

      8.10.2 individual

      8.10.3 marital/family

   8.11 training

   8.12 vocational/career

9 Cognition

   9.1 attention/perception

   9.2 memory

   9.3 modeling

   9.4 problem solving/reasoning/comprehension

10 Community

   10.1 service delivery

   10.2 rural/urban

11 Comparative

12 Computer Applications

13 Creativity

14 Crime/Delinquency

15 Cross-Cultural

16 Death Studies

   16.1 death and dying

   16.2 bereavement

17 Depression/Suicide

18 Developmental

   18.1 gender roles

   18.2 stages

      18.2.1 infant

      18.2.2 child

      18.2.3 adolescent

      18.2.4 adult

   18.3 family

   18.4 cognitive

19 Disabilities

   19.1 physical

   19.2 emotional

   19.3 cognitive/learning

20 Disasters/Crisis

21 Education

   21.1 teaching

   21.2 learning

   21.3 professional training

22 Emotion

23 Environment

24 Ethics

25 Ethnic Minority Studies

   25.1 African Americans

   25.2 Asian/Pacific Islanders

   25.3 American Indian/Alaska Natives

   25.4 Hispanic Americans

26 Ethnic Studies

   26.1 Cross-Cultural

27 Exercise Behavior

28 Experimental (General)

29 Family

30 Gay and Lesbian Issues

   30.1 bisexual

   30.2 transgender

(continued)

TABLE 1.2   (continued)

31 Health Psychology/Behavioral Medicine
   31.1 etiology
   31.2 diagnosis
   31.3 treatment
   31.4 health promotion/prevention
   31.5 health service systems
32 History
33 Human Factors Studies
34 Hypnosis
35 Industrial/Organizational
   35.1 management/administration
   35.2 consumer studies
   35.3 personnel
36 Information Processing
37 Injury Prevention
   37.1 intentional injuries
   37.2 unintentional injuries
38 International
39 Law
   39.1 clinical/forensic
40 Learning
   40.1 animal
   40.2 human
41 Measurement/Statistics/Methodology/Computer
   41.1 program evaluation
   41.2 test construction
42 Media/Public Information
43 Men's Studies
44 Mental Retardation
45 Military
46 Motivation
47 Neuropsychology
48 Peace
49 Personality
   49.1 humanistic theory
   49.2 psychoanalytic theory
   49.3 personality measurement
50 Pharmacology

51 Philosophy
52 Political
53 Population
54 Prevention
55 Psycholinguistics
56 Psychology Policy Issues
   56.1 ethics
   56.2 professional issues
   56.3 public policy
   56.4 scientific issues
   56.5 training and education
57 Psychophysiology
58 Rehabilitation
59 Religion
60 Rural
61 School
62 Sensation/Perception
63 Sexual Behavior/Functioning
64 Social
   64.1 attitude/attitude change
   64.2 attribution
   64.3 conflict resolution
   64.4 decision making
   64.5 group processes
   64.6 relationships
   64.7 sex roles
   64.8 social cognition
65 Sports
66 Stress
67 Substance Abuse
68 Teaching of Psychology
69 Violence/Aggression
   69.1 assault
   69.2 homicide
   69.3 suicide
70 Women's Studies
71 Work/Employment/Careers
   71.1 academic
   71.2 business/government
   71.3 practice/research

Source: Reprinted with permission of the American Psychological Association, © APA.

of subtopics. Are you surprised by the wide variety? Are there any topics that you never heard of before? As you can see from Table 1.2, psychology is a large and varied enterprise that studies animals and people, old and young, abstract and applied topics, and many other interesting aspects of behavior and cognition. Psychology has grown tremendously since 1879 and that growth will likely continue. Fifty years from now, this list certainly will contain topics we cannot foresee today.

SCIENCE AND TECHNOLOGY

Technology consists of the tools and artifacts that humans create to make their lives easier. Throughout history, humans have crafted technological devices to augment their strength, lengthen their grasp, and increase their understanding. Examples of ancient human technology abound in the archeological record. Indeed, those ancient technologies have become symbolic of the peoples who used and developed them. Anthropologists characterize ancient peoples by their technology with terms such as "stone age," "bronze age," and "iron age," which refer to the materials the groups used to create the artifacts they used.

Technology, of course, is much older than science. Early technologies developed and improved through trial and error and without the benefit of scientific understanding. After the rise of science, technology and science slowly fused into a synergistic partnership called engineering. Today, engineers outnumber scientists. Engineers use science to solve practical problems. In the process, their technologies change the world. Think of how computers went from costly, room-sized business machines to inexpensive, pocket-sized necessities in less than 50 years.

Relationship of Science and Technology

As an ideal, scientists seek to understand how the world works. Engineers, on the other hand, are more interested in using the discoveries of science to make the world a better place to live. Many basic technologies are constantly at work to preserve health and maintain life. Only when they fail or are disrupted by natural catastrophes or human malice are these technologies missed. For instance, sewer design is based on the scientifically simple principle that water flows downhill. Sewer structures, however, are technologically complex systems that can cost many millions of dollars. But sewers are directly responsible for lowered rates of waterborne illnesses and indirectly responsible for increased average life spans. Other basic technologies, such as electric power grids and transportation networks, are similar in their beneficial effects for human beings. However, no technology is without drawbacks. Power generation that uses coal, for example, denudes large tracts of land and endangers miners. Highways displace people and divide communities. Technology can also be harmful by design. Humans have always crafted weapons such as swords, and they later engineered weapons such as nuclear bombs and biological toxins. Cipolat (2004) estimates that simply maintaining our present nuclear arsenal costs American taxpayers $18 million a day. The cost of creating and maintaining weapons of mass destruction is high. The cost of using them will be higher still. The constructive and destructive effects of technology are of great psychological interest.

Technology and the History of Science

Science and technology developed together over the past 500 years. The instruments of science show the relationship nicely. Galileo's telescope enabled him to see the moons of Jupiter. The microscope enabled Leeuwenhoek and others to magnify a previously invisible world. Clocks and compasses enabled accurate navigation. Inventions such as the steam engine led to locomotives and steamships. Similarly, simple tools such as the plow revolutionized agriculture. The telegraph, telephone, and computer quickly followed basic discoveries in electricity and magnetism. These technological developments were just as essential to the development of science as were the intellectual surprises discussed earlier.

Technology and Psychology

Because technology changes behavior, psychologists study technology. For example, most college students (and nearly everyone else, it seems) now own and use cell phones. Changes in behavior caused by cell phones have happened very quickly, and have become a topic of interest to many psychologists.[7]

What other life-altering technologies have you witnessed in your lifetime? What future technologies do you anticipate seeing?

STOP & Think

Certainly, digital devices of all kinds come quickly to mind. Medical technologies seem to constantly improve as well. It's risky, however, to predict the appearance of future technologies. We have yet to see the flying cars or automated roadways predicted 40 years ago. Still, many technological surprises await us.

Technology has changed the behavior of psychologists as well. Thirty years ago, almost all teachers used blackboards and chalk in class. Now, many bring laptop computers and video projectors to class. Researchers, too, have benefited from technology. They make more precise measurements

---

[7]PsycINFO, a database of psychological research, shows 105 studies for the search string "cell phone." The first study cited was published in 1998. We cover the use of PsycINFO in chapter 11.

and thus collect better data using devices such as a global positioning system (GPS). Researchers can track animal migrations remotely using GPS transmitters attached to a few animals. New imaging techniques such as the functional magnetic resonance imaging (fMRI) allow researchers to study the brain in real time by changing the stimulus situation and watching changes in blood flow in specific parts of the brain. Technology is used also in applied areas of psychology, such as assessment and therapy. Therapists, for example, may host a Web page where their patients can confirm that they are taking their prescribed medicines. Technology profoundly affects behavior and cognition, and many psychologists investigate how technology affects us for good or ill. Such applied research began early in the history of psychology as researchers attempted to apply their laboratory findings to real-world situations.

Research in industrial or organizational psychology, for instance, led to the creation of sophisticated personnel-selection instruments and vocational aptitude batteries. Employers use these tools to recruit, hire, and retain employees. Individuals seeking employment take vocational aptitude batteries to find out what careers or occupations fit with their abilities and interests. Similarly, research in educational psychology moved that field from its 19th-century model of rigidly structured classrooms filled with rote learners to a 21st-century model composed of flexible learning environments where students learn by doing. Behavioral psychology, too, has influenced a wide variety of everyday situations that range from classrooms to therapy. For example, behavior modification, the application of learning contingencies to the real world, brings principles of learning into many practical situations. Parents use reinforcement to successfully modify their children's behavior. Therapists eliminate their clients' fears using counterconditioning and flooding. Teachers make their classrooms better by establishing conditioned reinforcers such as stars and stickers. The applied areas of psychology today account for the employment of most psychologists. We promised early in this chapter that the things you learn in this book will take you beyond the laboratory or the classroom. By becoming a scientific thinker you will be able to apply psychology's methods to many real-world circumstances.

PHILOSOPHY OF SCIENCE

To prepare you for our discussion of how theory operates in science, we examine three important 20th-century philosophers of science: Karl Popper, Thomas Kuhn, and Paul Feyerabend. In the early 1900s, as science became a prominent part of the intellectual world, philosophers began to study it from their own perspective. Karl Popper (1902–1994) proposed a method to determine the worth of scientific theories. Thomas Kuhn (1922–1996) discovered that the traditional way of thinking about science's progress had

FIGURE 1.8
Karl Popper.

been largely unrecognized. Paul Feyerabend (1924–1994) doubted that science could be studied at all because he found no consistent methodological rules that applied, without exception, to science.

Karl Popper

Karl Popper (**Figure 1.8**) believed that some of science's theories were not really scientific. He believed that Einstein's general relativity theory was scientific but that Freud's psychoanalytic theory was not. General relativity hinged upon gravity bending light, a suggestion that violated existing (that is, Newtonian) physical theory. Eddington's 1919 confirmation of Einstein's prediction about bending light (Coles, 1999) inspired Popper. Using Einstein's theory as a model, Popper proposed that all scientific theories be judged as to how **falsifiable** they were. Falsifiable theories made predictions that could be shown to be false. On the other hand, nonfalsifiable theories made ambiguous predictions that were difficult or impossible to test. For Popper, authors of scientific theories should state their predictions in a way that data could destroy the entire theory. Such theories were falsifiable and, thus, were good scientific theories. Falsifiability became Popper's method for determining the worth of a scientific theory. Unlike the majority of scientists, Popper reversed their usual order of observation, experiment, theory. Instead, Popper argued that theory should be the first step in science. A falsifiable theory points the scientist to the observations and experiments necessary to falsify the theory. The more the theory resists scientists' attempts at falsification, the better it is.

falsifiable Karl Popper's criterion for deciding the worth of a scientific theory. Falsifiable theories allow their predictions to be tested.

Thomas Kuhn

The inspiration for Thomas Kuhn's description of the growth and death of scientific theories came after he read old science textbooks. Kuhn (**Figure 1.9**) wondered how someone as smart as Aristotle could have had such wrongheaded ideas about motion. Aristotle believed that moving objects traveled in straight lines only. For Aristotle, the path of an arrow shot into the air was an upside-down *V*. Galileo's observations, however, showed that the arrow's path was a parabola. As van Gelder (1996, p. B7) noted, Kuhn eventually realized that Aristotle's views were not "bad Newton"; they were just different. From then on, Kuhn looked for historical evidence of intellectual conflict; he found it. Science, he claimed, was normally a peaceful enterprise whose practitioners agreed about the problems to be addressed and the methods to use. Those scientists, he said, shared a **paradigm,** a shared viewpoint that determines what questions are asked and what methods are used. Every now and then, however, a discipline might go through a period of doubt and strife when a new theory challenged an existing paradigm. Kuhn called those periods of intellectual conflict *scientific revolutions*. For Kuhn, revolutions occurred when an old paradigm no longer worked and was replaced by a new paradigm. Over time, the theorists supporting the new paradigm became more numerous whereas those supporting the old paradigm either converted or retired. Eventually the scientific revolution was complete. Very soon after the publication of Kuhn's book, *The Structure of Scientific Revolutions* (1962), other philosophers began to address (and criticize) Kuhn's views of science and its progress.

FIGURE 1.9
Thomas Kuhn.

paradigm A global viewpoint that determines which scientific questions are asked and the methods used to answer them.

Kuhn's ideas about scientific progress have sparked debate about how they apply to psychology. Some psychologists believe that, as a young science, psychology has yet to develop any paradigms at all. Psychology is preparadigmatic, to use Kuhn's terminology. Other psychologists, how-ever, believe that Kuhn's idea of scientific revolutions is not applicable to psychology. Instead, psychology's wide variety of topics (see Table 1.2) reflect a tradition of independent research and theorizing, none of which is amenable to the kind of synthesis suggested by Kuhn. Recently, Stern-berg and Grigorenko (2001) argued for a unified conception of psychol-ogy based on phenomena and not on methods of inquiry. Furthermore, they see "unified psychology" as a multiparadigmatic, multidisciplinary, and integrated approach in which researchers should attempt to break free of smaller and restrictive mindsets.

Paul Feyerabend

Paul Feyerabend (**Figure 1.10**) was a student of Popper's and a colleague of Kuhn's who gradually drifted away from Popper's view of science. An Austrian, he served in the German army during World War II on the Russian Front. After the war, he received his PhD at the University of Vienna where he met Popper whom he followed to the London School of Economics. After teaching in England, he moved to the United States where he met Kuhn. While teaching at the University of California, Berkeley, in the early 1960s, Feyerabend began to question the very roots of knowledge itself. As

FIGURE 1.10
Paul Feyerabend.

he taught newly enfranchised minority students, he wondered what right he had to tell them how to think. Moreover, he began to question his own scientific training. He eventually wrote a manifesto, *Against Method* (1975), in which he doubted all method, including science's. Feyerabend was a relativist[8] of the highest order and thus could not force himself to decide whether one method of finding truth is better than another. Science was too complex to be explained by any single methodology. Because science had so many methods and no way of deciding which method to use beforehand, it did not deserve its unique status among methods of inquiry, he argued. Feyerabend represents a small group of philosophers who question science's generality and applicability. Obviously, your authors do not share Feyerabend's views; otherwise, we would not have written this book! We believe that scientific methods are superior to others for investigating the natural world. However, we agree with Feyerabend that the methods of science and psychology must always be scrutinized and not simply accepted because of tradition.

THEORY IN SCIENCE

One of the characteristics of science is theory, which serves two main functions. Theory provides a cognitive framework for the data that scientists collect. That is, theories help scientists make sense of their data by providing a way to find patterns in the data. Without theories, the sheer mass of data that scientists collect would overwhelm their capacity to organize and understand their findings. A second function of theories is that they guide future research. Theories help point scientists toward new problems.

The oldest theories in science are the **ideal theories** of the physical sciences. Ideal theories deduce theorems (rules and laws) from axioms (essential observations), and correspond precisely to the observed data (Mjøset, 2001). Physical science theories explain complex physical systems by postulating relationships among a small number of variables. For example, Hawking (1988) noted that Newton's theory of gravity depended on only two variables, mass and distance, but that gravity explains a diverse group of phenomena, including oceanic tides and the motion of planets. Successful physical theories may end up as "laws of nature" such as the law of gravity or the second law of thermodynamics. The success of physical science and its theories has been so spectacular that biologists and social scientists naturally tried to imitate them. However, theories in biological science and in social science differ considerably from the ideal theories in physical science.

Unfortunately, the nature of biological and social science is such that it is impossible to simply apply physical science's way of theorizing.

ideal theory Traditional theory in physical science that creates generalizable models and laws from observations of the universe.

---

[8]Relativism is the philosophical doctrine that maintains that truth is not absolute or unchangeable. Instead, truth varies according to historical time and culture.

Neither biology nor social science has yet discovered any laws as universal as those of the physical sciences. That lack of success has led to conceptions of theory that are narrower or different entirely from those of ideal theory. Let's start with a survey of your conceptions about social science theory.

Psychological Theories and You

Before you read about social science theories, take this survey. It will reveal what you think psychological theory is (or what you think it should be).

1. It is only a matter of time and effort before psychology discovers laws like those in physical science theories. True or false?

   If you answered true, see Number 1 in **Table 1.3**. If you answered false, go to question 2.

2. Psychological theories will always be narrowly defined, more restricted versions of physical science theories. True or false?

   If you answered true, see Number 2 in Table 1.3. If you answered false, go to question 3.

3. Using simpler models of complex psychological processes is a good way to study psychology. True or false?

   If you answered true, see Number 3 in Table 1.3. If you answered false, go to question 4.

4. Psychology is a kind of exclusive club that I want to join because it will allow me to understand the world in a way that nonmembers of the club cannot. True or false?

   If you answered true, see Number 4 in Table 1.3. If you answered false, go to question 5.

5. The world is a bad place, but by becoming a psychologist I can help make it better. True of false?

   If you answered true, see Number 5 in Table 1.3.

If you answered false to all five, our effort to classify you as a theorist has failed!

TABLE 1.3	Psychological Theories and You—What Your Answers Mean

1. You are waiting for psychology to move from law-oriented to ideal theories.

2. You are a law-oriented theorist.

3. You are an idealizing theorist.

4. You are a constructivist.

5. You are a critical theorist.

THEORY IN PSYCHOLOGY

In the face of the difficulty of using physical science's ideal theory in social science, Mjøset (2001) described four alternative views of social science theorizing. All of these alternatives modify ideal theory to a lesser or greater extent. Two alternatives, law-oriented theory and idealizing theory, make relatively minor changes to ideal theory. **Law-oriented theories** restrict the universality of ideal theories to more narrow domains whose theories apply only within those domains. Chapter titles of a general psychology textbook such as development, learning, and cognition are basically a list of law-oriented theories. **Idealizing theories,** on the other hand, attempt to discover the perfect (or ideal) situation. Unfortunately, that search is doomed because it requires complete knowledge beforehand. The compromise here is to restrict the number of variables considered in order to create working models that explain the phenomena under observation. The economic "law" of supply and demand is a good example of idealizing theory. It predicts prices accurately only when variables outside the model (such as taxes or government controls) are kept constant. In this view of these two theoretical approaches, psychological "laws" apply only within restricted domains (e.g., law-oriented theories) or when only the most critical or salient variables are included (idealizing theory).

Mjøset's two other categories of social science theory, constructivism and critical theory, reject natural science's ideal theory entirely. **Constructivism** characterizes science and scientific work by asserting that the gap between scientific knowledge and general knowledge is closer than ideal theory holds it to be. At the same time, constructivism is unwilling to give greater credence to scientific findings than to other findings. **Critical theory** makes ethical behavior the key to theorizing and sees observation as an intermediate step toward creating a better world. For critical theorists, observations are a starting point for social change motivated by universal ethical principles. Let's look at these four types of theories more closely.

Law-Oriented Theory

Law-oriented theories restrict the scope of a theory to a narrow aspect of behavior instead of trying to create a universal theory that applies in all situations. Piaget's cognitive developmental theory and Maslow's hierarchy of needs are examples of law-oriented theory. From the perspective of law-oriented theory, most of psychology can be viewed as a disjointed collection of law-oriented theories with each theory covering its own narrow domain. Instead of universal laws, law-oriented psychological theories offer local "ordinances" that may or may not be applicable in the next "jurisdiction." Law-oriented theories preserve the methodological rigor of physical science ideal theories, but lose their broad applicability. Most of the psychological theories that you learn about in undergraduate psychology courses are of this type. Many law-oriented theorists believe (or hope) that psychology will eventually discover ideal theories.

law-oriented theory Modification of the ideal theory that limits the universality of its theoretical constructs.

idealizing theory Modification of the ideal theory that creates models based on a few, core variables.

constructivism Rejects the ideal theory; proposes that science is just one of many approaches to knowledge.

critical theory Rejects the ideal theory; uses ethical principles as its main theoretical guide.

FIGURE 1.11
Rodent Skinner box.

Idealizing Theory

Idealizing theories attempt to find the core variables that determine a behavior. Theorists who create idealizing theories set up models of reality that preserve only selected parts of the behavioral situation. A rat in a Skinner box (or operant chamber) is a good example of a restricted behavioral situation (see **Figure 1.11**). In the chamber, nearly all of the variables that affect learning in the real world have been removed. The only things left are an uncluttered box, a lever connected to a food dispenser, and of course, a hungry rat. Eventually, the rat learns to operate the lever to get food because the reinforcer (the food) has a powerful influence on learning. But what does this situation tell us about learning when more variables are added? The original model may not work as well when more variables are added.[9] The problem with idealizing theory is that the simpler models they create sometimes fail as more variables are added.

---

[9]In urban environments, rats learn to swim through sewers. Residents who live in rat-infested areas must keep their toilet lids closed to keep rats out of their houses. An observer of rats in a Skinner box would have difficulty predicting, ahead of time, that rats could learn to swim through sewers, but could explain the behavior nicely after the fact.

Constructivist Theory

Constructivist theory rejects the idea that scientific knowledge is special or different from everyday knowledge. It also rejects scientists' traditional intellectual status as "superior." Instead, constructivist theory sees science as a set of socializing principles and scientists as members of a group who have accepted these principles. To a constructivist, a scientist is someone who has been admitted into the "tribe" of scientists through ceremony and practice. Think of graduation exercises, academic gowns, and sheepkins as examples of such tribal ceremonies and practices in the academic world. In constructivist theory, reality and ethics are relative. Men and women thus experience similar situations differently because their biological sex, psychological experiences, and social environment all interact to create separate and distinct realities. Similarly, ethical decisions vary depending on a number of factors including historical time, culture, and situation. To constructivists, scientific reality is only one of many realities, and constructivists see no way to declare scientific reality any better than other similarly constructed but nonscientific realities. Thus, constructivists reject ideal theory's search for universal truths as impossible and misguided. Instead, constructivists maintain that psychological data are best explained within frameworks than include variables such as gender, culture, historical time, and the effect of social processes.

Critical Theory

Critical theorists reject the relativism of constructivist theory. They insist on a universal foundation for social science, a foundation based on ethics. Critical theory is the only theory that makes the attainment of universal ethical principles the standard for scientific work. In addition, critical theorists see the world as imperfect. Data collected by critical theorists are used to demonstrate how much distance still remains between the unjust present and the just world of the future. Critical theorists use the historical success of social movements such as racial justice, feminism, and universal suffrage to demonstrate that an ethical world is an attainable goal. That humans still resort to violence such as guns and suicide bombs should not be viewed as a flaw in critical theory. Critical theorists see a future in which such violence is avoided through the use of language. Settling conflicts through communication instead of physical confrontation is a goal of critical theory. Critical theorists, unlike most scientists, see themselves as agents of social and ethical change.

Summary of Social Science Theories

Our main goal in differentiating between the ideal theory of natural science and the social science theories is to give you a more sophisticated understanding of how theory and research interact with each other. Most psychological theorizing is law oriented or idealizing, and most researchers realize that the likelihood of discovering universal laws of behavior or cognitive processing is very slim. They understand that researching narrow areas of psychology is much more likely to yield important, but limited, results and theories to explain those results. Some psychologists, though, are more willing to cast aside the ideal theory model and characterize psychology in terms of constructivism or critical theory. Those who create constructivist theories see psychology as less amenable to reduction to universal or even local laws. To them, psychology is both complex and dynamic. Thus, constructivist theories will also be complex and dynamic. Critical theorists also question the use of ideal theory and its near relatives, law-oriented and idealizing theories, in psychology. In addition, critical theorists reject constructivism's endorsement of relativism. The eventual goal of a just and ethical world appeals to critical theorists. In summary, theory in psychology is a complex topic. Our discussion is designed to just introduce you to this complexity.

RESEARCH METHODS AND YOU

We hope you recognize that we are rather excited about research methods and psychology. In this last section, we'd like to get you a little excited about research methods too. We believe that learning research methods will bring you far more than a grade and a few credits toward your degree. In fact, we believe that you will take things from this course that will last a lifetime and will be applicable in a wide variety of settings. For some of you the payoff will come on the job, for others it will come in graduate school, and for still others it will benefit you in your daily life. Lots of data support these contentions of ours.

Table 1.4 lists some of the skills that are considered useful by employers. Your research methods course will help you develop many of these skills.

So, who are these employers who value these skills? **Table 1.5** shows fields of employment and types of work performed by research-trained psychologists. Note the wide variety of work settings in which research methods are important.

TABLE 1.4	Useful Skills According to the National Association of Colleges and Employers
• Communication skills	• Flexibility/adaptability
• Honesty/integrity	• Interpersonal skills
• Teamwork skills	• Motivation/initiative
• Strong work ethic	• Computer skills
• Analytical skills	• Detail oriented

Source: From Job Outlook 2006, National Association of Colleges and Employers, copyright holder.

TABLE 1.5	Nonacademic Careers for Scientific Psychologists: Today's Careers for Research-Trained Psychologists

Field of employment

Advertising	Health
Aerospace	Human Resources (e.g., personnel)
Architecture & Design	Human Services (e.g., social service)
Banking/Finance	Industry
Business	Insurance
Computer Hardware & Software	Manufacturing
Consumer Products	Military
Criminal Justice System	Museums, Zoos
Education	Sports
Employment	Startup Companies
Entertainment, the Arts	Telecommunications
Environment	Transportation/Traffic
Government	

Type of work performed

Administration	Motivation
Advising	Negotiation
Analysis	Performance Evaluation
Assessment	Polling
Business Process Engineering	Public Policy
Computer/Human Interface	Recruiting
Consulting	Rehabilitation
Counseling	Research
Data Analysis	Safety
Design	Sensory Evaluation/Perception
Editing	Software Engineering
Ergonomics	Statistics
Evaluating	Strategic Planning
Experimental Design	Stress Evaluation
Facilitation	Teaching/Training
Focus Groups	Time-Motion Study
Forensics	Work Design
Interviewing	Writing
Market Research	

Source: From APA Online, http://www.apa.org/science/nonacad-jobs.html.

Graduate training in psychology provides many opportunities to learn other skills that are useful inside and outside academic and scientific settings. Perhaps the most widely applicable skills are in information gathering, analysis and synthesis, methodology, and statistical reasoning. Graduate training can prepare you for a career at a college or university, of course, but it can also prepare you for a wide variety of nonacademic careers. For example, psychologists design cockpits for NASA and furniture for manufacturing companies. Psychologists create incentive systems for brokerage houses and personnel evaluation systems for police departments. They develop ways to alleviate dental pain, and stress of those working crime scenes. Their research impacts jury selection, prison design, toy advertising, and interactions with computers.

Even outside work and the classroom, the benefits of a research methods course are valuable. All of us are consumers and should learn to make intelligent choices in the marketplace. Marketers flood everyone with products and statistics. What you learn in this course will help you navigate those data. Many of you are or will become parents, and your children will challenge you in ways you never thought possible. Knowledge of research methods will help you as parents, too. Finally, it's fundamentally satisfying to know that when you are asked a question, you will always be able to say "I may not know the answer now, but I know how to find it!"

In chapter 2 we describe how psychology investigates behavior and cognitive processes using scientific methods. We introduce many of the basic concepts and terms that are used in psychological research.

Chapter Review _____

1. Science is about _____ years old.

2. Name the four characteristics of science that the text identifies.

3. Before scientific explanations existed, _____ , _____ , and _____ were used to explain the world.

4. Place Aristotle, Plato, and Socrates in the correct chronological order.

   a. Socrates, Aristotle, Plato

   b. Plato, Aristotle, Socrates

   c. Socrates, Plato, Aristotle

   d. Aristotle, Plato, Socrates

5. Universities were first established in about _____ ; they were places where _____ were trained.

6. Two models of the solar system are the _____ and _____ models.

7. The scientific discovery that first caused Galileo trouble with the Inquisition was:

   a. his discovery of the four moons of Jupiter

   b. experiments with falling bodies

   c. switching careers from medicine to mathematics

   d. publishing *Dialogues Concerning the Two Chief World Systems*

8. Darwin's theory of evolution caused people to:

   a. believe that the earth revolved around the sun

   b. believe that gravity bent light

   c. rethink their relationship with the natural world

   d. believe the mind could be studied empirically

9. Match the person with the accomplishment.

   1. Einstein   a. explained how populations changed over time

   2. Galileo   b. showed that matter and energy were equivalent

   3. Darwin   c. studied the mind using introspection

   4. Wundt   d. discovered new bodies in the solar system

10. The text identifies _____ as the first psychologist; the year he founded the first laboratory in psychology was _____.

11. Match the theorist with the phrase.

    1. Thomas Kuhn   a. falsifiability

    2. Karl Popper   b. paradigm shifts

    3. Paul Feyerabend   c. all method is flawed

12. Match the type of theory with its characteristic.

    1. idealizing   a. ethical behavior is a necessary foundation of science

    2. constructivist   b. a restricted number of variables account for a restricted range of phenomena

    3. critical   c. science is just one way to explain the world

    4. law-oriented   d. laws are universal, but apply only to restricted situations

Thinking Critically About Research

1. Identify which one of the four characteristics of science each statement relates to.

   a. I like science because there are no secrets and everything is above board.

  b. The thing I like about science is that undiscovered things are predicted by principles.

  c. I'm going to take a scientific approach and look for myself.

  d. It is easy to find scientific stuff because so much is online.

  e. The neat thing about science is that the facts are explained by an overarching idea.

  f. The facts that get put into textbooks have been observed several times at least.

2. In a few sentences, describe the kind of scientific surprises that resulted from the work of Galileo, Darwin, and Einstein.

3. Distinguish between good and bad scientific theories, according to Popper.

4. Identify which type of theory is being described in each sentence.

  a. I know my little law doesn't cover much ground, but that's the way it is in psychology; there are no big laws that encompass several little ones.

  b. We should emulate Einstein and search directly for laws as big as $E = mc^2$.

  c. We should start and finish our scientific efforts ensuring that what we do is ethical.

  d. I know my little law doesn't cover much ground but someday someone will incorporate lots of little laws into a big one.

  e. You may see it differently and that is just fine, but my training tells me how to explain these results.

Answers to Chapter Review

1. 500
2. empiricism, public nature, replication, theory
3. myth; magic; mystery
4. c. Socrates, Plato, Aristotle
5. the Middle Ages or the late 12th century; clerics or clergy
6. geocentric; heliocentric
7. a. his discovery of the four moons of Jupiter
8. c. rethink their relationship with the natural world
9. 1. b; 2. d; 3. a; 4. c
10. b. Wilhelm Wundt; 1879
11. 1. b; 2. a; 3. c
12. 1. b; 2. c; 3. a; 4. d

Answers to Thinking Critically About Research

1. a. public nature; b. theory; c. empiricism; d. public nature; e. theory; f. replication

2. Galileo discovered the moons of Jupiter using his telescope. This discovery challenged the existing worldview because there were supposed to be only seven "heavenly bodies." Darwin used evidence from plants and animals to create a theory of evolution with natural selection as the mechanism. His ideas challenged the conception that nature is static. Einstein's theory of relativity showed that our universe is quite different than it appears and that very small or very fast particles follow rules unlike those of the observable world. Einstein's efforts changed our view of how the universe is put together.

3. For Popper, good and bad scientific theories were distinguished by their falsifiablity. A falsifiable theory is good because it makes specific predictions that can be proven wrong. If the data do not confirm the predictions, the theory, though scientific, is incomplete or mistaken. An unfalsifiable theory is bad because its predictions are so vague or contradictory that no result can prove the theory wrong.

4. a. law-oriented; b. ideal; c. critical; d. idealizing; e. constructivist

Know for Sure

Aristotle, 9

constructivist theory, 30

critical theory, 30

Darwin, Charles, 13

Einstein, Albert, 15

empiricism, 4

falsifiable, 23

Feyerabend, Paul, 25

Galileo, 12

geocentric model, 12

heliocentric model, 12

ideal theory, 26

idealizing theory, 29

Kuhn, Thomas, 24

law-oriented theory, 28

natural selection, 14

paradigm, 24

Popper, Karl, 23

publish, 5

replication, 5

science, 2–6

theory, 6, 26

Wundt, Wilhelm, 16

2

Research in Psychology

OVERVIEW

This chapter provides an overview of psychological research.[1] It covers topics that range from getting an idea to presenting the conclusions. The basic elements of research are explained using published research articles, including some conducted by undergraduates. The format that psychologists use to present their findings and many of the terms they use are introduced. All of the topics in this chapter turn up in more detail in later chapters.

OBJECTIVES

After studying this chapter and working through the exercises, you should be able to:

1. Distinguish among experimental research, correlational research, and meta-analytic research

2. Identify nine components of the research process

3. Describe the logic of a model experiment

4. Distinguish among confounded variables, controlled variables, and extraneous variables and identify what they have in common

5. Distinguish between: random samples and convenience samples; internal validity and external validity; and descriptive statistics and inferential statistics

6. Define *independent variable, dependent variable, nuisance variable,* and *peer review*

7. List the seven sections of the format that psychologists commonly use in their presentations

---

[1]Because this chapter is an overview of research in psychology, it has lots of terms and concepts. Many, however, are ones that you already have at least some familiarity with. An overview is helpful because it provides a context for specific topics such as ethics, measurement, and statistics when those topics are explained in detail in later chapters. The pedagogical technique of providing an overview followed by more detailed explanation is sometimes referred to as the *spiral method*.

Modern science has been developing for five centuries. During this time it has compiled an impressive catalog of facts and a number of theories that help explain the facts. One result of this development is that *applications* of our scientific understanding have transformed our world into one where space travel, artificial organs, and manufactured materials stronger and lighter than anything that occurs naturally are commonplace and even expected.

In psychological science during the 20th century, scientists discovered many new phenomena. The application of this knowledge has transformed the ways that we treat mental illness, structure organizations, and educate children. As one example, the counseling provided to children with behavior problems is quite different today from what it used to be.

What does the future hold? One possibility is that psychological problems could be prevented rather than just treated. The *American Psychologist* devoted a special issue to the prevention of psychological problems that occur among youth. The problems addressed were those such as mental health, violence, drug abuse, delinquency, and adolescent pregnancy. In that issue, Weissberg, Kumpfer, and Seligman (2003) noted that 20% of children and adolescents exhibit symptoms of mental disorder during the course of a year and that about three fourths of these do not receive treatment. Some 30% of youths 14 to 17 years of age engage in more than two high-risk behaviors. The long-term effect is that a significant proportion of youth fail to mature into adults who contribute positively to their families, communities, and society. Psychologists now believe that these problems can be *prevented*. By applying psychological principles and methods in a preventive fashion, youth (and later, adults) will be healthier and more successful in school and in life; all of society will benefit.

Many psychology-based prevention programs have been implemented in recent years and most of them have been formally evaluated to determine how effective they are (Nation et al., 2003). Successful programs had several characteristics in common. They used multiple interventions in a variety of settings, emphasized the learning and practice of new skills, and were theory driven. Successful programs were also implemented by teams of people working together. The determination of whether or not a program was successful was based on data. Understanding how to obtain data (research methods) and how to analyze them (statistics) are important skills for those who want to contribute to prevention research. Let's move from a description of the topic of prevention to a scenario that might appeal to you:

Imagine that you were attracted to the topic of prevention of youth problems. Suppose that you believed that if a prevention science were developed and applied to youth problems, your children and grandchildren (and nieces, nephews, neighborhood children, and others) would be healthier and more successful in school and in life (and, of course, that you would be safer and happier as well). Suppose that you decided to get in on the ground floor of this exciting, developing field of prevention science. How might you get started? Remember, the successful programs were those with several people working together as a team.

What do you know about problems that can arise when a team of individuals work together to reach a common goal?

As you probably know, social psychologists (among others) specialize in studying how groups of individuals work. If we posed the Stop & Think question to social psychologists, they would identify a number of problems that occur among team members. The problem(s) you wrote down would probably be listed. In this chapter, we focus on a particular problem that we are sure social psychologists would identify—social loafing. **Social loafing** is a phenomenon that sometimes occurs when individuals work together. In particular, social loafing occurs when people don't work as hard when they are in a group as they do when working alone.

Having identified social loafing as a potential problem that goes with teamwork, the next step is to find out more. Does it always occur? How much of a problem is it, really? If it is a big problem, can it be prevented? To answer these and other questions, researchers begin by reading the literature. *Reading the literature* means that they read studies on social loafing that were published in psychology journals. We have detailed directions and advice on searching the literature for topics of interest in chapter 11.

AN EXAMPLE OF PSYCHOLOGICAL RESEARCH

To make this overview of research more engaging and more specific, we describe three studies that were conducted by students. We begin with a portion of a study published by undergraduate students at Widener University in *Psi Chi: Journal of Undergraduate Research.* The reference to this study is:

Welter, W., Canale, S., Fiola, C., Sweeney, K., & L'Armand, K. (2002). Effects of social loafing on individual satisfaction and individual productivity. *Psi Chi Journal of Undergraduate Research, 7,* 142–144.

In this research on social loafing, groups of 3 to 6 people were formed by random assignment from a total of 51 participants. Each group was told that it would participate in a brainstorming activity.[2] One member

---

[2]Brainstorming is a group technique for soliciting ideas. Participants express their ideas freely and no judgments or doubts are expressed. All ideas are written down.

social loafing Working less as a group member as compared to working alone.

in each group was a **confederate** of the researchers. For some groups, the confederate was a *loafer* who made disparaging remarks about the project and contributed no ideas. For other groups, the confederate was a *worker* who contributed both ideas and positive comments about the project. The task for each group was to think of unusual uses for a paper clip. About half of the participants were women and about 80% were traditional students (ages 18 to 22). When an idea was expressed, group members wrote it down, putting an asterisk by their own contribution(s). Brainstorming sessions lasted 8 minutes.

The researchers' hypothesis was that the number of unique uses of a paper clip would be greater in groups with a confederate worker than in groups with a confederate loafer. Of course, the contributions of the confederates were not included in the analysis of the data. The researchers' hypothesis was based on an earlier study by Mulvey, Bowes-Sperry, and Klein (1998). The data collected by Welter and colleagues (2002) favored their hypothesis; the mean number of uses in groups with workers ($M = 5.67$ uses) was greater than the mean for groups with loafers ($M = 4.57$ uses). When the two means were analyzed with a statistical test, the difference (1.10 uses) was not statistically significant, which means that it is reasonable to think that chance might account for the difference observed. Thus, support for their hypothesis was weak.

What questions, comments, or uncertainties do you have about the social loafing study? Write down your thoughts now. We will likely address some of them as the chapter progresses; resolution for others may require you to talk with other students or your instructor.

One attitude about the social loafing study might be expressed as, "Paper clips? Who cares about paper clips?"

The response might be, "Well, nobody actually, but the study is really about creativity. Thinking up new uses for a paper clip is just a handy way to measure a person's creativity."

Thus, for Welter et al. (2002), *uses of a paper clip* was the **operational definition** of creativity. Psychologists are quite interested in topics such as creativity, intelligence, and depression, but to use scientific methods of investigation, they must be able to measure those topics. An operational definition tells how the researchers measured a concept.

CATEGORIES OF RESEARCH IN PSYCHOLOGY

Let's step back from the close analysis of the social loafing study for a few pages so we can examine the whole field of psychological research. Although the number of different topics investigated by psychologists is

confederate Member of the research team who appears as a naïve participant but instead plays a predetermined role.

operational definition Procedures or operations used to measure a variable or establish a condition.

enormous, the number of methods used is much smaller. In turn, it has been common to group the methods into three categories: experimental research, correlational research, and meta-analytic research.

Experimental Research

In **experimental research,** the outcome of one treatment (or condition) is compared to the outcome of a different treatment to determine if one is better or worse than the other and by how much. Experimental research is characterized by a focus on *differences in groups*. The social loafing experiment is an example of experimental research. Some participants brainstormed with a loafer; others brainstormed with a worker. Thus, there were two groups of participants in different conditions. The effect of these two conditions was assessed by measuring the number of paper clip uses that the participants thought of. Experimental research is very common and is used in many disciplines.

At the heart of an experiment is a comparison—a comparison between treatments, conditions, or experiences. In a model experiment, the groups that are compared differ in only one clearly defined way. However, in conducting an experiment there is no checklist of procedures that *guarantees* only one difference. Different combinations of procedures produce greater or lesser correspondence to the one-difference ideal. Unfortunately, there is no consistent terminology that distinguishes among the combinations of procedures. The terms that are used include *random assignment, true experiment, randomized experiment, quasi-experiment, natural experiment, correlation experiment, field experiment,* and *ex-post facto experiment*. Of course, all this inconsistent terminology makes it difficult for beginning research methods students (and for their professors). Here is our solution to this terminology problem:

In this textbook, we use the word *experiment* in a broad, unrestrictive fashion to mean any comparison of treatments, conditions, or experiences. One category of experiments is **random assignment** experiments. In such experiments, participants are randomly assigned to the groups that are compared. Random assignment is a procedure that comes closest to guaranteeing a one-difference comparison. Our second category of experiments is **quasi-experiments,** which are those that do not use random assignment. Quasi-experiments vary in how well they accomplish the one-difference ideal. Where appropriate, we introduce the terms in the italicized list above and show their relationship to random assignment experiments or quasi-experiments.

Correlational Research

In **correlational research,** the *degree* of relationship between variables is measured rather than the difference that results from different treatments. In a simple case of correlational research, all participants are treated the

experimental research Scientific research to compare two or more groups that received different treatments.

random assignment Procedure that uses chance to assign participants, procedures, or materials to groups.

quasi-experimental design Experimental design in which participants are assigned to levels of the independent variable according to a known characteristic.

correlational research Scientific research that predicts the outcome of one variable based on the scores of one or more other variables.

same and then measured on two or more variables. The goal is to predict an individual's score on an outcome variable based on that person's score on the other variable(s). An outcome such as happiness, drug abuse, or schizophrenia is predicted on the basis of a person's score on variables such as family history and personality tests. Variables that help predict the outcome become labeled *risk factors* if the outcome is undesirable (drug abuse and schizophrenia) and *predictors* if the outcome is a good thing (happiness). Thus, correlational research focuses on predictions. Here is our first caution about words and phrases: *correlation(al) experiment* is used by some to refer to experimental research that does not use random assignment of participants to treatments. This book, however, joins those for whom correlational research is a category of research rather than a type of experiment.

Meta-Analytic Research

Meta-analytic research focuses on synthesizing the results of several studies that report investigations of one topic. Thus, meta-analysis is the analysis of analyses. Until about 30 years ago, scholars doing meta-analytic research used a qualitative approach. They collected all the relevant research on a topic, studied it thoroughly, and drew conclusions based on their analysis. As one example, Eysenck (1952) reviewed 24 studies on the effectiveness of psychotherapy. He concluded that psychotherapy for nonpsychotic disorders was no more effective than no treatment at all.

About 30 years ago researchers began using a quantitative technique called **meta-analysis,** which was introduced and named by Gene Glass (1976). Using the meta-analytic technique, Smith and Glass (1977) reexamined the question of the effectiveness of psychotherapy. They applied meta-analysis to 475 studies and concluded that about 80% of those who receive treatment are improved as compared to the average untreated individual. Because of the Smith and Glass meta-analytic study, psychologists today can recommend psychotherapy with confidence. Meta-analysis is a technique that can be used for any topic that has been investigated quantitatively. It can be applied to both experimental and correlational research.

Commonalities and Cautions

meta-analysis
A quantitative technique that summarizes the results of many studies of a single topic.

Our description of three kinds of psychological research emphasized how they are different. Of course, they have elements in common as well. Foremost, all three approaches are empirical. In every case, the data analyzed come from observations. Also, all three involve comparisons among the empirical observations; there is never a comparison to an outside absolute authority. Finally, all three approaches contribute in different ways to our understanding of cause-and-effect relationships among variables.

We have two cautions about the three-category classification of psychological research. One caution is that a particular research project may include elements of both experimental and correlational research. A second caution is that this three-category classification, though a widely used organizational scheme, is not used by all researchers. As you encounter other sources of information on research methods, you'll just have to read carefully and be alert for alternative categorization schemes.

AN OVERVIEW OF THE RESEARCH PROCESS

Research projects from a wide variety of fields and for a wide variety of topics have many elements in common. The nine topics that follow provide an overview of the components of successful empirical research projects. If you are faced with the task of proposing and conducting a research project of your own, this overview will help.

1. The Work of Others

Knowing about work of others is valuable at every stage of the research process and not just at the beginning. Knowing about others' research gives you ideas about design and materials for your own research; it can guide your interpretation of the completed results. Your instructor, other faculty members, and graduate students in your department are often good sources of information about the work of others. If you already have an interest in a topic, encyclopedias such as *The Encyclopedia of Psychology* and the *International Encyclopedia of Social and Behavioral Sciences* are superb sources of information. Articles in professional journals usually have the most specific information and their references guide you to additional articles. The experiment on social loafing by Welter et al. (2002) cited six references to other journal articles. Chapter 11 explains how to find the work of others.

2. The Idea

Sometimes the idea for a research project comes from a journal article. It also might come from your instructor or a conversation with a fellow student. Your own experience or curiosity is often a starting point for a process that leads to a research project. If you have an interest in a particular area, then almost any topic in that area works well because your interest guarantees that you will stay engaged. The task of finding an idea to research sometimes appears difficult to beginning researchers, but it turns out not to be that hard; in fact, thousands of students do it quite successfully every semester. One technique that provides a good start is to sit for 10 minutes with a pen and paper, writing down all the ideas that come to you. In chapter 11, there is a section on getting ideas.

3. Design

In general conversation, the word *design* is used in many different ways. Among researchers, however, it refers to the broad plan that shows the main features of a study. The **design** of a research project includes the number of groups, how they are treated, and how the behavior is measured. The dependent variable, independent variable, levels of the independent variable, and how extraneous variables are controlled are all aspects of a research design. These terms are explained later in this chapter. Who the participants are and how they are assigned to groups is an important aspect of design. The order of events and the planned statistical analyses are part of the research design. Design is perhaps the most important component of any research project because it not only describes what goes on, but it also determines the kind of conclusions that are permissible when the experiment is completed.

4. Ethical Issues

Ethical issues are pervasive. Ethical problems are present before Day 1 of any research project and continue to be present after the project is completed. Many of these ethical problems are common; they occur in many kinds of research. Over the years, solutions to ethical problems have been devised and are available for you to use. In fact, most ethical issues can be anticipated and prepared for. However, unanticipated ethical problems can arise at any stage of the research process. You should remain alert for ethical issues and recognize that dealing with them has the potential to alter your plans. Chapter 3 covers ethics.

5. Logistics

Logistics refers to the details of conducting a project and the order in which they are completed. Recruiting participants, arranging for facilities, obtaining supplies, and securing permissions are all problems of logistics. Logistics might also include recruiting an assistant, practicing presentations, and writing thank-you notes. Creating a planning timeline that includes as many details as you can think of is a helpful tool as you assemble materials, permissions, and personnel. As you might imagine, the logistics of research are quite variable from one study to another.

design Part of a research plan that identifies the independent and dependent variables, tells how they are measured, and explains procedures for collecting data.

6. Data Collection

Collecting data should not begin until the details of design, research procedures, and known ethical issues are resolved. Collecting data, like logistics, is quite variable from one study to another. During our own careers we have watched gerbils foot-thump and pigeons spin; we have read clocks, counted pencils, and noted interracial contacts in school lunchrooms. One important aspect of collecting data is preserving it. Many times the data you collect can be used for other projects—yours or someone else's.

7. Data Analysis

Statistics are very helpful as you move from collecting data to understanding how the variables in your study are related. Descriptive statistics (such as means and graphs) often allow you to form preliminary conclusions. Inferential statistics (such as a *t* test) may confirm your preliminary conclusions. We address both descriptive and inferential statistics in chapters 5 and 6.

8. Conclusions

Based on the outcome of data analyses, design used, and procedures actually followed, the next step is to arrive at conclusions that the research supports. Contrary to a common saying, the data do not speak for themselves. It is the researcher who speaks. The researcher's conclusion, of course, must be supported by the data analysis.

9. Presentation of Research

The last step for the researcher is to present the findings to others. In cases of most student research, *others* is just one person, the course instructor. However, for some students, the presentation might be to a larger audience such as class members, an audience at a professional meeting, or the readers of a journal article. Certainly, the larger the audience, the greater the feedback. A common experience of researchers is that valuable, long-lasting lessons come from discussions and reflections that occur after formal and informal presentations of research.

List the components of a research plan. Which component of the research plan do your authors describe as perhaps the most important one?

STOP
& *Think*

The answer to the first Stop & Think question is shown in the left column in **Table 2.1.** In addition to the components of research, we added a column that shows chapters in this book where each component is explained in more detail. This additional column directs you to helpful information should you have to start a research project before you have finished this book. Note that four chapters are devoted to design, which we described as perhaps the most important component.

TABLE 2.1	Nine Components of Research and Chapters in the Text Where They are Addressed
Element of research	*For additional explanation. see:*
1. The work of others	Chapter 11, Planning Research
2. The idea	Chapter 11, Planning Research
3. Design	Chapter 7, Design I: Between-Subjects Designs
	Chapter 8, Designs II: Within-Subjects Designs and Pretests
	Chapter 9, Complex Designs
	Chapter 10, Observational, Qualitative, and Small-*N* Research
4. Ethical issues	Chapter 3, Ethics
	Appendix B, *Ethical Principles of Psychologists and Code of Conduct* (2002)
5. Logistics	Chapter 11, Planning Research
6. Data collection	Chapter 4, Measurement
7. Data analysis	Chapter 5, Data Exploration and Description
	Chapter 6, Statistical Tests
	Chapter 9, Complex Designs
8. Conclusions	Chapter 5, Data Exploration and Description
	Chapter 6, Statistical Tests
	Chapter 9, Complex Designs
9. Presentation of research	Chapter 12, Conducting and Reporting Research Appendix A, A Sample Student Manuscript in APA Style

STOP & *Think* Before we brought up the issue of social loafing, we asked you to stop and think of a topic associated with groups of individuals who were working toward a common goal. Recall your answer. Using the list in Table 2.1, think your way through a study of your topic.

Our description of the research process summarized in Table 2.1 is an overview and not a recipe that must be followed. For a particular research project, the order of activities may vary from the order in Table 2.1. For every research project, some of the activities occur more than once. Understanding all the components of the big picture allows researchers (and students) to use them whenever they are appropriate. We expect that this list will be helpful for your own research projects regardless of whether you conduct them in this class or later.

EXPERIMENTAL RESEARCH IN PSYCHOLOGY

This book, which is designed as an introduction to research methods, is focused principally on experimental research rather than correlational or meta-analytic research. In many ways, experimental research is the most basic of the three. Once you understand the terminology and techniques of experimental research, it is not too difficult to learn the terminology and techniques of correlational and meta-analytic research.

Let's begin by attending to the word *experiment*. To scientists *experiment* means something different from what it means in casual conversation. In casual conversation *experimental* conveys the idea of doing something new and important, but not knowing how to go about it. *Experiment* also often implies that you don't know what you are doing. In science, however, neither of these meanings holds. In science, an **experiment** is a specific set of procedures that are designed to establish, to a greater or lesser degree, a cause-and-effect relationship between two variables. A scientific experiment is one in which two or more treatments or conditions are compared. To experiment is a good thing in science.

The experimental method is well established and well understood; lots of books explain it, including this one. Of course, the experimental method sometimes produces surprising outcomes. Unexpected outcomes and the subsequent challenge to explain them make science attractive and engaging.

Although scientists believe that an experiment is a good thing, they don't all agree on what particular procedures should be honored by being called *experimental methods*. Some scientists want to restrict the word *experiment* to only the very best methods for establishing cause-and-effect relationships. Other scientists are less restrictive; for them any comparison of conditions or groups constitutes an experiment. In this book, we adopt the latter, less restrictive approach to the word *experiment*. For us, any comparison can be called an experiment. In your situation as a student who often encounters the word *experiment,* you'll have to be alert to the definition used by the particular writer or speaker.

Earlier in this chapter, you read about an experiment on social loafing. Two additional experiments, also conducted by undergraduates, are described below. In the section that follows these experiments, we explain the general concept of an experiment and identify elements that are common to all experiments.

TWO EXAMPLE EXPERIMENTS

Motivation and Performance in Sports

Melissa Frahm was interested in factors that affect the performance of motor skills. Frahm (2002) reported two experiments in her article; we

experiment A comparison of two or more conditions in search of differences.

describe part of the second one in which 28 undergraduates participated. One of the factors in her experiment was motivation to achieve, which she measured by administering the Mehrabian Achieving Tendency Scale (MATS) (Mehrabian, 1968). The MATS is a 36-item questionnaire with items such as, "I believe that if I try hard enough, I will be able to reach my goals in life." Participants respond to each item by indicating their degree of agreement. High scores mean high achievement motivation.

The particular motor skill Frahm studied was golf ball putting. Participants, who were all novice golfers, began the experiment by taking the MATS and then attempting to sink 20 putts from a point 6 feet from the cup. The number of successful putts out of 20 became the pretest number. Over the next 3 weeks, participants had six 10-minute practice sessions followed by a final test session in which they again attempted twenty 6-foot putts. The number of successful putts out of 20 was the posttest number. A participant's score was the posttest number minus the pretest number, a difference score.

After the pretest training and posttest, the MATS scores were used to divide participants into a high achievement motivation group and a low achievement motivation group. The scores of the low achievement motivation participants were positive, showing that they improved; their mean difference score was 5.2 putts. The high achievement motivation group improved even more; their mean difference score was 7.9 putts. The difference between the means of the two groups (2.7 putts) was statistically significant. Thus, both groups improved with practice but those with high achievement motivation improved more. The reference to Frahm's study, arranged in the correct format, is:

Frahm, M. J. (2002). Effects of mental imagery, physical practice, and achievement motivation on sport performance. *Journal of Psychological Inquiry, 7*, 7–12.

Music Tempo and Productivity

Jeffery Miller and his advisor, Blaine Peden, had participants listen to music while working arithmetic problems (Miller & Peden, 2003). Their hypothesis was that changes in the tempo of music affect the number of arithmetic problems completed and the number of errors made. We describe the part of their experiment in which 33 undergraduates mentally added three 3-digit numbers and wrote answers, working for 2 minutes. The arithmetic problems were simple; they required no "carrying" to the next column. While performing the mental arithmetic, all of the participants heard Bach's Brandenburg Concerto No. 3 in G Major. For one third of them, the tempo was 96 beats per minute (bpm) and there was no increase in tempo while the concerto was playing (0% increase). For another third of the participants, the tempo increased from 96 bpm to 120 bpm during the 2 minutes (a 25% increase). For the final third, the tempo increased 50% (from 96 to 144 bpm). Special software changed the tempo of the music without changing the pitch. Each participant's answer sheet was scored two ways. One score was the number of problems worked (which ranged from 11 to 42), and the other score was the number of errors made (which ranged from 0 to 5).

As the music tempo increased, the number of problems worked decreased. At the 0% increase, 25.0 problems were completed, on average. For the 25% increase in tempo, the mean was 20.7 problems and for the 50% increase, the participants worked 16.2 problems, on average. This reduction in the number of problems worked was statistically significant. As for the number of errors, the change in tempo did not produce any significant differences. In fact, few errors were made at any tempo. Thus, an increase in music tempo produced a decrease in the number of problems worked but had no significant effect on the number of errors. The reference to this article is:

Miller, J. M., & Peden, B. F. (2003). Complexity and degree of tempo modulation as factors in productivity. *Psi Chi Journal of Undergraduate Research, 8,* 21–27.

The three studies by undergraduates that we've discussed have elements that are common to all experiments. Our next step is to identify the elements and to explain the terms that psychologists use for these elements. Learning to identify the elements and use the terms allows you to understand research and thus, to join the community of those who conduct and discuss research.

ELEMENTS OF EXPERIMENTAL RESEARCH

To provide an additional context for the elements of an experiment and the terms that are used to describe them, consider the "model experiment." We use this model experiment and the three experiments discussed earlier to illustrate the elements of experimental research.

The Model Experiment

Begin by identifying or creating approximately equivalent groups of participants. Except for one particular treatment that varies from group to group, treat the participants exactly alike. Measure each participant on a variable of interest. If there are statistically significant differences among the groups on the variable of interest, attribute these differences to the different treatments that the groups received.

Independent Variables and Dependent Variables

Perhaps you are already able to identify independent and dependent variables. If so, test yourself by underlining once the phrase in the paragraph above that refers to the independent variable. Underline twice the phrase that refers to the dependent variable.

In the model experiment, the independent variable is the particular treatment that varies from group to group. Underlining <u>one particular treatment</u> once is correct. (It is also correct to underline <u>varies from group to group</u>.) The dependent variable is <u>a variable of interest</u>.

The **independent variable (IV)** and the **dependent variable (DV)** are selected by the researcher when the study is first designed. They are the two most important elements of an experiment. The purpose of the experiment is to find out if there is a relationship between these two variables. Specifically, the purpose is to see if values of the DV are related to (that is, dependent on) the IV.

When the IV is selected, the researcher also determines how many values it will have and what the values will be. To be an experiment, the IV must have at least two values (also called levels). Although the researcher also chooses the DV, its values are not known before the experiment begins.

In psychological research, the values of the DV are typically quantitative; qualitative DVs are not common. Variables such as test scores, errors, and productivity yield quantitative scores as do measures of time, distance, and frequency. Qualitative (nonnumerical) dependent variables are discussed in chapter 10 in the section on qualitative research. As for the IVs, quantitative and qualitative values are both common.

For the social loafing experiment by Welter et al. (2002), identify the IV and the DV. For the music tempo experiment by Miller and Peden (2003), identify the IV and DV.

independent variable (IV) Variable whose values are controlled by the researcher.

dependent variable (DV) Variable that is expected to change as a result of changes in the independent variable.

To express the IV and DV of an experiment, choose a word or short phrase that captures the essence of the variable. Sometimes two or three possibilities present themselves to you. Choose the alternative that seems the best, but recognize that other words or phrases may be just as good. In the social loafing experiment by Welter et al. (2002), our choice for the IV is confederate's role. The DV was uses of a paper clip. In the Miller and Peden experiment, the IV was tempo increase. Because each participant's answer sheet was scored two ways, there were two DVs. One DV was problems worked and the other was errors.

Levels of the Independent Variable

The values of the IV are usually referred to as the **levels** of the IV or **treatments**. When the general concept of an experiment is being discussed, the levels of the IV are often referred to as the **experimental group** and the **control group**. *Experimental group* and *control group* are very helpful generic terms, but for a specific experiment it is usually much more informative to refer to the groups with terms from the experiment. For example, in the social loafing experiment, if the IV is labeled confederate's role, the levels of the IV are loafer and worker. An alternative label for that IV is presence of a loafer. The two levels then become present and absent.

For Frahm's golf ball putting experiment and Miller and Peden's music tempo experiment, identify the IV, tell the number of levels of the IV, and name the levels.

For the putting experiment, the IV was achievement motivation; there were two levels, high and low. For the music tempo experiment, the IV was tempo increase. The three levels were *0%, 25%,* and *50%.*

The requirements for a good experiment are clear: Keep everything the same except for the IV and then measure the DV. Of course, keeping everything exactly the same is a tall order, and as a practical matter, is impossible. However, a number of research methods techniques allow valid comparisons even though variables other than the IV are operating. Indeed, much of the information in this text is about techniques that refine the design so that the final comparison of groups corresponds more closely to the levels of the IV. What are these variables other than the IV that might influence the DV?

Confounded Variables

If an experiment has a third variable that changes as the IV changes, the logic of the experiment is compromised. Any change in the DV that accompanies a change in the IV might be due to this third variable rather than the IV. If a third variable in an experiment is linked with the IV, the experiment is said to be confounded. **Confounded variables** are unfortunate. Although saying that they ruin an experiment is too strong, confounded variables do keep interpretations from being straightforward statements about the relationship between the IV and the DV. When a confounded variable could have been removed from an experiment but was not, the expression Confound it! is appropriate. For some topics that psychologists investigate, however, confounded variables are unavoidable, as will be explained in chapter 7.

levels   Values of the independent variable that the researcher chooses for an experiment.

treatment   Values of the independent variable that the researcher chooses for an experiment.

experimental group   Generic name of the group in an experiment that receives a treatment.

control group   Generic name of the group in an experiment that does not receive a treatment.

confounded variable   Variable whose values change in step with changes in the independent variable.

Controlled Variables

Many experiments are designed to ensure that particular variables are not confounded with the IV. In many places in this book, we describe techniques that prevent a variable from being confounded with the IV. When a potentially confounded variable is controlled, the logic of an experiment remains intact. The term ***controlled variable*** is used to identify a variable that does not vary in step with changes in the IV. In Frahm's experiment on achievement motivation, practice is a variable that affects putting scores. In that experiment, however, practice was a controlled variable because all participants received the same amount of practice. Thus, differences in achievement motivation (the IV) were not associated with a difference in practice.

Extraneous Variables

The term ***extraneous variable*** is a general term for variables that affect the DV and are linked to the IV. When extraneous variables are recognized during the design stage of the experiment, researchers use techniques that are described in chapters 7, 8, and 9 to turn them into controlled variables. If extraneous variables go unrecognized, they become confounded variables.

Nuisance Variables

A **nuisance variable** is one that increases the *range* of the DV scores but does not affect the levels of the IV differentially. The reason that these variables are a nuisance is that when scores become more variable, differences between the levels of the IV are more difficult to detect. **Figure 2.1** illustrates this problem. The panel on the left shows DV scores from a two-treatment experiment with no nuisance variables. The two distributions are fairly compact. You can see at a glance that open-circle scores are generally greater than closed-circle scores. The

controlled variable An extraneous variable that does not vary in step with the independent variable.

extraneous variable General term for a variable that varies concomitantly with the independent variable.

nuisance variable A factor that causes the dependent variable scores to be more variable.

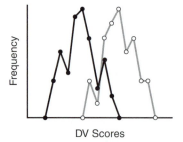
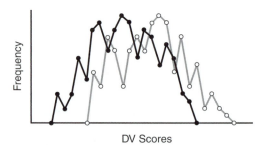

FIGURE 2.1   Both panels show the DV scores from a two-group experiment. *Left panel:* No nuisance variable operating; *right panel:* Nuisance variable increases overlap of the two distributions.

panel on the right shows what happens when nuisance variables are added to the experiment. The range of both distributions is increased, making the difference between the two much more difficult to see. In both panels the difference between the means of the two distributions is the same. Incidentally, statistical tests have the same problem that your eyes do—they are much less likely to detect the difference in treatments for the scores in the right panel.

Let's look at some examples of nuisance variables. In the social loafing experiment, the DV was the unique uses of a paper clip. What characteristic of the participants might increase the range of the scores? How about creativity? Indeed, participants differ in creativity and that is reflected in their DV score. Thus, the more variable the creativity of the participants, the more variable the DV scores. In the putting experiment, the natural athletic ability of the participants is a nuisance variable. Agree? In the music tempo experiment, the participants' varying ability to do mental arithmetic is a nuisance variable.

Besides participant differences such as those just described, variations in the environment can be nuisance variables. In the music tempo experiment, interruptions reduce the number of arithmetic problems worked. Thus, noise is a nuisance variable as is visual distraction. Equipment, too, can contribute to changes in DV scores. In Frahm's putting experiment, the inevitable variations in putting surfaces are a nuisance variable that produces variation in the number of successful putts. Variation in the balls and golf clubs is another nuisance variable.

Fortunately, nuisance variables do not compromise the logic of an experiment. If the experiment is designed well, the effect of a nuisance variable falls equally on all levels of the IV. That is, the scores of all groups are spread out equally. This leaves the logic of the experiment intact; the groups differ only on the IV. It's just that the effect of the IV is more difficult to detect when there are nuisance variables. To qualify as a nuisance variable, changes in the variable must *not* correspond to or accompany changes in the IV.

The terms *confounded, controlled,* and *extraneous* refer to variables that can influence the DV for one level of the IV differently than they do for another level of the IV. Nuisance variables affect the DV, but all levels of the IV are affected equally. **Table 2.2** lists terms that are used in experimental research and their definitions.

POPULATIONS AND SAMPLES

A **population** is the entire group; a sample is just one part of the group. The goal of research is to tell a story about the population. As a practical matter, however, populations are almost always unmeasurable. In the face of an immeasurable population, the solution is to conduct research on a

population An entire set of scores.

TABLE 2.2	Experimental Research Terms and Their Definitions
Term	*Definition*
Dependent variable (DV)	The behavior or outcome that is measured. It is expected to change as a result of changes in the IV.
Independent variable (IV)	Variable with two or more levels chosen by the researcher. Changes in the IV are expected to be related to changes in the DV.
Confounded variable	Variable that changes along with changes in the IV. The DV is affected by both the IV and the confounded variable.
Controlled variable	Variable that changes along with changes in the IV, but whose effects can be distinguished from those of the IV.
Extraneous variable	General term for a variable that changes along with changes in the IV.
Nuisance variable	Variable that causes DV scores to be more variable.

sample and then generalize the results to the population. The worry that goes with this approach is that the sample won't be an accurate mirror of the population. Fortunately, there are two ways to reduce this worry. One way is to use a random sample.

Random Samples

Random samples are obtained from a population by following a precise procedure that is described in chapter 7. The advantage of random samples is that their mathematical properties are well understood. By analyzing the characteristics of a random sample, characteristics of the population are revealed with a degree of certainty that can be measured quantitatively. Unfortunately, for many populations that are interesting to researchers, it is a practical impossibility to obtain random samples. To give you an idea about the prevalence of random samples, we examined the articles in the most recent six months of the *Journal of Consulting and Clinical Psychology,* a highly respected journal. We found that only 7% of the studies reported using random samples.[3] If random samples are so rare, what kind of samples are researchers using? Aren't they concerned about generalization?

Convenience Samples

Researchers who do not obtain random samples often refer to the samples they use as **convenience samples**. The procedures that researchers use to

sample   A subset of the population.

random sample   A sample from a population obtained by applying a random sampling technique.

convenience sample   A sample that was not obtained randomly from the population.

---

[3]In some areas of research, random or randomlike samples are more common. Examples include national survey research and research on limited populations.

secure convenience samples vary widely; there are no established procedures like those for random samples. To call a sample a convenience sample is simply to acknowledge that it isn't a random sample.

What about the issues of representativeness and generalizability? Can researchers who use convenience samples determine the degree of certainty that the sample mirrors the population? No, they can't, but researchers give two justifications for their use of convenience samples.

1. The first question in a researcher's mind is whether or not there is a relationship between the IV and the DV. Only after this relationship is established does the question of generality become relevant. Thus, a convenience sample is perfectly adequate for answering questions of whether or not there is a relationship at all.

2. The second justification for convenience samples is based on a characteristic of science that we discussed in chapter 1, the characteristic of replication. When a 3rd, 5th, or 10th study produces results similar to the first one, researchers become much more confident that the story found in all the samples is also the story of the population, even if the results are based on convenience samples.

INTERNAL VALIDITY AND EXTERNAL VALIDITY

Imagine an experiment with rats. Charlie and Charlene's project involves training rats in a Skinner box to perform an auditory discrimination task to get reinforcement. The IV in their experiment is diet. One group of rats eats rat chow enriched with the trace mineral selenium; the other group eats regular rat chow. Every morning for 2 weeks, Charlie tests the rats that ate the enriched chow, carefully recording each rat's discrimination score. Every afternoon for the same 2 weeks, Charlene tests the rats that ate the regular chow, carefully recording each rat's score. Imagine that the results show that the mean score of the rats that consumed the selenium-enriched chow is significantly higher than the mean score of the rats that ate regular chow. The researchers conclude that adding selenium to the diet improves sensory discrimination in rats and people.

Write at least two reasons why the conclusion in the rat discrimination study is not justified.

STOP & *Think*

We constructed the imaginary experiment above so we could illustrate internal validity and external validity. If you noted that the variable *experimenters* was confounded with the IV or that time of day was confounded with the IV, you are saying that the experiment is not **internally valid**. The rats with the selenium-enriched diet were trained by Charlie and the regular chow rats were trained by Charlene. Thus, the difference observed could be due to a difference in the experimenters. Differences in the two such as their smell or the way they handle rats might reasonably affect the outcome. Likewise, morning training and afternoon training might result in different performances because laboratories can differ in noise, light, and temperature over the course of a day. Of course, in a well-equipped laboratory, environmental differences associated with time of day can be eliminated. Even with the environment controlled, rats may learn better in the morning than in the evening. In summary, an experiment with internal validity is one that has no extraneous variable confounded with the IV.

Perhaps you noted that the researchers' conclusion generalized from a rat study to humans, or that they did not say whether the rats were a random sample. Perhaps you wondered whether the results of an auditory discrimination task should lead to a conclusion about sensory discrimination in general. All three of these complaints indicate you were questioning whether the experiment was **externally valid**. External validity is about generalization of the results to other species, situations, or times. What about generalizing from rats to people? Is it OK? In general, it is quite acceptable among scientists. Unless there are reasons to believe that selenium metabolism is different for rats and humans, generalization is permissible. In a similar way, without evidence that the sample or the task is unrepresentative, scientists are comfortable with generalizing. Thus, to raise a legitimate complaint about the external validity of a study, you must present evidence or reasoning that makes generalization suspect.

STATISTICAL METHODS

The relationship between research methods and statistical methods is an intimate one. Research methods are about collecting data; statistical methods are about analyzing data. The conclusions from a study depend on both the design that is used and the statistical results that are obtained. Thus, to conduct research or even to understand it requires knowledge of methods of gathering data and the statistics necessary to analyze them. Statistical methods are often classified as either descriptive statistics or inferential statistics.

Descriptive statistics summarize a set of scores from a sample or from a population. Descriptive statistics convey characteristics of a data set by reducing it to one number, two numbers, or a graph. Examples of descriptive statistics that you may be familiar with include the mean, standard deviation, correlation coefficient, and frequency polygon.

internal validity No extraneous variables are confounded with the independent variable.

external validity Results can be generalized to other populations, situations, or conditions.

descriptive statistics Numbers or graphs that summarize a data set.

Inferential statistics are techniques that permit you to draw conclusions about populations by analyzing sample data. Of course, samples always have a degree of chance built into them, so a conclusion about a population includes a degree of uncertainty. Fortunately, inferential statistics provide a quantitative measure of the uncertainty that comes with the conclusion. If there is little uncertainty, researchers assert the conclusion with confidence (while acknowledging that there is a small chance that it is wrong). If there is a great deal of uncertainty, researchers avoid drawing a conclusion from the sample.

As an example of an inferential statistics technique, Frahm (2002) analyzed the putting improvement scores for high and low achievement motivation participants with an F test. (F tests are covered in chapter 9.) The F test revealed that there was little uncertainty about the conclusion so Frahm concluded: "the group with high achievement motivation made significantly more putts than the group with low achievement motivation" (p. 10).

When it comes to calculating descriptive and inferential statistics, the two tasks for students are to get the right answer and to explain what is going on. Tools include paper and pencil, calculators, and computer software. Of course, the big benefit of computer programs is that their arithmetic calculations are always error-free. If the data entry into the program is correct, the only task you are left with is explaining the output. Explaining is harder than getting the right numbers, so be alert when reading explanations.

In this book we explain statistics in several chapters. In addition to words, graphs, and formulas, we illustrate statistics with computer software output from the Statistical Package for the Social Sciences (SPSS). Although SPSS is probably the most popular statistical software program used by social and behavioral scientists, other programs produce equally valid results. Regardless of the source of your output, we think that SPSS output and our explanations of it will help you understand descriptive and inferential statistics.

PUBLICATION AND PERSUASION

After a research project is completed, researchers often want to share the results with as many people as possible. The traditional and most prestigious format for sharing is publication in a scholarly journal. Other ways to share include oral presentations, poster presentations, and informal communication with like-minded researchers. We discuss all these possibilities in chapter 12. In addition to a desire to share, researchers usually have hopes for persuasion. That is, they hope that their publications will influence others and become part of what is accepted as psychological science.

inferential statistics Method of reaching conclusions using samples and probability.

Peers are important for both publication and persuasion. Peers, of course, are those who have equal standing with each other. Scientists are fond of the terms *peer* and *peer review* because *peer* conveys the idea that there is no supreme boss over scientists.[4] One way to enhance acceptance among peers is to use their language.

A Seven-Point Outline

In psychology and other disciplines, the style manual of the American Psychological Association (APA) dictates organization and language. The APA outline that follows is required by most psychology journals. Presenters often choose this seven-point outline for oral and poster presentations as well because their audiences expect to hear or see particular kinds of information in particular places.

1. *Title* The title should summarize the overall topic of the research in 12 words or less. Often, putting the independent variable, the dependent variable, or the theoretical issue investigated in the title helps capture readers.

2. *Abstract* The abstract is a concise summary of the information in the article in 120 words or less. It includes a statement of the problem, the independent and dependent variables, the main results, and the principal interpretation. A well-written abstract invites a person to read the whole article.

3. *Introduction* The Introduction section provides organized background information that leads up to the problem that was investigated. Theoretical issues, if any, are discussed here. Introductions often state the reason that the research was conducted and what the researcher's hypotheses were.

4. *Method* The Method section contains the details of how the study was conducted. It has information about the number and characteristics of the participants and what they did. In the Method section, the design of the study is explained, including independent and dependent variables. Test materials and apparatus are described here.

5. *Results* Descriptive statistics are reported in this section as are the results of any inferential statistical tests. Data tables and figures that display data go in the Results section.

6. *Discussion* Whereas the rest of the article is nonevaluative (only the facts are given), the Discussion section contains evaluation and interpretation. If the author(s) proposed a hypothesis in the

---

[4]Of course, some peer scientists are held in higher esteem than others.

Introduction, this section tells how well the hypothesis predicted the results. If the hypothesis fared poorly or if the results were contrary to those of previous research, the author may offer an explanation. Any confounded variables or limitations of the study are identified here. Applications of the results, statements of generalization, and suggestions for future research are found in the Discussion section.

7. *References* All studies cited anywhere in the article are listed alphabetically by first author in the references list.

Publication

The process of publication begins when the researcher sends a **manuscript** to the editor of a journal. The editor sends the manuscript out for **peer review** to a small number of reviewers (two to four) who independently critique the study and the manuscript. These reviewers, typically professors or researchers, make suggestions and render a judgment as to whether the manuscript should be published. Among dedicated researchers, publication is the most public part of their research program. Research programs are usually focused on particular aspects of fairly broad questions such as how to prevent youth violence or how individuals work together in groups.

In the Know

In the old days when an author sent material to an editor, *manuscript* was an accurate word; the report was written by hand with a pen. When typewriters came into use around the turn of the 20th century, the term *typescript* didn't catch on and *manuscript* continued to be used. Today, material to be published is submitted as a word-processed, electronic file. So far, we still refer to the file as a *manuscript*.

Persuasion

What happens after publication? How does the research community respond? Do they accept the findings? Cite the results in later publications? Send a check?

Only the last of these questions has a clear-cut answer: No check. Authors do not get paid directly for their research efforts. Scientific research is supported by institutions that are committed to producing new knowledge. Universities are the most important example of such

manuscript A typewritten report or an electronic file of a research project.

peer review Formal process in which scientists judge colleagues' work submitted for publication or funding.

institutions. They pay the salaries of researchers and also supply space (laboratories) and workers (students and staff). Researchers often receive additional financial support in the form of grants from other institutions such as governments, foundations, and corporations. Governments and foundations support research for the common good, and corporations support research in part because they expect that the results will have commercial applications. Actually, our explanation here is too simple. The relationships among universities, governments, foundations, and corporations are rather complicated.

Let's return to the question of whether or not the research community embraces the findings of a particular study. Once again, peer review is important. After publication, much of peer review consists of judgments that professors and researchers make when they read an article, hear a presentation at a professional meeting, or converse with authors and colleagues. One characteristic that makes a study acceptable is that it was conducted in an ethical manner, which is the topic of the next chapter.

Although the process of acceptance of a research finding is complex and not well understood, there is a commonly used measure of whether an article or book achieved acceptance. If a publication is widely cited by subsequent researchers, it has been accepted (or is controversial). Reference sources such as the *Social Sciences Citation Index* and *PsycINFO* tally the number of times an article or book appears in the reference section of other articles and books. As examples of accepted research, the two studies of the effectiveness of psychotherapy by Eysenck (1952) and Smith and Glass (1977) had 725 and 804 citations, respectively, in the *Social Sciences Citation Index* in August 2006. Of course, the influence of an individual article starts at near zero. Some studies become more influential over time, but then their influence declines. Other publications never begin that upward climb.

We don't want you to think that peer review is merely a matter of subjective opinion. A study's acceptance depends heavily on whether or not it meets the standards and practices of the profession. Many of these standards and practices are well known and documented in textbooks such as this one. Of course, because science is a human endeavor, its standards and practices are always being refined, a point made by Wilkinson and the Task Force on Statistical Inference (1999). As they point out, standards and practices evolve; today's standards and practices are different from what was acceptable in earlier years.

The typical story of a research project is that it leads to another research project. The researcher who completes the project incorporates what was learned from the original project into plans that often include a revised hypothesis and adjustments in the design. Often the new project serves to replicate some or all of the results of the previous project. You can see how a research *program* might get started!

CONCLUSION

This chapter is an overview of research in psychology. Understanding each component in the chapter requires elaboration—our elaboration is this textbook; your elaboration will be your engagement in your course. No doubt your instructor will contribute other valuable elaborations as well. But what is the purpose of learning about research in psychology?

At the beginning of the chapter, we asked you to suppose that you were attracted to the topic of prevention of youth problems because the world would be a better place if there were a well-developed science of prevention. If you are attracted, your path leads directly through this book. On the other hand, if you are attracted to another worthy endeavor in psychology or other behavioral science, your path also leads through this book because these methods are widely used. Even if you believe that you don't have a future as a researcher, a benefit of working your way through this course is that you will learn many of the ins and outs and ups and downs of psychological research. What you learn will make you a more informed consumer of research. Our prediction is that what you learn will be very helpful as you judge the many research findings that you come in contact with in the future.

Figure 2.2 shows a portion of a fanciful research methods tool room. Of course, few students have access to fully equipped tool rooms. Even so, perhaps the most important element in the tool room in Figure 2.2 is the ideas drawers.

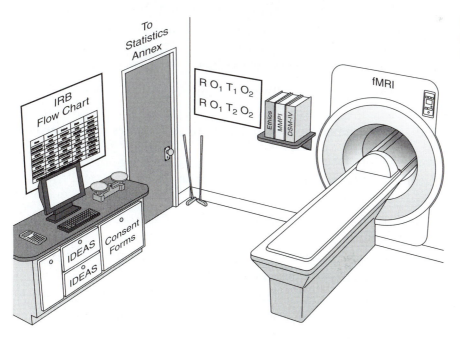

FIGURE 2.2
Research methods tool room.

Chapter Review

1. Complete each sentence with *independent* or *dependent* as appropriate.

   a. The _____ variable is the cause and the _____ variable is the effect.

   b. Values of the _____ variable are determined by the researcher; values of the _____ variable are determined by the participants.

   c. The _____ variable has an effect on the _____ variable.

2. Identify the type of variable that is described.

   a. variable that increases the range of scores but does not violate the logic of the experiment

   b. general name for a variable that varies in connection with the IV and may have an effect on the DV

   c. variable that changes in step with the IV, violating the logic of experiments

3. Identify the type of research that is described.

   a. research combines the results from many separate studies to arrive at a conclusion

   b. research compares two or more conditions and produces a conclusion about the relative position of the conditions

   c. research predicts an individual's score and gives the degree of relationship between variables

4. The text's overview of research included nine components. List them.

5. The two types of experiments identified by the text are _____ and _____.

6. Random sample and replication are two techniques that researchers use to help ensure _____.

7. The two broad categories of statistics are _____ and _____.

8. Identify the name of the section of an APA paper by its description.

   a. name of the paper

   b. bibliography of the sources cited

   c. section that describes the background for the study

   d. section that explains the implications of the study

  e. section that gives the details of how the data were collected

  f. section that reports the analysis of the data

  g. overall summary of the paper

9. Research that can be generalized to new situations has _____ validity. Research that is free of variables that are confounded with

 the independent variable has _____ validity.

Thinking Critically About Research

1. Identify the category of research described in each scenario.

  a. Forty studies on the relationship of wealth and happiness were analyzed.

  b. Four factors that predict a person's happiness were determined.

  c. The happiness scores of men and women were compared.

2. Determine whether the experiments in your text were random assignment experiments or quasi-experiments.

  a. Welter, Canale, Fiola, Sweeney, and L'Armand (2002)

  b. Frahm (2002)

  c. Miller and Peden (2003)

3. For each scenario identify the DV and the IV, and name the levels of the IV.

  a. Amber's participants read a handout about a company executive and looked at a photograph of her. From a list of 25 adjectives, participants circled those that seemed to apply to the executive. A participant's score was the number of positive adjectives circled. For half the participants the executive was smiling; for the other half the expression was neutral.

   DV

   IV

   Levels of the IV

  b. Brian entered 14 stores wearing business casual, 12 stores wearing preppy clothes, and 11 stores wearing a grunge outfit. At each store he recorded the time in seconds from entering the door until a salesperson offered assistance.

   DV

   IV

   Levels of the IV

4. This experiment is modified from that of Triplett (1898) who published the first social psychology experiment, which was on competition. Ten-year-old children reeled line onto a fishing reel.

Forty children were tested individually before school using brand-new reels. They were told to "reel as fast as you can." Thirty children were tested after school with the same reels. They were divided into groups of three and told to "be the fastest in your group." The students who competed against others reeled in an average of 65 feet of line. Those who reeled individually averaged 50 feet of line. The conclusion was that competition improves performance.

    a. Identify features of this experiment that cause problems for internal validity.

    b. Identify aspects of the experiment that could lead to questions about its external validity.

    c. Identify one extraneous variable that is explicitly the same for both groups.

    d. What effect does the difference in the size of the two groups have on internal validity? External validity?

5. Write a one-paragraph scenario that describes a specific experiment. For your scenario, identify the IV, DV, and levels of the IV. Include an extraneous variable that is controlled by being the same for both groups.

Answers to Chapter Review

1. a. independent, dependent; b. independent, dependent; c. independent, dependent

2. a. nuisance; b. extraneous; c. confounded

3. a. meta-analysis; b. experimental; c. correlational

4. 1. the work of others; 2. the idea; 3. design; 4. ethical issues; 5. logistics; 6. data collection; 7. data analysis; 8. conclusions; 9. presentation of research

5. random assignment experiments; quasi-experiments

6. external validity

7. descriptive; inferential

8. a. title; b references list; c. Introduction; d. Discussion; e. Method; f. Results; g. abstract

9. external; internal

Answers to Thinking Critically About Research

1. a. meta-analytic research; b. correlational research; c. experimental research

2. a. random assignment experiment; b. quasi-experimental design; c. random assignment experiment

3. a. DV—positive adjectives, IV—facial expression, Levels of the IV—smiling and neutral; b. DV—seconds, IV—clothing (or outfit), Levels of the IV—business casual, preppy, and grunge

4. a. Internal validity is compromised by the before-school and after-school difference and to some degree by the difference in new reels and used reels; b. External validity issues include whether results for 10-year-old children generalize to others, the generalization of reeling behavior to other competitive behaviors, and whether competition with no reward generalizes to competition with reward (in Triplett's study, the children who reeled the most line got to keep the reel); c. The age of the participants was the same for both groups; d. That the number of participants in the groups was unequal has no effect on internal or external validity

5. Many scenarios qualify as good answers; grade yourself.

Know for Sure

3

Ethics

OVERVIEW

Ethics is a commitment to follow particular, established behaviors while conducting research. Both ethical attitudes and behaviors are specified in the American Psychological Association's *Ethical Principles of Psychologists and Code of Conduct,* which is discussed in this chapter. Also covered are a brief history of ethics, three historical ethical cases, and research with animal subjects.

OBJECTIVES

After studying this chapter and working through the exercises, you should be able to:

1. Discuss the historical importance of ethics and moral codes
2. Describe how scientific ethics emerged
3. Describe the function of institutional review boards (IRBs)
4. Identify a researcher's responsibilities to participants as covered by psychology's *Ethics Code*
5. Identify a researcher's responsibilities to psychology as covered by the *Ethics Code*
6. Identify differences in the ethics of research with humans and research with animals
7. Conduct ethical research

LOST IN THE MALL

Picture this: The year is 1991 and you are taking a cognitive psychology class at the University of Washington. Your teacher emphasizes that memory is sometimes quite mistaken. She adds that some people have a completely false memory of an event but do not realize it. She suggests a class project: You are to go home and attempt to plant a completely false memory into one of your family members. The memory must be for something that never happened.

A few weeks later, Jim, one of your classmates, reports that he has managed to convince (with support from their parents) his 14-year-old brother Chris that he had been lost in a shopping mall when he was 5 years old. Jim told the following story:

> It was 1981 or 1982. I remember that Chris was 5. We had gone shopping in the University City shopping mall in Spokane. After some panic, we found Chris being led down the mall by a tall, oldish man (I think he was wearing a flannel shirt). Chris was crying and holding the man's hand. The man explained that he had found Chris walking around crying his eyes out just a few moments before and was trying to help him find his parents. (Loftus, 1993, p. 532)

On several occasions afterward, Jim got Chris to write a sentence or two about being lost. After 2 weeks, Chris told the following story about his "memory of being lost in the mall":

> I was with you guys for a second and I think I went over to look at the toy store, the Kay-Bee toy and uh, we got lost and I was looking around and I thought, "Uh-oh. I'm in trouble now." You know. And then I . . . I thought I was never going to see my family again. I was really scared you know. And then this old man, I think he was wearing a blue flannel, came up to me . . . he was kind of old. He was kind of bald on the top . . . he had like a ring of gray hair . . . he had glasses. (Loftus, 1993, p. 532)

Weeks later, Jim and his parents told Chris the truth about his false memory. Chris was quite surprised and, at first, did not believe them. Eventually, however, he came to believe that he had never been lost in a mall. Later, Chris reported that the experience, on the whole, had been pleasant. He was pleased that his story had made national headlines (in *The New York Times, The New Yorker, Newsweek,* and the *Ladies Home Journal*) and had helped spark subsequent research (Loftus, 1997).

Jim's teacher was Dr. Elizabeth Loftus, a well-known researcher in the psychology of memory. After the class project, Loftus, Jim Coan (Chris's brother), and Jacqueline Pickrell, another of Loftus's students, planned a formal experiment that involved implanting false memories. They submitted the proposed research to the Human Subjects Committee at the University of Washington, which approved after revising their plan some (Loftus, 1999). Soon thereafter at the 1992 meeting of the American Psychological Association, Loftus reported the classroom findings about the Lost in the Mall research. She referred to Chris and others as pilot subjects (Crook & Dean, 1999b), not as students participating in a class-room exercise.

PRISON GUARDS AND PRISON INMATES

Let's move to a different time and place. Picture this: It is 1971 at Stanford University and you volunteer to participate in a 2-week prison simulation study for $15 per day. (Today, the equivalent amount is about $75.) You and 24 other volunteers are chosen because you have no criminal record, no medical or psychological problems, and no his-tory of drug abuse. For the 2 weeks, you are to serve as either a prisoner or as a guard, a role determined by a coin flip at the beginning of the study. You are slated to serve as a prisoner. On a Sunday afternoon and in full view of your neighbors, the local police come to your home and arrest you, charge you with armed robbery and burglary, advise you of your legal rights, handcuff you, and take you to the city jail with lights flashing and siren blaring (see **Figure 3.1**). You are booked, fingerprinted, blindfolded, and put into a holding cell. From the holding cell you are moved to "prison." The prison is in the basement of the Stanford psychology building. Three rooms have been converted into cells, each of which has three cots and real bars instead of a door. The hall is the prison's "yard" and a small closet serves as the "hole," which is used

FIGURE 3.1
Arrest of a
"prisoner."

to discipline unruly prisoners. There is a bathroom. The walls are bare and there are no clocks.

You are assigned a number, and you are called by it instead of your name during the study. You are stripped naked and sprayed for lice and bacteria. You wear a smock, rubber sandals, and a cap made from women's nylon hose (to simulate having your head shaved). No underwear is issued. A heavy piece of chain is padlocked to your right ankle. The guards (fellow students, remember) wear khaki uniforms and sunglasses. They carry clubs and whistles and are untrained. You are one of nine prisoners. There are nine guards, three per shift, with three shifts per day. When the guards are not on duty, they are free to go anywhere they please. They, too, are paid $15 daily.

The first day is uneventful until 2:30 a.m. when the guards conduct a prisoner count, forcing the inmates to stand in the yard. On the morning of the second day, the prisoners riot during the guards' shift change. Prisoners remove their caps, barricade the barred doors with cots, and tear off their identification numbers. The other guards are called in and all nine move against the prisoners using fire extinguishers. The guards lock the leaders of the rebellion in the hole. The prisoners who participated least are placed in a new special privileges cell, given back their cots and uniforms, and fed better food. Twelve hours later, however, the guards move some leaders of the rebellion into the special privileges cell and move some of the others to the regular cells. The action breaks the prisoners' solidarity and intensifies the differences between prisoners and guards.

According to plan, parents and friends visit for 10 minutes on the third day. Before the visit, the guards clean the prison and issue fresh uniforms. All visitors are forced to register and then made to wait 30 minutes. During the visit, a guard is always present. After the visit, the guards hear a rumor about a mass-escape attempt that is to be aided by students on the outside. The guards respond by temporarily moving all prisoners, blindfolded and chained together, to a fifth-floor storage room. The rumor proves false. Over the next 2 days, the guards become more dominant as the prisoners become meeker and more disorganized.

After 5 days, prisoners, guards, staff, and visitors had fallen into the experiment completely. Dr. Phillip Zimbardo, head of the project, reported that he felt more like a warden than like a research psychologist. When his fiancé (also a social psychologist) visited and protested vigorously, he decided it was time to halt the experiment (Zimbardo, 1973). On the sixth day, all of the participants attended two encounter sessions (a two-way debriefing session encompassing information and emotions): one for the prisoners, one for the guards, and one for prisoners and guards together. All of the prisoners were glad that the experiment was over, but most of the guards were not.

WOULD YOU SHOCK A STRANGER?

Now, let's move to an even earlier time. Picture this: It is the early 1960s and you are a student at Yale University. You volunteer to participate in an experiment on learning and teaching. Another student volunteer arrives at the lab at the same time. Drawing a slip of paper from a hat makes you the "teacher" and him (at that point, Yale did not accept female students) the "learner." The learner is taken to a nearby room, but you can hear him easily.

As teacher, you sit in front of a wide instrument panel with many switches **(Figure 3.2).** Your task is to ask the learner questions and if the learner gets the answer wrong, to flip a switch that delivers an electric shock. Each switch is labeled with a voltage; the lowest is 15 volts and the highest is 450 volts. Beneath the switches are warnings that range from "Mild Shock" on the left to "Danger: Severe Shock" on the right. The experimenter senses your concern and tells you not to worry. He gives you the 15-volt shock that is delivered by the first switch. The mild shock is not very painful. The experimenter instructs you to administer a shock to the learner for each incorrect answer, increasing the shock level each time.

The experiment starts and after a few trials, the learner makes his first mistakes. He seems not to mind the pain from the lower-voltage shocks. Later, however, as additional mistakes are made, he begins to complain. When you flip the switch labeled 180 volts, he yells that he can no longer stand the pain. You look at the experimenter nearby, but he says to continue. Reluctantly, you go on. When you flip the switch labeled 270 volts, the learner screams in agony. You look at the experimenter again; he says you must continue. Soon afterward, the learner stops answering your questions. You don't know what to do when the

FIGURE 3.2
Milgram's
apparatus.

learner doesn't respond. The experimenter tells you to treat no response as an error and to deliver the appropriate shock. Finally, you get to the last switch and pull it. The study is over at last. You feel drained and exhausted. You also feel lucky; except for the luck of the draw, that could have been you in there.

What do you think about the examples above? How would you feel had you been one of the participants in one of those studies? Before you read further, write down some thoughts about each of the studies. Do you think there was anything ethically wrong with the studies? If you do, list the specifics. At the end of the chapter, we ask you to compare your thoughts at that point to the ones you have now (and are about to write down).

HISTORY OF ETHICS

Questions of right and wrong have accompanied us since our emergence as a species more than one million years ago. Much of our moral and religious training is concerned with answering questions about proper behavior. Both primitive and civilized groups have created a variety of **ethical codes**—written or widely accepted prescriptions of proper behavior and morality—and inculcated them into their children. Systems of laws that govern moral behavior emerged from those ethical codes. Throughout human existence, laws, religions, and other spiritual pathways have focused on thorny questions of morality. Thus, ethics and concern about ethical standards are older than science and psychology by thousands of years. Part of being human is to be concerned with ethical questions and their resolution.

> ### In the Know
> *Morality* and *ethics* are nearly synonymous. *The American Heritage Dictionary of the English Language* differentiates between these words as follows. *Morality* relates to personal and sexual behavior according to societal strictures. *Ethics,* on the other hand, is derived from philosophy and attempts to provide objective and idealistic standards for human conduct.

ethical codes   Written or widely accepted prescriptions of proper behavior and morality.

As civilizations emerged, many ancient peoples transformed their ethical codes into written laws, and some of them survive today. The core of the ancient Hebrew ethical code is the Ten Commandments. Those basic moral rules became the seeds for an extensive set of laws that governed the ancient Hebrews. Indeed, some of those laws such as "Thou shalt not kill" are incorporated into current civil and criminal law codes. Later, in classical Greece (600–300 BCE), the study of ethics became a branch of philosophy. Socrates attempted to answer questions about morality and virtue but later Greek philosophers disagreed with many of his arguments. Those disagreements led to a flowering of different points of view about ethics. When the Roman world was converted by Christianity, its newer and divinely inspired form of ethics (codified in the Bible) shaped the European worldview for two millennia. In the Middle East, another divinely inspired ethical code arose as Islam swept into existence some 500 years after the emergence of Christianity. The words of Mohammed (570–633 CE) became the Koran, Islam's moral code. Of course, peoples in other parts of the world also created moral codes. In Asia, codes derived from the writings of Confucius (551–479 BCE) survive. Confucius's writings are known as *The Analects* or *The Analects of Confucius*. Much of the practice of any religion consists of learning and living by its particular moral code.

In the 20th century, relativistic thinking challenged older absolutist forms of thinking. In absolutist thinking, moral decisions are based on traditional laws or rules that are usually codified in sacred books. In contrast, relativistic thinking's moral decisions are based on local norms or specific historical contexts. To explore the difference between the two modes, think of the prohibition against killing other humans. An absolutist thinker would ban all killing under all circumstances. However, a relativistic thinker might allow killing under special circumstances. For instance, a convicted murderer might be put to death ethically in some jurisdictions. Or, consider soldiers in a combat zone. Based on their rules of engagement, they may ethically kill enemy combatants, but not enemy civilians. Like many seeming dichotomies, absolutist and relativistic positions turn out instead to be points along a continuum. The advent of relativistic thinking, along with the emergence of nations with large, pluralistic, and diverse citizenries, has made the study of ethics more interesting and more difficult than in the past. When you add the development of high-speed communications networks, including the Internet, you have a world in which ethical choices are both more difficult and more important than ever before. Today, as in the past, ethics is part of everyone's daily life. Now let us turn to ethics in psychological research.

Until about 60 years ago, researchers in psychology were guided by their own personal ethics. No published ethical code existed. Occasionally, there were lapses in ethics. For example, in Watson and Rayner's (1920) study of Little Albert, an infant was classically conditioned to fear a white rat by using a loud sound as an aversive stimulus. Landis (1924) investigated emotion by administering electric shocks to participants without warning or consent. Neither study would be considered ethical today.

Psychology's attention to written codes of ethics began during the Nuremberg trials (1946–1947) that followed World War II. One of those trials, the Doctors' Trial, revealed atrocities committed by Nazi medical doctors and others (Lifton, 1986). Cohen (no date) summarized some of the horrible violence perpetrated on Jews and other victims of the Holocaust during World War II. Experiments at the Nazi death camps tested humans' response to freezing temperatures, high altitudes, drinking sea water, tuberculosis, and poisons. Many suffered pain and death as a result of these experiments. The Doctors' Trial exposed the depth and scope of the Nazi experiments to a shocked world. Those experiments were so repugnant that recent attempts to use the data have met with nearly universal disapproval. The U.S. Environmental Protection Agency ruled that the data from those studies could not be used in any way (Sun, 1988). After the Nuremberg trials, the psychological community understood that scientific methods alone do not define science; ethics is also part of the definition.

Despite Nazi atrocities and the creation of the **Nuremberg Code,** ethics was not a commonplace concern in psychological research until the last quarter of the 20th century. A strong and persistent concern about ethics emerged in psychology after 1974 because of a changing social climate and the APA's revision of its earlier, informal ethical code (McGaha & Korn, 1995). The most recent document, the *Ethical Principles of Psychologists and Code of Conduct* (American Psychological Association [APA], 2002) is the fourth revision since its publication in 1977. In the sections that follow, we examine the portions of the *Ethics Code* that guide research and publication. The entire *Ethics Code* is reprinted in appendix B. Around that same time, the U.S. Department of Health and Human Services (USHHS) published the Belmont Report, which included recommendations for research with human participants. The three main areas covered by the report were: respect for persons, beneficence, and justice. By 1991, the Belmont recommendations had been codified into U.S. law for USHHS under Title 45 Part 46. In addition, 14 other federal departments share the same regulations under different sections of the *Code of Federal Regulations* (U.S. Department of Health and Human Services [USHHS], 2005). Thus, psychology is not alone in its concern with ethics and research. The U.S. government requires researchers and their institutions to follow formal procedures that ensure ethical research. All scientific and medical disciplines that interact with human participants must conform to certain principles and procedures in conducting research.

Today, many psychologists are concerned with ethics in general and with the ethics of research in particular. The major issues of research ethics are how to conduct research, how to analyze data, and how to report results (Rosenthal, 1994). No statement of ethical principles, scientific or otherwise, covers all possible situations. So, as you conduct and present research, you will have to make ethical decisions. The *Ethics Code* gives you guidance, but it is not a complete list of do's and don'ts. Learn the basic principles and implement the checks and balances built into them so that you will practice scientific integrity and avoid scientific misconduct.

Nuremberg Code Ten recommendations about permissible medical research released after the Nuremberg Doctors' Trial.

> ## *In the Know*
> Psychology is not alone in its concern for ethics. Nearly every professional organization has its own code of ethics. Look at the Web page that accompanies this book to find ethics codes published by other professional organizations.

THE INSTITUTIONAL REVIEW BOARD (IRB)

Formal regulations and processes apply to the planning and conduct of research. All institutions in the United States that receive federal funds and conduct research are required to have an **institutional review board (IRB).** IRBs meet to review proposed research that is submitted by a researcher. Membership of IRBs includes faculty members with appropriate research expertise, other faculty members, and representatives from outside the institution. Sometimes, students are members too. During its deliberations, the IRB assesses whether participants are truly giving informed consent, anticipates risks and benefits to participants, and reviews how the data will be safeguarded, among other things. IRB review is pervasive. Most journals now require authors to stipulate in writing that the research submitted was approved by an IRB. Most colleges and universities have one or more IRBs, although they are sometimes called human subjects committees, animal subjects committees, institutional animal care and use committees, or other similar names. Depending on your institution's IRB rules, you may have to submit your personal research to an IRB. If you are required to submit your proposal, take heart from the report of Kallgren and Tauber (1996). They found that undergraduates who submitted research proposals to an IRB viewed the experience positively and believed that the process improved their research.

THE *ETHICAL PRINCIPLES OF PSYCHOLOGISTS AND CODE OF CONDUCT (ETHICS CODE)*

The *Ethical Principles of Psychologists and Code of Conduct* (APA, 2002) contains 5 general principles and 10 ethical standards. The *Ethics Code* covers most of the situations in which psychologists and student researchers find themselves. The intent of the general principles is "to guide and inspire psychologists toward the very highest ethical standards" (APA, 2002, p. 3). Research is the activity we cover in this textbook. Therapy, education, and assessment are examples of other areas addressed by the *Ethics Code*.

The 5 general principles of the *Ethics Code* are summarized in **Table 3.1**. They provide broad guidelines that apply to all psychologists. Indeed,

institutional review board (IRB) Group that reviews research proposals for ethical propriety.

TABLE 3.1	Five General Principles of The *Ethics Code*

A. Beneficence and Nonmalificence—This first principle urges psychologists to do no harm, to be aware of their influence on others, to use their professional positions for good, and to monitor their own physical and mental health so those factors will not negatively affect their work.

B. Fidelity and Responsibility—This principle tells psychologists to be aware of their professional and scientific responsibilities, to interact collegially with colleagues, and to donate a portion of their expertise to others *pro bono*.[a]

C. Integrity—Psychologists are accurate, honest, and truthful. They keep their promises, and correct any consequences that arise from the ethical use of deception.

D. Justice—All people should have access to and enjoy the benefits of psychological research and services. Psychologists should be aware of their own biases and professional limitations.

E. Respect for People's Rights and Dignity—Psychologists value people and their dignity. They respect diversity, people's right to privacy, confidentiality, and self-determination. They do not condone others who fail to live up to this principle.

[a]For no charge.

Source: Reprinted with permission of the American Psychological Association, © APA.

they are broad enough to apply to anyone who works with people. The 10 ethical standards **(Table 3.2)** provide specific guidelines to psychologists about their activities. Because the standards are specific, they may not apply to every psychologist (or student of psychology).

As you can see from Tables 3.1 and 3.2, the *Ethics Code* addresses many issues. As mentioned, the entire *Ethics Code* is reprinted in appendix B. If you plan to pursue a career in psychology, you should read the entire *Ethics Code*. We begin by examining Ethical Standard 4.01, a standard that applies to all psychologists.

Ethical Standard 4.01, Maintaining Confidentiality

Conducting research and working with people are both a privilege and a serious business. Perhaps the most important thing to learn is the importance of maintaining **confidentiality**—keeping research data about individual participants private. We believe that maintaining confidentiality is so important that we quote Ethical Standard 4.01 in full (APA, 2002, p. 7).

> Psychologists have a primary obligation and take reasonable precautions to protect confidential information obtained through or stored in any medium, recognizing that the extent and limits of confidentiality may be regulated by law or established by institutional rules or professional or scientific relationship.

confidentiality
Requirement to keep research data about individual participants private.

The ethical conduct of research requires researchers to protect the information they obtain from others. In practice, this means that no

TABLE 3.2	Ten Ethical Standards of The *Ethics Code*

1. **Resolving Ethical Issues**—This standard governs general issues related to ethics and the law. It outlines psychologists' responsibility to their organization and the reporting and resolving of ethical complaints.

2. **Competence**—This standard ensures the competence of psychologists as they pursue their work. It ensures that they work within the boundaries of their expertise, maintain an appropriate level of training, delegate work to others appropriately, and not enter into situations likely to cause personal conflicts.

3. **Human Relations**—The human relations standard governs psychologists' relationships with others. It mandates that issues of discrimination, harassment, conflicts of interest, and exploitation be avoided. This standard also defines informed consent (as does Standard 8.02).

4. **Privacy and Confidentiality**—The fourth standard describes how psychologists should communicate information received as part of their work and to whom such communications should be made.

5. **Advertising and Other Public Statements**—This standard covers how psychologists may represent themselves to the public through statements, publications, media, or by word of mouth.

6. **Record Keeping and Fees**—The sixth standard deals with situations in which psychologists receive payment for services rendered and how records of such payments must be handled.

7. **Education and Training**—This standard refers to psychologists who teach. It covers assessment, evaluation, accuracy, privacy, and personal relationships with students.

8. **Research and Publication**—This standard addresses issues related to research in psychology.

9. **Assessment**—The assessment standard applies to psychologists who test or assess others; it governs issues such as release of test data, test construction, test interpretation, and test security.

10. **Therapy**—The last standard governs psychologists who provide therapy. It covers such aspects of therapy as informed consent, sexual intimacy, and termination of therapy.

Source: Reprinted with permission of the American Psychological Association, © APA.

information about the participants should be shared with anyone who is not directly associated with the research project. Furthermore, the reporting of results must be done in a manner that does not identify individual participants.

Ethical Standard 8, Research and Publication

As you can see in **Table 3.3,** Ethical Standard 8 has 15 sections that address specific issues of research and publication. All the topics are important, but they don't apply equally to students in research methods

TABLE 3.3	Section Headings of Ethical Standard 8, Research and Publication

8.01	Institutional Approval
8.02	Informed Consent to Research
8.03	Informed Consent for Recording Voices and Images in Research
8.04	Client/Patient, Student, and Subordinate Research Participants
8.05	Dispensing With Informed Consent for Research
8.06	Offering Inducements for Research Participation
8.07	Deception in Research
8.08	Debriefing
8.09	Humane Care and Use of Animals in Research
8.10	Reporting Research Results
8.11	Plagiarism
8.12	Publication Credit
8.13	Duplicate Publication of Data
8.14	Sharing Research Data for Verification
8.15	Reviewers

Source: Reprinted with permission of the American Psychological Association, © APA.

courses. We arranged the topics that apply to students into two sections: Responsibilities to Participants and Responsibilities to Psychology.

Responsibilities to Participants

You have a number of ethical responsibilities to the participants in your research. Three important ones are informed consent, deception, and debriefing.

Informed Consent   The relationship between researchers and participants and the transactions that occur between them during the process of research are governed by **informed consent.** Except for situations in which informed consent may be dispensed with (described below), psychologists *must* inform participants:

1. of the purpose, duration, and procedures of the study;
2. that they may decline to participate or withdraw from the research;
3. of any possible consequences of declining or withdrawing;
4. of any risks, discomfort, or adverse effects related to the research;
5. of any possible benefits related to the research;
6. about limits of confidentiality of the research;

informed consent
Agreement, usually written, to participate in a study after being informed of the consequences of participation.

7. of any incentives, such as money or grades, for research participation;

8. of their rights and whom to contact for answers to questions about the research.

Table 3.4 shows a sample informed consent form that Dawn Branch used in her project, which was designed to determine if there was a relationship between personality traits and self-inflicted wounds. Informed consent forms like hers are used routinely to document that informed consent was obtained. A research project is unethical if the principles of informed consent are not followed. However, there are occasions when you need not provide informed consent.

TABLE 3.4	Sample Consent Form

Consent Form

For this study, the researcher cannot give you information about its purpose until after the study is finished. If you would like, the researcher will e-mail you a description and the results when the study is completed.

This survey may ask you personal details about your life. However, there will be no way to link the information you provide to your name. In addition, any information about your participation will be kept confidential.

Please complete this survey honestly. If at any time you feel uncomfortable, you are free to withdraw from the study and none of your information will be used in the results. There is no penalty for withdrawing, but you are encouraged to complete the survey for the sake of the study.

By signing this form you agree not to discuss this survey with others until the researcher has contacted you. If you discuss this survey with others who complete it at a later date, it may influence their responses. By signing, you are agreeing to complete this survey honestly and accurately.

Thank you for participating. If you have any questions please ask one of the researchers or you may contact Dawn Branch by phone (--) or e-mail (address.edu) or Dr. Spatz by phone (--).

_____   _____
Signature   Date

_____
E-mail address

Dispensing With Informed Consent   There are three situations that allow researchers to dispense with informed consent. The first occurs "where research would not reasonably be assumed to create distress or harm" (APA, 2002, p. 11). Dispensing with informed consent is permissible when the research involves:

1. the study of normal activities in a school setting related to teaching practices, curricula, or classroom management.
2. anonymous questionnaires, naturalistic observation, or archival research. (Naturalistic observation and archival research are covered in chapter 10.)
3. jobs or organizations where there is no risk to participants' employability and their confidentiality is protected.

Even in these situations, participants must not be placed at risk for legal liabilities, financial damages, employability, or reputation. Also, the participant's confidentiality must be protected. Dispensing with informed consent is also allowed in situations covered by federal law or institutional regulation. Whether or not informed consent is required, participants are always free to withdraw from research participation.

In the Know

An exception to informed consent involves U.S. military personnel. Executive Order 13139 (September 30, 1999) allows the Department of Defense (DoD) to administer "new investigational drugs" to members of the military without their consent. On October, 28, 2004, federal judge Emmett Sullivan ruled that the order did not apply to anthrax vaccines (Judge halts forcing of anthrax shots, 2004). Later, (DoD) filed to resume the vaccine (Files, 2004) and administered it to at least 250 service members. Sullivan later sanctioned resumption of the shots, but only to troops who voluntarily agree (Anthrax vaccinations allowed to resume, 2005). Late in 2006, the U.S. Food and Drug Administration found that the shots were safe and DoD planned to resume inoculating troops going to Iraq, Afghanistan, and South Korea (Baldor, 2006).

Deception in Research   The standard that covers **deception** has three parts. The first part prohibits deception unless researchers determine that deception is justified by "the study's significant prospective scientific, educational, or applied value," *AND* that "effective nondeceptive alternative procedures are not feasible" (APA, 2002, p. 11). The second part of the standard prohibits deception if the research might cause pain or significant

deception   Deliberately misleading participants about any aspect of the research.

emotional distress. The third part requires psychologists to explain any and all deceptions to participants as early as possible after their participation. This process is called debriefing, and is explained below. Furthermore, participants who so desire may withdraw their data from the study after the deception has been explained to them. To summarize, to use deception researchers must demonstrate two things: the high prospective value of the proposed research and that there is no way to carry out the research without deception.

Of all the standards, deception is the most controversial. The use of deception in psychology has been tracked and analyzed over the years (Dunston & Ross, 1986; Nicks, Korn, & Mainieri, 1997; Sieber, Iannuzzo, & Rodriguez, 1995). These reports reveal an ebb and flow in the percentage of deceptive studies over time. But the frequency of deceptive studies was above 30% in all of the analyses. A similar proportion of today's psychological research probably involves deception. Researchers engaged in a debate over deception that was published in the *American Psychologist* over a period of months (Broeder, 1998; Kimmel, 1998; Korn, 1998; Ortmann & Hertwig, 1998). Ortmann and Hertwig's article was first and they argued for a complete ban on deception in psychological research. The authors who responded, however, argued that *some* deception must remain permissible in psychology. The APA's standard on deception reflects a view similar to those of Broeder (1998), Kimmel (1998), and Korn (1998). The important ethical question in psychological research is not *if* deception should be used but *when* and *how* it should be used.

Debriefing   **Debriefing** informs participants of the "nature, results, and conclusions of the research" (APA, 2002, p. 12). A debriefing session usually ends with a question such as "Do you have any questions about the study?" which allows researchers to correct misconceptions that participants may have acquired. Debriefing is useful to researchers because it allows them to monitor their studies. Through debriefing, researchers may learn how participants perceive the study and if any procedures did not work.

Debriefing is also an excellent time to explain psychology to nonpsychologists. Nearly all research that uses human participants requires debriefing. However, the second section of the standard allows researchers to delay or withhold debriefing information from participants, but only for scientific or humane reasons. Finally, psychologists who discover after the fact that their research procedures have harmed participants must act to minimize that harm.

Other Responsibilities to Participants   Other standards that cover your responsibilities to participants include obtaining informed consent before recording data. In cases other than naturalistic observation (see chapter 10), researchers must obtain consent from participants before making audio or visual recordings. When conducting research with students, clients,

debriefing Explaining to participants the nature, results, and conclusions of the research they participated in and correcting any misconceptions.

patients or subordinates, researchers must ensure that the participants are not being coerced in any way when they consent to participation. The use of **inducements** is also covered in the *Ethics Code.* Inducements are things that researchers may offer to participants in order to secure participation. Typical inducements include cash, grades, or prizes. Inducements as such are ethical. However, inducements that are "excessive or inappropriate" (APA, 2002, p. 11) are unethical.

Responsibilities to Psychology

Reporting Research Results   "Psychologists do not fabricate data" (APA, 2002, p. 12). The point? Report the data you get. As we explained in chapter 1, science depends on reliable results. Many scientists consider violations of this standard to be the most heinous of all ethical violations because publishing false data undermines the entire scientific enterprise. The actual data are what must be reported. We provide more information on instances of falsified data reports and some suggestions to reduce their rate in a section that follows titled Scientific Integrity and Scientific Misconduct.

Plagiarism   **Plagiarism** is using a written or other intellectual work of someone else and claiming it as your own. Plagiarism is a serious ethical breach. One problem in academic institutions is that many students do not know what constitutes plagiarism, nor do faculty always provide a clear definition (Murray, 2002a).

Martin (1994) identifies four types of plagiarism of interest to students: (1) word-for-word plagiarism, (2) paraphrasing plagiarism, (3) plagiarism of secondary sources, and (4) plagiarism of ideas. You can prevent these types of plagiarism in your work by knowing that they are wrong and actively avoiding them. Certainly, plagiarism caused by carelessness or incompetence is curable by skill building. For example, many students do not realize that cutting and pasting from the Web without acknowledging the original author is plagiarism. In response, some instructors use software tools that detect plagiarism from Web sources (Young, 2001).

Why are we so concerned about plagiarism? One reason is that we want to teach correct scientific procedures. Properly acknowledging the work of fellow scientists is important not only as a basic procedural characteristic of science but also as a safeguard for science itself. Science suffers when research results are plagiarized. Healthy science requires that all people trust scientific results. Another reason is to protect the scientists who think up research ideas, conduct studies, and publish data. They are valuable to society. Plagiarizers threaten scientific procedures, public confidence in science, and scientists' livelihoods. So, learn what plagiarism is and how to avoid it. Cite previous scientific work properly.

inducements   Cash, grades, prizes, or recognition to encourage or reward research participation.

plagiarism   The unintentional or intentional use of words or ideas of others without attribution.

Other standards that cover your responsibilities to psychology relate to obtaining institutional approval, practices related to the publication and handling of data, and reviewing others' data for publication. No research can be conducted ethically without prior institutional approval. Ethical research also requires careful and proper handling of results. A careful reading of all of Section 8, Research and Publication, reveals additional responsibilities of researchers. Before you plan and conduct a personal or class research project, you should familiarize yourself with all of the standards in Section 8. The six standards above receive special attention because they affect so many student research projects.

Ethical Standard 8.09, Animal Research

This standard (**Table 3.5**) on the ethical conduct of animal research contains seven sections. It and the APA booklet *Guidelines for Ethical Conduct in the Care and Use of Animals* (APA, n.d.) provide guidance for researchers who conduct research with animals. Both publications document researchers' responsibilities.

TABLE 3.5	APA Standard 8.09, Humane Care and Use of Animals in Research

(a) Psychologists acquire, care for, use, and dispose of animals in compliance with current federal, state, and local laws and regulations, and with professional standards.

(b) Psychologists trained in research methods and experienced in the care of laboratory animals supervise all procedures involving animals and are responsible for ensuring appropriate consideration of their comfort, health, and humane treatment.

(c) Psychologists ensure that all individuals under their supervision who are using animals have received instruction in research methods and in the care, maintenance, and handling of the species being used, to the extent appropriate to their role. (See also Standard 2.05, Delegation of Work to Others.)

(d) Psychologists make reasonable efforts to minimize the discomfort, infection, illness, and pain of animal subjects.

(e) Psychologists use a procedure subjecting animals to pain, stress, or privation only when an alternative procedure is unavailable and the goal is justified by its prospective scientific, educational, or applied value.

(f) Psychologists perform surgical procedures under appropriate anesthesia and follow techniques to avoid infection and minimize pain during and after surgery.

(g) When it is appropriate that an animal's life be terminated, psychologists proceed rapidly, with an effort to minimize pain and in accordance with accepted procedures.

Source: Reprinted with permission of the American Psychological Association, © APA.

Table 3.5 shows APA's standard 8.09. Note that the standard covers a variety of ethical concerns including legal issues, training of personnel who handle animals, animal care guidelines, pain and stress avoidance or reduction, and termination of animal subjects. The appropriate IRB must approve animal research before it is conducted. In addition, the use of animals for educational purposes such as classroom demonstrations is subject to more stringent requirements than is the use of animals for research purposes. Again, an IRB must approve the use of animals for educational purposes beforehand. Federal, state, and local laws and regulations that apply to animal research must be followed. Thus, there are more requirements (such as required visits from veterinarians and housing standards for particular species) for ethical research with animals than there are with humans.

Debate on Ethics

At a recent professional meeting, your authors debated the ethics of a proposed student project that involved smokers outside campus buildings.

Read **Table 3.6** and identify the ethical issues involved. Write them down.

We see three ethical issues here. The first issue concerns secondhand smoke. At School A, the removal of the signs may increase the likelihood that nonsmokers breathe additional secondhand smoke. The experimenters, then, could be responsible for causing distress or harm by removing the existing signs. At School B, of course, the installation of signs could actually reduce the risk of secondhand smoke. A second issue is whether or not the researchers obtained permission to install or remove signs at the two institutions. A third issue is whether or not the IRBs of both institutions approved the research. Did you identify any of these three issues? Did you raise others not mentioned?

SCIENTIFIC INTEGRITY AND SCIENTIFIC MISCONDUCT

The vast majority of scientists conduct themselves in an ethical manner, follow ethical standards, avoid plagiarism, and are conscientious researchers. Still, scientists make honest mistakes. Bolton (2002) classifies scientific errors into four categories: honest mistakes, unethical behavior, noncompliance, and deliberate deceit. In her classification scheme, only deliberate deceit qualifies as scientific misconduct. Examples of scientific misconduct include falsified results (scientific fraud) and plagiarism. Unfortunately, it is sometimes hard to tell the difference between scientific misconduct

TABLE 3.6	Smoker Compliance With Newly Moved "No Smoking" Signs

In this field experiment smoker compliance with newly moved or newly installed "No Smoking" signs will be observed. Two buildings on two campuses will be used. On one campus, School A, smokers must not smoke within 25 feet of any campus building. Signs at School A inform smokers of this regulation. On the other campus, School B, smokers may smoke just outside any campus building. There are no signs prohibiting smoking outside the buildings at School B.

In the first part of the experiment, smokers will be observed on each campus to determine their average distance from the building. In the second part, signs will be moved or added on each campus. At School A, the signs prohibiting smoking within 25 feet of any building will be temporarily removed. At School B, new signs prohibiting smoking within 25 feet of any building will be installed. Again, smokers will be observed to determine their average distance from the building. In the final part of the experiment, the signs on each campus will be returned to their original positions (Campus A) or removed (Campus B). The final data collection will measure smokers' average distance again.

Because data will be collected by naturalistic observation, no informed consent by smokers will be required. On each campus, researchers will remove and add signs as described above.

and honest mistakes. Gould (1989), for instance, distinguishes between scientific fraud and the errors made by honest scientists in the pursuit of new findings. He characterizes good science as a risky business. Many errors committed by scientists are by-products of the creative aspects of science, not fraud.

Although the overall rate of scientific misconduct is low, scientists have increased their efforts to reduce that rate (Shore, 1995). Psychology and the other sciences police themselves with a process known as **peer review.** Peer review means that fellow scientists review the work of their colleagues when it is proposed, submitted for publication or presentation, and when funds are applied for. No external, higher-level mechanism beyond peer review exists. Thus, scientists work under a system of self-regulation to read, edit, and pass judgment on the work of their colleagues. Peer review is a very rare and unusual system of quality control. It depends on honesty and good will among members of the scientific community who cooperate with each other to ensure that science's published results are reliable and accurate.

In peer review, as in any system devised by human beings, there are those who seek to take advantage of others. Scientists who commit scientific misconduct risk the loss of their jobs, reputations, and access to funds, and they may even be prosecuted. Murray (2002b) maintains that scientific misconduct could be minimized if both institutions and individuals adopted a few basic rules. For institutions, she suggests that educating students about ethics, conducting unannounced audits of research projects, and thoroughly and even-handedly investigating cases of fraud

peer review Formal process in which scientists judge colleagues' work submitted for publication or funding.

would create a climate more conducive to ethical science. For individuals, she suggests that establishing clear rules for data collection and analysis, reviewing data before drafting reports, and explaining data analysis procedures would make unethical science easier to detect. In 1993, the U.S. federal government created the Office of Research Integrity whose principal mission is to prevent scientific misconduct and promote research integrity through investigative oversight and education. Similarly, Keith-Spiegel, Aronson, and Bowman (1994) published a bibliography of instances of scientific misconduct in psychology.

> ## In the Know
>
> The United States Public Health Service (USPHS) project, the Tuskegee Syphilis Study (Thomas & Quinn, 1991), studied 399 syphilis-infected African American men for nearly 40 years instead of 6 months as originally planned. The USPHS prevented the infected men from receiving antibiotic therapy, misinformed them about the nature of the research, and did not allow physicians to inform them of their syphilitic condition. After the study ended, the federal government provided free medical and burial services to all remaining participants and their families. In 1997, President Clinton apologized to the seven surviving participants.

One point you should take from this chapter is that psychological research is not just data collection, analysis, and reporting. Ethics is an essential component of research. Simply using the techniques of research without attending to ethics is not science.

RETURN TO SHOCKING STRANGERS, THE PRISON, AND THE MALL

Let's return to the three studies described at the beginning of this chapter. By examining them in chronological order, we show how the *Ethics Code* emerged and developed over time.

Milgram and Obedience

Criticism of the ethics of Milgram's (1963) obedience study began shortly after he published his results. The criticism focused on his treatment of the participants (Baumrind, 1964). Baumrind argued that Milgram had caused so much anxiety in his participants that some were permanently harmed. She predicted that future research involving deception would not be effective because participants would know about Milgram's study and behave differently because of that knowledge. That is, participants would no longer trust psychologists. Milgram (1964) responded by noting that his debriefing procedure, combined with psychiatric referrals where necessary, removed any effects of his anxiety-producing procedure. Furthermore, he pointed out that only a few participants believed that they had been harmed when they were asked after the study was completed. Milgram believed that he was acting properly as a psychologist. All of his actions fell within the normal social role of a research psychologist at the time. Psychology in the 1960s was unaware of the unique relationship between researcher and participant. Later, when researchers realized that participants suspended their normal cautions in research situations, it became the responsibility of researchers to protect their participants. As a result of this realization, ethical standards for research changed. Milgram's research stimulated a concern for how research psychologists and participants should interact. Today's requirement that participants be free to withdraw from a study stems partially from Milgram's obedience studies.

Zimbardo and the Stanford Prison Experiment

When Zimbardo (1973) suspended his famous prison study, he was acting ethically within the new and evolved ethical context created by Milgram's work. IRBs had been established at some universities as a result of earlier studies such as Milgram's. Stanford had an IRB and Zimbardo obtained permission from it to conduct the prison study. Unfortunately, the prison study worked all too well, sucking both participants and researchers into uncertainty as to what was research and what was real life. When Zimbardo began to fear for the welfare of his participants, he cancelled the remainder of the study. Retrospectively, Zimbardo stated that he should have called off the experiment sooner (O'Toole, 1997).

Neither Milgram's nor Zimbardo's studies would be approved by an IRB today. Neither study provided for informed consent, which would be required now. Also, both studies required participants to remain throughout the study and only excused participants after the most vigorous protests on their part. Ethics is a dynamic process and ethical standards will continue to change.

Loftus and the Lost in the Mall Studies

Loftus and Pickrell (1995) deceived their participants about their childhood memories. The researchers believed that deception was necessary and that the potential scientific benefits were important enough to warrant including the deception. Loftus and many others later demonstrated that false memories could be implanted in about 20 to 25% of participants (Loftus, 1997). The University of Washington IRB that reviewed Loftus and Pickrell's proposal approved their plan for deception. Crook and

Dean (1999a, 1999b), however, questioned Loftus's original reports on Chris, the 14-year-old who believed the lost in the mall story told by his brother, Jim. Crook and Dean maintain that Loftus presented the data about Chris as a pilot study and that the pilot study had not received the required approval from an IRB. A **pilot study** is preliminary research designed to evaluate aspects of a planned experiment. Loftus (1999) responded that the original data on Chris resulted from a classroom assignment, and thus was not subject to IRB review. Both Loftus (1999) and her critics (Crook & Dean, 1999a) agree that the definition of what constitutes psychological research in classroom situations is unclear and that guidelines may have to be written to cover those situations.

Look at the notes you made after reading the three examples at the beginning of this chapter. Is your opinion of the ethics of those studies changed? Here are some additional questions to consider.

When does a class assignment become research?

Are today's ethical standards likely to change in the future?

Will concern over ethics make the discovery of new and important results difficult or impossible?

As you have seen, the *Ethics Code* differentiates between teaching and research. A classroom assignment can become research, but the necessary steps must be taken and those may include review by an IRB. Ethical standards will continue to evolve. Researchers will have to monitor those changes. Researchers and IRBs will continue to weigh the benefits of expanding scientific knowledge against the ethical costs of conducting research.

ETHICS AND YOUR PERSONAL RESEARCH

As we noted near the beginning of this chapter, concern with ethics has been around since the beginning of recorded history and is an issue in everything we do, including research. The inseparability of ethics from research methods is one reason this chapter comes early in this book. Full-fledged psychological researchers have adopted and internalized the basic ethical standards discussed in this chapter. You may be conducting your first research project soon. The seven basic ethical responsibilities that we discussed were confidentiality, informed consent, dispensing with informed consent, deception, debriefing, reporting data, and plagiarism. Practice these ethical responsibilities now as part of your transition to becoming a more fully trained scientist.

pilot study   A preliminary. abbreviated experiment to evaluate aspects of a planned experiment.

FIGURE 3.3
First things first.

As you think of potential research projects, discuss them with your classmates. Be sure to include ethical topics and issues in these discussions. As your ideas for research projects become clearer, reread the *Ethics Code* and ask yourself how your project meets the ethical standards. Ask your classmates to assess your project for ethical as well as methodological flaws. In summary, use all of these methods of science including ethics.

The line between ethical and unethical research is not always clear and that line may change over time. Good scientists take risks, but they take them only after carefully considering alternatives and consequences. They know that they should not take risks to answer trivial questions. They also depend on their peers beforehand, using consultations and IRBs as tools to help prevent ethical problems before they occur. In today's scientific research, ethical decisions are woven into the fabric, not stitched on later. Refer to this chapter often as you conduct research and let the *Ethics Code* whisper in your ear always as you plan your research activities (see **Figure 3.3**).

Chapter Review

1. Match the researcher with the study.

    1. Zimbardo   a. lost in the mall

    2. Loftus   b. would you shock a stranger?

    3. Milgram   c. Stanford prison experiment

2. In ethics, the _____ approach values written laws or rules that are considered universal. The _____ approach values local norms or is specific to a particular historical era.

3. The _____ Code was established after World War II as a response to Nazi atrocities during the war.

4. The group that judges and may grant approval for a research project is the institution's _____ , which is abbreviated _____.

5. The *Ethical Principles of Psychologists and Code of Conduct* consists of 5 _____ and 10 _____.

6. Your text arranged the elements of Standard 8 into two responsibilities: those to _____ and those to _____.

7. Recall from memory at least five ethical responsibilities that you incur when you conduct research.

8. Match the concept with the responsibility.

   1. confidentiality

   2. debriefing

   3. plagiarism

   4. reporting results

   5. informed consent

   6. permitting participants to withdraw

   a. Explaining the risks and benefits of participating in a research project.

   b. Allowing participants to exit the research situation at any time.

   c. Informing participants of the nature of the study and its results.

   d. Keeping information and scores of participants secure.

   e. Not modifying data from a study.

   f. Not using another's words or ideas without acknowledgment.

9. The process in which scientists examine other scientists' request for funds or for publication is called _____

10. A proposed study can use _____ if there is no alternative procedure and the study causes no pain or psychological harm and might produce important results.

Thinking Critically About Research

1. For each scenario, identify the responsibility that was not met.

   a. Alberta shared with her roommate the phone number of one of her participants.

   b. Bertram left the study he participated in without the name of a contact person.

   c. Conrad put his name on a sign-up sheet that was passed in class. When he arrived to participate, he was told to sit down and fill out the forms at his desk.

   d. Darla was told to just continue working when she asked to leave during the study.

   e. For the Introduction section of his paper, Ephram used the same references and organization as those of the research article he based his study on.

   f. Fred told his friend that a mutual friend of theirs had the lowest motor coordination score of all the participants in his study.

   g. To ensure that only motivated participants were included, Ginny analyzed only the scores of participants who signed up to receive the results.

2. Why were institutional review boards (IRBs) established?

3. Why is scientific misconduct a problem to science and psychology?

4. What was it about Loftus's lost in the mall report that aroused ethics complaints?

Answers to Chapter Review

 1. 1. c; 2. a; 3. b

 2. absolutist; relativistic

 3. Nuremberg

 4. institutional review board; IRB (other answers can be correct here)

 5. general principles; ethical standards

 6. participants; psychology

 7. confidentiality, informed consent, allow participants to withdraw, debriefing, report data correctly, avoid plagiarism, and avoid deception except when permitted and necessary

 8. 1. d; 2. c; 3. f; 4. e; 5. a; 6. b

 9. peer review

10. deception

Answers to Thinking Critically About Research

 1. a. confidentiality; b. debriefing; c. informed consent; d. freedom to withdraw; e. plagiarism; f. confidentiality; g. reporting results

2. IRBs were established after it became obvious that human participants abandoned their usual cautions when placed in research situations. Researchers, in turn, realized that they had much more power over participants than they had previously believed. IRBs and ethical codes evolved to meet the social dynamics of the research situation.

3. One rogue scientist who publishes false data threatens the entire trustworthiness of science.

4. Loftus reported the results of a classroom exercise, which does not require IRB approval, as pilot research, which does require IRB approval.

Know for Sure

absolutist thinking, 73
animal research, 83
confidentiality, 76
debriefing, 81
deception, 80
ethical codes, 72
Ethics Code, 75
inducements, 82

informed consent, dispensing with, 80
informed consent, 78
institutional review board (IRB), 75
Nuremberg Trials, 73
Nuremberg Code, 74

peer review, 85
pilot study, 88
plagiarism, 82
relativistic thinking, 73
scientific misconduct, 85

4

Measurement

OVERVIEW

Measurement is a fundamental characteristic of science, although every measurement has some degree of error in it. Operational definitions and four different ways to categorize measurement are explained. Reliability, validity, and sensitivity, the three characteristics of trustworthy measures, are covered as is the correlation coefficient, which is used to assess reliability and validity. Sources of instruments that measure psychological characteristics are listed. Some directions for creating your own instrument are provided.

OBJECTIVES

After studying this chapter and working through the exercises, you should be able to:

1. Explain operational definitions and create examples of your own
2. Distinguish among continuous variables, discrete variables, and dichotomous variables
3. Distinguish between quantitative variables and qualitative variables
4. Distinguish among categorical variables, ranked variables, and scaled variables
5. Know the characteristics of nominal, ordinal, interval, and ratio scales of measurement
6. Define *reliability, validity,* and *sensitivity* as they are used in measurement
7. Interpret correlation coefficients
8. Explain the difference between test–retest reliability and split-half reliability
9. Know the minimum correlation coefficient that establishes reliability
10. Calculate an interobserver reliability coefficient
11. Distinguish between content validity and criterion-related validity
12. Know some rules for writing test items
13. Define *random error, systematic error, ceiling effect,* and *floor effect*

I van Pavlov was almost in a rage. Valuable time was wasting. Pavlov's assistant struggled to attach the collecting tube to the opening in the dog's cheek, but the dog was already salivating and everything was a gooey mess. Finally, the tube was secured and the experiment began. Dried food powder was blown into the dog's mouth, and the assistant counted drops of saliva as they fell from the tube into a graduated beaker.

Later, Pavlov pondered the problem. Early in the experiment dogs didn't salivate before the tube was attached, but as an experiment progressed, salivation began when the dogs were brought to the lab. The only biologically sound reason to salivate is food powder in the mouth, but after a few trials, dogs were salivating in anticipation of food. Sort of a "psychic secretion," Pavlov mused.

You probably recognize that this story is a version of how Pavlov discovered what is today called *classical conditioning*. The part of this scenario that we want you to focus on is that Pavlov noticed a difference—a difference in the way the dogs salivated at the beginning of an experiment and the way they salivated after some experience. That is, the way they salivated was *variable*. Measuring differences in salivation was central to Pavlov's research.

In some situations, however, noticing a difference and then measuring it is not as easy. Consider an 8-year-old, third-grade student who asks two questions that interrupt the teacher's directions for a writing assignment. The teacher is exasperated because both questions had just been answered by the teacher's directions. The teacher has other reasons to be exasperated: this child sometimes practices karate moves during the spelling lesson! This 8-year-old behaves differently from other children. And this child is not alone. In classroom after classroom all over the world, teachers are frustrated by the disruptive behavior of one or two students. What is the underlying variable that the teachers are observing? Can measurement help?

In fact, measurement has already begun. The first step in measurement is to notice a difference. The next step is to measure what has been noticed. Perhaps, based on the few details we've supplied, you have anticipated what's going on with the 8-year-old. The child is exhibiting a behavioral syndrome characterized by inattention, hyperactivity, and impulsiveness. The syndrome is *attention-deficit/hyperactivity disorder (ADHD)*. (Feldman, 2001; Whalen, 2001). ADHD is a controversial and evolving topic in psychology. We won't have the last word for you, but by learning the material in this chapter, you'll be better able to evaluate measures of ADHD. You will also be better able to evaluate measures of other variables, whether controversial or not.

Perhaps all this talk about measuring variables brings to mind concepts such as independent variables (IVs), dependent variables (DVs), and extraneous variables. If so, good! The purpose of this book is to explain research methods and those concepts are central to research. To thoroughly comprehend IVs, DVs, and extraneous variables, however, you must understand some of the basics of measurement. We begin with operational definitions.

OPERATIONAL DEFINITIONS

Scientists are masters at measuring. They measure distances as large as the diameter of the Milky Way (100,000 light years) and as small as the diameter of an atom (one ten-billionth of a meter). Of course, those distances are measured with different methods. Scientists measure time as long as the age of the universe (13.7 billion years) and as brief as the duration of a computer's command (a nanosecond, one billionth of a second). Like distances, long and short times are measured with different methods. In psychology, scientists measure the memory of animals as simple as mollusks and as complex as humans. In the case of measuring the memory of mollusks, consider *Aplysia,* a beautiful salt-water snail about the size of your fist. When conditioned to withdraw from a light touch, they will withdraw 2 weeks later, even without a reminder. In the case of human memory, college sophomores recall words they studied days before and their memory or lack of it is revealed in functional magnetic resonance images (fMRI) of the brain. Memory is being measured in both cases, but the methods are different. To completely understand a concept such as distance, time, or memory, you must understand how the measurements are made.

An explanation of how to make a measurement is called an operational definition. More formally, an **operational definition** is a description of the procedures used by the researcher to measure a variable or create levels of a variable. These procedures are connected in a logical way to the concept or condition that is being operationally defined. We introduced operational definitions in chapter 2 (page 40).

To illustrate operational definitions of psychological concepts, we contrast them with their dictionary definitions. **Table 4.1** lists six psychological variables, their dictionary definitions, and one or more operational definitions. You already know that dictionary definitions almost always help us understand a concept better. An operational definition adds to that understanding in a special way by telling how the concept is measured. Notice in Table 4.1 that several variables have two or more operational definitions. A variable such as ADHD can be measured in different ways by different researchers. Thus, not all studies that refer to ADHD are referring to the same thing. However, in every case, the operational definition of ADHD tells you what the researcher meant by that concept.

Table 4.1 shows several operational definitions of psychological variables, including two of hunger, three of memory, and five of ADHD. In

operational definition Procedures or operations used to measure a variable or establish a condition.

| TABLE 4.1 | Dictionary and Operational Definitions of Psychological Terms |

Psychological variable	Dictionary definition[a]	Operational definition (to measure or create)
Frustration	State of insecurity and dissatisfaction arising from unresolved problems or unfulfilled needs	1. abruptly remove toys that a child is playing with 2. withhold reinforcement for performing a previously reinforced behavior
Hunger	Craving or urgent need for food	1. hours of food deprivation 2. percent of *ad libitum* weight
Depression	State of feeling sad	Beck Depression Inventory score[b]
Happiness	State of well-being and contentment	Subjective Happiness Scale score[c]
Memory	Power or process of reproducing or recalling what has been learned and retained	1. trials to relearn 2. custom-made multiple-choice test 3. fMRI activity
Attention-deficit/ hyperactivity disorder (ADHD)	Syndrome of learning and behavioral problems not caused by a serious underlying physical or mental disorder and characterized especially by difficulty in sustaining attention, by impulsive behavior (as in speaking out of turn), and usually by excessive activity.	1. ACTeRS checklist 2. ADDES-2 checklist 3. ADHD-IV checklist 4. ADHDT checklist 5. CPR-S checklist[d] 6. TOVA[e]

[a]*Merriam Webster's Collegiate Dictionary,* 11th edition (2004).

[b]Beck, Steer, and Garbin, 1988.

[c]Lyubomirsky, 1999.

[d]Demaray, Elting, and Schaefer, 2003, describe and compare the five checklists.

[e]www.tovacompany.com/about.

every case, additional operational definitions could be listed. As you may already know, different researchers at times use different operational definitions for the same concept. For example, researchers agree on how to measure hunger but they disagree on the best way to measure ADHD. However, in every case, the operational definition tells you what the researcher meant by the concept.

As you can see in Table 4.1, we listed two operational definitions for *frustration*. The first one gives the procedures that have been used to create frustration in children: "abruptly remove toys that a child is playing with." The second operational definition has been used with rats: "withhold reinforcement for performing a previously reinforced behavior." The procedures to follow to create frustration are fairly clear and there is a logical connection between the procedures and concept. A satisfactory operational definition is one that leaves you saying "I understand what you mean," or "I can measure it the same way" or "I can create the same conditions."

Let's acknowledge that operational definitions have an incomplete quality about them. They tell you exactly what to do to replicate an experiment, but they don't produce feelings of assurance. Hunger seems to be more than hours without food. Happiness seems to be more than a score on a test. However, operational definitions communicate clearly, which is such an important element of mutual understanding.

In any journal article in psychology, descriptions of the IV and the DV are accompanied by their operational definitions. If EVs are discussed and controlled, their operational definitions are given as well. Often these operational definitions are provided in the Method section of the article.

> ## In the Know
> Perhaps the most important step you can take if you want to move from confusion to confidence about a scientific topic is to find out how the concepts are measured. Knowing how schizophrenia, intelligence, or subjective well-being is measured gives you a big boost toward understanding the topic.

VARIABLES

A variable is a characteristic that has two or more values. In psychology characteristics of individuals such as putting skill, creativity, and arithmetic ability are variables. The word *variable* gets used in many different situations. When experiments are being discussed, the terms *independent variable, dependent variable, extraneous variable,* and *nuisance variable* are helpful. These terms all describe the role that a variable has in an experiment. In this section, we focus on characteristics of variables themselves and not on any function they might serve.

Here are some terms you might have encountered when variables were discussed:

continuous	ranked
discrete	scaled
dichotomous	nominal
qualitative	ordinal
quantitative	interval
categorical	ratio

Unfortunately, there is no scheme that satisfactorily reduces these dozen, overlapping terms into a smaller coherent catalog. Some words may not work well in a particular context, but all are useful in some context. Our solution to this problem is to group the terms into four different lists. Later, we use the list that is appropriate for that context.

Continuous, Discrete, and Dichotomous Variables

Continuous variables have, in theory, an infinite number of different values between the highest and lowest score. Thus, continuous variables can have any number of decimal places. In practical experiments, the scale values are not infinite, although the number is still large. Length, time, and cognitive ability are all examples of continuous variables that, in theory, could have an infinite number of different values between the lowest and highest value on the scale. **Discrete variables** have only a limited and countable number of distinct steps between the highest score and the lowest score, both in theory and in practice. Discrete variables include birth order (first born, second born), college class standing (sophomore, junior), and the number of people in your research methods class. **Dichotomous variables** have only two levels. Gender (male and female), performance (pass or fail), and psychiatric diagnoses such as schizophrenic and not schizophrenic are examples of dichotomous variables. Testing a child for ADHD results in a diagnosis of ADHD or not ADHD, even though everyone recognizes that there are variations in children with an ADHD diagnosis.

Quantitative and Qualitative Variables

Quantitative variables are those whose levels are characterized by numerical differences. Scores on a quantitative variable tell you something about the amount or degree of the variable. Time, distance, and size are typically measured on a quantitative scale. Psychological measures such as intelligence, shyness, and attitudes are also measured quantitatively, using tests that are designed to measure a particular trait. **Qualitative variables** are those whose levels are characterized by differences in kind. Each level has a different label, but the labels do not indicate an amount or degree of difference. For some qualitative variables, the levels are ordered (military rank and college class) and for others there is no inherent order (gender, political affiliation, and race).

Categorical, Ranked, and Scaled Data

This list of variables is most useful when deciding what statistical test is appropriate for a particular set of data. **Categorical data** consist of frequency counts of defined groups. Examples include the number of participants who cheat on an exam and the number who do not cheat. The categories of *cheater* and *noncheater* represent values on a qualitative

continuous variable Variable that is theoretically infinitely divisible; for any two values, you can imagine an intermediate value.

discrete variable Variable with a limited number of values; many intermediate values are not possible.

dichotomous variable Variable that can have only two values.

quantitative variable A variable whose values indicate different numerical amounts.

qualitative variable A variable whose values differ in kind rather than in amount.

categorical data Frequency counts of the events observed in designated categories.

variable. Another example is the number of students with grade point averages in the categories of

less than 0.99,
1.00 to 1.99,
2.00 to 2.99,
3.00 to 3.99,
4.00

The categories of GPA are divisions of a quantitative variable. The critical point about categorical data is that the measurement of the participant is simply that the participant is counted in a category. **Ranked data** show each participant's position among all participants. Children's artwork that is judged and ranked by a professional artist produces ranked data. Class ranks among the graduates at your university this year are ranked data as is order of finish of participants in a race. **Scaled data** are what we usually think when the word *measurements* is used. Scaled data are quantitative data for which a participant's score does not depend on other participants' performances. Whereas a person's rank depends on other participants, a person's scaled score stands on its own. Measures of time, distance, and psychological characteristics are scaled data.

Scales of Measurement

A final way to distinguish among variables is to determine the variable's *scale of measurement*. To determine scale of measurement, focus on the object that is being measured and not on the numbers themselves. To illustrate, look at **Table 4.2**, which shows three different measurements for two teams participating in an adventure race.[1] Look at the first line, an 8 and a 16, which are the identification numbers of the two teams. What can you say about the two teams based on these two numbers? The

TABLE 4.2	Measurements of Two Teams on Three Variables in an Adventure Race	
Thing measured	*Team A*	*Team B*
Identification #	8	16
Order of finish	8	16
Hours required	8	16

ranked data Each observation is a rank score.

scaled data Numerical measurements that are not ranks.

[1]Adventure races have coed teams that travel by foot, water, and bicycle for hours and hours across rugged terrain with only a map and a compass to guide them.

two numbers tell you only that they are two different teams and nothing more. Agree?

Now look at the next pair of scores which are also 8 and 16. These two numbers indicate the order of crossing the finish line. Of course, the two different orders also tell us that there were two different teams. Team A finished before Team B, but these two numbers tell nothing about the time between the two crossings.

Finally, the bottom row again shows an 8 and a 16, which are the number of hours required to finish the race. The interpretation of these two numbers is that Team A was twice as fast as Team B (and also that it was faster and different). The three 8s for Team A are all the same, but each 8 carries different information. The take-home message about scales of measurement is that the interpretation of numbers such as 8 and 16 depends on the scale of measurement. Four different scales of measurement are typically identified. They are *nominal, ordinal, interval,* and *ratio* scales.

Nominal Scale   On a **nominal scale,** numbers carry the same information as names—the numbers carry no quantitative information. Examples of psychological variables that are measured on a nominal scale are psychological disorders, personality types, and gender. The variable psychological disorders, for example, consist of different categories. One person might be classified as a paranoid type schizophrenic (which is numbered 295.30) and another as having obsessive-compulsive disorder (which has a numerical classification of 300.3). The numbers associated with these two diagnoses are from the *Diagnostic and Statistical Manual of Mental Disorders* (4th ed.), which describes different psychological disorders and gives them numbers (American Psychiatric Association, 1994). The numbers are just substitute labels and carry no quantitative information, either about amount or order. In Table 4.2, the numbers used to identify the teams are from a nominal variable.

Ordinal Scale   Numbers that result from ordinal measurement indicate *more than* and *less than* (in addition to *different*). If a participant is asked to rank animals from most frightening to least frightening, then fear of animals is being measured with an **ordinal scale.** Scores based on checklists in which the score is the sum of the number of items checked are ordinal scores. Judgments of recovery such as *much improved, improved, no change,* and *worse* produce an ordinal scale. Ordinal scales are characterized by rank order. In Table 4.2, the numbers used to identify the order of finish of teams are from an ordinal variable.

Interval Scale   For an **interval scale** measurement, equal intervals between numbers indicate equal amounts of the thing being measured and the zero point (if any) is arbitrarily defined. To illustrate, we turn to

nominal scale   Measurement scale in which numbers or names serve as labels and do not indicate a numerical relationship.

ordinal scale   Measurement scale in which numbers indicate rank order, but equal differences between numbers do not indicate equal differences between the thing measured.

interval scale   Scale in which equal differences between measurements indicate equal differences in the thing measured.

a nonpsychological example: temperature. Everyday thermometers that measure temperature use an interval scale. The amount of heat needed to increase the temperature from 35° to 45° F is the same amount of heat that is needed to raise the temperature from 80° to 90°F. Any two temperatures that differ by 10 degrees indicate equal amounts of heat. Note that a value of *zero* on the Fahrenheit scale does not mean that no heat exists.

Turning to psychological variables measured on an interval scale, we have to acknowledge a problem. We know of no measurement of a psychological variable that definitely has the characteristics of an interval scale. Many concepts measured by psychologists produce numbers that clearly carry more than ordinal scale information, but proving equal intervals requires assumptions that are not universally accepted. Nevertheless, most researchers treat these measurements as if they were interval data, even though they cannot prove that equal intervals indicate equal amounts of the variable being measured. Thus, variables such as intelligence, depression, happiness, sociability, and many others are usually treated as an interval scale variable.

Ratio Scale   The characteristic that distinguishes a **ratio scale** from the others is that zero on this scale means that there is a zero amount of the thing being measured. Variables such as reaction time, errors, height, and weight are all measured with ratio scales. In each case, zero means that none of the thing measured was detected. With ratio scale measurements, interpretations such as "twice as much" or "a 10% increase" are permissible. Such statements are inappropriate for the other three scales. In Table 4.2, the numbers used to identify the hours required to finish are from a ratio variable. The differences among these four scales of measurement are summarized in **Table 4.3**.

| TABLE 4.3 | Characteristics of the Four Scales of Measurement |

		Scale Characteristics		
Scale of measurement	Different numbers for different things	Numbers convey more than and less than	Equal differences mean equal amounts	Zero means none of what was measured was detected
Nominal	Yes	No	No	No
Ordinal	Yes	Yes	No	No
Interval	Yes	Yes	Yes	No
Ratio	Yes	Yes	Yes	Yes

Source: Based on Spatz, 2008.

ratio scale   Measurement scale with the characteristics of an interval scale plus the characteristic of a true zero: zero means that none of the thing measured is present.

Using Scales of Measurement   Knowing a variable's scale of measurement is important when you determine what descriptive statistic to use. For example, nominal scale data permit only a mode. Ordinal scale data permit the use of the median or the mode. Interval and ratio scale data permit the calculation of the mean (as well as the median and the mode). Interval or ratio data are required if a standard deviation is to be meaningful. As for determining an NHST statistical test to use, those decisions should be made on the basis of the assumptions of the test, which are explained in chapter 6, rather than on the scale of measurement.

> ## In the Know
> The question of how to use the information in Table 4.3 is one that has produced different answers at different times. When this catalog of scales of measurement was first presented by Stevens (1946), it was promoted as a way to determine what inferential statistical tests were appropriate for a particular set of data. The idea was that different classes of inferential tests required a particular scale of measurement. Over the years (but with occasional resurgence), this idea has lost adherents. Our position is that the distinctions among scales of measurement are *not* helpful in deciding what statistical test to use. What is required is knowledge of the nature of the distributions of the numbers and not the scale of measurement.

ERRORS IN MEASUREMENT

2 + 6 = ?

A three-sided figure is a(n) _____ ?

For these two problems, there are right answers, which are 8 and triangle. An answer of 9 or 8.2 or 8.01 is just wrong. For the second question, using a polygon as an answer is quite permissible in some situations, but it isn't the most accurate answer. In these two examples, no measuring was required to get the answer.

My friend's Beck Depression Inventory score was 21[2]

My brother has ADHD

We may want to attribute the same preciseness to 21 and ADHD that we attribute to 8 and triangle, but that would be a mistake. Any score or

---

[2]Scores 19 to 29 indicate moderate to severe depression.

label obtained by measurement is always subject to some degree of error. The classic way to convey the error that exists in a measurement is a formula that shows the obtained measurement (X) as a sum of a true score plus some error. One version of this formula is:

$$X = T + e$$

With this formula in mind, obtaining more precise measures depends on reducing error. Experts in measurement find it helpful to distinguish between two kinds of error, systematic error and random error. **Systematic errors** are variations in the data for which a cause can be specified. Examples of systematic errors include transposing two numbers, making a checkmark in the wrong column, and always rounding numbers down. It is also a systematic error if a participant's response on a questionnaire fails to acknowledge behavior that actually occurred (but now seems too embarrassing to admit). As you might expect, researchers develop and use procedures that reduce systematic errors, but despite their best efforts, research data are not error-free.

Random error results from the chance fluctuations that accompany every set of measurements and from undetected systematic error. Even the measurements of the 10 gram weight at the U.S. National Bureau of Standards show random variation. As reported by Freedman, Pisani, and Purves (2007), five consecutive weighings under very controlled conditions by experienced employees produced weights of

9.999591 grams
9.999600 grams
9.999594 grams
9.999601 grams
9.999598 grams

In these five weighings, the effects of random error show up in the last three decimal places. In the case of biological and psychological measurements, where data are gathered under less than very controlled conditions, random error is even more apparent. Fortunately, there are statistical methods that allow the measurement of random error. Of course, the greater the size of the error, the less trust we should put in a particular measurement.

TRUSTWORTHY MEASURES

Many of the topics in this chapter were originally researched by psychologists who worked in a subfield called *testing*. As a result of that research, we know how to develop tests and how to determine if they are trustworthy.

systematic error Variation in data set from causes that can be specified.

random error Variation in a data set that comes from uncontrolled variables that cannot be specified.

Undergraduate and graduate courses with titles such as *Tests and Measurements* and *Assessment* cover this information in some depth. For this course in research methods, we introduce some of the topics and show you how to use a few of the tools that help determine if a test is trustworthy. The topics and tools we've included are those that are most commonly used by researchers who are conducting experiments—that is, researchers who are choosing IVs and DVs, gathering and analyzing data, and presenting conclusions.

Three of the more important issues that determine the trustworthiness of measurements are reliability, validity, and sensitivity. **Reliability** refers to the degree that chance influences the scores. Tests that are reliable produce consistent scores; that is, the same people make about the same score if they are measured a second time. Random error plays only a small role in a reliable score. **Validity** refers to whether the test measures what it claims to measure. Scores on a valid test of memory, for example, are related to actual evidence of memory. The scores on a valid test of depression or happiness or procrastination show a relationship to other independent measures of depression, happiness, or procrastination. **Sensitivity** refers to a test's ability to make fine distinctions. A test that divides participants into two personality types is not as sensitive as one that gives each person a quantitative score.

You can imagine that parents who have been told that a test indicates that their 8-year-old son has ADHD might ask, "Is the test for ADHD a trustworthy test?" What a reasonable question! Fortunately, measures of reliability, validity, and sensitivity provide an answer to the question. To assess reliability and validity, psychologists use a statistical tool, the Pearson correlation coefficient, which we explain next.

Correlation Coefficient

The Pearson correlation coefficient (symbolized r) is a widely used descriptive statistic that shows the degree of relationship between two variables. Correlation coefficients range from -1.00 to 1.00, with $.00$ in the middle.

The strongest degree of relationship is indicated by $r = 1.00$ and $r = -1.00$. Both coefficients indicate that the relationship is perfect, which means that changes in the scores of one variable are accompanied by perfectly predictable changes in the scores of the other variable. The middle value, $r = .00$, means that there is no relationship between the two variables. When $r = .00$, the changes in one variable give no clue as to changes in the other variable.

Positive correlation coefficients (from $.01$ to 1.00) indicate that the two variables vary in the same direction. That is, as scores on one variable increase, scores on the other variable increase as well. Negative correlation coefficients (from $-.01$ to -1.00) mean that the variables change in opposite directions. As scores on one variable increase, scores on the other

reliability The consistency or dependability of a measure.

validity The extent to which a test measures what it claims to measure.

sensitivity The ability of a test or measure to make distinctions.

variable decrease. The closer r is to 1.00 or -1.00, the more predictable the increase or decrease is.

Correlated data are often graphed on a **scatterplot.** One of the variables is plotted on the x axis and the other on the y axis. Each dot of a scatterplot represents a pair of scores, one for the x variable and one for the y variable. **Figure** 4.1 shows six scatterplots; three perfect positive ones ($r = 1.00$) are on the left and three perfect negative ones ($r = -1.00$) on the right. In the top two panels of Figure 4.1, the changes in y that accompany the changes in x are identical—one unit each time. In the middle two panels, the changes in y are one half the size of the change in x. In the lower two panels, the change in y is twice the change in x. In all cases the change in y is perfectly predictable from the change in x, resulting in a perfect correlation.

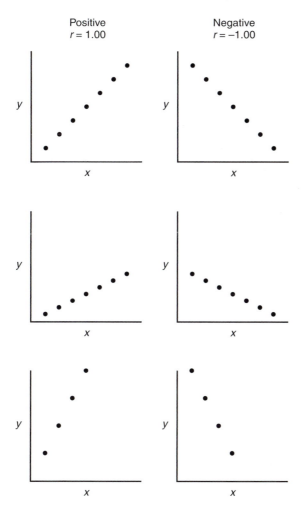

FIGURE 4.1 Scatterplots of three perfect positive rs (left) and three perfect negative rs (right).

scatterplot A graph of participants' scores on two variables.

Figure 4.2 shows four scatterplots with *r*s of .00, −.20, .80, and .50. Scatterplot 1 (*r* = .00) shows something like a snowstorm; changes in *x* are associated with no discernible pattern in *y*. Scatterplot 2 (*r* = −.20) shows a low negative correlation. There is a tendency for *y* scores to decrease as *x* increases, but there are many exceptions. Scatterplot 3 (*r* = .80) shows a high positive correlation. As *x* increases, *y* increases and the range of the increase is restricted. Finally, Scatterplot 4 (*r* = .50) shows a moderate positive correlation. With *r* = .50, changes in *y* are more restricted than when *r* = −.20, but they are less restricted than those when *r* = .80. In chapter 5, we address the calculation of *r*. Correlation coefficients are used in the assessment of both reliability and validity.

FIGURE 4.2   Scatterplots of *r* = .00, *r* = −.20, *r* = .80, and *r* = .50.

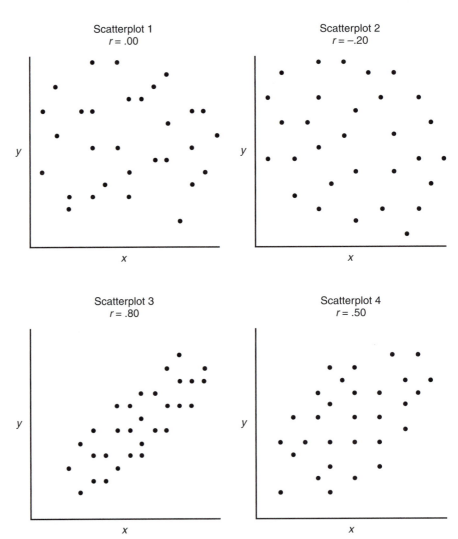

In the Know

In 1896 Karl Pearson published the mathematics for calculating a product-moment correlation coefficient that today bears his name. In the more than 100 years since its introduction, this mathematical approach has been expanded to cover more than two variables and to remove the effects of a variable from the outcome. Pearson's versatile statistic and its derivatives are used in many disciplines.

Reliability

A reliable test gives the same score again and again when it is applied to the same situation. Thus, reliable tests are characterized by *consistency*. Reliability can be assessed several ways. We begin by describing a method that conveys the essence of reliability very clearly.

Test–Retest Reliability   One way to determine the reliability of a test is to administer it to a group of individuals and then, after a period of time ranging from days to months, administer it to them again. This is referred to as **test–retest reliability.** If the instrument is reliable and the individuals have not changed, the scores from Time 1 to Time 2 will be consistent. That is, individuals with low scores the first time will get just about the same low scores the second time, and high-scoring individuals will get similar high scores the second time.

A correlation coefficient with test scores as variable x and retest scores as variable y provides a scaled measure of consistency of the test. How high does r have to be before researchers describe a test as reliable? The generally accepted rule-of-thumb is that tests are reliable if they have a test–retest correlation coefficient of .80 or higher. Instruments with reliability coefficients less than .80 are not treated with the respect that is accorded to those with higher correlation coefficients.

You probably won't be surprised to find out that r is very high for measures such as height and lower for measures such as happiness and depression. Johnson et al. (1985) found that when height was measured on two different occasions, $r = .98$. For intelligence tests, rs of about .90 are common. College entrance examinations such as the SAT and ACT have test–retest reliability coefficients above .90.

In many research situations, the second administration that is required for a test–retest reliability check is either impractical or impossible. For a memory experiment in which participants are tested on a three-page passage from the *Encyclopedia Britannica,* retesting the participants after several hours or days just isn't practical. In experiments observing animals in their natural habitat, retesting isn't even possible. Nevertheless, for a reliable study, reliable measurements are required.

test–retest reliability
Determining reliability by administering a test a second time and correlating the two scores.

Fortunately, reliability can be determined when behavior is measured just once.

Split-Half Reliability   Psychologists call techniques that measure reliability with just one testing session *measures of internal consistency.* One of the simplest of these is **split-half reliability.** To determine split-half reliability, divide the items that make up the test into two halves. A common way to do this is to separate the even-numbered items from the odd-numbered items. The scores on the even-numbered items could be the *x* variable and the odd scores the *y* variable. Each test taker has two scores. A Pearson *r* measures the degree of consistency between the odd scores and the even scores. Even if the even scores are generally higher than the odd scores, *r* is a measure of consistency. A high correlation (.80 or higher) indicates that the test is internally reliable. One of the problems with the split-half reliability coefficient is that its value depends on whether you divide the items by odd-even, or first half-second half, or some other method.

Other Measures of Internal Reliability   Two other popular measures of internal consistency are Cronbach's *alpha* (also known as *coefficient alpha* or just *alpha*) and the Kuder-Richardson formula known as K-R 20. The formula for Cronbach's alpha produces a coefficient that is a corrected average of all possible split-half correlation coefficients. Thus, Cronbach's alpha overcomes the "how to divide into halves" problem we noted above. The K-R 20 formula is useful when each item of a test is scored as right or wrong, as is the case with multiple-choice and true-false tests. As with the test–retest method of assessing reliability, internal consistency coefficients of .80 or higher indicate an acceptable measure of reliability. Textbooks for courses in tests and measurements and assessment provide formulas and descriptions of these measures of reliability. One such reference is Cohen and Swerdlik (2002). Look at **Table 4.4,** which shows reliability coefficients for five well-known tests.

Interobserver Reliability   In some research situations, measurement of the participants does not involve a test. Indeed, the participants may not even know they are in an experiment. Instead, they are simply observed for a period of time by a researcher who looks for particular behaviors such as head swaying, approaching, retreating, touching, or trumpeting (if the participants are elephants in a zoo). After the observation period, the researcher has a record of the elephant's behavior, but is it a reliable record? A technique called **interobserver reliability** can answer that question.

  Let's switch from elephants in a zoo to couples in a park being observed by Albert and Victoria for their social psychology class project. Some couples were seated on benches in the shade and some were on

split-half reliability
Determining reliability by dividing a test in half and correlating the two part scores.

interobserver reliability   Method of detecting inconsistent measuring by comparing observations of two independent observers.

benches in the sun (the IV). The question the students were researching is whether couples are more intimate in the shade or in the sun. The DV of intimacy was measured by the students with a checklist of behaviors and a watch that beeped every 10 seconds. The checklist had five behaviors on it: she smiles, he smiles, she touches, he touches, and legs touching. Both student researchers observed a couple for 2 minutes. If one or more of the five behaviors occurred during a 10-second period, the observer placed a checkmark by the behavior for that period. After 2 minutes, Albert and Victoria each had a record of the behaviors observed and the time period they occurred in.

Although this procedure sounds simple enough, the decision making during observation is not so easy. The accuracy of either record would be questionable to anyone experienced in naturalistic observation studies such as this one. Fortunately, because both students recorded the same behavior simultaneously, an interobserver reliability coefficient may settle the question.

An interobserver reliability coefficient is the percentage of times that the two observers are in agreement. The formula for this percentage is

$$\frac{\text{Number of times observers agree}}{\text{Number of opportunities to agree}} \times 100 = \text{Percentage of agreement}$$

Table 4.5 shows the checklists of both Albert and Victoria for 12 periods. This example is for illustration only because 12 opportunities for the two observers to agree is too few for an assessment of reliability. Fifty to 100 or more are needed. In Table 4.5 the number of agreements between the two observers is noted by the checkmarks below the two records. As you can count, there were 9 agreements out of the 12 opportunities to agree: $9/12 = 75\%$.

TABLE 4.4	Reliability Coefficients for a Variety of Measures
Test or measure	*Reliability coefficient*
SAT college admission test	.92[a]
ACT college admission test	.96[b]
Beck Depression Inventory (BDI)	.86[c]
Wechsler Adult Intelligence Scale (WAIS)	.87[d]
Minnesota Multiphasic Personality Inventory (MMPI)	.84[d]

Sources:

[a]www.collegeboard.com/prod_downloads/about/news_info/cbsenior/yr2005/10_test_characteristics_sat_0506.pdf

[b]ACT (1997)

[c]Beck, Steer, and Gabin (1988)

[d]Parker, Hanson, and Hunsley (1988)

TABLE 4.5	Checklists Filled Out by Two Observers, Albert and Victoria

Albert's Checklist　　　　　　　　　　*10-Second Periods*

Behavior	1	2	3	4	5	6	7	8	9	10	11	12
He smiles	✓											
She smiles				✓	✓						✓	
He touches		✓	✓									✓
She touches							✓	✓			✓	
Legs touching						✓	✓	✓	✓	✓		

Victoria's Checklist　　　　　　　　　　*10-Second Periods*

Behavior	1	2	3	4	5	6	7	8	9	10	11	12
He smiles	✓											
She smiles					✓						✓	
He touches		✓	✓									✓
She touches							✓	✓				
Legs touching							✓	✓	✓	✓		
Agreements	✓	✓	✓	×	✓	×	✓	✓	✓	✓	×	✓

✓ = yes
× = no

$$\frac{9 \text{ agreements}}{12 \text{ opportunities to agree}} \times 100 = 75\%$$

The interpretation of an interobserver reliability coefficient of 75% is that it does not quite indicate the degree of reliability that researchers strive for. Researchers strive for interobserver reliability coefficients of 80% or higher. If this data gathering was a practice run by the two students, then an interobserver reliability coefficient of .75 suggests that they should specify more clearly what constitutes a smile or a touch so they can be more consistent. Additional practice usually guarantees a higher rate of agreement. If the data gathering was not preliminary, but was the actual study, Albert and Victoria risk not discovering that sunlight helps (or hinders) intimacy because their measure of intimacy contains too much random error. For situations where two records show high interobserver reliability, either can be used for the data analysis.

Other Assurances of Reliability The authors of most journal articles don't report reliability figures for the dependent variables they use unless the DV is a published test or a custom-made test. For many DVs, such as reaction time, percent correct, number of bar presses, or key pecks, reliability is not mentioned. In these cases, researchers usually know from experience or from the literature that their measures are reliable. How do they know?

In many areas of research, the same DVs are used in study after study. In operant conditioning experiments, bar presses and key pecks are common. In sleep research, the height of brain wave recordings is used. Pavlov's assistants must have measured gallons of saliva, drop by drop. Thus, in developed research areas, experimenters become convinced that measures are reliable because they observe consistent results in their own studies and replication is common.

Validity

A valid test or measurement is one that measures what it claims to measure. To establish validity some kind of standard or criterion must be accepted against which the test can be compared. Because there are several acceptable standards, the topic of validity is complex. In keeping with this book's focus on topics that are of immediate concern to many researchers, we discuss only two aspects of validity: content and criterion-related validity. For a more complete treatment of validity, we recommend Cohen and Swerdlik (2002) or Rosnow and Rosenthal (2005).

Content Validity A test has **content validity** if the items on the test are clearly related to the characteristic or trait that the test is measuring. For example, the purpose of a test in a college course is to measure whether the students learned the assigned material. If the test has items about material that was not assigned, then those items have zero content validity because they are measuring something other than whether the students learned the assignment. Content validity is not just a concern for conventional tests; it is also a concern for researchers.

Imagine an experiment in which a student uses salespeople in a mall to determine the effect of fashion (the IV) on service (the DV). The three levels of the IV are grunge, casual, and geek, which are accomplished with three outfits worn by the same student. The DV is the time from entering the store until a salesperson offers assistance.

To ask if the costumes were "really" grunge, casual, or geek is to ask if content validity was established. To be sure that the outfits were conveying the fashion they claimed, the student might ask friends who are knowledgeable about fashion to judge the three costumes. If all agree, then the costumes are conveying what they claim to convey: grunge, casual, and geek. Such a check on content validity typically would be

content validity Determined by the degree to which the test items represent the characteristic tested.

reported in the student's writeup of the experiment. In the case of the test on the material from three pages in an encyclopedia, content validity can be ensured by comparing the test (item by item) to the article (paragraph by paragraph) to be sure that the test covers thoroughly the content of the article and only that article.

Of course, for some measures, the connection between the test and what it claims to measure is obvious. No check for content validity is necessary. If the DV in an experiment is the number of eye contacts in the first 3 minutes of conversation, then there is no question that eye contacts are what is being measured and that the test has content validity. In an experiment on speed of cognitive processing, the time in milliseconds that it takes participants to respond is a valid way to measure speed.

Criterion-Related Validity   To establish **criterion-related validity,** a researcher must have an independent, outside-the-experiment standard to compare the test to. This standard (or criterion) is a measure of the same thing as the test, and it is one whose validity has already been established. If there is a match between the test and the criterion, then the test is measuring what it was intended to measure.

If the criterion is a quantitative measure, the validity of the test can be evaluated by calculating a Pearson r between the test and the criterion. As an example, consider college entrance examinations such as the SAT and the ACT. What do these tests claim to measure? At a basic level, they claim to measure and predict how well a person will do in college. What criterion is appropriate for judging the validity of these tests? One appropriate criterion is first-year student grade point average (GPA). That is, unless students maintain an adequate GPA, they cannot stay in college. Thus, the criterion-related validity of college entrance tests can be evaluated by knowing the r between the test and first-year student GPA. The size of this r varies from school to school, but is generally in the .40 to .50 range (Sternberg, 1997).

Is there a rule-of-thumb for the size of the r that establishes criterion-related validity that is comparable to the reliability rule of .80? Cronbach and Gleser (1965) caution that such rules-of-thumb for validity coefficients are inappropriate because values for validity are not context free. A question about validity is always a question about validity *for what?* A test might be valid for one purpose but not valid for another purpose. In any case, validity coefficients are typically much lower than reliability coefficients. See Cohen and Swerdlik (2002) or Murphy and Davidshofer (2005) for more on validity.

Sensitivity

criterion-related validity Determined by the degree to which the test correlates with other measures of the same variable.

Suppose you are in possession of what might be an important aid to human memory. Perhaps your aid is a memory pill you've invented or a relaxation technique you've modified or a new twist to posthypnotic suggestion. Whatever your memory aid, an experiment is needed if you are to establish the value of your aid. In your experiment, one group gets the treatment and a control group does not. Participants in both groups then read a three-page passage from the *Encyclopedia Britannica* and take a test on the material. The dependent variable is the recall score on a test that you make up that covers the *Britannica* material.

How hard should the test be? To be more specific, what would you think the mean score for the control group should be? How about 90%? Would you rather have the mean at 75%? 50%? One of these figures is the right answer!

Which answer do you think is correct, 90%, 75%, or 50%?

Remember that the purpose of your experiment is to show that the treatment has an effect on memory. Although you expect the experimental group to do better, you probably would be quite interested in finding just the opposite—that your treatment *reduces* recall. (After all, understanding how to reduce memory is a step toward improving memory.) With this reasoning in mind, the best average test score for the control group is 50%. With the control group scoring 50%, there is room for the effect of the IV to show up in the scores of the experimental group, regardless of whether the treatment enhances or reduces recall.

Suppose, however, that the mean score of the control group is 90% and the treatment improves recall. The test doesn't allow much room for the improved recall to reveal itself. If the mean score of the control group is 90%, the DV suffers from a **ceiling effect.** A ceiling effect occurs when the measure of a characteristic is limited by the upper boundary of the measure used. In the Miller and Peden (2003) experiment discussed in chapter 2, the arithmetic errors measure suffered from a ceiling effect. Because very few participants made them, errors were not sensitive to the effect of music tempo. Fortunately, Miller and Peden also counted the number of problems worked, which was a sensitive measure.

The opposite of a ceiling effect is a **floor effect.** A floor effect occurs when the measure of a characteristic is limited by the *lower* boundary of the measure used. If a test is too hard and the control group scores 10%, there isn't room for a deleterious treatment to reveal that it reduces memory. A test in which the control group scores 50% is maximally sensitive and will avoid both ceiling and floor effects.

TESTS AND MEASUREMENTS

In this final section, we turn from measurement characteristics of tests to tests themselves. We include advice on both finding published tests and creating custom-made tests.

ceiling effect Scores clustered near the maximum possible score prevent the detection of variables that raise scores.

floor effect Scores clustered near the minimum possible score prevent the detection of variables that lower scores.

Often, a test is the DV in an experiment. However, the measures that we describe below can also serve in the creation of an IV. If you want to compare high-anxious students to low-anxious students on their attitude toward the physical discipline of children, you need two tests, one for anxiety (to establish the IV) and one for attitude toward physical discipline (the DV). By administering both tests to participants, you can later separate the high anxious from the low anxious (the two levels of the IV) using the anxiety test scores. Now, with two groups established, you can compare them on the DV, the attitude measure. In a similar way, tests are used to separate participants into IV levels according to learning styles, GPA, attitudes, health practices, and other characteristics. Using a test to establish levels of the IV precludes random assignment of participants to groups. The distinction between random and nonrandom assignment is covered in chapter 7.

Some of the ways that researchers establish levels of the IV and measure DVs don't need to be explained in a textbook. IVs of gender, age, and group membership are either obvious or easily determined in a reliable, valid manner. DVs of frequency counts, time, or automatic recordings by equipment are similarly not covered, although questions about reliability are always appropriate.

Published Tests

The number of tests that have been published by psychologists over the past 100 years is enormous. Tests have been developed to measure psychological traits that range from anxiety to zoophobia. Probably the principal advantage of using a published test in your research is that you can compare your results to those of others who used the same test. Thus, your research adds to overall knowledge of a topic. Scores that are similar to those obtained by others give you confidence in the reliability of your work. On the other hand, if your results are quite different from those of others, you are faced with a challenge, which, if you accept it, can be quite exciting. The task, of course, is to determine why the results are different.

Finding a specific test that meets the purpose of your own research project may take a little detective work, but we have suggestions for you. Also, once you find a test, you must determine if you can get permission to use it for your own research.

Sometimes the source of a test is found easily. If your literature search turns up an article that captures your attention, the DV (or DVs) used in that article might become your DV. Most of the time the actual test will not be part of the article, but the reference section will give you the source of the test. Another readily available source of information about tests is your professor. Professors often can direct you to a test, and they sometimes have tests themselves.

There are a number of print and electronic references that either provide tests or direct you to tests. The Buros Institute publishes *Tests in Print* and the *Mental Measurements Yearbook,* which are reference books that are probably in your university library. *Tests in Print* is a comprehensive bibliography of all available commercial tests. Each entry explains what a test measures, how to obtain it, and other information. The *Mental Measurements Yearbook* (which is reissued about every 2 years) provides reviews of new and revised tests. Reviews always have information about reliability and validity. The Institute's Web site (http://www.unl.edu/buros/) has free information on almost 4,000 tests.

The American Psychological Association (APA) maintains an electronic database that allows you to search for both published tests sold by commercial publishers and unpublished tests (which are usually the work of individual researchers). The APA Web site is http://www.apa.org/science/faq-findtests.html/. Another electronic database is maintained by the Educational Resources Information Center (ERIC). You can search the database at http://www.eric.ed.gov/ for tests and questionnaires. In addition, your library might have an APA publication, the *Directory of Unpublished Experimental Mental Measures,* which lists tests used by researchers since 1970.

Some sources of information include actual copies of the tests. The instructor's manuals that come with introduction to psychology textbooks often have tests and scoring keys. Your professors will likely have copies. Ask. Two other references that include copies of tests, scoring keys, and test information are Robinson, Shaver, and Wrightsman (1991) and two volumes by Fischer and Corcoran (2000a, 2000b).

Here are two cautions that go with published tests. One caution is to check the test manual or reviews to determine the reliability of the test. Even published tests sometimes have marginal reliability coefficients. The second caution concerns the right to use the test. If the test is copyrighted, you may not use the test without permission. In the case of tests copyrighted by commercial publishers, you get permission when you buy the test. Other copyright holders, however, may grant you permission for limited use, such as to conduct a research project for a class. Individual researchers, if they hold the copyright to tests they have written, are usually happy to grant students and other researchers the right to use their test. We offer advice on how to contact researchers by e-mail in chapter 11.

Custom-Made Tests

At various times, students and other researchers cannot find a published test that is satisfactory for their project. In our earlier example of the student project in which the DV was memory for a three-page passage from an encyclopedia, there is no published test on that material. The student has to construct a test. In a similar way, a project to investigate attitudes about a local event or a local issue needs a custom-made measuring device. The topic of constructing custom-made tests is a complex one; a full discussion is beyond the scope of this book. Our solution is to give you a brief example—the construction of a test to measure a person's attitude toward the use of physical discipline with children. Our test has only five items; an actual test would require more items to be reliable, valid, and sensitive.

The most common format for tests that measure respondents' attitudes is a Likert scale (named after its developer, Rensis Likert). A Likert scale presents an item and a range of responses such as *strongly disagree, disagree, no opinion, agree,* and *strongly agree.* A respondent simply checks the response that is closest to his or her attitude.

Read the five first-draft items in **Table 4.6** and circle the response that best expresses your attitude. Do this exercise before continuing.

TABLE 4.6	First Draft of a Five-Item Test of Attitude Toward Physical Discipline of Children

1. Spanking and paddling are effective methods of child discipline.
   Strongly disagree   Disagree   No opinion   Agree   Strongly agree

2. Sometimes when a child misbehaves, physical punishment should be used.
   Strongly disagree   Disagree   No opinion   Agree   Strongly agree

3. Revocation of privileges is an effective form of discipline that should be used judiciously.
   Strongly disagree   Disagree   No opinion   Agree   Strongly agree

4. Parents should not spank children.
   Strongly disagree   Disagree   No opinion   Agree   Strongly agree

5. We should have laws that prohibit physical discipline.
   Strongly disagree   Disagree   No opinion   Agree   Strongly agree

Scoring   We use Table 4.6 to illustrate how to score items and how to edit them. Let's score the items so that high scores indicate high approval of physical punishment. For Items 1 and 2, give points according to the scheme:

Strongly disagree = 1, Disagree = 2, No opinion = 3, Agree = 4, Strongly agree = 5

For Items 3, 4, and 5, use reverse scoring:

Strongly disagree = 5, Disagree = 4, No opinion = 3, Agree = 2, Strongly agree = 1

The advantage of reverse scoring is that it helps break up a respondent's mental set. That is, after two or three items in which a respondent checks *strongly agree* (or *disagree*), there is a tendency to continue to check the same response. An item that is reverse scored encourages a closer reading by the respondent.

Editing   We now turn to editing the items in Table 4.6, each of which has a flaw.

For each of the items in Table 4.6 identify one or more problems or rewrite it to improve it. Remember, the purpose of the test is to determine a person's attitude toward the physical discipline of children.

The problem with Item 1 in Table 4.6 is that it asks about two methods of physical discipline, spanking and paddling. Such items are referred to as *compound items*. It is easy to imagine a person who believes that a quick swat on the behind is acceptable, but that using a paddle is not. How should such a person respond? Thus, one rule is that an item should be about only one thing. Hint: The word *and* is one tip-off that an item is a compound item. The solution to this problem is to write two separate items, one for spanking and one for paddling.

The problem with Item 2 is the word *sometimes* which creates ambiguity. Imagine a person who thinks that children should always be physically punished when they misbehave. Such a person would respond strongly disagree. (They should always be punished.) Another person who does not approve of physical punishment at all would also respond "strongly disagree." (They should never be punished.) Thus, this item has two people with very different attitudes who respond the same way. The solution is to remove the word *sometimes*. A good way to detect ambiguities is to play a game with yourself. For each item, adopt a succession of quite different attitudes and write your response. If a strange result occurs (as happens with the *sometimes* item), you have an ambiguity. An easier way to detect ambiguities is to get friends to read and discuss items with you.

There are several problems with Item 3. To begin with, it is hard to comprehend. It is a long item that has two uncommon words, *revocation* and *judiciously*. Another problem is that, like Item 1, it is a compound item. It asks whether revocation of privileges is an effective form of punishment and it also asks if revocation should be used judiciously. A simple shorter form is "Loss of privileges is an effective form of discipline." In addition, another problem is that the item may not measure attitude toward physical discipline. The item is about discipline that is not physical, which may or may not give an indication of attitude toward physical discipline. Thus, Item 3, even in its improved form, lacks content validity.

Item 4 includes a negative, *not,* which creates a problem. Readers often miss the *not* in a sentence. (You may have had this experience yourself.) Besides the possibility of missing an important word, respondents who favor physical discipline have to comprehend a double negative to correctly register their opinion. They are saying, "I disagree that parents should not spank their children." Double negatives are difficult to understand. Best to rewrite the item to remove the negative. The rewritten item becomes, "It is acceptable for parents to spank their children."

The problem with Item 5 is that it evokes attitudes about the judicial system as well as attitudes about physical discipline. It may be that such an item can be a reliable measure of attitude toward physical discipline, but additional testing is required.

The rules we have illustrated in this exercise are summarized in **Table 4.7.** For more complete instruction in how to write test items, see Babbie (2007). The best overall advice we know of is that of Ira Bernstein (1988). "The most important thing to keep in mind about constructing items is to *keep the wording simple*" (p. 377). Indeed, the best published tests in psychology are characterized by short and simple items.

Look again at the test in Table 4.6. Ignore the wording and the short length of the test. What other comments, either positive or negative, can you make?

On the positive side, we think that the layout of the questions and responses is good. Participants are not likely to become confused about which responses go with which items. On the negative side, there are no instructions for the participant. Instructions usually provide an example dealing with some other topic. The example shows how a person would respond (perhaps, by circling the response).

TABLE 4.7	Summary of Rules for Writing Test Items

- Separate items with compound elements into two separate items.
- Avoid ambiguities.
- Use simple words.
- Eliminate unnecessary phrases.
- Avoid negative phrasing.
- Be cautious of items that are not directly on the topic.

Note: Rules are based on the test items in Table 4.6.

> ## In the Know
>
> Magazines and the Internet are the source of many tests. People like to take tests. Using tests published in magazines, you can determine your score as a friend, lover, or intellectual. You can determine whether you are right-brained, depressed, or destined to become rich or lose weight. Unfortunately, most of these tests have not been checked for reliability or validity. Their purpose is entertainment, not measurement. Of course, now that you know the basics of reliability, you can check a test's reliability yourself.

Item Testing   As we will discuss in detail in chapter 12, clear and understandable prose is prose that has been revised a number of times. As illustrated in our analysis of Table 4.6, the same is true for test items. Good writers edit to remove ambiguities. One of the most efficient ways to discover ambiguities is to test the items. After writing the test and editing it to remove ambiguities that you detect, give the test to other people such as friends and classmates. After (or during) the test, have them explain any uncertainties or questions they have about items. Item testing always provides information about other ways to interpret a question. Usually, editing or rewriting an item reduces the number of other interpretations.

This chapter is about how to measure and how to determine the trustworthiness of the measures. The next chapter shows ways to extract more meaning from the numbers by applying statistics.

Chapter Review

1. A(n) _____ tells how the researcher measured a variable.

2. Match the term with its definition.

   1. continuous
   2. discrete
   3. dichotomous

   a. a variable whose adjacent values do not have intermediate values

   b. a variable that has only two values

   c. a variable with adjacent values that could have intermediate values

3. Match the term with its definition.

   1. quantitative
   2. qualitative

   a. a variable whose values differ from each other on a continuum

   b. a variable whose values differ from each other in kind

4. Match the term with its definition.

1. categorical data
2. ranked data
3. scaled data

a. obtained when participants are ordered from highest to lowest
b. consists of the frequency of observations that fall in different classes
c. obtained when participants are measured and given a quantitative score

5. A formula that separates a measured score into two components is _____.

6. Distinguish between systematic and random errors.

7. The three characteristics of trustworthy measures that your text identified were _____ , _____ , and _____ .

8. Match the numerical value with its description.

1. .00
2. +1.00
3. −1.00

a. a perfect one-to-one relationship between two variables
b. no relationship between the variables

9. Your text identified several kinds of reliability. Name three of them.

10. A test has _____ validity if it correlates highly with a different test on the same topic. A test has _____ validity if a careful examination of the test items reveals that each item is related to the topic being tested.

11. A test that is so difficult that the scores cluster near zero suffers from a(n) _____ effect, whereas a test that is so easy that the scores cluster near 100 percent suffers from a(n) _____ effect.

12. Name the two general sources of tests that your text identified.

13. Name three sources that could lead you to a published test on a topic that interests you.

14. A(n) _____ scale measures attitudes by having participants evaluate statements by circling responses such as *agree, neutral,* or *disagree.*

15. Give two of the rules for writing clear test items.

Thinking Critically About Research

1. Create an operational definition that divides college students into two groups who differ in procrastination.

2. Match the measurement with the type of measurement scale

1. university degrees—BA, MS, PhD   a. nominal
2. dollars—5, 15, 28   b. ordinal
3. clothes—hat, shoes, pants   c. interval
4. seconds—1, 2, 3   d. ratio
5. degrees Fahrenheit—5, 15, 28
6. Olympic metals—gold, silver, bronze
7. psychiatric disorders—anxiety, phobic, adjustment

3. Calculate the interobserver reliability coefficient for two observers who were watching an elephant at the zoo. Are the two observing reliably?

Observer 1's Checklist   *5-Minute Periods*

Behavior	1	2	3	4	5	6
Head swaying	✓	✓	✓	✓	✓	✓
Approaching		✓				✓
Retreating			✓		✓	
Trumpeting						✓

Observer 2's Checklist   *5-Minute Periods*

Behavior	1	2	3	4	5	6
Head swaying	✓	✓	✓	✓	✓	✓
Approaching		✓				✓
Retreating			✓		✓	
Trumpeting						

4. The following items are for an inventory that measures procrastination in college students. For each item, identify one or more problems using the list in Table 4.7. Rewrite the item. The response choices are *frequently, occasionally,* and *never.*

a. Procrastination is not a problem for me.

b. Often I find myself doing less important tasks when there are more important tasks to do.

c. I use written goals as a prophylaxis against procrastination.

d. I come to class late and turn in papers after the deadline.

e. I have been known to forget when assignments are due.

Answers to Chapter Review

1. operational definition
2. 1. c; 2. a; 3. b
3. 1. a; 2. b
4. 1. b; 2. a; 3. c
5. $X = T + e$
6. Systematic error is variation in scores that can be attributed to an identified cause. Random error is variation in scores that cannot be attributed to an identifiable cause.
7. reliable; valid; sensitive
8. 1. b; 2. a; 3. a
9. Correct choices include: test–retest, split-half, interobserver, Cronbach's alpha, K-R 20, and results consistent with past results
10. criterion-related; content
11. floor; ceiling
12. published tests and custom-made tests
13. Correct choices include: articles in journals, references in articles, professors, and any of the reference sources mentioned in the text
14. Likert
15. Correct choices include: avoid ambiguities, use simple words, eliminate unnecessary phrases, avoid negative phrasing, and use items that are on the topic

Answers to Thinking Critically About Research

1. Many answers are appropriate, but a correct one describes a procedure that forms two groups and has a logical connection to the concept procrastination. One example is to ask students if they have turned in two or more assignments late in the past school year. The "yes" group becomes *procrastinators* and the "no" group becomes *not procrastinators*.

2. 1. b; 2. d; 3. a; 4. d; 5. c; 6. b; 7. a

3.

Observation periods	1	2	3	4	5	6
Agreements	✓	✓	✓	✓	✓	✓

There were five periods of agreement and one period of disagreement. The interobserver reliability coefficient is $5/6 = .83$. The interobserver reliability coefficient is greater than the rule-of-thumb requirement of .80.

4. You may have additional improvements beyond our answers.

Item 1: negative phrasing. *Procrastination is a problem for me.*

Item 2: ambiguous, wordy. Remove the word often. *I do less important tasks before more important tasks.*

Item 3: use simple words. *I use written goals to prevent procrastination.*

Item 4: compound elements. Separate into two items. *I come to class late. I turn in paper after the deadline.*

Item 5: wordy. *I forget when assignments are due.*

Know for Sure

categorical data, 98

ceiling effect, 113

content validity, 111

continuous
variable, 98

correlation
coefficient, 104

criterion-related
validity, 112

dichotomous
variable, 98

discrete variable, 98

floor effect, 113

interobserver
reliability, 108

interval scale, 100

nominal scale, 100

operational
definition, 95

ordinal scale, 100

qualitative
variable, 98

quantitative
variable, 98

random error, 103

ranked data, 99

ratio scale, 101

reliability, 104, 107

scaled data, 99

scatterplot, 105

sensitivity, 104, 112

split-half
reliability, 108

systematic error, 103

test–retest
reliability, 107

validity, 104, 111

5

Data Exploration and Description

OVERVIEW

This chapter and the one that follows are about descriptive and inferential statistics. In this chapter we cover about 20 descriptive techniques that are used for scaled data and categorical data. Calculation of these statistics is explained using definitional formulas and computer software. In all cases, there is a heavy emphasis on the interpretation of the results.

OBJECTIVES

After studying this chapter and working through the exercises, you should be able to:

1. Distinguish between descriptive statistics and inferential statistics
2. Distinguish between scaled data and categorical data
3. Construct and explain stem-and-leaf displays
4. Calculate and explain the mean, median, and mode
5. Calculate and explain the range, interquartile range, standard deviation, and standard error of the mean
6. Calculate and explain a confidence interval about a sample mean
7. Construct and explain frequency distributions, frequency polygons, histograms, line graphs, and bar graphs
8. Identify the direction of skew in a distribution
9. Construct and explain a boxplot
10. Know the percentages of the normal curve that are associated with 1 and 2 standard deviations from the mean
11. Identify three questions that are prompted by a difference between two sample means
12. Calculate and interpret the effect size index, d
13. Calculate a correlation coefficient, r
14. For categorical data, calculate percentages, construct bar graphs, and interpret the effect size index, phi (φ)

Research generates data. Sometimes, research generates lots of data. **Figure 5.1** shows researchers drowning in data. Fortunately for them, there is a rescue procedure—statistics. Statistical techniques guide researchers as they plan their research; later, statistical techniques help them make sense out of the mounds of data that research produces. This chapter and the next summarize some of the statistics that scientists use to help them understand the meaning of the data from experimental research. Some of these techniques are also used in correlational research and meta-analytic research.

You may recall from chapter 2 (page 49) that a simple model experiment compares two approximately equal groups that have been treated exactly alike except for one particular treatment. The statistics we discuss in this chapter and the next are often used in the analysis of such simple experiments. After the data are gathered, statistics are used to help make the decision about the treatment.

Understanding statistics is necessary for both producers of research and knowledgeable consumers of research. Producing research, however, requires not only that you be able to interpret statistics but also that you be able to plan statistical analyses for data that are

FIGURE 5.1
"Help! we're covered up with data—it's so confusing . . ."

generated by your experiment. Once the analysis is planned, the confused researchers in Figure 5.1 can become the organized researchers in **Figure 5.2**, whose plan for the data was already in place even before the data were generated.

As we said earlier, the goal of research is to tell a story about the population. In experiments, researchers want to compare parameters in two (or more) different populations. Parameters, of course, are unchanging characteristics of populations. If researchers could obtain population data, they could calculate parameters and there would be no uncertainty. However, researchers are almost always stuck with samples, which give only approximate measures of the parameters.

One of the beauties of some statistical techniques is that they allow you to measure the *degree of uncertainty* that goes with sample data. Because you can measure it, you can include the degree of uncertainty in your conclusions about population parameters. If uncertainty is low, you can have confidence in your conclusions; if uncertainty is great, more caution is warranted. Although you may have heard that the data speak for themselves, this isn't true. It is the researcher's (and others') explanations that speak for the data.

FIGURE 5.2
"Ahhh. A planned statistical analysis sure helps."

DESCRIPTIVE AND INFERENTIAL STATISTICS

Statistical techniques are often divided into two categories: descriptive statistics and inferential statistics. A **descriptive statistic** is a number, numbers, or graph that conveys a characteristic of a sample or population. Descriptive statistics of samples carry an intuitive degree of uncertainty with them, but they do not provide a measure of that uncertainty. **Inferential statistics** are techniques that use sample data and probability to arrive at conclusions about populations. Inferential statistics help generate conclusions, and they also provide a measure of the uncertainty that goes with the conclusion.

SCALED DATA AND CATEGORICAL DATA

In chapter 4 we described the distinctions among scaled, ranked, and categorical data. This categorization scheme is particularly useful when you decide what descriptive and inferential techniques are appropriate for a particular set of data. **Scaled data,** as you may recall, include both continuous variables and discrete variables. Measuring responses in seconds or distances in meters produces continuous scaled data. The number of children in a family, college enrollment figures, and the number of unique uses of a paper clip are examples of discrete scaled variables. For both continuous and discrete data, the transition between levels of the variable is a transition in amount, rather than in kind. Researchers generally do not distinguish between continuous and discrete scaled data when they select statistical techniques. For variables that produce scaled data, descriptive statistics are covered in the first part of this chapter; inferential statistics are covered in chapter 6.

    For **categorical data,** the transition between levels is a transition in kind rather than in amount. Categorical data always have discrete levels. Gender, color, and psychiatric diagnoses are categorical variables whose levels are discretely different from each other. Some categorical variables such as college standing (first-year student through senior) and military officer rank (lieutenant through general) have an ordered aspect to them, and others such as gender and personality type do not. Descriptive statistics for categorical data are explained in the last section of this chapter; one inferential statistical technique for categorical data is covered in chapter 6.

    Of course, scaled data and categorical data might be from a sample or from a population. In some cases, the formula for a sample statistic is the same as the formula for its corresponding population parameter (the mean is an example). In other cases, the formula for the sample statistic is a little different from the formula for the population parameter (the standard deviation is an example). Because most psychological research uses samples, the explanations that follow focus on the formulas for *sample* statistics.

descriptive statistics Numbers or graphs that summarize a data set.

inferential statistics Method of reaching conclusions using samples and probability.

scaled data Numerical measurements that are not ranks.

categorical data Frequency counts of the events observed in designated categories.

EXPLORING AND DESCRIBING SCALED DATA

To have scaled data to explore and describe, we return to the social loafing experiment by the Widener University students that we described in chapter 2 (Welter et al., 2002). In that experiment, the dependent variable (DV) was a scaled variable—the number of uses of a paper clip. The independent variable (IV) was the confederate's role as a group member. There were two levels of the IV: loafer and worker. The group's task was to dream up creative ways to use a paper clip. To illustrate descriptive statistics, we turn to the scores of the participants whose group included a worker.

> ### In the Know
>
> For both descriptive and inferential statistics, there is more than one way to calculate a correct answer. One method is to use a hand calculator or a pencil and a *definitional formula* of the statistic. The best way to develop an understanding of what's going on is to use definitional formulas. Another way to get answers is to use a computer with *statistical software* or a *programmed calculator*. Computers and calculators are the most efficient way to get the correct answer for a reasonably large data set. Your task as a student, however, is not only to get right answers, but also to understand what's going on and to write interpretations. This chapter and the next use both approaches to calculating statistics.

We created two data sets for you to work with. **Table 5.1** is a small data set ($N = 7$) that we use to illustrate definitional formulas. Using definitional formulas, you get to see all the computational steps and

TABLE 5.1	A Small Data Set, Unorganized and Ordered
Unorganized	*Ordered*
5	9
3	8
8	6
9	5
1	3
3	3
6	1
Σ 35	35

TABLE 5.2	Paper Clip Use Scores by 30 Participants Whose Group Included a Worker		

Unorganized	Ordered	Unorganized	Ordered
5	10	9	5
7	10	8	5
2	9	3	5
10	9	3	5
5	8	4	5
6	8	10	5
4	8	7	4
1	8	6	4
8	7	4	4
0	7	5	4
5	7	5	3
6	6	9	3
8	6	6	2
4	6	7	1
5	6	8	0
		Σ 170	170

develop an understanding of what's going on. **Table 5.2** is a larger data set ($N = 30$). For several of the examples that rely on the larger data set, we just give you the answers. You can use the answers to verify the procedure you use for work with computer software or calculators. The data in Table 5.2 produce answers that are similar to the answers produced by the worker scores in the social loafing experiment. We expect that this two-data-set approach will produce both understanding (from using definitional formulas) and efficiency (from working with statistical packages such as SPSS).

The best way to begin any analysis of data is to start with exploratory techniques such as simple descriptive statistics and graphs. We use the data in Tables 5.1 and 5.2 to illustrate several statistical techniques that are helpful as you develop an understanding of an experiment. After using these techniques to reach a preliminary understanding of what the data mean, inferential statistics are applied. The next chapter provides examples of a particular inferential approach, null hypothesis statistical testing (NHST).

Arrange the Scores in Order

In both Table 5.1 and Table 5.2, the left-column scores are unorganized; they appear in the order they were generated, participant by participant. The first task is to create some organization! The right-column scores in Tables 5.1 and 5.2 are sorted in descending order. It is traditional to order the scores in a descending fashion, but this is a tradition that is often ignored (especially by statistical software).

Examine the Scores

One of the most helpful things you can do to begin to understand a data set is to look at the organized scores. Here are some specific things to look for.

1. Are there any impossible scores? In the case of a DV such as the number of uses of a paper clip, negative scores are impossible. For some DVs, the scores must be within a particular range. For example, Frahm (2002) had participants putt a golf ball 20 times before training and 20 times after training. The DV was the posttraining score minus the pretraining score. Negative scores are possible (but not less than -20), and positive scores are possible (but not greater than $+20$). If you discover an impossible score, determine why it is there. Is it a typographical error or a scoring error? An impossible score is a warning that something was not done properly.

2. Are there any outliers? An outlier is a very high score or very low score widely separated from other scores that meets the definition on page 134. None of the scores in Table 5.1 are outliers, according to that definition. When outliers exist, they require investigation. Is the number a typographical error? If so, correct it. Is there an explanation such as equipment failure for an extreme score? If so, discard the data. Is there no explanation for the outlier? Then include it in the analysis. Sometimes outliers deserve to be explained to readers; they may require adjustments in the statistical analysis.

Most experiments generate a sizable amount of data. For such data sets, an informal frequency distribution called the *stem-and-leaf display* is a very effective way to begin. Stem-and-leaf displays are easy to construct and give you an overall view of the data quickly. John Tukey, a prominent 20th-century statistician, was a proponent of stem-and-leaf displays. He said that "scratching down numbers" in a stem-and-leaf display organizes the numbers so you can begin to make some sense of them. **Table 5.3** is a simple stem-and-leaf display of the 30 scores from Table 5.2. You can see how it can be constructed easily from the ordered scores column in Table 5.2. A stem-and-leaf display gives you a picture of the form of the distribution and the scores that occur frequently (or infrequently). Table 5.3 shows a distribution with the bulk of the scores in the middle and with fewer scores at the extremes. For advice on constructing stem-and-leaf displays for more complex data, see Howell (2004, pp. 35–39) or Runyon, Coleman, and Pittenger (2000, pp. 54–57).

TABLE 5.3	Stem-and-Leaf Display of Scores in Table 5.2

Scores
10, 10, 10
9, 9
8, 8, 8, 8
7, 7, 7, 7
6, 6, 6
5, 5, 5, 5, 5, 5
4, 4, 4
3, 3
2, 2
1
0

Central Tendency

You are probably already familiar with the three most common measures of **central tendency.** They are the mean, median, and mode. We illustrate their calculation with definitional formulas and the small data set in Table 5.1.

Mean   The **mean** (which is also known as the arithmetic average) is the sum of the numbers divided by the number of numbers. Among researchers, the most common symbol for the mean of a sample is M.[1] In formula form:

$$M = \frac{\Sigma X}{N}$$

Where: ΣX is the sum of the scores

N is the number of scores

Thus, for the small data set,

$$M = \frac{\Sigma X}{N} = \frac{35}{7} = 5.0 \text{ uses}$$

Stop for a moment and think about the meaning of $M = 5.0$ uses. In the social loafing experiment, participants worked in groups of 3 to 6 persons

central tendency
Descriptive statistics that indicate a typical or representative score. Examples are mean, median, and mode.

mean   The arithmetic average; the sum of the scores divided by the number of scores.

---

[1]In the field of statistics, the symbol most commonly used for the mean is $\overline{X}$ rather than M. A bar over any letter symbol typically indicates a mean. Thus, $\overline{X}$ is the mean of the X scores.

for 8 minutes. During those 8 minutes the average participant created five unique uses for a paper clip. Pretty impressive creativity, it seems to us.

The mean for the large data set in Table 5.2 is 5.67 uses, which is the same value found by Welter et al. (2002) for participants whose group included a hard worker. You can confirm this value with a calculator or a computer software program and the data in Table 5.2.

Median   The **median** is a point that divides a distribution into an upper half of larger scores and a lower half of smaller scores. Stated another way, the median is the 50th percentile. Finding the median requires two steps. The first step is to locate the position of the halfway point in a distribution. The second step is to simply note the score that is at that halfway point location. To find the *location* of the median, use the formula,

$$\text{Median location} = \frac{N + 1}{2}$$

In the small data set, $N = 7$, so the location of the median is the 4th number. Agree? By examining the descending scores in Table 5.1, you can see that the 4th number is 5. Thus, the median number of uses generated by those who participated with a hard worker was 5.0 uses.

In the large data set (Table 5.2), the median location is the 15.5th score. Agree? That score is halfway between the 15th score (which is a 5) and the 16th score (which is a 6). The median is the average of the two scores. Thus, the median of the data in Table 5.2 is 5.5 uses.

Mode   The **mode** is the score that occurs most frequently. In the small data set, 3 occurs more frequently (twice) than the other numbers (which appear only once). In the large data set a score of 5 uses occurs more frequently (6 times) than any other score. You can determine the mode from a stem-and-leaf display or SPSS can find it for you.

Variability

Measures of variability indicate the degree of spread in a distribution of numbers. Thus, the scores 1, 5, and 9 are more variable than 1, 3, and 5. Both sets of scores are more variable than 10, 11, and 12. Like central tendency, there are several ways to measure the variability of a set of scores.

Range   The simplest measure of variability is the **range,** which is the distance from the highest score to the lowest score. In formula form,

$$\text{Range} = X_H - X_L$$

Where: X_H is the highest score

X_L is the lowest score

median The point that divides a distribution into equal halves; half the scores are above the median and half are below it; 50th percentile.

mode The score that occurs most frequently in a distribution.

range The highest score minus the lowest score.

For the small data set (Table 5.1), the range is 8 (9 − 1 = 8). For the larger data set (Table 5.2) the range is 10 (10 − 0 = 10). It is common when reporting the range to give the lower and upper scores. Thus, for the data in Table 5.2, the range might be reported as: The number of unique uses of a paper clip ranged from 0 to 10.

Interquartile Range   The **interquartile range** (IQR) is also a statistic of two numbers. Between these two numbers lie the middle 50% of the scores. That is, half the scores are in the interquartile range. The upper bound (the larger number) of the IQR is the 75th percentile score and the lower bound (smaller number) is the 25th percentile score. The IQR is useful for larger data sets, but not for smaller ones such as the one in Table 5.1.

To find the IQR, begin by multiplying 0.25 times N. This number is used to find the location of both the 75th percentile and the 25th percentile. For the data in Table 5.2 with $N = 30$, $0.25 \times N = 7.5$. For the distribution in Table 5.2, the 75th percentile score is at the location 7.5 scores from the top, which is halfway between two 8s. Thus, 8 is the 75th percentile score. The location of the 25th percentile score is 7.5 scores from the *bottom* of the distribution. The 25th percentile score is 4. The formula for the interquartile range (IQR) is

$$IQR = \text{75th percentile} - \text{25th percentile}$$

Thus, for the larger data set, $IQR = 8 - 4 = 4$ is often reported as two scores (just like the range). For the data in Table 5.2, the IQR for unique paper clip uses was 4 to 8.

IQRs are often helpful when comparing the variability of two distributions. You can see that small IQRs indicate that most of the scores are closely bunched together, whereas larger IQRs mean that the scores are more spread out. All popular computer software programs calculate IQR under the Descriptive statistics menu.

IQRs are used in the most popular definition of **outlier** scores (Hogan and Evalenko, 2006). Upper and lower outliers are defined as

$$\text{Upper outlier} = \text{75th percentile} + 1.5\ IQR$$
$$\text{Lower outlier} = \text{25th percentile} - 1.5\ IQR$$

interquartile range   A range of scores that captures the 50% of a distribution that is between the 25th and 75th percentiles.

outlier   A score separated from others and 1.5(IQR) beyond the 25th or 75th percentile.

In our earlier discussion of outliers we said that there are no outliers in Table 5.2. What scores (or scores more extreme) would qualify as outliers?

$$\text{Upper outlier} = 8 + 1.5\ (4) = 14$$
$$\text{Lower outlier} = 4 - 1.5\ (4) = -2$$

TABLE 5.4	Steps in Calculating the *SD* for the Small Data Set in Table 5.1		
X	M	$X - M$	$(X - M)^2$
9	5	4	16
8	5	3	9
6	5	1	1
5	5	0	0
3	5	-2	4
3	5	-2	4
1	5	-4	16
Σ 35		0	50

$$SD = \sqrt{\frac{\Sigma(X - M)^2}{N - 1}} = \sqrt{\frac{50}{7 - 1}} = \sqrt{8.333} = 2.887 = 2.89 \text{ uses}$$

What if there was a score of 14 or greater in Table 5.2? If the 14 was not a typographical error or a miscount on the data sheet, it should be included in the analysis. As for the lower outlier limit, all negative scores are impossible in the paper clip experiment.

Standard Deviation   A third descriptive measure of the variability of a distribution is the **standard deviation** (*SD*). The *SD* is the most widely used measure of variability in research. The definitional formula for *SD* of a sample is

$$SD = \sqrt{\frac{\Sigma(X - M)^2}{N - 1}}$$

Where: $X - M$ is each score minus the mean of the scores

N is the number of scores

We illustrate the calculation of *SD* in **Table 5.4,** using the seven scores from Table 5.1.[2] The columns show the steps that lead to $(X - M)^2$. The sum of this right-hand column is the value of the numerator in the formula. Work through each of the columns. In the lower portion of Table 5.4, the formula and the completed calculation of *SD* are shown. *SD* = 2.89 uses. For the large data set in Table 5.2, *SD* = 2.51 uses.

---

[2]The formula for the standard deviation of a population (σ) is $\sigma = \sqrt{\frac{\Sigma(X - M)^2}{N}}$. For an explanation of why the population standard deviation formula has N in the denominator and the sample standard deviation has $N - 1$, see Spatz (2005, p. 63).

standard deviation A measure of the dispersion of scores around the mean of a distribution.

STOP
& *Think*

Do you get $SD = 2.51$ uses when you use a calculator or statistics package to find the standard deviation of the scores in Table 5.2?

In the Know

The numerator of the standard deviation, $\Sigma(X - M)^2$, is a component of several other statistical formulas. It turns up so often that it has a name of its own—*sum of squares.*

The standard deviation, like the range, is a measure of how spread out the scores are; large *SD*s indicate that the scores are widely distributed; small *SD*s indicate that the scores are grouped together closely. As a rule-of-thumb for research data, the relationship between the range and the standard deviation is that the range is usually three to six times larger than the *SD*. For the data in Table 5.2, the range (10) is almost 4 times the *SD* (2.68). In any data set, the range is always at least twice as large as the standard deviation. We provide more explanation about the standard deviation later in this chapter in the section The Normal Curve.

Look at the formula for the mean (p. 132) and the formula for the standard deviation (p. 135). You can see that there is some similarity in that both are averages. The mean is the average of the scores. The *SD* is an average of the deviations of the scores from the mean. Thus, the *SD* gives you a kind of average of how far the scores are from the mean.

Standard Error of the Mean   Every set of sample scores has some inherent randomness and the sample mean incorporates this randomness. That is, another sample from the same population will most likely produce a larger mean or a smaller mean. One of the most important developments in statistics was the discovery of ways to measure the uncertainty that comes with the sample mean. One of those measures is the *standard error of the mean.* The larger the standard error of the mean, the greater the uncertainty that goes with a sample mean.

To help understand the standard error of the mean, imagine many random samples being drawn from a population. For each sample, its mean is calculated. Of course, the sample means are not all the same.

STOP
& *Think*

How could the variation among all these means be measured?

standard error of the mean   Standard deviation of the sampling distribution of the mean.

A standard deviation calculated from all the sample means produces a measure of the variability of the means. This particular standard deviation is so important that it has a special name, the **standard error of the mean.** Thus, in the same way that the standard deviation is a measure of the variability of a group of scores, the standard error of the mean is a measure of the variability of sample means that were all drawn from the same population.

Don't let the word *error* obstruct your understanding. When used in statistics, *error* means *expected variation* and not *mistake*. Thus, the standard error of the mean is the standard expected variation of the mean.

The symbol for the standard error of the mean is SE_M.[3] The formula for SE_M is

$$SE_M = \frac{SD}{\sqrt{N}}$$

Where: SD is the standard deviation of the sample

N is sample size

The data in Table 5.2 on uses of a paper clip produced a mean of 5.67 uses. The standard error of the mean gives a measure of the expected variation about that mean:

$$SE_M = \frac{SD}{\sqrt{N}} = \frac{2.510}{\sqrt{30}} = \frac{2.510}{5.477} = 0.458 = 0.46 \text{ uses}$$

The larger the standard error of the mean, the greater the uncertainty that goes with a particular sample mean. If the standard error of the mean is quite small relative to the mean, there is very little uncertainty. As with our promise to explain more about the interpretation of the standard deviation in the section on the normal curve, we'll cover more on interpretation of the standard error of the mean in that section. For the small data set in Table 5.1, SE_M is 1.29.

The standard error is a measure of uncertainty about a sample mean. How can this measure of uncertainty be reduced?

STOP
& *Think*

By examining the formula for SE_M, you can see that as the size of the sample increases, SE_M decreases. Thus, uncertainty about the mean is reduced. Indeed, with very large samples, you can be quite certain that the sample mean is very close to the population mean.

Confidence Interval About a Mean

A **confidence interval about a mean (CI)** is a useful statistic that conveys both the precision of a sample mean and the uncertainty that is

confidence interval about a mean   A range of scores that is expected with a specified degree of confidence to include the population mean.

---

[3]Another common notation for the standard error of the mean is $s_{\bar{x}}$.

inherent in a sample. A CI about a mean is a range of values with an upper limit (UL) and a lower limit (LL). CIs are calculated for a specified amount of confidence. CIs of 95% are the most common, but 90 and 99% CIs are not unusual. The sample mean is always exactly in the middle of any confidence interval.

A CI is calculated from sample data, but the interpretation is about the population mean. Suppose sample data produced an LL of the 95% CI of 8 and a UL of 12 (and a mean of 10). The interpretation is that you have 95% confidence that the mean of the population the sample came from is between 8 and 12. Put another way, the probability is .95 that the interval 8 to 12 contains the population mean.

The formulas for the lower and upper limits of a CI are:

$$LL = M - t_c(SE_M)$$

$$UL = M + t_c(SE_M)$$

Where: M is the mean of the sample

t_c is a t value for c% confidence

SE_M is the standard error of the mean for the sample

The only element in the formula that has not been explained so far is t_c. The value for t_c comes from the table of t values in **Table C.2**, appendix C.

The t values in Table C.2 are used for a number of different statistical problems, but for any use, you must determine the number of degrees of freedom (df) in the problem. For the CI about a mean, the formula for df is simple: $df = N - 1$, where N is sample size. The first header in Table C.2 is for confidence intervals, where you can see entries for 80, 90, 95, 98, 99, and 99.9% confidence intervals. The t values are at the intersection of the amount of confidence you want and the degrees of freedom for the sample.

We illustrate with a 95% CI about the sample mean of the 30 scores in Table 5.1. From previous calculations, you know that

$$M = 5.67 \text{ uses}$$

$$SE_M = 0.46 \text{ uses}$$

Because $N = 30$, $df = N - 1 = 30 - 1 = 29$. The t value from Table C.2 is 2.045. This is expressed as

$$t_{95}(29 \ df) = 2.045$$

which shows the t value (2.045) for 29 degrees of freedom and 95% confidence.

Applying the numbers that we have to the formula for the confidence interval:

$$LL = M - t_c\,(SE_M) = 5.67 - 2.045(0.46) = 4.73 \text{ uses}$$

$$UL = M + t_c\,(SE_M) = 5.67 + 2.045(0.46) = 6.61 \text{ uses}$$

Thus, for those who brainstormed for uses of a paper clip with a confederate who was a worker, we are 95% confident that the population mean is between 4.73 and 6.61 uses.

Calculate a 90% CI about a mean for the seven scores in Table 5.1.

The 90% CI about a mean for the scores in Table 5.1 is 2.88 to 7.12. The t value for t_{90} (6 df) is 1.943.

Frequency Distributions

In some ways, frequency distributions describe a data set more completely than other descriptive statistics. After some practice, you can look at frequency distributions and make fairly accurate estimates of the mean, median, mode, range, and standard deviation. With more experience, you can make rough estimates of the standard error of the mean.

A **frequency distribution** shows both the score values that participants obtain and the number of participants who obtain each score value. **Table 5.5** is a frequency distribution of the scores in Table 5.2. By examining Table 5.5,

TABLE 5.5	Frequency Distribution of the Paper Clip Scores in Table 5.2

Score	Frequency
10	2
9	2
8	4
7	3
6	4
5	6
4	4
3	2
2	1
1	1
0	1
Σ	30

frequency distribution
Arrangement of scores from the highest to the lowest with the frequency of each score shown.

FIGURE 5.3

Frequency polygon
of the frequency
distribution in
Table 5.5.

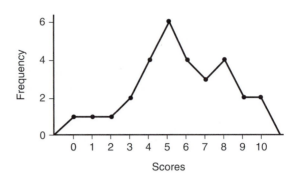

you can see that the distribution is roughly symmetrical with a greater number of scores in the middle and fewer on both ends. The central tendency values are about 5 (the mode is exactly 5). An experienced eye would probably estimate the standard deviation as about 3 or 4. Stem-and-leaf displays such as Table 5.3 are frequency distributions.

Graphs

Graphs are especially helpful when it comes time to understand the data. The role of graphs as a way to help others understand data has been recognized for a long time; their role as a guide to the researchers themselves is more recent (see Wainer & Velleman, 2001). In this section we explain graphs that are used to display frequency distribution data for one variable. As you probably already know, frequency distributions are often graphed as a frequency polygon or as a histogram. For both graphs, scores are plotted on the x axis and frequencies of the scores on the y axis. For more information on constructing graphs, look at the practical guide by Nicol and Pexman (2003).

Frequency Polygon   A **frequency polygon** is a series of straight lines that connect the points where scores and frequencies intersect. **Figure 5.3** shows the frequency distribution in Table 5.3 graphed as a frequency polygon.

Four characteristics of well-constructed frequency polygons are that

- the lines that connect the points are straight
- the polygon is closed at the ends; that is, the polygon ends at the point where the frequency is zero
- the axes are each labeled with the name of the variable that is graphed
- the variable on the x axis is a scaled variable

frequency polygon A frequency distribution graph of a scaled variable with frequency points connected by lines.

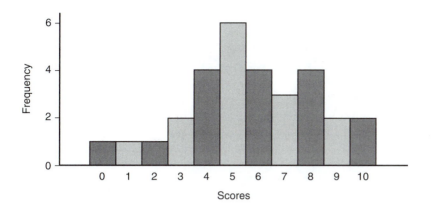

FIGURE 5.4
Histogram of the frequency distribution in Table 5.5.

Histogram   Histograms are another way to present data from a frequency distribution. A **histogram** is constructed by drawing rectangles that extend from the x-axis scores to the frequency levels of the scores on the y axis. **Figure 5.4** shows the frequency distribution in Table 5.3 graphed as a histogram.

Three characteristics of well-constructed histograms are:

- the bars are not separated by spaces
- the axes are each labeled with the name of the variable that is graphed
- the variable on the x axis is a scaled variable

There are no hard-and-fast rules that govern when to use a frequency polygon and when to use a histogram. Depending on the pattern of the data, one or the other may look less cluttered or easier to read. Frequency polygons and histograms are not limited to showing only the raw scores from an experiment. The frequency of other statistics can be plotted as well.

Skew   If a distribution has fewer scores at one end of the scale than the other, it is described as **skewed.** A distribution with few large scores and a greater number of small scores is *positively skewed.* One with few small scores and more larger scores is *negatively skewed.* The degree of skew depends on how far the few scores are from the bulk of the rest of the distribution. There is a mathematical way to measure skew but it is not commonly used. **Figure 5.5** shows a positively skewed frequency polygon on the left and a negatively skewed histogram on the right.

Boxplots   Unlike frequency polygons and histograms, which have been used since the 19th century, **boxplots** are a recent invention. They were first described by John Tukey (Tukey, 1972).

histogram   A graph of frequencies of a scaled variable constructed with contiguous vertical bars.

skewed   Scores clustered at one of a distribution.

boxplot   A graph that shows a distribution's range, interquartile range, skew median, and sometimes other statistics.

FIGURE 5.5
A positively skewed
distribution (left)
and a negatively
skewed distribution
(right).

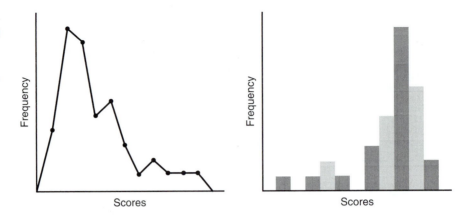

> ### *In the Know*
> John Tukey (1915–2000) was a champion of exploratory data analy-
> sis. Exploratory data analysis is best characterized as an attitude
> toward data rather than a set of procedures. The attitude is, "What
> can I discover from these data?" rather than the usual, "What pro-
> cedures must I follow to confirm my conclusions?" Quickly con-
> structed graphs such as stem-and-leaf displays and boxplots are
> characteristic of exploratory data analysis. (The original name for a
> boxplot was *box-and-whisker plot.*)

A boxplot presents precise information about central tendency, variability, and skew in one graph. A basic boxplot shows the median, range,
interquartile range, and skew. Boxplots can also show the mean, outliers,
and other characteristics of a distribution.

We illustrate boxplots with **Figure 5.6**, which was constructed from
the frequency distribution in Table 5.5. The score values in the distribution
are on the *x* axis along with their label. The horizontal rectangle represents
the *IQR*, which extends from the score at the 25th percentile to the score
at the 75th percentile. Thus, you can tell at a glance that 50% of the participants had paper clip use scores of 4 (25th percentile), 5, 6, 7, or 8 (75th
percentile). The vertical line in the box is the median, which is 5.5 uses.
The lines (whiskers) extend from the interquartile range box to the lowest

FIGURE 5.6
Boxplot of the
paper clip scores of
participants whose
group included a
worker.

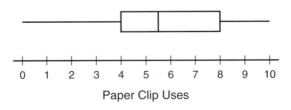

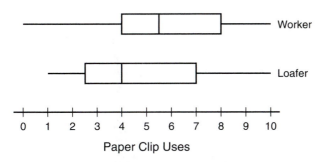

FIGURE 5.7
Boxplots of the
two groups in the
social loafing
experiment.

score (0) and to the highest score (10). The longer line over the low scores is indicative of a negatively skewed distribution. Boxplots can show the distribution's mean (usually with a dot aligned with the mean), and outlier scores can be indicated with asterisks at either end beyond the line.

Boxplots are a superb way to display several distributions on one graph because each distribution appears separately. To illustrate, we constructed **Figure 5.7**, which shows boxplots based on the scores of both groups in the social loafing experiment. The upper boxplot shows the scores of those participants whose group included a worker and the lower one shows the scores of those whose group included a loafer.

Inspect the loafer distribution in Figure 5.7 and determine the median, IQR, and range.

The loafer distribution in Figure 5.7 has a median of 4, an *IQR* from 2.5 to 7, and a range of 9 (10 − 1 = 9).

To compare the two conditions shown in Figure 5.7, begin by noting that the middle 50% of the worker scores are somewhat higher than the middle 50% of the loafer scores. Similarly, the median of the worker boxplot (5.5 uses) is higher than the median of the loafer boxplot (4 uses). The range is about the same for both groups. The differences observed are suggestive of a difference caused by the different treatments, but they might also be the result of chance. Ruling out chance as a cause for differences observed requires a statistical test, which is the topic of the next chapter. Boxplots can be arranged vertically rather than horizontally. Most computer programs produce vertical boxplots, with the scores on the y axis.

Graphs of Means and Error Bars   Probably the most popular way to present the central tendency and variability of a sample is with a graph of the mean and an **error bar.** Error bars extend from the mean; they indicate the variability in the scores that produced the mean. An error bar might represent a confidence interval about a mean, the standard error of the mean, or the standard deviation of the sample. You have to consult a figure's legend or its caption to determine what the error bar indicates. The best choice for an error bar is a confidence interval (Cumming & Finch, 2005).

error bar   A line the length of which indicates degree of variability.

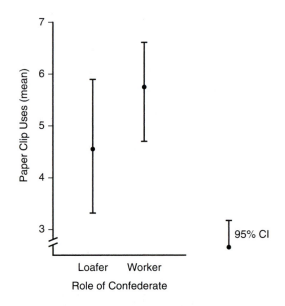

FIGURE 5.8
Means and 95% confidence intervals for the social loafing experiment.

Figure 5.8 shows the social loafing data as a graph of the means and 95% CI error bars. The mean for those who brainstormed with a worker is greater than the mean for those whose confederate group member was a loafer, but there is a great deal of overlap in the error bars. The value of Figure 5.8 is that it shows at a glance both the group means and the uncertainty that comes with sampling. Under certain conditions, a graph with CIs can even show whether chance can be ruled out as an explanation for the difference in means (Cumming & Finch, 2005).

Line Graphs   The graph most frequently used in psychology textbooks and journal articles is the **line graph,** which is a picture of the relationship between *two* variables. Two thirds of the graphs in psychology textbooks (Peden & Hausmann, 2000) and two thirds of the data graphs in psychology-related journal articles (Boehner & Howe, 1996) are line graphs. **Figure 5.9** is an example of a line graph. Line graphs are not closed at the end as frequency polygons are. Figure 5.9 shows how long it takes to perform a task when you do it again and again. The first trial takes a considerable amount of time, but each succeeding completion requires less time. The take-home lesson—keep trying, you are improving.

The Normal Curve

Figure 5.3 is an **empirical frequency polygon;** that is, the graph is based on observed data. Frequency polygons that are based on mathematical formulas or logic rather than on data are **theoretical frequency polygons.** One of the most frequently displayed theoretical frequency polygons is

line graph   A graph that shows the relationship between two variables with lines rather than bars.

empirical frequency polygon   A frequency polygon of observed scores.

theoretical frequency polygon   A frequency polygon of hypothesized scores.

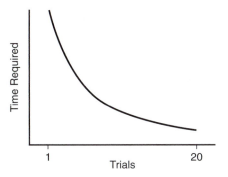

FIGURE 5.9
Twenty trials on a
task and the time
required to
complete it.

the **normal curve. Figure 5.10** is an example. The normal curve occupies a prominent position in the history of statistics. It will also prove very helpful as we deliver on our promise to explain more about the standard deviation and the standard error.

In the Know

The term "normal" was adopted in the 19th century as the name for a curve that was proving important as mathematical statistics developed. Among some statisticians, the curve was thought of as an ideal; that is, it was the way the data should be distributed if there were no errors in measurement. This idea was quite mistaken, but it provides a clue to the selection of the term *normal*. The Latin adjective, *normalis,* means built with a carpenter's square or built exactly right. Thus, the ideal or proper curve should be called the *normal curve* according to those who adopted the name.

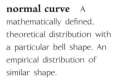

normal curve   A mathematically defined, theoretical distribution with a particular bell shape. An empirical distribution of similar shape.

The *mean* of the normal curve is the score that corresponds to the peak of the curve. Of course, the peak of the curve indicates the most frequently

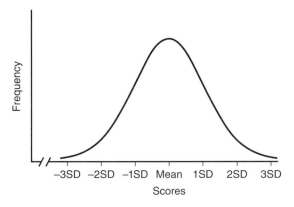

FIGURE 5.10
The normal curve.

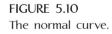

FIGURE 5.11
Normal curve
divided into
approximate
percentages
according to *SD*
units.

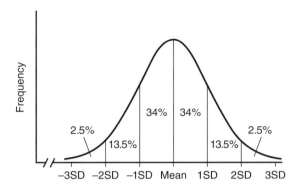

occurring score, so the *mode* is the same score as the mean. Note that the normal curve is symmetrical; half of it is to the right of the mean and half to the left. Thus, the *median* is the same score as the mean and the mode.

In Figure 5.10, the *x* axis is marked in *scores,* which could be any scaled measurement. The *x* axis is also marked off in *SD* units from −3 *SD* to +3 *SD*. For fairly large data sets, the general rule is that the range $(X_H − X_L)$ is about six times as large as the *SD*. For small data sets, however, the range is often only two to four times as large as the *SD*.

The value of knowing about *SD* units on the normal curve is that there is a mathematical relationship between the *SD* units and the proportions of the curve. Rounded numbers of those proportions are shown in **Figure 5.11.** Thus, for a score that is two *SD*s below the mean, only about 2.5% of the participants have lower scores. Similarly, a score 1 *SD* above the mean has 84% of the participants with lower scores (50% + 34% = 84%).

There are two percentages of the normal curve that you will encounter frequently. One is that about 95% of the scores lie between a score that is 2 *SD* below the mean and one that is 2 *SD* above the mean. Thus, about 2.5% of the curve is above +2 *SD* and about 2.5% is below −2 *SD*. (The exact number of standard deviations that separate the most extreme 2.50% of a normal curve from the rest is 1.96.)

The other commonly encountered percentage is that 68% (about two-thirds) of normally distributed measures fall between −1 *SD* and +1 *SD*.

Describing a Difference Between Sample Means

It is very common for a two-group experiment to produce means that are different. With a difference in hand, researchers have three questions that help determine if the difference is meaningful:

1. *Is the difference reliable?* Can chance be ruled out as an explanation for the difference observed? This question is answered using NHST techniques such as those in the next chapter. NHST answers are in the form of *significant* (the difference appears reliable) or *not significant* (not reliable).

2. *Is the difference a large one or a small one?* Compared to other differences observed in the social and behavioral sciences, how big is this difference? This question is answered using an effect size index, the topic of the next section.

3. *Is the difference an important one?* This is a question about the practical effect of knowing that there is a difference. To ask this question implies that the answer to the first question is "Yes, the difference is reliable and not due to chance fluctuation." The question of importance is answered by people who are knowledgeable about the topic being studied. Learning how to answer the question "Is the difference an important one?" is best done at the elbow of someone who is knowledgeable in the field you are interested in. Perhaps it is obvious, but information beyond statistics is required to determine importance. (For another version of the ideas in this section, see Kirk, 2001.) We return to the second question, "Is the difference large or small?"

An Effect Size Index

Effect size is a common concern when there is a comparison of two circumstances. A way to convey the size of the effect, however, differs from one situation to the next. Consider the following two conversations:

"I got a raise at work."

"Good, how much of a raise?"

"25%."

"Wonderful!"

"My sales were up this week."

"Good, how much were they up?"

"25%."

"Is that unusual?"

In both cases, the initial announcement was greeted with a question about the size of the change. In both cases, an answer was given as a percent change. In the first case the reaction was, "Wonderful" because we know that a 25% increase in wages is unusual. In the second case, the reaction was to ask whether 25% was unusual. Let's listen to one more conversation.

"People have more ideas when their group has a worker rather than when their group has a loafer."

"How many more ideas?

"An average of 1.1 ideas, or 24% more."

"I don't know what to make of that."

Although percentages are meaningful when we know their usual range, the scores of most research instruments are new to us. For such cases, an effect size index is valuable.

There are several ways to calculate an **effect size index;** one of the most common effect size indexes is the statistic d.[4] The formula for d is

$$d = \frac{M_1 - M_2}{SD'}$$

Where: M_1 and M_2 are the means of the two groups

SD' is a weighted standard deviation based on the SDs of the two groups

The calculation of SD' requires knowledge of degrees of freedom, a topic that will be explained in the chapter on statistical tests that follows. Although we don't illustrate the calculation of d until the next chapter, we discuss its interpretation here. Researchers use the following conventions to interpret whether an effect size is small, medium, or large:

Small	$d = 0.20$
Medium	$d = 0.50$
Large	$d = 0.80$

These conventions were first suggested by Jacob Cohen (1969) and are widely used.

The effect size index in the social loafing experiment shows the effect of the confederate (worker or loafer) on the number of uses of a paper clip that the participants thought of. In that experiment, $d = 0.40$. Thus, the effect that the kind of worker in a group has is about midway between a small effect and a medium effect.

Here are some other values of d for phenomena you are more familiar with than paper clip uses. For the heights of 20- to 29-year-old American men and women, $d = 1.92$. This huge effect size index corresponds to the fact that gender has an easily noticeable effect on height. You may know that the average verbal ability of women is higher than the average verbal ability of men. The difference, however, is very small: $d = 0.09$. Psychotherapy, on the average, produces an improvement in those with emotional problems: $d = 1.00$, a very large effect.

Correlation Coefficient

In chapter 4 we introduced the correlation coefficient (r) and its interpretation. In this section we discuss its calculation. **Table 5.6** shows two

effect size index The amount or degree of separation between two distributions.

---

[4]See Kirk (2005) for an extensive exposition on effect size measures.

TABLE 5.6	Eight Pairs of Scores That Can Be Correlated	
Pairs	Variable X	Variable Y
1	1	4
2	3	2
3	4	6
4	6	4
5	7	8
6	8	8
7	10	13
8	12	9

columns of data (labeled X and Y) that can be correlated. To calculate a correlation coefficient, you must have two sets of scores that are paired for some logical reason. When r was used to assess test–retest reliability, the X variable was test score and the Y variable was retest scores. The scores on each line are logically paired because they belong to the same person. If variable X was years of education and variable Y was annual income, the scores might be paired on the basis of individuals (or cities or countries).

The sample size for a correlation coefficient is the number of pairs. Thus, for Table 5.6, $N = 8$. Computers and calculators with statistical packages all have programs that compute r. The Web site http://calculators.stat. ucla.edu has a function to calculate r under the button *correlation and regression*. **Table 5.7** shows the output from the SPSS program for *Correlate*. In Table 5.7, the correlation coefficient (.801) appears twice.

TABLE 5.7	SPSS Output for the Correlation Coefficient of the Data in Table 5.6		

Correlations

		Variable X	Variable Y
Variable X	Pearson correlation	1	.801[a]
	Sig. (2-tailed)		.017
	N	8	8
Variable Y	Pearson correlation	.801[a]	1
	Sig. (2-tailed)	.017	
	N	8	8

[a]Correlation is significant at the .05 level (2-tailed).

EXPLORING AND DESCRIBING CATEGORICAL VARIABLES

As we mentioned at the beginning of this chapter, it is often helpful to classify dependent variables as scaled variables or categorical variables. For categorical variables, the appropriate descriptive and inferential statistics are different from the ones for scaled variables, but the process that you go through to understand the data is much the same. Thus, the headings that follow are similar to those we used for scaled data. As an example of a study in which the DV was categorical data, we turn to the *Psi Chi Journal of Undergraduate Research*.

Brad Jurica, Kelly Alanis, and Shirley Ogletree (2002) investigated the popularity of violent and nonviolent video games among female and male game players at six video arcades in Texas. Each of the 183 participants was observed for one minute. The participant's gender and the name of the video game were recorded. Later, the games were classified as violent or nonviolent. Thus, the categories for the data were gender (female and male) and games (violent and nonviolent). The "score" of each participant was that he or she was counted as a frequency in a category.

The operational definition of *violent games* was that they involved kicks, punches, or hand-to-hand combat with weapons or they involved killing an opponent with missiles, lasers, or artillery. Games that included none of these characteristics were classified as nonviolent. Gender was determined by observation. **Table 5.8** shows the data that the investigators observed.

Examine the Scores

Just as for scaled data, begin by examining the scores. Are there any numbers in Table 5.8 that are impossible? Are any unlikely? Are any wrong?

The only impossible numbers would be negative numbers, and there are none. Are there any numbers that are unlikely? It is hard to know for sure, but unlikely numbers might be that more females than males were observed playing video games. The row totals in Table 5.8 reveal that more males were observed than females. Are there any numbers that are

TABLE 5.8	Categorical Data from Study of Gender and Video Games		
	Type of Game		
Gender	Nonviolent	Violent	Total
Female	24	7	31
Male	87	65	152
Total	111	72	183

TABLE 5.9	Data from the Study of Gender and Video Games, Presented as Percentages

	Type of Game		
Gender	Nonviolent	Violent	Sum
Female	13%	4%	17%
Male	48	36	83[a]
Sum	61%	39%[a]	100%

[a]Due to rounding, adding the two cell percentages does not equal the sum.

wrong? Although we cannot detect mistakes in the frequency counts, we can check the arithmetic. All margin totals in Table 5.8 are correct.

There are two benefits from examining the numbers. The first is that you may detect errors very early in your analysis. Often arithmetic errors, transposed numbers, or mislabeled tables can be corrected, preventing later embarrassment. The second benefit is that your examination *guarantees* that you will understand the study and the data better.

Percentages

Probably the most informative descriptive statistic that you can calculate for categorical data is a percentage. **Table 5.9** shows each cell in Table 5.8 converted to a percentage by dividing the observed frequency by 183, the total number of observations. A glance at Table 5.9 shows that more than 80% of the participants were males and that with both groups, nonviolent games were more popular than violent games. These same facts could be gleaned from Table 5.8, but not as easily.

Table 5.9 shows each of the four data cells as a percentage, but it doesn't highlight the issue that Jurica, Alanis, and Ogletree (2002) set out to investigate. That issue is the comparison of the two genders in playing violent and nonviolent games. The percentages in **Table 5.10** make the comparison more apparent.

TABLE 5.10	Data from Table 5.8 Arranged in Percentages That Illustrate the Issue Addressed by Jurica et al. (2002)

	Type of Game		
	Nonviolent	Violent	Sum
Female	77%	23%	100%
Male	57	43	100

The percentages in Table 5.10 are the cell frequencies in Table 5.8 divided by the row totals. Table 5.10 shows that males preferred nonviolent games by a majority of 57% to 43%. However, for females those playing nonviolent games were a more pronounced majority of 77% to 23%. The question is whether there is a relationship between gender and type of game; that is, do females prefer nonviolent games more than males do? Table 5.10 shows descriptive data that support this conclusion. A question remains, of course, as to whether the difference in Table 5.10 could be due to sampling fluctuation. Evaluating sampling fluctuation is a job for inferential statistics.

Do you think that the difference observed in the preferences of the two genders is so large that it cannot be attributed to sampling fluctuations? Or do you think that such a difference is fairly likely if there really is no difference between the genders in their preferences?

The answer to this Stop & Think question is in the next chapter in the explanation of the chi-square test, which is used to analyze categorical data.

Percentages are especially valuable for conveying information to others because most people understand them. Percentages make categorical data comparable regardless of the number of observations involved. Of course, percentages sometimes do not sum to 100% due to rounding, but this is a minor inconvenience.

Bar Graphs

The traditional graph for presenting categorical data is the **bar graph.** Categories are shown on the x axis. Rectangular bars extend up to the height of the frequency of a category. Frequencies are shown on the y axis. Bar graphs have space between the bars of different categories. Histograms are similar to bar graphs, but the bars all touch, which conveys the more or less continuous nature of scaled data. By shading some bars and not others in a bar graph, a second (or third) variable can be included. The categories conveyed by the different shadings are explained in a legend.

Figure 5.12 is a two-category (gender and games) bar graph of the data in Table 5.8. Note that the bars of the two categories on the x axis are separated and that Figure 5.12 shows the number of observations, not percentages. An examination of Figure 5.12 yields several observations. Considerably more males than females were observed playing video games. Nonviolent games were preferred over violent games for both genders.

Bar graphs are the usual way to present categorical data. In common with other graphic techniques, bar graphs are so engaging that they lead easily to conclusions, speculation, and understanding. Bar graphs are sometimes presented with the axes reversed. That is, the categories are

bar graph   A graph of the frequency distribution of nominal or qualitative data.

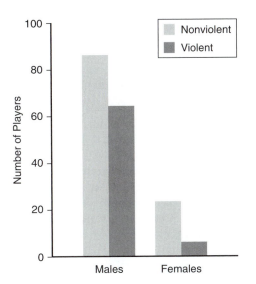

FIGURE 5.12
Male and female
video players who
were playing
violent and
nonviolent games.

listed horizontally on the y axis and frequency is on the x axis. This arrangement is especially preferred if the names of the categories are long because horizontal words are easier to read.

Effect Size Index

We introduce an effect size index for categorical data that is appropriate for 2 × 2 tables such as Table 5.8. Although Table 5.8 may appear to be more than a 2 × 2 table, the cells for gender and game type contain all the data. The other cells are summation cells. The symbol for the effect size index for 2 × 2 categorical data is φ (**phi,** pronounced *fee* by researchers). Like the interpretation of *d,* there are conventional guidelines for the interpretation of φ that were proposed by Cohen (1969). They are:

small	φ = 0.10
medium	φ = 0.30
large	φ = 0.50

For the data reported by Jurica and colleagues (2002), φ = 0.16. Thus, the size of the relationship between gender and type of game is small. That is, whether a person is male or female has only a small effect on whether the person chooses a violent or nonviolent video game. This interpretation of φ = 0.16 assumes that the difference in the two genders that was observed is known to be a reliable difference. As we mentioned a few paragraphs back, the issue of whether or not the difference is reliable will be resolved in the section on chi-square in chapter 6.

By using the techniques in this chapter to explore and describe sample data from experiments, you can reach preliminary conclusions about

phi   An effect size index for categorical data.

the relationship of an IV to a DV. By applying statistical tests to the data, you can arrive at a final conclusion (even though some uncertainty will remain). Statistical tests are the topic of the next chapter.

EXPLORING AND DESCRIBING RANKED DATA

Ranked data are a third kind of data. Unlike scaled data and categorical data, there isn't an array of descriptive statistics that help describe a distribution of ranked data. In fact, only one statistic is helpful. That statistic is N, the number of observations. The meaning of a rank varies depending on the number of items ranked. For example, being valedictorian (graduating first in the class) may or may not warrant an interpretation of *very superior*, depending on whether N is large or small. If $N = 1,000$, *very superior* seems appropriate. If $N = 10$, *very superior* doesn't seem justified. For inferential statistics, however, there are a large number of tests available that analyze ranked data. Some of these tests are listed in chapter 6.

The statistical techniques in this chapter are quite helpful as a first step in understanding the results of experiments. A second step is covered in chapter 6—statistical tests. Statistical tests always involve a comparison of sample data that received a treatment to other sample data or to some standard. Of course, there is almost always a difference. The important question is whether this difference could be due to chance. Statistical tests provide a measure of the effects of chance. If chance can be eliminated as an explanation, the difference might be attributed to the treatment.

Chapter Review _____

1. Statistical techniques can be separated into two broad categories,

   _____ statistics and _____ statistics.

2. Dividing data into three categories of _____ , _____ ,

   and _____ is helpful when choosing what descriptive statistic
   to use.

3. Three measures of central tendency are _____ , _____ ,

   and _____.

4. Name four statistical measures of variability. _____ ,

5. *Error* in statistics means _____.

6. Scores less than the one calculated from the formula _____
   are outliers.

7. A range of scores that is expected to capture the population mean is called a(n) _____.

8. A frequency polygon with a long skinny point to the right is _____ skewed.

9. A graph that displays central tendency, variability, and skew is the _____.

10. A graph that displays the relationship between two scaled variables is a(n) _____ graph.

11. About _____ of the normal curve is between -1 SD and $+1$ SD. About _____ of the normal curve is below -2 SD.

12. The symbols for two effect size indexes are _____ and _____.

13. Five values of d follow. Using Cohen's conventions, interpret the size of each.
    a. 0.50   b. 1.50   c. 0.20   d. 0.35   e. 0.80

14. Five values of φ follow. Using Cohen's conventions, interpret the size of each.
    a. 0.30   b. 0.40   c. 0.50   d. 0.05   e. 0.10

Thinking Critically About Research

1. For each of the six variables listed, three levels are shown. Identify each variable as scaled, continuous (SC); scaled, discrete (SD); or categorical (C).
   a. colors (red, blue, magenta)
   b. grams (2.3, 4.6, 10.0)
   c. drops of saliva (1, 5, 21)
   d. places (New York, Los Angeles, New Orleans)
   e. SAT scores (990, 1100, 1240)
   f. species of fish (bluegill, bass, perch)

2. Arrange the scores that follow into descending order and find M, median, mode, range, SD, and SE_M.
   7   4   8   3   8

3. Undergraduates responded to four items using a Likert scale. Each item required one of five responses that ranged from *strongly disagree*

(scored 1) to *strongly agree* (scored 5). Arrange the following scores in descending order, examine them, and tell what your examination shows.

10	6	16	11	5	9	22	8	8	17	19
1	10	8	5	17	12	11	15	7	0	2
10	8	18	9							

4. The mean legibility score for instructions printed in capital letters was 28; $SE_M = 1$. The mean score for instructions in lowercase letters was 30; $SE_M = 5$. Higher scores indicate greater legibility. Write an explanation of letter case and legibility based on these statistics.

5. Remove the two impossible scores from the data in problem 3 (0 and 22) and use the remaining 24 scores to compute the *IQR*.

6. Using the scores in problem 5, construct a frequency distribution.

7. Construct a boxplot for a distribution that has a high score of 11, a 75th percentile score of 8, a median of 5, a 25th percentile score of 3, and a low score of 1.

8. For the legibility statistics in problem 4, construct a bar graph of the two means and their 95% confidence intervals. Assume that each sample has 15 scores.

9. The experiment by Jurica, Alanis, and Ogletree (2002) included 138 video game players who were age 18 or less and 45 who were 19 or more. What percentage of the players was 19 or older?

10. Researchers have three questions that help determine if a difference between two groups is meaningful. List the questions and the statistic that answers each question, *if* there is a statistic that answers the question.

11. Comment on descriptive statistics that are useful for ranked data.

Answers to Chapter Review

1. descriptive; inferential
2. scaled; categorical; ranked
3. mean; median; mode
4. range, interquartile range, standard deviation, standard error of the mean
5. expected variation
6. 25th percentile—1.5 *IQR*
7. confidence interval
8. positively

9. boxplot

10. line

11. 68% (or two thirds); 2.5%

12. *d*; φ

13. a. medium; b. very large; c. small; d. intermediate between small and medium; e. large

14. a. medium; b. intermediate between medium and large; c. large; d. very small; e. small

Answers to Thinking Critically About Research

1. a. C; b. SC; c. SD; d. C; e. SD; f. C

2. 8   8   7   4   3

   $M = 6.00$; median = 7; mode = 8; range = 5; $SD = 2.35$;
   $SE_M = 1.05$

3. 22   19   18   17   17   16   15   12   11   11   10
   10   10   9   9   8   8   8   8   7   6   5
   5   2   1   0

   When you examined the scores, did you find an impossible score? More than one? If either of your two answers is "No," go back and examine the arranged scores again. The examination shows that there are 26 scores, not 24. Two of the scores (0 and 22) are impossible.

4. Instructions written in lowercase letters are more legible than instructions in capital letters. Because the standard errors are so different, we are more uncertain about the mean for lowercase instructions than the mean for uppercase ones.

5. $0.25 \times 24 = 6$. The 6th score from the top is 15; from the bottom, the 6th score is 7. $IQR = 15 - 7 = 8$.

6.

X	f
19	1
18	1
17	2
16	1
15	1
12	1
11	2
10	3
9	2
8	4
7	1

7.

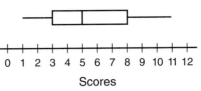

8.

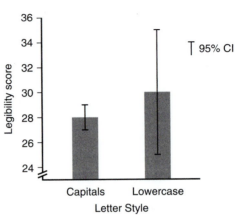

9. 45/183 = 25%

10. 1. Is the difference reliable? NHST techniques.

2. Is the difference big or small? Effect size index.

3. Is the difference important? No statistic for this question.

11. The only descriptive statistic that is useful for ranked data is *N*.

Know for Sure

6

Statistical Tests

OVERVIEW

Statistical tests are used to assess the effect that chance might have had producing differences found in sample data. The logic of null hypothesis statistical testing (NHST) is explained along with six tests that use NHST logic. The tests are appropriate for categorical data (chi-square) and scaled data (correlation coefficient and t tests). Statistical power is covered and meta-analysis is introduced.

OBJECTIVES

After studying this chapter and working through the exercises, you should be able to:

1. Explain negative inference logic and how it applies to chi-square problems of independence
2. Distinguish among null hypothesis, alternative hypothesis, and research hypothesis
3. Explain the logic of null hypothesis statistical testing (NHST)
4. For the statement $p < .05$, name the event that has a probability of less than .05
5. Describe a sampling distribution and the part it plays in NHST
6. Distinguish between a one-tailed and a two-tailed statistical test
7. Distinguish between Type I and Type II errors
8. Interpret the outcome of studies analyzed with chi-square, Pearson r, and t tests
9. Calculate and interpret the effect size indexes, φ and d
10. Determine the effect size index for a Pearson r
11. Calculate and interpret a confidence interval about a mean difference
12. Define the power of a statistical test
13. Identify the four factors that determine the power of a statistical test
14. Identify the conventional cut-off probability values that signify statistical significance and adequate statistical power
15. Explain the concept of meta-analysis and its statistic, $\bar{d}$

This chapter on statistical testing explains additional ways that psychologists analyze quantitative data. As you saw in the previous chapter, there are many statistical techniques you can use to describe a set of data. Descriptive techniques are very informative when you want information about central tendency, variability, degree of relationship, effect size, and such. However, sample-based descriptive statistics such as means always have a built-in degree of uncertainty about them. This uncertainty is reflected in the question, "How close is the descriptive statistic to the population parameter?" Fortunately, researchers can measure uncertainty using inferential statistics. Although uncertainty cannot be eliminated, measuring it with a statistical test tells you how much or how little uncertainty there is.

Inferential statistics is a big topic—much bigger than can be covered in an introductory research methods book. In addition, although one approach to inferential statistics has been dominant, other approaches are also used. In this chapter we direct most of our explanation to the popular inferential statistics approach.

The popular inferential statistics approach that has dominated quantitative data analysis in psychology and many other disciplines is **null hypothesis statistical testing (NHST).** NHST techniques are designed to analyze *differences* that are observed between sample statistics. The result of this analysis is that the differences in the samples may or may not be attributed to the populations the samples are from. The end result of the calculations for all NHST techniques is a probability figure such as $p = .05$. On the basis of this p value, researchers decide whether or not the differences are **statistically significant.** Null hypothesis statistical testing and statistical significance are fundamental concepts for the statistical tests that we discuss in this and later chapters.

Here are some NHST phrases that you have probably heard before. These are usually desirable outcomes, regardless of the researcher's discipline:

"I got significant results."

"The statistical test produced a $p < .05$."

"The two groups were significantly different."

null hypothesis statistical testing (NHST) An inferential statistics technique that produces accurate probabilities about samples when the null hypothesis is true.

statistically significant Sample data with a probability less than alpha (α).

By the end of the chapter, you should be able to explain such statements. In addition, you should be able to answer these two questions as well:

1. What event has a probability of less than .05 when $p < .05$?
2. How is statistically significant different from important?

In chapter 4 we discussed three classes of dependent variable scores: categorical data, scaled data, and rank data. As we noted there, this classification scheme is useful because each of these three kinds of data require different NHST techniques. We begin with categorical data.

A STUDY WITH CATEGORICAL DATA

In chapter 5 we discussed a study by Jurica and colleagues (2002). They recorded the gender of 183 arcade video game players who were playing either violent or nonviolent games. Each participant was observed and then classified into one of four categories:

- females playing nonviolent games
- males playing nonviolent games
- females playing violent games
- males playing violent games

In this experiment, there were two variables, gender and type of game. **Table 6.1** shows the data (which you saw in the previous chapter as Table 5.6).

The research question is whether or not there is a relationship between gender and type of game in the population. To put the question another way, is the type of game that people play contingent to any degree on gender? In the sample data, females preferred nonviolent games over violent games by a sizable margin of 77% to 23%, but for males this preference for nonviolent games was less pronounced (57% to 43%). At the end of the last chapter we left unanswered the question of whether the differences observed were because females and males are different or whether the differences observed could be the result of sampling fluctuation.

SAMPLING FLUCTUATION

Sampling fluctuation (or sampling uncertainty) is a fairly simple idea. Suppose there is *no* relationship between gender and type of game. If there is no relationship, the preference for nonviolent games would be the same for females and males. But of course, no one would be surprised

sampling fluctuation
The chance differences between samples and the population the samples are from.

TABLE 6.1	Observed Frequencies From Study of Gender and Video Games		
	Type of Game		
Gender	*Nonviolent*	*Violent*	*Total*
Female	24	7	31
Male	87	65	152
Total	111	72	183

Note: Total frequencies are in the margins.

sampling fluctuation
The chance differences between samples and the population the samples are from.

if particular samples showed small differences. Small differences are an expected feature of samples because of sampling fluctuation. Large differences, however, are rare when there is no relationship between gender and type of game. Questions of what is a small difference and what is a large difference can be answered with NHST techniques. For the categorical data gathered by Jurica et al. (2002), the proper NHST technique is a **chi-square test.**

Chi-square is the most commonly used test for frequency count categorical data. There are several situations that call for a chi-square test. The most common situation that calls for a chi-square test is when researchers want to determine if the frequencies of one variable are contingent on (related to) a second variable. This chi-square test is called a *test of independence.* In the video game study, the question is whether the variable kind of game is related to the other variable, gender. Before discussing the details of the chi-square test of independence, we explain the logic that all NHST techniques use. All of the tests discussed in this chapter, those in chapter 9, and others that you will encounter in the future are based on this logic.[1]

A NEGATIVE INFERENCE LOGIC PROBLEM

If a situation is either A or B and it is not A, what is it?

We didn't bother to put the italicized question on a Stop & Think box; it's too easy. Even so, please keep this problem and the answer in mind. *If either A or B and not A, then B.* In logic, this kind of reasoning is called *negative inference,* which in Latin is *modus tollens.* Note that the problem is set up so that there are only two possibilities. By rejecting one of the two, you establish the other as true. You use negative inference in everyday decision making if, when faced with two alternatives, you think of the downside effects of each choice and then choose the alternative with the lesser downside effects. Travel decisions are often made using negative inference. Given two routes to a destination, thoughts about traffic congestion, poor road conditions, and longer travel time indicate that negative inference is at work because reasons to eliminate a route are being assessed. As another example, the architects of political contests know that many people use negative inference to choose between two candidates. As a result, they give the electorate reasons not to vote for the opposing candidate. To choose the lesser of two evils is to use negative inference.

---

chi-square test NHST technique that is appropriate for category data.

[1]The second-most-common situation that calls for a chi-square test is when researchers want an objective way to determine how well frequencies that were predicted by a theory match those that are actually observed. This situation calls for a *goodness-of-fit* test. Explanations of goodness-of-fit tests can be found in statistics texts such as Spatz (2008) and Howell (2004).

CHI-SQUARE LOGIC

Now, let's apply the logic of negative inference to the video game experiment. For situation *A*, we substitute the idea that there is *no* relationship between gender and type of game. That is, *A* becomes "type of game is not contingent on gender." For *B*, we substitute the idea that there *is* a relationship between gender and type of game. That is, *B* becomes "knowing a person's gender helps predict the game being played." The negative inference in chi-square logic is that if the "no relationship" hypothesis is eliminated, then the "there is a relationship" hypothesis becomes the conclusion.

In logic you can often *prove* that *A* is not true, which leaves you with the certain conclusion that *B* is true. In most statistics problems (and travel decisions, too), you only have probabilities, so completely disproving *A* is impossible. The data, however, can lead to the conclusion that *A* is highly unlikely. Reasonable people, of course, are willing to conclude that *B* is true, even though there is a small possibility of being wrong. Reasonable people may agonize over the choice of political candidates or travel routes, but eventually they do make decisions.

We use the chi-square test to introduce NHST because chi-square involves fewer unfamiliar concepts than other statistical tests. In addition, chi-square was the first NHST technique developed that was applicable to small-sample research such as that usually conducted by students.

> ### In the Know
>
> Chi-square was invented in 1900 by Karl Pearson (of Pearson product-moment correlation coefficient fame). It is used by researchers in almost every discipline that uses quantitative data. The importance of chi-square was recognized when it was listed as one of the 20 greatest discoveries of the 20th century by the editors of a popular science magazine (Hacking, 1984).

Statistical Independence

Statistical independence means no relationship. For any table (such as Table 6.1) that has row totals and column totals, there is just one set of cell entries that shows complete statistical independence. For the video game study, a statistically independent set of cell entries would be expected if there was no relationship between gender and type of game. To illustrate statistical independence, we constructed a special 2 × 2 table of numbers **(Table 6.2)**. Tables such as Table 6.1 and Table 6.2 are often called *contingency tables* because they reveal whether one of the variables is contingent on the other. If two variables are contingent, they are not independent. As you will see, the ideas that we derive from these tables can be used to establish statistically independent entries for any table.

statistical independence
Two variables that, as their own levels change, do not produce changes in the other variable.

TABLE 6.2	A 2 × 2 Table of Statistically Independent Cells		
	Column 1	*Column 2*	*Total*
Row 1	8	12	20
Row 2	4	6	10
Total	12	18	30

The characteristic that makes a table of cell entries statistically independent is that corresponding proportions are exactly equal. To explain this "equal proportions" idea, find the number 8 in row 1 of Table 6.2. Row 1 has a total of 20, so 8 represents a proportion of .40 because $8/20 = .40$. In a similar way 12 in the first row represents a proportion of .60 $(12/20 = .60)$. Are these same proportions found in row 2?

Find the two proportions in row 2, using the row 1 illustration as a model.

In row 2, the proportion in column 1 is $4/10 = .40$ and the proportion in column 2 is $6/10 = .60$. Thus, in column 1, the row 1 and row 2 proportions are exactly equal (.40) and in column 2 the row 1 and row 2 proportions are also exactly equal (.60).

This illustration that a textbook table shows statistical independence may leave you with a nagging, but important question: "Fine, but how can I find cell entries for research data that are statistically independent?" Fortunately, it's not hard.

To calculate the entry for one particular cell, multiply three numbers—the proportion that the row is of the grand total, the proportion that the column is of the grand total, and the grand total. Thus, for the cell at row 1, column 1 in Table 6.2, $\left(\frac{20}{30}\right)\left(\frac{12}{30}\right)(30) = 8$. In a similar way, for the cell at row 2, column 1, $\left(\frac{10}{30}\right)\left(\frac{12}{30}\right)(30) = 4$.

Use the examples above to calculate statistically independent cell entries for row 1, column 2 and row 2, column 2.

You may have recognized that the arithmetic above can be simplified by canceling out a 30 in the numerator with a 30 in the denominator. The simplified version of a calculation of a statistically independent cell entry is $\frac{\text{(row total)(column total)}}{\text{grand total}}$. Thus, for row 1, column 2, $\frac{(12)(18)}{30} = 12$ and for

| TABLE 6.3 | Row, Column, and Grand Totals for the Video Game Experiment | | |

| | Type of Game | | |
Gender	Nonviolent	Violent	Total
Female	——	——	31
Male	——	——	152
Total	111	72	183

row 2, column 2, $\dfrac{(10)(18)}{30} = 6$. Note that all of the numbers that are used to calculate the cell entries are row totals, column totals, or the grand total.

Here's a reminder about chi-square logic: Statistically independent data result when there is no relationship between the two variables, Thus, when there is no relationship, statistically independent cell entries are *expected*.

Now let's return to the question of what the data would look like in the video game study if there was no relationship between gender and type of game. **Table 6.3** shows the row, column, and grand totals that we began with. The task is to use these totals to calculate cell entries that satisfy the requirement of statistical independence.

Perhaps you would like to calculate the cell entries yourself, before you look at our calculations. Use the row and column totals in Table 6.3.

Table 6.4 shows the arithmetic for calculating statistically independent cell entries for the margin totals in Table 6.3. Examine all of the entries in **Table 6.4.**

| TABLE 6.4 | Calculation of Statistically Independent Cell Entries for the Margin Totals in Table 6.3 |

Cell	Calculation
Row 1, column 1	$\dfrac{(31)(111)}{183} = 18.80$
Row 1, column 2	$\dfrac{(31)(72)}{183} = 12.20$
Row 2, column 1	$\dfrac{(152)(111)}{183} = 92.20$
Row 2, column 2	$\dfrac{(152)(72)}{183} = 59.80$

| TABLE 6.5 | Expected Cell Frequencies for the Video Game Experiment | | |

	Type of Game		
Gender	*Nonviolent*	*Violent*	*Total*
Female	18.80	12.20	31
Male	92.20	59.80	152
Total	111	72	183

Table 6.5 combines Table 6.3 with the cell entries calculated in Table 6.4. Table 6.5 shows the cell values that are expected if there is no relationship between gender and type of game. Now compare Table 6.5 to Table 6.1. They are different. That these two tables are different nudges us away from the "no relationship" hypothesis. However, the difference may be just an example of sampling fluctuation.

Probabilities

NHST techniques provide probabilities. In the case of a chi-square test, probabilities indicate the likelihood of particular cell arrangements if it is true that the two variables are statistically independent in the populations the samples come from. **Table 6.6** shows two other examples of 2 × 2 cell entries that are not like Table 6.5 but also have grand totals of 183. Note that the numbers in the left table (X) are closer to statistical independence than the numbers in the right table (Y). Note also that the cell entries in the actual data (Table 6.1) are intermediate between the X and Y displays in Table 6.6. The probability associated with the numbers in table X of Table 6.6 is .38, a figure that comes from an SPSS analysis. This means that if the two variables are statistically independent, sampling fluctuation would produce a 2 × 2 table such as X or a table more extreme than X 38 times in a hundred tries. (Table 6.1 and table Y of Table 6.6 are examples

| TABLE 6.6 | 2 × 2 Tables With the Same Margin Totals as Tables 6.1 and 6.5 | | |

	X		*total*	y		*total*
	21	10	31	29	2	31
	90	62	152	82	70	152
total	111	72	183	111	72	183

of more extreme numbers.) The probability of obtaining table Y or one more extreme is less than .0001. (There are only two tables more extreme than table Y. One has a 1 in the upper right corner and the other has a 0.) Remember that these probabilities are accurate *only* if the two variables are actually independent of each other.

Returning to our video game data, what probability is associated with the observations in Table 6.1? The probability is .036 if there is actually no relationship between gender and type of game. Researchers consider an event with a probability of .036 as unlikely. But in reality, the event did occur. Those were the data that were observed. Faced with the question of whether the sample was a rare event or whether the premise that the probability is based on is false, researchers conclude that the premise is false. Thus, they reject the hypothesis that there is no relationship and conclude that there is a relationship.

Conclusions

The final step is to say what the relationship is. This very important step requires an examination of the descriptive statistics and a decision of how best to tell the story. You probably recall that the descriptive statistics of the video game data showed that both males and females preferred non-violent rather than violent video games, but that the preference of females (77% to 23%) was greater than the preference of males (57% to 43%). The conclusion can be written simply: Females have a greater preference for nonviolent video games than males have, $p = .036$.

"Well," you might say, "that's what I thought in the first place!" But, of course, the chi-square analysis has eliminated (or at least substantially reduced) the possibility that the differences observed could be the result of sampling fluctuation. All of us have an idea of what the data will show before the study is conducted. This predication is called a **research hypothesis.** A research hypothesis is a working expectation of what the data will show. It is sometimes referred to as a *working hypothesis* or the *experimental hypothesis*.

In summary, here's the logic of chi-square expressed in terms of the video game study. If gender and type of game are either independent or related and data are obtained that are unlikely if the two variables are independent, conclude that gender and type of game are related.

NULL HYPOTHESIS STATISTICAL TESTING (NHST) LOGIC

In this section, we explain null hypothesis statistical testing (NHST) using a general vocabulary that applies to all NHST techniques and not just chi-square. NHST begins with two hypotheses about the population the data are from and a criterion for deciding between the two. One hypotheses is the **null hypothesis** (symbolized H_0) and the other is the

research hypothesis
The researcher's expectation of what the data will show; often the alternative hypothesis.

null hypothesis   Usually a hypothesis that there is no relationship or that population means are equal.

alternative hypothesis (symbolized H_1). The criterion is a probability value (symbolized **alpha,** α). The sample data are analyzed with a statistical test that produces a probability figure, p. If the probability p is equal to or less than α, H_0 is rejected and H_1 is accepted. Once H_0 is rejected, researchers write a conclusion about the relationship between (or among) the variables, basing this conclusion on descriptive statistics from the samples.

If the sample data result in rejecting H_0, the data are said to be **statistically significant.** Statistically significant means that the null hypothesis was rejected when an NHST technique was performed on the sample data.

The null hypothesis (H_0) is always a statement about independence or equality in populations. H_0 is rejected when the observed sample data are unlikely if H_0 is true. But what probabilities qualify as unlikely? That is, what value should α have? The consequences of rejecting H_0 or not rejecting H_0 differ greatly in different kinds of research and some researchers can choose α based on considerations peculiar to their own research. Nevertheless, the general rule is that probabilities of .05 or less are considered unlikely and only those probabilities lead to rejection of H_0. A phrase such as "$p < .05$" (or some lower probability figure) generally accompanies conclusions that are supported by NHST.

The Meaning of $p < .05$

At this point we think that you are prepared to answer one of the questions we posed in the introduction to this chapter.

What event has a probability of .05 when $p < .05$?

The sample data that were observed have a probability of less than .05, and this probability is accurate if the null hypothesis is true. The probabilities that NHST produce are *conditional probabilities.* A conditional probability is correct only if specified conditions hold. In NHST, the specified condition is that the null hypothesis is true. If H_0 is true, then data such as those that were observed have the probability that is indicated. When NHST produces $p < .05$, then if the null hypothesis is true, the data observed occur less than 5% of the time.

If the probability of the data is greater than .05, you cannot reject H_0, so H_0 is retained. This leaves you back where you started—you have two hypotheses. Let's explore this further. Suppose the data produce a probability much larger than .05. Perhaps the probability is .75. If so, then .75 is the probability of the data, if H_0 is true. Although the data are certainly consistent with the null hypothesis, they are consistent with other hypotheses as well. For example, any hypothesis that is close but not exactly the null hypothesis is supported by data that produce NHST probability

alternative hypothesis
A hypothesis that two variables are related or that two population means are not equal.

alpha The probability that is the criterion for rejecting the null hypothesis.

equal to .75. In summary, an NHST technique that produces a probability greater than α leaves you with both the null hypothesis and the alternative hypothesis. Of course, you do have descriptive statistics for the sample, which are informative and helpful, even if the NHST technique does not permit you to rule out sampling fluctuation as a cause of the difference.

NHST allows a strong statement of support for the alternative hypothesis when the probability of the sample data is less than α because the null hypothesis has been eliminated. However, under no conditions does NHST logic permit a strong statement of support for the null hypothesis. Failure to eliminate the null hypothesis leaves it in contention but is not evidence that permits a strong statement of support.

> ### *In the Know*
> Ronald A. Fisher introduced the null hypothesis concept in 1925 in an influential for book research workers. He proposed $\alpha = .05$ as a guideline but later researchers treated it as a rule. Today, the exclusive reliance on NHST techniques for analyzing quantitative data is under attack. In the 1990s there was a move to ban its use. A group of influential researchers recommended not banning NHST but supplementing it with alternatives such as confidence intervals and exploratory data analysis (APA, 1996). Other explanations of the problems with NHST are in Dillon (1999), Nickerson (2000), and Spatz (2000). Recently, Killeen (2005) introduced a new statistic, p_{rep}, which gives the probability of replicating the observed data. Its use, rather than p, is encouraged by a leading journal, *Psychological Science*. Science continues to evolve.

Many different statistical tests use NHST logic, and chi-square is one of them. In this chapter we discuss other NHST techniques: correlation coefficients, the independent-samples t test, and the paired t test. In chapter 9 we cover three analyses of variance that are also based on NHST logic. Additional NHST techniques are covered in intermediate and advanced statistics textbooks.

The question of which statistical test to use for a particular set of data depends on a number of considerations. One consideration is the kind of data. Categorical data, scaled data, and ranked data all require different tests. In addition, various characteristics of experimental design such as the number of independent variables and dependent variables, number of levels of the independent variable, and other considerations lead to different tests. Although the tests differ, every NHST technique of sample data results in a probability figure. We turn now to the source of these probability figures.

FIGURE 6.1
Normal curve
sampling distribution
showing frequency
of different samples.

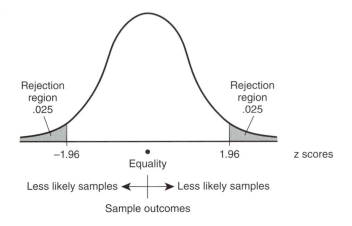

Sampling Distributions

The probabilities produced by NHST come from **sampling distributions.** Sampling distributions come in different forms, but every NHST technique has an accompanying sampling distribution. Chi-square tests use the chi-square distribution, the various *t* tests use the *t* distribution, and ANOVA uses the *F* distribution. A number of tests use the normal distribution, which we discussed in chapter 5.

In practice, researchers do not calculate a sampling distribution for each batch of sample data they analyze. Instead, computer software programs use sampling distributions to give them a probability figure or they use a table that shows the probability of their sample data. However, the better you understand sampling distributions, the better you will understand NHST. We'll illustrate with a sampling distribution that you already have some familiarity with, the normal curve.

Figure 6.1 is a sampling distribution that is a normal curve. Several different NHST techniques use the normal curve (or an approximately normal curve) as the sampling distribution. For these tests, a normal curve results when samples are repeatedly taken from a population in which the null hypothesis is true. As always, samples vary, and in this case they vary in the form of a normal curve.

In Figure 6.1, the null hypothesis is a hypothesis of equality. A sample result of exact equality falls at the center of the normal curve in Figure 6.1. As actual samples depart from equality in either direction, they are less and less likely to occur. The sample results in the two tails of the distribution are quite unlikely. The least likely 5% of the samples are in the tails of the curve, 2.5% in each end. The point that separates the extreme 2.5% of the curve is 1.96 standard deviations from the midpoint of the curve. Points along the normal curve are commonly expressed as *z* scores. A **z score** indicates the number of *SD* units a point is from the mean. Thus, *z* scores

sampling distribution
A theoretical distribution based on random sampling that shows probabilities of actual sample outcomes.

z score Score expressed in standard deviation units.

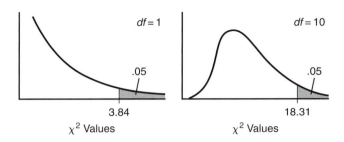

FIGURE 6.2
Two chi-square sampling distributions with different degrees of freedom.

of -1.96 or less and 1.96 or more signify that the null hypothesis should be rejected if $\alpha = .05$. If $\alpha = .01$, the z scores that separate the lower .005 and upper .005 of the curve are ± 2.58. Values such as 1.96 and 2.58 come from a table that shows the proportions of the curve that are associated with various z scores. For the normal curve and all other sampling distributions, the points associated with an α level are called **critical values.** Thus, if $\alpha = .05$, the critical values for the normal curve are ± 1.96.

The more general point is that a portion of every sampling distribution, regardless of its shape, includes sample results that occur only 5% of the time or less. Because such results are rare when H_0 is true, actually obtaining them calls into question the truth of H_0. When this happens, researchers conclude that H_0 is probably false rather than conclude that a rare event occurred. You can see that they are reasoning using negative inference.

As indicated in Figure 6.1, the region of a sampling distribution that includes samples that are less likely than α is called the **rejection region.** For some sampling distributions the rejection region is in the two extremes of the curve but for other sampling distributions the rejection region is in just one tail of the curve.

Degrees of Freedom

Sampling distributions other than the normal distribution have one additional consideration—**degrees of freedom** (*df*). A sampling distribution such as the chi-square distribution is not one curve but a family of curves. Likewise, the F distribution is a family of curves and so is the t distribution. **Figure 6.2** shows the χ^2 curves for 1 *df* and 10 *df*. As you can see, the rejection region is associated with a different critical value in each curve. The correct critical value depends on the number of degrees of freedom that the data have. Once a *df* figure is known, you can use a table to find the p value associated with the sample data.

Degrees of freedom for NHST techniques such as χ^2, t, or F can be determined from simple formulas, which we provide where the tests are discussed. Statistics textbooks such as those by Spatz (2008), Howell (2004), and Aron, Aron and Coups (2006) provide elementary explanations of degrees of freedom. A full understanding requires knowledge of mathematical statistics.

critical value The number from a sampling distribution that determines whether the null hypothesis is rejected.

rejection region The portion of a sampling distribution that includes sample data that are less probable than alpha (α).

degrees of freedom Concept used by mathematical statisticians to determine the sampling distribution that is appropriate for a set of data.

Two-Tailed Tests and One-Tailed Tests

The null hypothesis is a hypothesis of equality. For example: Males = Females. The two alternatives to the null hypothesis are Males > Females and Males < Females. If the null hypothesis of equality is rejected, **two-tailed tests** allow you to conclude either of the two remaining possibilities. Thus, if the data show that $M_{male} > M_{female}$, you can conclude Males > Females in the population. On the other hand, **one-tailed tests** restrict you to just one of the two possibilities, and you must choose which one before the data are gathered. Thus, if you believe that Males > Females and you choose a one-tailed test, you can reject the null hypothesis only if the data produce $M_{male} > M_{female}$. A one-tailed test does not permit you to reject H_0 if $M_{male} < M_{female}$, no matter how large the difference. Our advice to beginning researchers is to use two-tailed tests. The critical values we explained in the previous section are critical values for a two-tailed test. When researchers choose a two-tailed test, the alternative hypothesis is expressed as Males ≠ Females. Thus, if the null hypothesis, Males = Females, is rejected, the alternative hypothesis, Males ≠ Females, is adopted, and the data determine if the conclusion is Males > Females or Males < Females.

This explanation may lead you to wonder why one-tailed tests were conceived of in the first place, but they are appropriate in some circumstances. For example, when comparing a new product or procedure to an old one, a researcher's only interest is whether the new is better than the old. For additional information on the issue of two-tailed and one-tailed tests, see Spatz (2005, pp. 182–184) or Howell (2004, pp. 154–156).

Type I and Type II Errors

You no doubt recognize that conclusions based on NHST can be erroneous. Indeed they can. Fortunately, the nature of NHST errors is well known. One kind of error can occur when the null hypothesis is true, and a second kind can occur when the null hypothesis is false. By knowing the nature of these errors, you can design your research to reduce the probability of errors.

Type I Errors   An NHST technique with $\alpha = .05$ assures us that some 5% of samples that actually come from a null hypothesis population will lead to a conclusion to reject H_0. Of course, rejecting H_0 in this situation is a mistake. Such a mistake is called a **Type I error.** Type I errors occur only when H_0 is true. The probability of a Type I error is symbolized α. As indicated earlier, researchers typically set α at .05, although sometimes it is set at a smaller figure such as .01.

Type II Errors   In many cases of research, the samples do *not* come from the null hypothesis population. In all of these cases, it is not possible to make a Type I error. If the samples don't come from the null hypothesis population, the correct thing to do is to reject H_0. That is, it would be a mistake if you did not reject H_0. However, if the data produce a probability greater than .05,

two-tailed test   A statistical test to detect a difference in population means, regardless of direction.

one-tailed test   A statistical test to detect a difference in population means, either positive or negative but not both.

Type I error   Rejecting the null hypothesis when it is true.

TABLE 6.7	Types of Errors That Can Occur in NHST Decisions		
		True Situation in the Population	
		H_0 *true*	H_0 *false*
Decision Based on Sample Data	Reject H_0	Type I error (probability $= \alpha$)	Correct decision
	Retain H_0	Correct decision	Type II error (probability $= \beta$)

H_0 will be retained. Such a mistake is called a **Type II error.** Type II errors occur only when H_0 is false. The probability of a Type II error is symbolized with a Greek beta (β). Several factors control the value of β. We return to the topic of β in the section on power near the end of this chapter.

A Table of Errors   Table 6.7 summarizes the kind of errors that are possible with NHST techniques. It also shows the circumstances that lead to correct decisions. Of course, in research situations you do not know whether the null hypothesis is true or false. The data guide your decision, but because data are subject to sampling fluctuation, any decision is tinged with a certain amount of uncertainty. Study Table 6.7. Understanding the table is necessary if you are to understand null hypothesis statistical testing.

Suppose that the conclusion about the video game study is wrong. If the conclusion the data led to is wrong, is the mistake a Type I or a Type II error?

STOP
& *Think*

The data in the video game study led to rejection of H_0. When you reject H_0, the only kind of error possible is a Type I error. You can confirm this by examining Table 6.7.

The task of detecting errors is an important one for researchers. The best check that researchers have for detecting Type I and Type II errors is *replication*. A research hypothesis that receives support from two or more independent data sets is fairly well protected from the charge that the results embody a Type I error. The importance of replication is captured in the saying "one replication is worth 1000 *t* tests."

Significant Results and Important Results

In statistics the word *significant* means only one thing: the null hypothesis was rejected. Outside of statistics, *significant* has additional meanings. In some contexts, significant means *important*. NHST techniques are designed to detect significant differences, but statistically significant differences may or may not be important. To determine the importance of a statistically significant difference, you must know the effect size index, alternative explanations of the difference, and perhaps some cost information.

Type II error   Retaining the null hypothesis when it is false.

As we said earlier in discussing importance, it helps to consult with someone who is knowledgeable about the specifics of the topic.

In the remaining sections of this chapter, we provide examples of four NHST techniques and four effect size indexes illustrated with research from the literature. Each section closes with an interpretation of the study.

In the Know

It is important to recognize that NHST is just an aid to decision making. The NHST technique results in one of two decisions:

1. Reject H_0, accept H_1 and write a strong conclusion that eliminates sampling fluctuation as an explanation
2. Fail to reject H_0, which leads to retaining both H_0 and H_1

In recent years a number of prominent researchers have questioned the value of the NHST technique. They argue that other approaches provide a more extensive analysis and will result in faster progress in our effort to understand behavioral and cognitive processes. The issues raised are not simple and are beyond the scope of this introduction to research methods. References that help explain this controversy are Dillon (1999), Spatz (2000), and Nickerson (2000). Many of the researchers who raised the questions about NHST contributed to a book whose title captures the problem, *What If There Were No Significance Tests?* (Harlow, Mulaik, & Steiger, 1997).

NHST TECHNIQUES

Chi-Square Test of Independence

Statistical Significance of χ^2   You studied the logic of chi-square in an earlier section. Near the end of that section, we said that the NHST probability associated with the data in Table 6.1 was .036, a probability that is statistically significant. In this section we explain the formula that takes you from the data to its probability. The symbol for chi-square is χ^2. The formula is

$$\chi^2 = \Sigma\left[\frac{(O - E)^2}{E}\right]$$

Where: O = observed frequencies (the observed data)

E = expected frequencies (statistically independent values)

The formula for χ^2 has two elements, O and E. The observed values (O) come from the data, Table 6.1. The expected values (E) are those that are

TABLE 6.8	Elements Needed to Calculate a Chi-Square Test			
O	E	$O - E$	$(O - E)^2$	$\dfrac{(O - E)^2}{E}$
24	18.80	5.20	27.04	1.438
7	12.20	−5.20	27.04	2.216
87	92.20	−5.20	27.04	0.293
65	59.80	5.20	27.04	0.452
Σ 183	183			$4.40 = X^2$

expected if the two variables are statistically independent. Calculation of the E values was shown in Table 6.4. The conventional way to combine these two elements to produce a X^2 value is with a table that begins with O and E values and proceeds through the arithmetic steps that lead to a X^2 value. **Table 6.8** is an example. Work your way across each of the columns in Table 6.8. Note that the sum of the right-hand column is 4.40. One way to get to the probability figure that is associated with $X^2 = 4.40$ is to determine df and then use **Table C.3** in appendix C. The df of any contingency table is determined by the formula

$$df = (R - 1)(C - 1)$$

Where: R is the number of rows

C is the number of columns

In the 2 × 2 table of the video game data, $df = (R - 1)(C - 1) = (2 - 1)(2 - 1) = 1$. Thus, every chi-square 2 × 2 contingency table has one degree of freedom.

With a X^2 value and its degrees of freedom, you are prepared to enter Table C.3 (in appendix C) to find the probability of the data that were observed. The header of Table C.3 shows five α levels that researchers use. The df column is on the left. The X^2 values at the intersection of an α level and df are critical values. For $\alpha = .05$ and 1 df, the critical value is 3.84. For the data in Table 6.1, the X^2 value (4.40) is greater than the critical value, so the probability of the data is less than .05. Therefore, the null hypothesis is rejected.

Once you understand and can explain how probabilities are calculated from contingency tables, you are better prepared to find X^2 values with a software program such as SPSS. **Table 6.9** shows SPSS output for the video games data. This SPSS output and others that we use show what appears on your screen if you analyze data with SPSS. These outputs always contain additional tests beyond those that we discuss. Table 6.9 shows the data that were analyzed in the top panel; the lower panel shows the chi-square value (4.395) and its probability (.036).

| TABLE 6.9 | SPSS Output for Video Games Experiment |

Gender Gametype Cross-tabulation*

		Gametype		Total
		Nonviolent	Violent	
Gender	female	24	7	31
	male	87	65	152
Total		111	72	183

Chi-Square Tests

	Value	df	Asymp. sig. (2-sided)	Exact sig. (2-sided)	Exact sig. (1-sided)
Pearson chi-square	4.395[a]	1	.036		
Continuity Correction[b]	3.590	1	.058		
Likelihood ratio	4.677	1	.031		
Fisher's exact test				.044	.027
Linear-by-linear association	4.371	1	.037		
N of valid cases	183				

[a]0 cells (.0%) have expected count less than 5. The minimum expected count is 12.20

A meaningful interpretation of any NHST probability incorporates the terminology of the research. In this case, the terms are *video games* and *gender*. Here's the conclusion we wrote before, but now with the supporting evidence of a chi-square test: Females have a greater preference for nonviolent video games than males have:

$$\chi^2(1, N = 183) = 4.40, p = .036$$

Effect Size Index for 2 × 2 Chi-Square Analyses   In chapter 5 you learned that the effect size index for a 2 × 2 chi-square is phi (φ). The formula for φ is

$$\varphi = \sqrt{\frac{\chi^2}{N}}$$

Where: χ^2 is the calculated value from a 2 × 2 contingency table

N is the total number of observations

For the data on the video games study, both Tables 6.8 and 6.9 supply the elements needed to calculate φ. Thus,

$$\varphi = \sqrt{\frac{\chi^2}{N}} = \sqrt{\frac{4.395}{183}} = \sqrt{0.0240} = 0.16$$

As you know from the guidelines stated earlier, a φ value of 0.10 is considered small, 0.30 is medium, and 0.50 is large. Thus, the effect of gender on the choice between violent and nonviolent video games is small. After calculating a statistical test and finding an effect size index, a conclusion can be written. You have seen parts of this conclusion already, but here is a final version:

Interpretation   Jurica and colleagues (2002) observed 31 females and 152 males playing video games at an arcade. Of the females, 77% were playing nonviolent games and 23% were playing violent games. Among the males, the preference for nonviolent games was not as great (57 to 43%). The difference in the preference for nonviolent games between the two genders is small (φ = 0.16) but statistically significant (χ^2(1, N = 183) = 4.40, p = .036).

Our explanation of the logic and the arithmetic of chi-square is more extensive than our explanations for the statistics that follow. Fortunately, the logic is the same for other NHST techniques and the calculations are typically handled by a computer's statistical package.

Pearson Product–Moment Correlation Coefficient

We explained the Pearson product–moment correlation coefficient (r) in chapter 4. As you will recall, r values range from −1.00 to 1.00. Values around zero indicate there is no relationship between the two variables and values of −1.00 and 1.00 indicate a perfect relationship.

Schaffer and Pritchard (2003) distributed questionnaires to 218 fellow students at the University of Evansville. From the questionnaires, they assessed each student's stress level and 28 different strategies for coping with stress. **Table 6.10** shows the correlation coefficients between stress and four of the coping strategies.

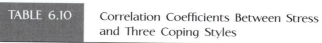 Put into words the relationship of stress to each coping strategy in Table 6.10.

 STOP & *Think*

TABLE 6.10	Correlation Coefficients Between Stress and Three Coping Styles
Coping strategy	*r*
Criticize oneself	.48
Use alcohol and drugs	.28
Look for something good in what happened	−.08
Prayer and meditation	−.22

The two positive *r*s in Table 6.10 indicate that the greater the use of this strategy, the greater the reported stress. The two negative *r*s indicate that the greater the use of this strategy, the less the reported stress. The larger the absolute value of *r*, the stronger the relationship.

Statistical Significance of *r*   The *r* values in Table 6.10 are calculated from a sample, which, of course, has uncertainty built into it. The NHST technique we illustrate answers the question: "What is the probability of obtaining a particular sample *r* if there is a zero correlation in the population the sample comes from?" To find such probabilities, use **Table C.4** in appendix C. Across the top of Table C.4 are α levels that researchers commonly use. The top row is for two-tailed tests and the second row is for one-tailed tests. We will use $\alpha = .05$ and a two-tailed test. The other requirement for entering Table C.4 is degrees of freedom, which are shown in column 1. The formula for *df* for correlation problems is

$$df = N - 2$$

Thus, for the Schaffer and Pritchard (2003) data with 218 participants, $df = 216$. You can see in Table C.4 that the largest listed *df* is 100. For $df = 100$ and $\alpha = .05$, an *r* value of .1946 or larger is statistically significant. Look at the other *r* values on the bottom line. Researchers usually report the smallest probability that is appropriate for a particular *r*. Thus, to be significant at the .001 level, an *r* must be equal to or greater than .3211. For the four correlation coefficients in Table 6.10:

$$r = .48, p < .001$$
$$r = .28, p < .01$$
$$r = -.08, p > .05$$
$$r = -.22, p < .05$$

As you might expect, software packages such as SPSS provide exact probability figures for *r* values that it calculates from raw data.[2] In the case of *r* values that are already calculated, use Table C.4.

Effect Size Index of *r*   Determining the effect size index for a sample *r* is much easier than calculating a value for φ or *d*. The effect size index for a correlation coefficient is just *r* itself. Unfortunately, interpreting this effect size index with adjectives such as small, medium, or large is not as

---

[2]Table 5.7 shows SPSS output for a correlation. An $r = .801$, based on $N = 8$, has a probability of .017 if there is a zero correlation in the population the sample came from.

simple as the 0.10, 0.30, and 0.50 guidelines for φ or the 0.20, 0.50, and 0.80 guidelines for d.

Cohen's 1969 book that established guidelines for φ and d also proposed guidelines for r. Values of .10, .30, and .50 were proposed as small, medium, and large effect sizes. These guidelines for r have not met with as much acceptance as the guidelines for φ and d. In fact, for some applications of r, Cohen's guidelines are clearly inappropriate. For example, you learned in chapter 4 that an r of .80 or greater is required if a test is to be considered reliable using the test–retest method. If you are testing the reliability of a test, an r value of .50 would be very small, not large. At the other end of the scale, an r value of .03 is the basis of the widespread recommendation to take a low dose aspirin as a preventative for heart attacks (Rosnow & Rosenthal, 1989). Part of the problem is that r is used in such a wide variety of ways. Whether an r is considered small, medium, or large depends on the reason it was calculated and the researcher's experience with the two variables. To the beginning researcher, our advice is to ask what values are considered small, medium, or large in each particular situation.

Hemphill (2003) addressed the question of establishing adjectives for r by cataloging thousands of correlation coefficients that were reported in hundreds of studies. Dividing the distribution of r values into thirds, he found:

Lowest third	rs were less than .20
Middle third	r values of .20 to .30
Highest third	rs were greater than .30

Using the division that Hemphill found, you can see that one of the rs in Table 6.10 is large enough to be in the highest third of correlation coefficients, two are in the middle third, and one is in the lowest third.[3] Having determined statistical significance and established effect size indexes, the last step is to write an interpretation.

Interpretation   Schaffer and Pritchard administered questionnaires to 218 undergraduates. From the questionnaires, they determined stress scores and scores for four strategies of coping with stress. Two strategies were positively correlated with stress and two were negatively correlated.

- The greater the participants' criticism of themselves, the greater their reported stress; $r(216\ df) = .48$, $p < .001$.

---

[3]Schaffer and Pritchard (2003) actually reported on 28 strategies. Four had correlation coefficients greater than .30, 9 were .20 to .30, and 15 were less than .20.

- The greater the participants' use of alcohol and drugs, the greater the stress; $r(216\ df) = .28, p < .01$.
- The greater the participants' use of prayer and meditation, the less the stress; $r(216\ df) = -.22, p < .05$.
- There was no significant relationship between participants' stress and their use of a strategy of looking for something good in what happened; $r(216\ df) = -.08, p > .05$.

t Tests

When an experiment has two treatments (two levels of the IV) and the DV is a scaled measure, researchers often analyze the data with a *t* test. The null hypothesis of a *t* test is that the two samples are from populations that have identical means. If the *t* test produces a probability figure that is less than α, researchers reject H_0. By comparing the two sample means, they determine which of the two population means is larger.

The probabilities for a *t* test come from a sampling distribution called the **t distribution.** The *t* distribution is actually a family of curves that vary according to their degrees of freedom. Compared to the normal distribution, *t* distributions have fatter tails and narrower peaks. As degrees of freedom increase, the *t* distribution becomes more like the normal distribution. In fact, when $df = \infty$, the *t* distribution and the normal distribution are identical.

Figure 6.3 shows two *t* distributions, one with 10 *df* and one with 2 *df.* For both curves (and for all *t* distributions), the larger the absolute value of *t*, the smaller the probability. The two curves in Figure 6.3 illustrate the general case. As degrees of freedom increase, smaller and smaller *t* values are required to reject H_0 at the .05 level.

FIGURE 6.3

t distributions with 2 *df* and 10 *df.* The shaded portions and *t* values are for 10 *df.*

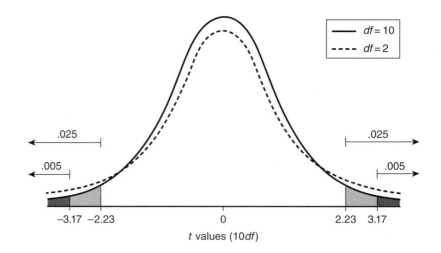

t distribution Sampling distribution used to determine probabilities for *t* tests.

In the two sections that follow, we explain independent-samples t tests and paired t tests. The choice of one or the other of these t tests depends on the design of the experiment. In both cases, however, you end with a t value based on a specific *df*. That t-test value is associated with a particular probability.

Independent-Samples t Test

The kind of experimental designs that call for an independent-samples t test are explained in chapter 7. As with all NHST techniques, an independent-samples t test gives you the probability of the difference that was observed, if the treatment has no effect on the scores. The formula for an independent-samples t test for two groups with equal Ns is

$$t = \frac{M_1 - M_2}{\sqrt{(SE_{M_1})^2 + (SE_{M_2})^2}}$$

$M_1 - M_2$ is called the *mean difference* and $\sqrt{(SE_{M_1})^2 + (SE_{M_2})^2}$ is called the *standard error of a difference*.

The steps that take you from the raw data of an experiment to the value of t can be done by a computer with a statistics software program. The result will be an accurate value of t. However, to really understand what is going on, you must understand the meaning of each of the elements in the formula. Understanding leads to satisfaction and confidence and also helps you write better interpretations.

Look at the formula for the independent-samples t test. Describe for yourself what the numerator is about and what the denominator is about.

Elements of the Independent-Samples t-Test Formula   The numerator of the t test is fairly simple; the mean of one sample is subtracted from the mean of the other sample. Thus, the numerator becomes the difference between the two sample means. This difference may reflect a difference in the two populations the samples come from.

The standard error of a difference, the denominator, is more complicated; it is the square root of the sum of two standard errors that have been squared. As a reminder about standard errors of the mean, the formula is

$$SE_M = \frac{SD}{\sqrt{N}}$$

Thus, a standard error of the mean depends on the variability of the sample scores (SD) and the size of the sample (N). Small values of SE_M occur when there is little variability in the sample data or when the sample size is large (or both). The standard error of a difference is a measure of the variability in the data.

To summarize, the numerator of the independent-samples t test is a measure of the variability between the means and the denominator is a measure of the variability within the samples and of N. The concept of *variability between means* divided by *variability within the samples* is a recurring one in NHST. This concept is at work in all t tests and all analysis of variance tests.

Assumptions of the Independent-Samples t Test   An independent-samples t test produces accurate probabilities when the two populations the samples are from are normally distributed and have equal variances. Of course, the whole reason for doing a t test is that you have sample scores and not population scores, so there is no way to know for sure that the probabilities from t tests are completely accurate. However, mathematical statisticians study the effects of sampling from nonnormal distributions and from distributions with unequal variances. Although there is some disagreement, the general conclusion is that unless the deviations from the assumptions are large, the probabilities that t tests produce are accurate enough for research. The mathematical term for statistical tests that produce reasonably accurate probabilities even when its assumptions are violated is **robust.** Thus, t tests are robust tests.

All NHST techniques are based on one or more assumptions about the populations the samples come from. Classical NHST such as Pearson r, t tests, and the analysis of variance (which is covered in chapter 9) are examples of *parametric* tests. Parametric tests have fairly restrictive assumptions. There are other NHST techniques that have much less restrictive assumptions. We discuss one such group, nonparametric tests, in a section that follows.

> ### *In the Know*
> The formula we presented for the independent-samples t test is the one that is most commonly used to compare two sample means. However, it is not the only one. Mathematical statisticians have known since at least 1938 that the commonly used formula can produce inaccurate probabilities when the assumptions are violated (Welch, 1938). Over the years various modifications were suggested that would improve its accuracy. This work continues; recently, Keselman, Othman, Wilcox, and Fradette (2004) offered "a new and improved t test."

robust A statistical test that produces reasonably accurate probabilities even when the assumptions the test is based on are not fulfilled.

Statistical Significance   Table 6.11 shows scores that closely reflect the data from the social loafing experiment described in chapter 2. **Table 6.12**

TABLE 6.11	Scores That Reflect the Data in the Social Loafing Experiment

Confederate

Worker		Loafer	
10	5	10	3
10	5	9	2
9	5	8	2
9	5	8	1
8	5	8	1
8	5	6	1
8	4	5	
8	4	5	
7	4	5	
7	4	5	
7	3	4	
6	3	4	
6	2	3	
6	1	3	
6	0	3	

TABLE 6.12	SPSS Output for the Independent-Samples t Test of the Social Loafing Experiment

Group Statistics

		N	Mean	Std. deviation	Std. error mean
Confederate	Worker	30	5.6667	2.50975	0.45822
	Loafer	21	4.5714	2.73078	0.59590

Independent-Samples Test

						95% confidence interval of the difference	
	t	df	Sig. (2-tailed)	Mean difference	Std. error difference	Lower	Upper
Equal variances assumed	1.479	49	.145	1.09524	0.74039	−0.39263	2.58311
Equal variances not assumed	1.457	40.805	.153	1.09524	0.75171	−0.42309	2.61356

t Test for Equality of Means

shows the SPSS output for an independent-samples t test of scores in Table 6.11. Descriptive statistics are in the top panel; t tests are in the lower panel. Use the t test in Table 6.12 that has equal variances assumed (the top line). The probability of obtaining the two sample means if the null hypothesis is true is .145. Thus, the p value is not as small as or smaller than .05, the commonly used α value.

When we explained the logic of NHST we used the following problem:

If a situation is either A *or* B *and it is not* A, *what is it?*

The answer, of course, is easy: *B.* But now let's change the problem:

If a situation is either A *or* B *and* A *cannot be dismissed, what is the situation?*

With this logic problem, you are back where you started from. You haven't eliminated an alternative so the situation is still either *A* or *B.* With NHST, however, the situation is not as bad as it is in logic because you have the data you gathered. Even if you cannot reject the null hypothesis, you do have all of the descriptive statistics such as means, standard deviations, and an effect size index. These are all valuable indicators of the true situation, although chance cannot be ruled out as an explanation for the differences observed.

For the social loafing experiment, the conclusion is that the two sample means are not statistically different. Although the participants who brainstormed with a worker created more unique uses for a paper clip than did those who brainstormed with a loafer (5.67 uses to 4.57 uses), the difference was not statistically significant.

Effect Size Index   The formula for the effect size index (d) for scores from an independent-samples experiment is

$$d = \frac{M_1 - M_2}{SD'}$$

Where: M_1 and M_2 are the means of the two groups

$$SD' = \sqrt{\frac{SD_1{}^2(df_1) + SD_2{}^2(df_2)}{df_1 + df_2}}$$

The df values in the formula for SD' can be obtained by applying the formula

$$df = N - 1$$

Where: N is the sample size of each separate group

The standard deviations of each group are shown in the computer output. Thus, for the data in Table 6.11, the value of SD' is

$$SD' = \sqrt{\frac{SD_1^2(df_1) + SD_2^2(df_2)}{df_1 + df_2}} = \sqrt{\frac{(2.51)^2(29) + (2.73)^2(20)}{29 + 20}} = 2.602$$

Thus,

$$d = \frac{M_1 - M_2}{SD'} = \frac{5.67 - 4.57}{2.60} = -0.42$$

It is conventional to use M_1 for the experimental group and M_2 for the control group when *experimental* and *control* are appropriate adjectives in an experiment. Thus, a negative d indicates that the experimental group scored lower than the control group. In the social loafing experiment, designating one group as the experimental group is arguable; either group could be considered the experimental group. In any case, values of d are interpreted according to their absolute value. Thus, an effect size index of -0.42 becomes 0.42, which is intermediate between small (0.20) and medium (0.50).

Interpretation   Participants who worked in a small group with a hard worker produced an average of 5.67 uses for a paper clip, which was not significantly more than the 4.57 uses produced by those who participated in a group with a loafer: $t(49) = 4.48$, $p = .15$. The effect size index was 0.42, a value intermediate between small and medium.

Suppose the independent-samples t test of the social loafing scores had produced $p = .04$ and $d = 0.75$. Write an interpretation.

STOP
& *Think*

Given the hypothetical outcome in the Stop & Think box, the conclusion is that brainstorming groups that include confederates who are hard workers produce significantly more unique uses of a paper clip than groups that include a loafer ($p = .04$), and the kind of confederate in the group has a large effect on output ($d = 0.75$).

In the Know

Synonymous terms for *independent-samples* in the context of t tests include *unpaired, uncorrelated, between-subjects,* and *randomized.*

Paired t Test

A paired t test is appropriate for two-group designs in which scores in one group are paired with scores in the other group. The kinds of experimental designs that call for a paired t test are explained more fully in chapter 8, but we note here that

1. Scores are paired if they belong to the same person.
2. Scores are paired if participants are matched for some reason such as being in the same family, the same income group, or because they had similar scores on a pretest.

To illustrate a paired t test, we examine the difference between males and females on a test that measures the importance of fairness in resolving moral dilemmas. This example is based on a meta-analysis by Jaffee and Hyde (2000). Here is the background information.

Psychologists began studying moral orientation in earnest after Lawrence Kohlberg (1969) proposed that moral reasoning develops in stages. According to Kohlberg, the highest level of moral reasoning is one that seeks fairness and justice, regardless of conventional rules that might apply to a situation. Carol Gilligan's (1982) response was that Kohlberg's analysis left out a very important characteristic of high moral behavior—care for others. An important issue in this debate was the expectation that there were significant gender differences in rating the relative importance of fairness and care for others.

For our paired t-test example, we focus on just one aspect of this topic: Do males and females differ on whether they consider fairness or care for others to be the better response to a moral dilemma? The DV for our example is scores on the Moral Orientation Scale (MOS), which was developed by Yacker and Weinberg (1990).

The MOS consists of 12 scenarios about children's activities and the responses that a parent or caregiver might make. Each scenario sets up a moral dilemma. People taking the MOS pick the choice they consider the best. For example, one scenario describes plans for a birthday party. The birthday child wants to invite most of his or her classmates, but not a nearby neighbor child who is also in the class. One response is that the neighbor child should be invited because it isn't fair to exclude just one child. Another response is that neighbors help each other, and especially because the neighbor child is unpopular, it would be best to be friendly and invite the child. You can see that the first alternative earns a score in the "be fair" column; choosing the second alternative raises your score on "care for others."

Table 6.13 shows data that reflect one of the conclusions of Jaffee and Hyde's (2000) meta-analysis. In our example, the scores are paired by family. The scores of 4 and 3 on the first line are a brother and sister in the Smith family. The scores of 3 and 0 on the second line are a brother

TABLE 6.13	Moral Orientation Scale Scores for Males and Females	
Family	Males	Females
Smith	4	3
Johnson	3	0
Williams	4	4
Jones	11	6
Brown	7	10
Davis	1	4
Miller	9	7
Wilson	0	3
Moore	5	6
Taylor	2	1
Anderson	7	5
Thomas	10	8
M	5.25	4.75
SD	3.57	2.86

Note: Higher scores indicate greater importance of fairness compared to care for others. (The surnames are the 12 most common in America, in order.)

and sister in the Johnson family, and so forth. The higher the score, the greater the importance of fairness.

Look at the data in Table 6.13 and arrive at a preliminary conclusion about how the two genders view the importance of fairness.

STOP & Think

A preliminary conclusion is that males judge fairness as more important than females do because the mean score of males is greater than that of females.

Paired-Samples *t* Test   The formula for a paired-samples *t* test is

$$t = \frac{M_1 - M_2}{SE_{\bar{D}}}$$

Where: $M_1 - M_2$ is a mean difference

$SE_{\bar{D}}$ is the standard error of a difference for paired samples

The formula for $SE_{\bar{D}}$ is $\sqrt{(SE_{M_1})^2 + (SE_{M_2})^2 - 2r(SE_{M_1})(SE_{M_2})}$. Notice that the standard error of a difference for paired samples is the same as the standard error of a difference for independent samples, except for the factor $\sqrt{-2r(SE_{M_1})(SE_{M_2})}$. The correlation coefficient, r, is the correlation of the paired values of the dependent variable.

TABLE 6.14	SPSS Output for a Paired *t*-Test of the Data in Table 6.13

Paired-Samples Statistics

	Mean	N	Std. deviation	Std. error mean
Males	4.7500	12	2.86436	0.82687
Females	5.2500	12	3.57071	1.03078

Paired-Samples Correlations

	N	Correlation	Sig.
Males & females	12	.700	.011

Paired-Samples Test

	Paired differences							Sig. (2-tailed)
	Mean	Std. deviation	Std. error mean	95% confidence interval of the difference		t	df	
				Lower	Upper			
Males & females	−0.50000	2.57611	0.74366	−2.13678	1.13678	−0.672	11	.515

SPSS Analysis   Table 6.14 shows an SPSS output for a paired *t* test of the data in Table 6.13. The descriptive statistics are shown in the top panel and the correlation coefficient *r* appears in the middle panel. The lower panel shows the paired *t*-test value (−0.672) and its probability (.515).

Effect Size Index   Calculation of an effect size index (*d*) for a two-group, paired-samples design is simpler than the calculation for an independent-samples design, although the formula may appear daunting at first. The formula for *d* for a paired-samples design is

$$d = \frac{M_1 - M_2}{SD'}$$

Where: $SD' = (\sqrt{N})\sqrt{(SE_{M_1})^2 + (SE_{M_2})^2 - 2r(SE_{M_1})^2(SE_{M_2})}$

N = number of pairs

Notice that SD' is $\sqrt{N}$ times the standard error of a difference, which is the denominator in the *t*-test formula. Although SPSS does not show you the standard error of a difference directly, it is easy to calculate it from the output. Since

$$t = \frac{M_1 - M_2}{SE_{\bar{D}}}, \text{ then}$$

$$SE_{\bar{D}} = \frac{M_1 - M_2}{t}$$

From the output in Table 6.14,

$$SE_{\bar{D}} = \frac{M_1 - M_2}{t} = \frac{0.50}{0.672} = 0.744$$

Thus,

$$d = \frac{M_1 - M_2}{SD'} = \frac{M_1 - M_2}{(\sqrt{N})(SE_{\bar{D}})} = \frac{0.50}{\sqrt{12}(0.744)} = 0.19^4$$

With the statistical calculations in hand, we can write an interpretation.

Interpretation   Brothers and sisters from 12 families filled out the Moral Orientation Scale, which gives a person's score on the importance of fairness when dealing with moral dilemmas. Males scored higher than females, but the effect size index ($d = 0.19$) indicates a small effect. A paired t test showed that the difference between means was not statistically significant: $t(11) = 0.67$, $p = .52$.

The conclusions based on the data in Table 6.13 are faithful to the meta-analysis results of Jaffee and Hyde (2000) for the effect size index but not for the paired t test. Based on more than 100 studies, Jaffee and Hyde found the same small effect size index of 0.19 between the genders for the moral orientation of fairness. However, unlike the small data set in Table 6.13, their meta-analysis showed a significant difference between males and females. Males value fairness more highly than females, but the difference in the two genders is small. To complete the picture, Jaffee and Hyde found that females' moral orientation toward care was significantly greater than that of males, but again, the effect size index was small ($d = 0.28$).

In the Know

Terms synonymous with *paired* t are *correlated* t, *related* t, *dependent* t, *within-subject* t, and *split plot* t.

---

[4]A shortcut for calculating d from SPSS output is that $d = \dfrac{t}{\sqrt{N}}$. For the scores in Table 6.13 and using the output in Table 6.14, $d = \dfrac{t}{\sqrt{N}} = \dfrac{0.672}{\sqrt{12}} = 0.19$.

STATISTICAL TESTS FOR RANKED DATA

To summarize the chapter so far, analyze categorical data with chi-square tests. Analyze scaled data that satisfy the assumptions required by parametric tests with *t* tests and Pearson *r*s. For the third category, ranked data, use nonparametric tests. Use nonparametric tests also for scaled data that do not meet the assumptions about the populations that are required for parametric tests. Nonparametric tests were invented to fill researchers' needs for NHST techniques that don't assume population data characteristics such as normally distributed or equal variances. For an explanation of assumptions made by parametric tests, see statistics textbooks such as Spatz (2008), Howell (2004) or Aron, Aron, and Coups (2006).

Many nonparametric tests have parametric counterparts. To give just a few examples, a Mann-Whitney test is a nonparametric counterpart of the independent-samples *t* test. A Wilcoxon Matched-Pairs Signed-Ranks test is a counterpart to the paired *t* test. A Spearman correlation coefficient (r_s) corresponds to a Pearson *r*. Descriptions of these and other nonparametric tests can be found in encyclopedia articles in the *Encyclopedia of Statistics in Behavioral Science* and in chapters of statistics textbooks such as Spatz (2008), Howell (2004), Aron, Aron, and Coups (2006), or Kirk (1999). SPSS provides probability figures for many nonparametric tests.

CONFIDENCE INTERVALS ABOUT A MEAN DIFFERENCE

A **confidence interval** (CI) consists of a lower limit and an upper limit. The two limits define an interval. With a specified degree of confidence, this interval captures a population parameter. Chapter 5 included information on the confidence interval about a population mean. In the case of an experiment with two samples, the parameter of interest is the *difference* in two population means. Using two sample means, you can calculate a CI about the mean difference in the two populations. The degree of confidence that researchers choose is most often 95%, but 99% and other values are used as well.

NHST techniques may give you assurance about the *ordinal position* of two population means. If H_0 is rejected with $\alpha = .05$, you can be 95% confident that the population mean of the sample with the larger mean is greater than the population mean of the sample with the smaller mean. A confidence interval uses the same sampling distribution as a *t* test but produces more information than just the ordinal position of the two population means. A CI gives you information about how much bigger the larger mean is than the smaller mean.

A CI also provides information that allows you to reject or retain the null hypothesis. The typical null hypothesis of an NHST *t* test is that the difference between population means is zero. A 95% CI about the

confidence interval (CI) Range of scores that is expected with a specified degree of confidence to capture a parameter.

difference in sample means allows you to test H_0 with $\alpha = .05$. Here is the rule: If zero is not in the confidence interval, reject H_0. If zero is in the interval, retain H_0.

The formulas for the lower and upper limits of a confidence interval are:

$$LL = (M_1 - M_2) - t_c \text{ (standard error of a difference)}$$

$$UL = (M_1 - M_2) + t_c \text{ (standard error of a difference)}$$

Where: LL and UL are the lower and upper limits of the confidence interval

$M_1 - M_2$ is the difference in two sample means

t_c is a t value for $c\%$ confidence from Table C.2

Standard error of a difference is a standard error whose value depends on whether the samples are independent or paired

Before discussing the calculation of CIs, let's look at their interpretation. Suppose that the mean of Sample 1 (M_1) is 45 and the mean of Sample 2 (M_2) is 42. The difference in sample means is 3. A CI about this sample difference answers the question, What is the difference in the two populations means? A good guess is 3, but nobody would be surprised if the value were a little less than 3 or a little greater than 3 because 3 is calculated from sample data, which are known to be variable.

Suppose a 95% CI about the difference resulted in a lower limit of 2 and an upper limit of 4. In this case, you can be 95% confident that the difference in treatments produces a difference in scores of 2 to 4 points. Now suppose that the CI is -2 to 8. You are still 95% confident that the difference between the two population means is in the interval, but the effect of the treatments is less certain than when the interval was 2 to 4. A CI of -2 to 8 means that the difference in treatments reduces scores by as much as 2 or increases them as much as 8. In the first case the effect of the difference increases scores; in the second case the effect of the difference is not clear from the sample data. As with NHST t tests, we turn to statistical software to calculate CI values for independent-samples and paired-samples experiments.

Independent-Samples Confidence Interval

In the social loafing experiment data, the mean for those who participated with a loafer was 4.57; for those whose group included a hard worker, the mean was 5.67. The difference is 1.10 uses. Note in the lower panel of Table 6.12 that SPSS calculated a 95% confidence interval about this difference. The 95% CI is -0.39 to 2.58. Thus, you can be 95% confident that the true difference between population means is between -0.39 and 2.58 uses. Because zero is in the 95% CI, retain H_0. This is the same conclusion the independent t-test produced.

Paired-Samples Confidence Interval

Table 6.14 shows the SPSS output for the MOS scores of males and females. The lower panel includes a 95% confidence interval about the difference in the two sample means. The difference between the sample means for males and females in Table 6.13 is -0.50. The 95% CI about the difference of -0.50 has lower and upper limits of -2.13 and 1.13. Thus, we can be 95% confident that the true difference between the population means is between -2.13 and 1.13 points on the MOS. Because zero is in this interval, the null hypothesis cannot be rejected for this textbook example, but recall that the conclusion based on many larger samples was that males rate fairness significantly more important than females.

A STUDENT'S GUIDE TO ANALYZING DATA

After you finish gathering data for your experiment, the next task is to analyze it. For most researchers, this is the most exciting part of the project. Here is our suggested order for analyzing the data.

- Explore the data using frequency distributions and graphs.
- Calculate descriptive statistics.
- Calculate an effect size index.
- Analyze the data with appropriate NHST techniques.
- At every step analyze the experiment for uncontrolled extraneous variables.

For paired- and independent-samples t-test experiments, **Table 6.15** gives a more detailed explanation of these steps. The order we show is just our suggestion; we prefer to include an effect size index as a part of the descriptive statistics approach to understanding the data.

POWER

power The probability of correctly rejecting a false null hypothesis

Statistical **power** is about rejecting a false null hypothesis. Of course, rejecting H_0 is usually the goal of researchers, so power is a topic of importance. If the populations are actually different (the null hypothesis is false), the sample data may lead the researcher to reject H_0 (a correct decision) or retain H_0 (a Type II error, the probability of which is β). Thus, the probability of a correct decision is $1 - \beta$. Mathematically, power is defined as $1 - \beta$. This means that the greater the power of a test, the higher the probability that it will detect that H_0 is false. To put this in terms of t-test values, if power is high the chance of a large t-test value is high; if power is low, you shouldn't be surprised at a small t-test value.

TABLE 6.15	Suggested Guide for Analyzing Data From a Paired- or Independent-Samples t-Test Experiment

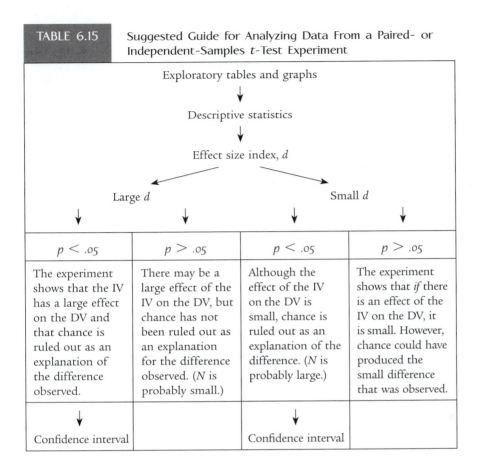

How much power should a statistical test have? The generally accepted rule-of-thumb probability is that .80 is adequate power. However, unlike α, which is set by the researcher, power is the result of a combination of factors. Unfortunately, researchers can control only some of the factors. Four of the factors that control the power of NHST are:

1. *Amount of difference between the populations.* The greater the difference between the populations the samples come from, the greater the power of the statistical test to detect the difference. This factor is sometimes referred to as the degree of falseness of H_0. In the context of an experiment, the greater the effect of the treatment on the experimental group population, the easier it is to detect that the treatment has an effect. Of course, you never actually know how different the population means are. After the experiment, however, you do have sample data and sample means. The difference between M_1 and M_2 is an estimate of the difference between the two population means.

To use this factor to your advantage in your research, choose levels of the IV that are far apart. For example, an experiment that compares strenuous exercisers with couch potatoes will probably be more powerful than one that compares moderate exercisers to occasional exercisers. Likewise, an experiment that compares dose levels of high and placebo will be more powerful than one that compares dose levels of medium and low.

2. *Sample size.* The larger the sample, the greater the power of the test. To see how increasing N leads to larger values of t and thus to a better chance of rejecting H_0, look again at the introduction to the independent-samples t test on page 181. The denominator, the standard error of a difference, consists of two $(SE_M)^2$ and

$$SE_M = \frac{SD}{\sqrt{N}}$$

Thus, as N increases, SE_M decreases. Smaller values of SE_M produce larger t values and the larger the t value, the more likely you are to reject H_0. You can use this factor to your advantage by increasing sample sizes.

3. *Sample variability.* Anything that reduces the variability in the data increases power. Look at the formula for the standard error of the mean above. Reducing the size of SD leads to a smaller SE_M and, thus, to larger t values. Researchers reduce the variability in their data a number of ways, including using exactly the same procedure with all participants, recruiting homogeneous participants, and using reliable tests. A sometimes overlooked method of reducing sample variability is to ensure that all scores are recorded correctly.

4. *Alpha.* The larger the value of α, the greater the power of the test. This is a relationship that is fairly easy to understand. Look at Figure 6.3. If the rejection region is increased from .01 to .05, the t values between 3.17 and 2.23 (and between -3.17 and -2.23) will all lead to rejection of the null hypothesis. Thus, increasing α from .01 to .05 increases the chance of rejecting H_0. Because an α of .05 is usually the largest level of significance that others will accept, researchers should not increase α beyond .05 to increase the power of their tests.

The relationships among the five factors—power, degree of falseness of H_0, N, SD, and α are such that once four factors are set, the fifth is determined. A **power analysis** consists of setting four values and solving for the fifth. The most common uses of a power analysis are to solve for sample size before the experiment is conducted and to solve for power after an experiment has produced differences that are not significant.

Cohen's (1992) five-page primer discusses power and provides a table of sample sizes required for eight different NHST techniques. Explanations of

power analysis
A statistical analysis that solves for one of the factors involved in rejecting a false null hypothesis with an NHST technique.

how to calculate power can be found in Spatz (2005, chapter 16 on the CD), Howell (2004, chapter 15), and Aron, Aron and Coups (2006, chapter 6). For a short textbook on statistical power analysis, see Murphy and Myors (2004).

META-ANALYSIS

At various places in this text, we emphasized the importance of replication in the scientific enterprise. Of course, when several studies all produce the same conclusion, people's concerns for Type I errors are eliminated and they are persuaded that the conclusion is reliable. However, it is not unusual for several studies to produce mixed results. Some reject H_0 and some retain H_0. In some studies, the experimental group scores higher than the control group and in other studies the reverse occurs. Mixed results produce confusion. **Meta-analysis** is a statistical technique that often creates a consensus and thus reduces or eliminates confusion.

Meta-analysis combines the results of many studies that all have the same IV and the same or similar DVs. The result is an average effect size index ($\bar{d}$) and a confidence interval about ($\bar{d}$). Interpretations of ($\bar{d}$) and its confidence interval follow the same reasoning as that used for the d and CI of a single study. The following meta-analysis used techniques that are explained in Lipsey and Wilson (2001).

To illustrate meta-analysis, we turn to data collected to compare reaction times. **Table 6.16** shows the results of five paired-samples experiments that measured the reaction time in seconds to an auditory stimulus (second column) and to a visual stimulus (third column). The rest of the table shows sample sizes, t-test values, p values, and effect size indexes for the five studies. As you can see from the p column, the null hypothesis should be rejected for two of the studies and retained for three. The results of the NHST tests leave us uncertain as to what to conclude.

TABLE 6.16	Results From Five Studies That Compared Reaction Times in Seconds to Auditory and Visual Stimuli					
	Paired-Samples Design					
Experiment	*Auditory* M	*Visual* M	N	*t test*	p	d
1	0.162	0.163	14	0.29	.778	0.07
2	0.135	0.161	6	2.87	.035	1.17
3	0.151	0.170	10	2.41	.039	0.76
4	0.166	0.175	14	1.08	.298	0.29
5	0.160	0.173	12	1.67	.123	0.48
M	0.155	0.168				

meta-analysis A quantitative technique that summarizes the results of many studies of a single topic.

A meta-analysis of the data in Table 6.16 produced a $\bar{d}$ value of 0.20 with a 95% confidence interval of 0.08 to 0.31. Because zero is not in the interval, H_0 can be rejected at the .05 level. Based on the meta-analysis, the confusion created by the five studies that had conflicting results is resolved.

Based on a meta-analysis of five studies, reaction time to an auditory stimulus ($M = 0.155$ second) is significantly faster than the reaction time to a visual stimulus ($M = 0.168$ second), $p < .05$. The effect size index for this difference is small (($\bar{d}$) = 0.20).

This chapter and the previous one are introductions to the most commonly used descriptive and inferential statistics. What we have emphasized, especially in this chapter, is the logic underlying NHST. Understanding this logic is necessary if you are to interpret tests correctly. Two other NHST techniques (one-way ANOVA and factorial ANOVA) are covered in chapter 9. Additional tests are explained in textbooks that focus entirely on statistics.

Chapter Review

1. *NHST* stands for _____.

2. In logic, the tactic of establishing two alternatives and then proving that one of them cannot be true, leaving the other alternative as proved, is called _____.

3. The p in "$p < .05$" is the probability of what?

4. For any NHST technique, the probability figure comes from a(n)

   _____.

5. Match the concept with the definition.

   1. Type I error
   2. Type II error
   3. H_0 (null hypothesis)
   4. H_1 (alternative hypothesis)
   5. researcher's hypothesis
   6. d
   7. φ

   a. the predicted or expected outcome of an experiment

   b. effect size index for a 2 × 2 contingency table

   c. retaining a false null hypothesis

   d. of the populations sampled, there is no difference in the means

   e. rejecting a true null hypothesis

   f. effect size index for the difference between two sample means

   g. of the populations sampled, there is a difference in the means

6. When the correlation coefficients in published research were divided into thirds, the lowest third was less than _____ and the highest third was greater than _____.

7. Match the kind of NHST technique to the *df* formula.
   1. independent-samples *t* test   a. $df = N - 1$
   2. paired-samples *t* test   b. $df = N - 2$
   3. Pearson *r*

8. Match the definition to the conventional number
   1. small effect size for a 2 × 2 contingency table   a. 0.10
   2. medium effect size for an independent-samples design   b. 0.20
       c. 0.50
   3. large effect size for a paired-samples design   d. 0.80
   4. large effect size for a 2 × 2 contingency table
   5. small effect size for a paired-samples design

9. NHST techniques that assume population characteristics such as normally distributed and equal variances are called _____ tests and those that do not make such assumptions are called _____ tests.

10. The mathematical definition of power is _____; a verbal definition is _____.

11. The amount of power that is conventionally considered adequate is _____.

12. The statistical technique that combines the results of several studies of one topic into an overall conclusion is called _____.

Thinking Critically About Research _____

1. If $p \leq \alpha$, _____ H_0. If $p > \alpha$, _____ H_0. (reject/retain)

2. Use Tables C.3 and C.4 in appendix C to determine if the following statistics are statistically significant. Use $\alpha = .05$.
   Pearson correlation coefficients
       a. $r = .30$ 50 pairs of scores
       b. $r = .30$ 40 pairs of scores
       c. $r = .46$ 17 pairs of scores

2 × 2 chi-square contingency tables

    d. $\chi^2 = 1.96$

    e. $\chi^2 = 3.85$

3. The two numbers are the limits of 95% confidence intervals. With $\alpha = .05$, write *reject* or *retain* beside each. In addition, write *largest* beside the CI that shows the largest effect of the IV on the DV.

   a. 2 to 6

   b. −2 to 1

   c. 5 to 6

4. Convert each description that follows into a paragraph interpretation of the results.

   a. Undergraduate volunteers provided their GPAs from which the researcher created 10 pairs with similar GPAs. One member of each pair was randomly assigned to the music group, leaving the other member in the quiet group. The music group worked eight difficult logic problems with music in the background. The quiet group worked the same problems under quiet conditions. Each answer was scored on a scale of 0 to 7. The music group mean was 24; the quiet group mean was 28. A paired-samples t test produced a $t(9) = 1.38, p = .20$.

   b. Bryan observed elementary school children at recess for 20 days, recording for each one the number of aggressive acts. He also had access to each family's report of the average number of hours of television the child watched each week. The correlation coefficient was .40; $p < .05$.

   c. Catherine had 100 participants read a story that involved several characters, including Rosemary, whose infidelity was for a noble cause. Afterward, participants named the character they considered the most noble. Sixty percent of the women participants named Rosemary; forty percent of the men named Rosemary. A chi square test showed that $\chi^2(1) = 4.00; p < .05$.

5. List four factors that affect power and explain how power changes as each factor changes.

Answers to Chapter Review

1. null hypothesis statistical testing (or tests)

2. negative inference or *modus tollens*

3. p is the probability of the data that were observed, if it is true that the null hypothesis is correct

4. sampling distribution

5. 1. e; 2. c; 3. d; 4. g; 5. a; 6. f; 7. b

6. .20; .30

7. 1. b; 2. a; 3. b

8. 1. a; 2. c; 3. d; 4. c; 5. b

9. parametric; nonparametric

10. $1 - \beta$; power is the probability of rejecting a false null hypothesis (or similar wording).

11. .80

12. meta-analysis

Answers to Thinking Critically About Research _____

1. reject; retain

2. a. $r = .30$; $df = 48$; significant

   b. $r = .30$; $df = 38$; not significant

   c. $r = .46$; $df = 15$; not significant

   d. $\chi^2 = 1.96$; $df = 1$; not significant

   e. $\chi^2 = 3.85$; $df = 1$; significant

3. a. 2 to 6, reject; b. -2 to 1, retain; c. 5 to 6, reject; largest

4. There are several ways to write a good answer. Example answers follow.

   a. Ten pairs of participants, matched for grade point average, worked eight logic problems while either listening to music or experiencing a quiet condition. The mean score in the quiet condition (28) was higher than the mean score in the music condition (24), but this difference was not statistically significant, $t(9) = 1.38$, $p = .20$.

   b. Based on data from elementary school children, there is a positive correlation of .40 between average hours of television watched and aggressive acts on the playground. This coefficient is significantly greater than zero. Thus, greater time with television is associated with larger numbers of aggressive acts.

   c. Of the 100 participants who read a story about a character who was unfaithful for a noble cause, a significantly greater percentage of the women (60%) named the character as the most noble, compared to 40 percent of the men; $\chi^2(1) = 4.00$; $p < .05$.

5. As the difference increases, power increases sample size; as sample size increases, power increases sample variability; as sample variability increases, power decreases alpha (α); as α decreases (such as .05 to .01), power decreases

Know for Sure

7

Design I: Between-Subjects Designs

OVERVIEW

This chapter explains the logic of comparing groups or conditions to arrive at a cause-and-effect conclusion. Both this chapter and the next (chapter 8) focus on two-group experiments. In this chapter two between-subjects designs, the quasi-experimental design and the random assignment design, are discussed. Problems that these designs have for establishing cause-and-effect conclusions are noted. Extraneous variables are explained and three of them are covered in detail. The capability of the two designs to remove the effects of each of the three extraneous variables is discussed.

OBJECTIVES

After studying this chapter and working through the exercises, you should be able to:

1. Describe the model experiment using the terms *independent variable, dependent variable,* and *extraneous variables*
2. Distinguish between the quasi-experimental design and the random assignment design and their capability of establishing cause-and-effect conclusions
3. Write an interpretation of an experiment
4. Randomly assign participants to groups
5. Identify four potential problems with the random assignment design
6. Describe the situation in which differential attrition might occur
7. Define *diffusion of treatment*
8. Describe methods that reduce the effect of differential attrition and diffusion of treatment
9. Discuss the issue of how to optimally separate the levels of the independent variable
10. Distinguish between between-subjects designs and within-subjects designs

We begin with an example from a state in the United States that shall remain unnamed. In 2005, 5 children died who were in legal custody of this state. These children had been removed from their homes by court order and placed in foster homes or in institutions that care for children. Here is a table showing this fact:

Children who died
5

What is your reaction to this fact? Does 5 seem "normal"? If 5 is normal, then there is nothing more to do. Does 5 seem like a lot? If so, perhaps an investigation is in order. Are you uncertain whether 5 is normal or a lot? If uncertain, perhaps follow-up information would help you reach a conclusion. Follow-up information usually means either confirming the fact or placing the fact into a larger context. For this exercise, please accept the number as a fact; we proceed to place the fact in a larger context.

Would it help you evaluate the fact if you knew the total number of children who were wards of the state in 2005? Of course! So, let's add another fact to the collection. The state was directly responsible for 500 children in 2005. Both facts are shown in **Table 7.1.**

With this additional information, we can calculate a percentage. Five out of 500 is 1.0% "One percent died" is more informative than "Five died." What is your reaction now? Is 1.0% "not much, let's forget it" or is it "lots, better investigate"? Or, do you need more information? If you want more information, what would be helpful?

What other numerical information would be helpful?

Two other numbers that help evaluate the 1.0% death rate are the number of children who were *not* wards of the state and the number of those children who died. Based on demographic data for 2005, there were 500,000 children in the state, ages 1 to 18. How many of those children

TABLE 7.1	Wards of the State Who Died and Didn't Die
	Wards of the state
Children who died	Children who didn't die
5	495

TABLE 7.2	Survival and Nonsurvival of Children in the State and Children Who Were Wards of the State	
	Children who died	*Children who didn't die*
Wards of the state	5	495
Other children in the state	400	499,600

died? Using state mortality figures, we calculated that 400 of them died. **Table 7.2** shows this additional information.

As we mentioned in chapter 5, percentages are more informative than raw numbers, so we converted the numbers to percentages. Four hundred out of 500,000 is 0.8% (eight tenths of 1%). Five out of 495 is 1.0%. **Table 7.3** shows the information in Table 7.2 as percentages. Table 7.3 focuses attention on the 1.0% and the 0.8%.

What is your reaction now to our starting fact: Five children whom the state was taking care of died?

We don't have a "correct answer" for you at this point, but keep your answer handy. We'll come back to this problem. Now, let's back away from specifics and examine the decision-making process we engaged in.

A CONCLUSION REQUIRES A COMPARISON

Any conclusion based on data requires a comparison. If your conclusion to "5 died" was "that's about normal," or if you concluded "that's too many," then at some point in your thinking, you made a comparison. Five was compared to some other number. That comparison might have been based on your knowledge about death rates in children, your belief in the importance of every human being, your knowledge or prejudices about how states handle foster children, or something else. Uncertainty about the fact that 5 died indicates a need for something more to compare 5 to.

Note the progression of comparisons in our example. These steps are often found when empirically minded thinkers puzzle out a conclusion.

TABLE 7.3	Death Percentages of Children Who Were and Were Not Wards of the State	
	N	*Percentage who died*
Wards of the state	500	1.0%
Other children in the state	500,000	0.8

The beginning point was a lone number (5). A comparison number was added (495) that placed the lone number on a more familiar scale (percentage). Finally, additional data from another source provided a comparison percentage. To put the progression another way, the example started with "5 died," which is the incidence of death. After comparisons were made, you had the prevalence of death. Knowing the incidence of a phenomenon is much more meaningful if you also know its prevalence.

You may still have concerns about a comparison based on the two percentages of 1.0% and 0.8%. In particular, you might complain that the comparison is not entirely valid. You might point out that children who are taken from their family are different and perhaps less healthy than children in general. You might note that the number of deaths of children in the general population is probably a less reliable number than the number of deaths among wards of the state. Perhaps you have other questions as well. The value of all these concerns is that they can help you identify a better comparison group and, thus, a more valid comparison number. One of the major characteristics of valid empirical research is excellent comparison numbers. Getting persuasive comparison numbers usually means planning for them as part of the basic design of your experiment.

As you can tell from the chapter titles on the Contents page, design is an important topic in this book. Probably the most important thing about a research design is that it dictates which groups will be compared to each other. Conclusions, as we have stressed, depend on what is being compared. As for the best way to create a comparison, many psychologists say that the ideal is the *model experiment*.

A MODEL EXPERIMENT

Here is a description of a simple, model experiment. This experiment has two conditions that are compared to each other.

> Set up two conditions that are *exactly alike* except that they *differ in one way*. Gather *data* in each condition. Apply appropriate statistical techniques to the data. Tell the story of the experiment; that is, explain the design, how the data were gathered and analyzed, and interpret of the results.

Match the italicized words and phrases in the description of a model experiment with the terms *independent variable, dependent variable,* and *extraneous variable.* After you make these associations, look at our answers in **Table 7.4.**

The model experiment is a goal to strive for. Unfortunately, it is a difficult goal to achieve in practice. However, if you develop an understanding of research methods, you will be able to design experiments that come closer to the model. In addition, you will be able to detect specific

| TABLE 7.4 | Matching Model Experiment Phrases to the Elements of an Experiment |

Phrases in the description of a model experiment	Elements of an experiment
exactly alike	Extraneous variables
differ in one way	Independent variable
data	Dependent variable

ways in which the experiments of others fall short of the model. The word *experiment* is used by some to be synonymous with the model experiment described here. However, we use *experiment* more broadly to mean comparisons between conditions, even if the comparisons do not meet the stringent requirements of the model experiment.

AN ACTUAL EXPERIMENT

Let's move from the model experiment to an actual one, complete with details. This experiment is to be conducted by two students in a research methods class. Your job as a fellow student is to understand their experiment and help them write the conclusion. In particular, you should be alert for any uncontrolled extraneous variables. We drop in on this experiment at the design stage, after the two students have sought help from others and have chosen an idea to investigate.

In this experiment, the independent variable is exercise and the dependent variable is mood. The researchers' hypothesis is that people's exercise level has an effect on their mood. In particular, they believe that those who exercise a lot experience better moods. In their discussions, the researchers tentatively decided that the independent variable of exercise should have two levels: More Active and Less Active.

To measure exercise level, they created their own questionnaire. The questionnaire listed 20 activities including walking; running; swimming; dancing; working out in the gym; basketball; volleyball; tennis; gardening; and 11 others. The instructions to the participants were "Several kinds of exercises are listed. Beside each one that you engaged in during the past 7 days, place a number that indicates the number of 20-minute periods that you engaged in this exercise." A participant's score was simply the sum of the numbers.

The researchers measured mood with the Profile of Mood States (POMS), a published test that they discovered during their literature review. The POMS (McNair, Lorr, & Droppleman, 1992) consists of a list of 65 adjectives such as *fatigued, cheerful, energetic,* and *exhausted.* Participants rate themselves on a 5-point scale, judging the degree to which the adjective describes their mood during the previous week. Although the POMS can be scored for five different moods, the researchers scored only the subscale that measures feelings of tiredness because they believed that this particular mood would be affected by a person's exercise level. On this subscale, high scores indicate a tired mood; low scores indicate a vigorous mood.

With materials in place, the researchers sought and received permission to use a classroom for their project. The participants in their experiment were their friends and acquaintances who agreed to come to the room at 4:00 p.m. for 10 to 15 minutes. On different afternoons, they tested different numbers of participants, debriefing each group afterward. By the end of the week, they had data from 25 participants. The participants' scores, arranged in the order of testing, are shown in the left panel of **Table 7.5**.

TABLE 7.5	Raw Data for 25 Participants in the Exercise–Tiredness Experiment		
Unsorted		Sorted by exercise	
Exercise	Tiredness	Exercise	Tiredness
0	42	10	45
3	60	7	50
1	53	6	58
3	53	6	49
4	55	6	38
0	52	5	42
10	45	5	36
0	58	5	43
1	54	4	55
1	46	4	47
4	47	4	34
6	58	4	48
1	70	3	60
7	50	3	53
2	47	2	47
6	49	2	58
6	38	1	53
0	63	1	54
5	42	1	46
4	34	1	70
5	36	0	42
2	58	0	52
0	49	0	58
5	43	0	63
4	48	0	49

Note: The left panel shows scores in the order they were compiled. In the right panel, scores are sorted by exercise.

TABLE 7.6	Stem-and-Leaf Display of the Tiredness Scores of the Less Active Group and the More Active Group	
More active N = 12	Tiredness scores	Less active N = 13
	70–74	0
	65–69	
	60–64	0, 3
5, 8	55–59	8, 8
0	50–54	3, 3, 4, 2
8, 7, 9, 5	45–49	7, 6, 9
3, 2	40–44	2
6, 8	35–39	
4	30–34	

The researchers' next step was to divide the participants into a More Active group and a Less Active group using the exercise scores. The 25 exercise scores, sorted from high to low, are shown in the right panel of Table 7.5. The 12 participants with scores of 4 or greater became the More Active group and the 13 with scores of 3 or less became the Less Active group.

Having established the independent variable and its two levels, the researchers turned to the dependent variable. To get a quick, overall view of the data, they compiled a stem-and-leaf display. Their handwritten version is shown in **Table 7.6.**

To construct their stem-and-leaf display, the researchers noted that the lowest score was 34 and the highest, 70. They grouped the scores into intervals 5 scores wide, (30–34, 35–39 . . . 70–74), which produced 9 intervals. (Seven to 15 intervals often produce useful stem-and-leaf displays.) With the 9 intervals written in the middle of the page (the *stem*), the digit value of each score was entered under its IV level and beside its interval. The digits that represent individual score are the *leaves*.

In Table 7.6 you can see that the two sets of scores overlap a great deal, although an estimated mean for the More Active group appears to be smaller than the mean of the Less Active group. Recall that a smaller mean indicates less tired. The researchers' next step was to calculate additional descriptive statistics. Means, standard deviations, and an effect size index are shown in **Table 7.7.**

Using the information in Table 7.7, write a tentative conclusion about the exercise–tiredness study.

STOP & Think

TABLE 7.7	Descriptive statistics for the tiredness scores of the two groups in Table 7.6

	Exercise Level	
	More active	Less active
M	45.42	54.23
SD	7.29	7.60
d		1.18

Based on the descriptive statistics in Table 7.7, the two students' tentative conclusion was: Exercise has a large effect on tiredness. Those who exercise more have lower scores on the POMS scale, which measures the mood of tiredness. The researchers' next step was to apply inferential statistics to the difference between the means of the two groups (8.81 points). Their choice of statistics was a 95% confidence interval about the mean difference. The lower limit of the 95% confidence interval about the difference in sample means is 2.64 points; the upper limit is 14.99 points.

The students' statistical conclusion was that they were 95% confident that the interval of 2.64 to 14.99 points on the tiredness scale contains the true difference between the More Active exercisers and the Less Active exercisers. Thus, they were 95% confident that the more active participants do not show as much tiredness on the POMS scale as do the less active participants. This difference, as measured by d, is quite large. The researchers also noted that because zero was not within the 95% confidence interval, they could reject at the .05 level of confidence, the null hypothesis that the two populations of more active and less active participants have identical means. Here is a paragraph summary of their experiment (except for the last sentence, for which they come to you for advice).

> The 25 friends and acquaintances of the researchers completed two surveys. On one survey they reported the number of 20-minute exercise periods they experienced in the past 7 days (exercise level). The other survey, the Profile of Mood Scales, yielded a score for the mood of tiredness. The tiredness scores of the more active participants ($M = 45.42$, $SD = 7.29$, $N = 12$) was significantly less than the tiredness scores of the less active participants ($M = 54.23$, $SD = 7.60$, $N = 12$). The effect size index ($d = 1.18$) indicates that this difference of 8.81 points is large. The 95% confidence interval about the mean difference of 8.81 points was 2.64 to 14.99 points. (Concluding sentence follows.)

Here are three possible concluding sentences. There is an important characteristic of the experimental design that makes one of the three sentences better than the others. The three sentences are:

i. Thus, we are 95 percent confident that exercise reduces tiredness

ii. Thus, we are 95 percent confident that if you exercise you will be less tired

iii. Thus, we are 95 percent confident that exercise and being less tired go together

This is a difficult question, but we ask it anyway: Which of the three sentences is better than the others?

The characteristic that distinguishes sentence *iii* (the most appropriate sentence) from the others is that the first two either state or imply that the experiment establishes a cause-and-effect relationship between exercise and tiredness. Although there *may* be such a relationship, the design of the experiment is not one that can establish a cause-and-effect relationship because it is a quasi-experimental design, the topic of our next section. As we mentioned earlier, the conclusion you draw depends on the design of the study as well as the data.

THE QUASI-EXPERIMENTAL DESIGN[1]

The defining characteristic of a **quasi-experimental design** is that participants are not randomly assigned to the different levels of the independent variable. Participants are selected for a level of the IV by some method that doesn't involve a formal, randomized process.

The simplest version of a quasi-experimental design has one independent variable with two levels and one dependent variable. More complex versions might have three or more levels of one independent variable, more than one independent variable, or more than one dependent variable. We'll discuss more complex versions in later chapters, but we concentrate on the simplest version in this chapter.

In the exercise–tiredness experiment, participants were assigned to the More Active or Less Active groups on the basis of their reported exercise during the previous week. The researchers did not assign exercise

---

[1]Unfortunately, there is no universal agreement on the names that are assigned to various designs. The concept that is generally referred to as *quasi-experimental* is also referred to with terms such as *correlational, ex-post facto, non-equivalent control group, static groups,* and *nonrandomized groups.*

quasi-experimental design Experimental design in which participants are assigned to levels of the independent variable according to a known charactersistic.

TABLE 7.8	Sampling of Independent Variables Usually Investigated With a Quasi-Experimental Design

Independent variable	Levels (conditions)
Gender	Male and female
Socioeconomic status	Lower, middle, and upper class
Culture	Chinese, Korean, Japanese
Age	10–12 years, 14–16 years, 18–20 years
Traumatic experience	Raped, automobile accident, neither
Personality	Highly hostile, moderately hostile, not hostile
Frontal lobe damage	Yes, no
College major	Natural science, humanities, other

levels, they simply assigned labels to the exercise levels that the participants reported.

In many research situations, experimenters *cannot* randomly assign participants to groups because they arrive at the experiment already in the condition that is of interest to the researcher. **Table 7.8** lists a sampling of independent variables and their levels (conditions). A quasi-experimental design is appropriate for these experiments and, as you can see, the list includes a number of interesting independent variables.

A quasi-experimental design can be described verbally as we did above; it can also be presented graphically. A two-treatment example is shown in **Table 7.9**. Table 7.9 indicates how participants are assigned (nonrandomly, or NR), the number of levels of the IV (two), and that the dependent variable measures are recorded after the treatments are applied (see time scale). By using other subscripts in place of the 1 and 2, and by substituting the name of the actual dependent variable, this graphic can be customized to illustrate a particular experiment. Such a graphic can be quite helpful

TABLE 7.9	Notation for the Quasi-Experimental Design for Two Treatments

Method of assignment	Independent variable	Dependent variable
NR	T_1	O
NR	T_2	O
Time ————————————————————⟶		

Where: NR = assignment to treatments is nonrandom

T_1 and T_2 = two treatment levels of the independent variable

O = observations that constitute the dependent variable

TABLE 7.10	Design of the Exercise–Tiredness Experiment	
Nonrandom assignment	*IV*	*DV*
Exercise score is 3 or less	Less active	POMS tiredness score
Exercise score is 4 or more	More active	POMS tiredness score
Time ⟶		

in explaining an experiment to others. **Table 7.10** shows one version of a table that illustrates the design of the exercise–tiredness experiment.

The quasi-experimental design is used in a variety of disciplines, but it has a limitation when it comes time to interpret the results. In particular, any interpretation that the change in the independent variable caused the change in the dependent variable is not warranted unless additional data or additional logic are included. The next two sections explain why.

EXTRANEOUS VARIABLES

You will recall from chapter 2 that extraneous variables that are not eliminated or controlled become confounded with the IV. If confounded, an extraneous variable prevents you from attributing changes in the DV to the IV because the changes could have been caused by the confounded variable. Identifying extraneous variables is one of the things that experienced researchers do best.

Let's examine the exercise–tiredness experiment, looking for examples of extraneous variables. Were there differences between the two groups of participants besides their exercise level? This may seem like an unfair question, but you have enough experience to reason out an answer. The trick to identifying additional differences is to think of a variable that you know is related to exercise. Is this variable related to tiredness as well? Could this variable and not exercise be causing the difference in tiredness?

Identify one variable that changes along with changes in levels of exercise. This variable must be one that affects tiredness.

STOP & Think

Several variables might be confounded (they co-vary) with exercise. One variable is sleep. If people who exercise also sleep more or sleep better, then the differences in tiredness may be the result of sleep differences and not exercise differences. Is there any evidence that sleep co-varies with exercise? Yes, there is (see Vitiello, Prinz, & Schwartz, 1994). Another variable that might be confounded with exercise is nutrition. If people who are conscientious about exercise are also conscientious about nutrition, then the differences in tiredness may be due to nutrition. Is there evidence?

Yes, (see Ford-Martin, 2006). A third variable is weight. If people who are overweight score higher on the tiredness measure and they do not exercise very much, then weight may be causing both tiredness and lack of exercise.

Note that this line of reasoning has us focusing on the lifestyle of the participants, not just on the independent variable identified in the experiment. Indeed, participants who exercise three or more times a week probably engage in other practices that promote good health. Any of these practices singly or in combination might be responsible for the observed reduction in tiredness. Finally, another reason to reject the conclusion that exercise reduces tiredness is that the relationship may be in the other direction. Rather than exercise reducing tiredness, it may be that tiredness reduces exercise. That is, participants who are tired to start with may become less active.

To summarize, extraneous variables are variables that co-vary with the independent variable. This means that when the IV changes, there is a corresponding change in the extraneous variable. The presence of an extraneous variable means that changes observed in the dependent variable could be due to the IV *or* to the extraneous variable *or* to a combination of the two. Thus, one of the consequences of using a quasi-experimental design is that it does not allow you to draw cause-and-effect conclusions between the IV and the DV. Let's move now from extraneous variables in general to a description of the first of eight particular extraneous variables that will be covered in this chapter and the next.

THE EXTRANEOUS VARIABLE OF SELECTION

One characteristic of the quasi-experimental design is that the extraneous variable of **selection** is never controlled. When this variable is operating, participants are assigned or selected for a treatment in such a fashion that there are differences in the groups other than the IV. The problem with selection is easy to understand. If the two groups could be different before the treatment, then any difference *after* treatments may not be due to the treatment. Selection (or *selection bias,* as it is sometimes called) is probably the most frequently encountered extraneous variable in actual research.

Psychologists have recognized the problems of interpretation that accompany the extraneous variable of selection for a long time. There is no way to eliminate the extraneous variable of selection after the data are gathered, but there are ways to reduce the problem. Statistical techniques such as analysis of covariance can remove the effect of confounded variables such as sleep, nutrition, and weight. Of course, you must have data on a variable to incorporate it into a statistical analysis.

selection An extraneous variable that occurs when participants for the different levels of the independent variable are not equivalent even before the treatment is administered

A second approach to the selection problem involves a literature search. If a literature search reveals that previous studies on similar topics found the same relationship you did, these studies strengthen the case for a cause-and-effect relationship. This is especially true if some of the other studies used a design in which selection was controlled.

The third approach to the selection problem is to gather more data on the topic. Of course, an exact **replication** won't help; the complaint that selection is uncontrolled will still be valid. However, a replication that reduces the plausibility of an extraneous variable such as sleep or nutrition increases your confidence that it was the IV that caused a change in the DV. For example, the exercise–tiredness researchers might gather additional data from participants whose exercise was prescribed by a doctor or physical therapist. Exercise that is prescribed is much less likely to correspond to changes in sleep or nutrition. Although the sleep and nutrition explanations seem reasonable if the participants are grouped according to what may be different lifestyles, they seem less likely explanations if participants are grouped on the basis of a doctor's or therapist's prescription.

Of course, a prescribed exercise experiment is also a quasi-experimental design. Thus, selection remains an uncontrolled extraneous variable. However, a nutrition difference between the two samples is a less plausible explanation for tiredness. Taken together, the two studies we've described both support a conclusion that exercise reduces tiredness. All three of these approaches to the selection problem allow you to strengthen an assertion that there is a cause-and-effect connection between the IV and DV. As we said earlier, scientific facts rest upon an accumulation of evidence and not on one study.

The most efficient way to eliminate selection as an uncontrolled extraneous variable is to gather data using a different design, the random assignment design. The random assignment design is considered the best design by knowledgeable researchers in most every field and they employ it whenever it is practical. The reason for its widespread popularity is that this design is better than any other design at balancing out not only selection, but other extraneous variables as well.

THE RANDOM ASSIGNMENT DESIGN

As the name implies, participants are assigned to treatments randomly in a **random assignment design.** In a research context, *random* is a technical word that refers to the process of assignment, which we explain below. **Random assignment** does not eliminate the many differences among participants; instead it balances them out so that the group means for many characteristics are approximately equal. Thus, by using random assignment and large enough groups, you are assured that individual

replication Repeating an experiment with the same procedures or with planned changes in the procedures to confirm the original results.

random assignment design Experimental design in which participants are randomly assigned to levels of the independent variable.

random assignment Procedure that uses chance to assign participants, procedures, or materials to groups.

TABLE 7.11	Notation for the Random Assignment Design for Two Treatments

Method of assignment	Independent variable	Dependent variable
R	T_1	O
R	T_2	O
Time	$\longrightarrow$	

Where: R = assignment to treatments is random

T_1 and T_2 = two treatment levels of the independent variable

O = observations that constitute the dependent variable

differences do not exert a bias that makes one group different from the others at the start of the experiment. In research, *random* does not mean haphazard, disordered, sloppy, or unplanned.

Table 7.11 shows the random assignment design for two groups. You can see how similar it appears on the surface to the quasi-experimental design (Table 7.9). The difference is that in the random assignment design, participants are assigned to groups randomly before the experiments starts. This difference is indicated by the letter *R* in the first column of Table 7.11.

Random Assignment Demonstrated

Any process that produces completely unpredictable outcomes can be used to create random assignment. One handy, easy-to-use method involves a table of random numbers. **Table C.1** in appendix C is an example. Table C.1 consists of thousands of one-digit numbers, 0 to 9, grouped into fives and arranged into rows (numbered on the left) and columns (numbered across the top). At any point, every digit is equally likely. Similarly, every two-digit combination, 00 to 99, is equally likely. The same is true for three or more digits.

Random Assignment From a Fixed Pool of Participants Table 7.12 shows a list of 40 college students who are available to participate in a two-group experiment. The students have ID numbers of 1 to 40. Three characteristics of each person are shown: gender, grade point average, and an optimism score on the Life Orientation Test—Revised (Scheier, Carver, & Bridges, 1994).

We demonstrate random assignment by dividing the 40 students in Table 7.12 into two groups of 20. Random assignment gives us some assurance (but not an iron-clad guarantee) that the two groups of 20 will (on average) be equal to each other on these three characteristics and on every other characteristic as well.

TABLE 7.12	Forty College Students and Three Variables		
Student ID no.	Gender	GPA	Optimism score
1	female	2.9	10
2	female	3.2	17
3	female	2.8	8
4	female	2.1	13
5	female	3.5	14
6	female	2.8	19
7	female	3.0	10
8	female	3.7	15
9	female	2.8	16
10	female	3.3	21
11	female	2.2	12
12	female	4.0	15
13	female	2.9	18
14	female	2.4	16
15	female	1.8	14
16	female	2.6	7
17	female	3.0	20
18	female	2.7	12
19	female	2.5	11
20	female	3.2	13
21	female	2.6	13
22	female	3.5	11
23	female	2.9	9
24	female	3.8	15
25	male	2.3	14
26	male	3.1	15
27	male	2.2	13
28	male	3.0	14
29	male	2.3	8
30	male	3.4	23
31	male	2.0	10
32	male	2.9	18
33	male	3.6	20
34	male	3.1	14
35	male	2.5	17
36	male	3.6	14
37	male	3.2	5
38	male	2.6	18
39	male	3.3	17
40	male	2.7	11

TABLE 7.13	General and Specific Instructions for Randomly Assigning a Pool of Participants

General instructions	*Random assignment of Table 7.12 participants*
1. Identify each potential participant with a code or number.	The students are numbered 1–40.
2. The largest number determines the size of the numbers you need from Table C.1.	The largest number, 40, means that two-digit numbers are needed.
3. Find a starting place in Table C.1.	Haphazardly point to a number. On page 441, the number is 86 (row 35, last two digits in columns 55–59).
4. Determine if this random number corresponds to an identifying number of a participant.	86 does not correspond to one of the identifying numbers in Table 7.13.
5. Move up or down, left or right to the next number.	Moving down, the number is 15.
6. Determine if this random number corresponds to an identifying number of a participant.	15 corresponds to a female with a GPA of 1.8 and an optimism score of 14.
7. If there is a correspondence, the person is selected for Group 1.	Student 15 is selected for Group 1.
8. Continue in the same direction, writing down random numbers that correspond to identifying numbers. *Skip repeats.*	04, 34, 24, 38, 10, 19, 29 (34 is repeated once).
9. When you reach the end of a row or column, change rows or columns and continue.	At the bottom of the page, skip to the right (first two digits of columns 60–64) and continue upward: 63 and 94 (not ID numbers), 29 (repeat), 02, 12, 08.
10. Continue until you obtain the number of participants that your plan calls for.	22, 05, 03, 32, 27, 06, 37, 11, 25.

To divide this fixed pool of participants into two groups, randomly select 20 to be in Group 1, which leaves the other 20 as Group 2. The first step is to obtain from the Table C.1 20 two-digit numbers that correspond to the student ID numbers. These 20 students become Group 1. Instructions for making random assignment are in **Table 7.13**. General instructions are on the left; the specific steps used for assignment of students in Table 7.12 are on the right. Read Table 7.13 carefully.

The two samples of randomly assigned participants ($N = 20$) are shown in **Table 7.14**. How well did random assignment work in this case? The mean GPA of Group 1 is 2.89; that of Group 2 is almost the same, 2.91. The standard deviations are not as close: 0.63 and 0.40. For the optimism scores, the two means are 13.75 and 14.25; the two standard

TABLE 7.14	GPAs and Optimism Scores (in descending order) for Two Randomly Assigned Groups of 20		
GPA		Optimism score	
Group 1	Group 2	Group 1	Group 2
4.0	3.6	21	23
3.8	3.6	19	20
3.7	3.4	18	20
3.5	3.3	18	18
3.5	3.2	17	17
3.3	3.1	15	17
3.2	3.0	15	16
3.2	3.0	15	16
3.1	3.0	14	15
2.9	2.9	14	14
2.8	2.9	14	14
2.8	2.9	14	13
2.6	2.8	13	13
2.5	2.7	13	12
2.3	2.7	12	11
2.3	2.6	11	11
2.2	2.6	11	10
2.2	2.5	8	10
2.1	2.4	8	9
1.8	2.0	5	7
N 20	20	20	20
M 2.89	2.91	13.75	14.25
SD 0.63	0.40	3.93	4.18

deviations are 3.93 and 4.19. As for gender, Group 1 was 65% female and group 2 was 55% female. For the most part, the descriptive statistics of the two groups are quite similar.[2]

Let's turn to an application of random assignment. Suppose that you want to evaluate some technique that might improve learning. The technique might be listening to music, using a highlighter, mentally summarizing points, or any one of the many techniques that students consider helpful while studying. For this experiment, participants study

---

[2]We hope that you repeat this exercise for yourself. In addition to practicing the procedure, it may help alleviate any doubts that you have about the adequacy of random assignment.

new material using or not using the technique. Afterward, they take a test of comprehension to measure how much they learned. Thus, the IV is study technique and the conditions (levels) are *yes* and *no.*

Can random assignment be used for this problem? Certainly. There is no reason not to assign participants to one of the two conditions in a random fashion. Will random assignment produce two groups that are equal in their ability to read and comprehend new material? That is, before any administration of the IV, will extraneous variables related to a person's ability to read and comprehend be balanced out?

Of course, you cannot know for certain, but Table 7.14 contains information that should alleviate your worries. The information is the similarity of the GPAs of the two groups. Because GPA is a partial measure of a person's ability to read and comprehend, you have some assurance that random assignment created two groups that are approximately equal in reading and comprehending because GPA is approximately equal for the two groups.

Random assignment can be accomplished in ways other than using a table of random numbers. A traditional method that is often very efficient is to write each identifying code (such as a student ID number) on a slip of paper. The slips are put in a container and thoroughly mixed. To randomly assign 40 participants to two groups, draw out 20 slips. These 20 identifying codes identify 20 participants whose scores constitute one sample. The remaining 20 scores constitute the other sample.

Random Assignment of a Stream of Participants   Sometimes potential participants arrive at your experiment one by one, rather than presenting themselves to you all together as in Table 7.12. Random assignment in this case is simpler, but equally effective in balancing out extraneous variables.

Before participants arrive for a two-group experiment, designate Group 1 as the "odds" and Group 2 as the "evens." Use a haphazard method of finding a starting place in Table C.1, finding a one-digit number. If the digit is odd, the first participant is assigned to Group 1; if even, the first participant is assigned to Group 2. Continue in one direction in Table C.1, writing down "odd" or "even." This procedure establishes the order in which participants receive particular treatments. To randomly assign a stream of participants to three groups, use the numbers 1 to 3, 4 to 6, and 7 to 9 to indicate the three groups. Ignore zeros.

If your plan calls for an equal number of participants in each group (which is usually a good idea), you may have to assign the last one or more participants to a particular group, ignoring the numbers in Table C.1. This "breach of procedure" from true randomness is seldom considered serious.

In the Know

The random assignment design is known by other names as well. In psychology, it is often referred to as a *true experiment.* In medicine, the random assignment design is called a *clinical trial.* Clinical trials are considered the "gold standard" in medicine because they provide the best support for cause-and-effect conclusions.

Problems With the Random Assignment Design

Although the random assignment design is the best design for establishing cause-and-effect conclusions, there are problems with it that you should know about. Our four-item catalog of problems follows. Two of the problems can be explained easily. The other two potential problems are extraneous variables that deserve separate sections.

Not Applicable for Some Variables   As we indicated in Table 7.8, many interesting and important questions cannot be investigated using the random assignment design. If the independent variable is gender, random assignment is not possible. If the independent variable is age, socioeconomic status, personality type, or psychiatric diagnosis, participants cannot be assigned randomly. Establishing cause-and-effect relationships in these situations requires the kind of accumulated evidence that we discussed earlier under quasi-experimental design.

   Let's return to our exercise–tiredness experiment. Using a quasi-experimental design, we were unable to draw a cause-and-effect conclusion. Could the experiment be redesigned so that random assignment could be used? If so, a cause-and-effect conclusion would be warranted if the two conditions were still significantly different on the dependent variable.

   A random assignment design is feasible, but additional resources would be required. Participants could be randomly assigned to a More Active or Less Active condition easily enough, but then the administration of the experiment begins. A more active condition might require four or more units on the exercise scale; the less active conditions would require a score of three or less. How long should the experiment last? One week? Two weeks? Will the participants stick with their assignment? Perhaps some method of monitoring should be used to assure that the participants comply with instructions. You can see that a random assignment design would require much more work than a quasi-experimental design.

Small Samples   A second problem with the random assignment design is that small samples do not give you assurance that extraneous variables are balanced out. This is particularly true when the distribution of the extraneous variable scores is skewed or has a large standard deviation. If the distribution is both skewed *and* variable, you have almost no assurance of equality with small samples.

The GPA scores in Table 7.12 are fairly compact and symmetrical, not skewed. Even so, when your authors randomly selected two samples of $N = 3$ from the scores in Table 7.12, we obtained mean GPAs of 3.2 and 2.5. The conclusion seems clear: Random assignment of small samples did not result in two groups that were equivalent in grade point average. Thus, the two samples are probably not equal on other variables that are correlated with GPA, such as ability to read and comprehend a passage of new material.

The reasonable question, "OK, but how small is small?" is not easy to answer. A complete answer requires analyses beyond those usually covered in a first course in research methods. In the meantime, here are three suggestions:

1. Consult with a faculty member or graduate student about sample size.
2. Use sample sizes reported in the literature by those working on your topic or on a similar topic.
3. Use this rule of thumb: In many situations, having groups with 12 to 15 scores is adequate, although there are many exceptions to this rule.

One general rule about sample size is, the larger the better (but sample sizes can become so large as to be unmanageable).

THE EXTRANEOUS VARIABLE OF DIFFERENTIAL ATTRITION

Attrition is the loss of participants from a study. Recruited participants may not show up for testing, or may not return for retesting, or may drop out during the experiment. Remember that the *Ethics Code* allows participants to drop out of a study without negative consequences. The consequences of attrition for the researcher depend on how many are lost, whether the losses are equal among the levels of the IV, and most important, why the participants are lost.

Picture this scene. Your assistant reports that several of the randomly assigned participants in your study did not complete the experiment. You recognize that this might be a small problem or it might be a big problem. Here are three scenarios that will help distinguish between small consequences and large consequences of losing participants.

Scenario 1

You: What groups lost participants?

Assistant: We lost them equally across groups.

You: Well, we'll be a little less likely to find a difference if there is one, but our experiment isn't biased. No big problem.

Scenario 2

You: What groups lost participants?

Assistant: We lost more from one group than from the other.

You: Uh-oh, we might have an experiment that is biased by differential attrition. If not, we're just a little less likely to find a difference if there is one. Let's check.

Scenario 3

You: What groups lost participants?

Assistant: We lost more from one group than from the other group, and the ones who dropped out are quite different from the ones who didn't.

You: Oh, no! We've got a biased experiment. Our poor experiment has been attacked by that dastardly extraneous variable, differential attrition! Big problem.

Differential attrition, which is also referred to as *mortality* or *experimental mortality,* is the third problem that can occur with the random assignment design; it can also affect the quasi-experimental design. To explain differential attrition, let's return to the proposed experiment about study techniques. As a specific IV, suppose we investigate a technique called *mental summaries.* Practicing mental summaries means that you read one short section of a textbook, close the book, and mentally summarize the material. Read the next short section, close the book, mentally summarize, and so on. For this example, the independent variable is mental summaries with two levels, *yes* and *no.* In the *yes* condition, participants receive instructions for mental summarizing. In the *no* condition, participants are told to use their best efforts to read and comprehend the material. Suppose that the written material is 12 pages about dinosaurs, taken from an encyclopedia. The DV is the participant's comprehension of a passage of the material as measured by a 25-item true-false test.

If participants are randomly assigned to groups, it is reasonable to assume that those who already know a lot about dinosaurs will be represented equally in both groups. Similarly, participants who regularly use mental summaries when studying should be found equally in both groups.

The experimental design calls for all participants to study the material for 30 minutes, be excused for 60 minutes, and return to take a true-false test. The 1-hour break allows forgetting to take place so that the test scores will not be subject to a ceiling effect (discussed in chapter 4). Unfortunately, several of the participants do not return for the test. If the dropouts come equally from the two groups, then Scenario 1 above applies. However, let's suppose that the dropout rate is not equal and that more of the participants

differential attrition An extraneous variable caused by a differential loss of participants from the levels of the independent variable in such a way as to bias the outcome.

from the mental summaries group failed to return. This is Scenario 2. Let's begin the check to see if we can discover any differential attrition.

Is there any reason to think that the difference in dropout rates might be due to the IV? Is there any reason to think that those who dropped out might be different from those who did not? There is.

Half the participants engaged in a technique that was new for them. It probably worked well for some of them, perhaps even most, but not so well for others. Who is likely to fail to return? Those for whom the technique did not work well and those who were frustrated by having to interrupt their study were most likely to drop out. If this is the case, scores of the mental summaries group will, on average, be higher than they would have been if all the participants returned. Thus, this difference in dropout rates of the two groups might produce a difference in means that is due to differential attrition and not to the IV. If this reasoning strikes you as valid, then Scenario 3 is true.

Figure 7.1 illustrates an admittedly fanciful version of differential attrition in the mental summaries experiment.

An experiment suffers from differential attrition not only if there are lots of dropouts and not only if the different levels of the IV have different dropout rates. Differential attrition occurs when the DV scores in the different groups are different *because* of the differential dropout rates. As one example, teacher evaluation forms turned in at the end of the semester may be affected in a positive way by differential attrition. Low ratings by students who drop a course because it is being taught poorly do not show up among the forms collected at the end of the semester. On the other hand, students who drop out for personal or financial reasons do not lead to differential attrition because their reasons for dropping out are not related to the quality of the course.

In general, there are two ways to address the problem of differential attrition. One is to prevent it in the first place. The other is to provide evidence that a differential dropout rate was not related to the conditions of the IV or that, if it was, you would not expect the DV to be affected.

If we had anticipated the problem of differential attrition in our mental summaries experiment, we could have altered our procedure to prevent it. Perhaps we could have kept the participants engaged during the hour between studying about dinosaurs and taking the test. Engagement tactics might include food, a video, supervised study of other topics, or perhaps best of all, engagement in another, unrelated experiment. If participants could not be detained for an hour, then reducing the hour to 10 to 15 minutes would prevent most dropouts. The cost of using a shorter break is that the DV scores might be limited by a ceiling effect because there was not enough time for forgetting to occur. Perhaps participants who don't return can be called and asked to return.

The second approach is to show that differential attrition did not occur, even though the potential for it was present. For example, in the mental

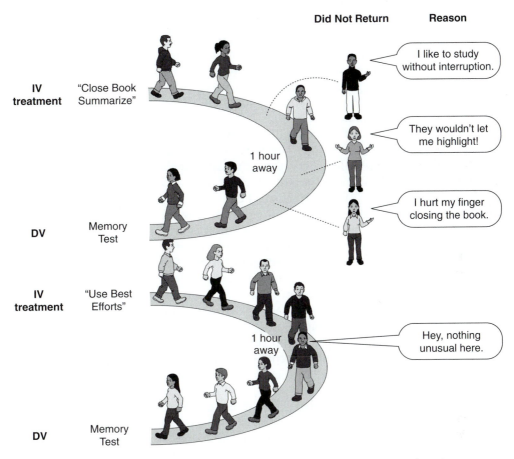

FIGURE 7.1   Differential attrition among the mental summaries–comprehension participants.

summaries experiment you might be able to show that those who failed to return would not be expected to score worse on the test. Had you asked the participants for their GPAs, you could use these data to evaluate the drop-outs. This approach makes the reasonable assumption that participants' GPAs are correlated with their comprehension of the dinosaur material.

THE EXTRANEOUS VARIABLE OF DIFFUSION OF TREATMENT

For an experiment to be an experiment there must be an IV with two or more conditions. If the conditions are not really different, then the groups will not be different on the DV. Thus, ensuring that the conditions of the experiment are truly different is a critical requirement for an experiment.

In some experiments, the IV is information; some participants get one version of the information and others get a different version. If the participants in one condition communicate their information to those in other conditions, the difference between conditions is reduced or eliminated. You can imagine that passing information is of particular concern when the participants are college students. College students attend class together, often live near each other, and are known for exchanging information.

When the conditions intended for only one group of participants are experienced by other groups, the experiment suffers from an extraneous variable called **diffusion of treatment.** Experiments that do not control for diffusion of treatment are unlikely to detect any differences that exist among different levels of the IV.

In the mental summaries experiment, diffusion of treatment could be a problem. You can imagine that if the experiment were conducted over a long period, college student participants who were instructed in mental summaries (and found it helpful) might describe the technique to fellow classmates, some of whom might be scheduled for the "use your best efforts" condition. Diffusion of treatment is especially easy to imagine if you think that to-be participants might ask their classmates, "What is that experiment about?"

Although diffusion of treatment could be a problem in the mental summaries–comprehension experiment, it is not a problem for the exercise–tiredness experiment. There is no way for the exercise level of either group to diffuse or influence the other group.

Preventing diffusion of treatment is usually easy. In many cases, conducting the experiment in a short time period (perhaps one day) prevents the problem from occurring. For experiments that require more time to conduct, the researcher can ask the participants not to talk with others about the experiment until a specified time in the future. Often such requests for confidentiality are made during the debriefing session. Finally, for some experiments, the researcher can embed the experimental conditions into the procedures in such a way that participants do not recognize what the experiment is about. Of course, if they don't know what the experiment is about, they cannot reveal important information when they are quizzed by their classmates. As one example of embedding, researchers with questionnaires sometimes include irrelevant questions that disguise the purpose of the questionnaire until a debriefing session reveals that purpose.

diffusion of treatment An extraneous variable that occurs when the conditions intended for only one group of participants are experienced by other groups.

A COMPARISON OF RANDOM AND QUASI-EXPERIMENTAL DESIGNS

The difference in the random assignment design and the quasi-experimental design is easily stated. Participants in the random assignment design are assigned randomly to groups; participants in the quasi-experimental design

TABLE 7.15	Control of Extraneous Variables by Different Research Designs		
	Extraneous Variables		
Design	*Selection*	*Differential attrition*	*Diffusion of treatment*
Quasi-experimental	Not controlled	Not controlled	Not controlled
Random assignment	Controlled	Not controlled	Not controlled

are not. (Compare Tables 7.9 and 7.11.) The effect of random assignment is that the extraneous variable of selection is controlled. Thus, statements of a cause-and-effect relationship between the IV and DV are much more secure if random assignment is used.

> ## In the Know
> When researchers refer to a *manipulated* IV, they generally mean that the participants were randomly assigned to conditions.

Table 7.15 shows the two designs covered in this chapter and their control of the extraneous variables selection, differential attrition, and diffusion of treatments. When we discuss other designs and extraneous variables in the next chapter, we expand this table.

INDEPENDENT VARIABLE VALUES

The two most important elements of an experiment are the independent variable and the dependent variable.

> ## In the Know
> When one researcher wants to explain an experiment to another researcher, one of the first sentences is about the IV and DV.

Most of what we have to say about the DV was said in chapter 4 on measurement. Here, we provide expanded coverage on the IV and the values that an IV can have. You have probably already recognized that the words *treatments, conditions, levels,* and *groups* are all synonyms to indicate that the

IV has different values. Each word's use depends on the situation. For example, *treatments* doesn't sound right for an IV of gender, but it works fine if the IV is a drug. Likewise, *conditions* sounds odd for age but fine for psychiatric diagnosis. *Groups* seems appropriate for gender and *levels* for age. *Groups* is the most general of the four words (and therefore the vaguest of the terms).

Whereas values of the DV are provided by the participants, values of the IV are selected by the researcher. If the IV is gender, values of male and female are the obvious selection. An IV of socioeconomic status leads to values of low, medium, and high. For some IVs such as culture or age, there is more room for choice. Faced with many possibilities for culture, a researcher might choose which values to use on the basis of practicality. For example, if your Taiwanese friend's brother will distribute questionnaires for you in Taipei, Chinese becomes one of the cultures you compare. IV value selection can be made on the basis of a theory. For example, Piagetian theory predicts a change in formal operations thinking between the ages of 10 and 14, so those ages might be used in a study of cognition. At times, the levels of the IV seem to be the "natural" ones. In the social loafing experiment, the two levels of the IV were the natural ones of worker and loafer.

One general principle for choosing levels of the IV is to select values that are not close together. The commonsense basis of this principle is that the more widely separated the IV values, the more likely you are to detect any difference the IV has on the DV. The scientific basis of this principle is statistical power, a topic covered at the end of chapter 6. One of the factors that affects power is amount of difference between the populations. The greater the difference, the greater the power of the test to detect the difference.

Given a choice between testing the effects of a placebo (0 mg) against 25 mg of caffeine or 50 mg, choose 50 mg.[3] Given the choice between a scenario that describes a person as a smoker or a two-pack-a-day smoker, choose the latter. For some research, a two-level IV is created by dividing the participants into a low-scoring group and a high-scoring group. How should they be divided? Although it is common to use the median to divide them into two groups, you can create a wider separation between two groups by using the lower third and the upper third of the participants (although you reduce the size of your samples). You'll notice that the data of the 25 participants in the exercise–tiredness experiment were all used. The division line was between activity scores of 3 and 4.

---

[3]Of course, there are ethical and practical limits to our advice about widely separating the levels of the IV. Too much caffeine can be harmful and amounts not normally consumed make generalization questionable.

BETWEEN-SUBJECTS AND WITHIN-SUBJECTS DESIGNS DISTINGUISHED

We end this chapter by distinguishing between two categories of designs, between-subjects (between-S) designs and within-subjects (within-S) designs.[4] We continue with this distinction in chapters 8 and 9. The two designs discussed in this chapter—random assignment design and quasi-experimental design—are both between-subjects designs. Within-subjects designs are covered in the chapter 8.

To explain the differences between these two kinds of designs, we focus on the simplest case, a design with two levels of the IV. For **between-subjects designs,** a comparison requires at least two participants—one who receives one level of the IV and another who receives the other level. The question is whether there is a difference between the two participants' scores. Thus, the comparison is *between* the subjects.

In the case of a **within-subjects design,** a comparison of DV scores can be made with just one participant; thus the comparison is *within* the participant. As a simple example of a within-subjects design, suppose that caffeine is the IV and there are two levels, 0 mg and 50 mg. The dependent variable is reaction time (*RT*) on some perceptual task. Imagine conducting this experiment so that each participant receives one level of caffeine and then is measured for *RT*. At a later time, the participant receives the other level of caffeine and is again measured for *RT*. Such an experiment is a within-subjects design because the comparison of the two conditions can be made with just one participant.

Although these two designs are different, their purpose is the same—to compare the levels of the IV, looking for a difference in the DV. The distinction between these two kinds of designs, however, is important. For example, choosing the appropriate statistical test depends on whether the design is between-subjects or within-subjects.

Near the beginning of this chapter, we did not give a final response to the fact that "5 children died who were wards of the state." We had taken the problem as far as showing that 1.0% of the children who were wards of the state died, but that only 0.8% of the other children in the state died. Is the difference one that could be the result of chance? Or is it too large to be attributed to chance? Sounds like an NHST question, doesn't it? It turns out that you studied a technique in chapter 6 that permits you to answer the question of whether or not the difference is too large to be attributed to chance.

---

[4]Until the 1990s the word *subject* was used for anyone or anything that provided data for a psychological experiment. *Subject* could mean people, animals, plants, or even cities or organizations. In recent years, however, people are always referred to as participants. The terms *between-subjects* and *within-subjects,* however, live on.

between-subjects design Any research design in which participants contribute scores to only one level of the independent variable.

within-subjects design A research design in which participants' scores are matched or paired on the basis of a similarity other than the independent or dependent variable.

STOP & Think

Determine what NHST technique is appropriate for the data in Table 7.2. Apply the technique and write a conclusion.

The NHST technique that is appropriate for categorical frequency count data is chi-square. An analysis of the data in Table 7.2 produced $\chi^2 = 0.0000227$, a value that is far from statistically significant. The conclusion is that the number of deaths of children who are wards of the state is not significantly different from the number of deaths among children who are not wards of the state.[5]

In the next chapter, we describe within-subjects designs more thoroughly and provide examples. In addition, we reveal additional extraneous variables to watch out for and ways to control them.

Chapter Review

1. The two kinds of designs described in this chapter were the

   _____ design and the _____ design; the one that is better for establishing cause-and-effect conclusions is the

   _____ design.

2. A table with the possible scores in the middle and actual scores on

   the edge is a _____ and _____ display.

3. Scores on the _____ variable come from the participants'

   behavior in the experiment. Values of the _____ variable are determined by the researcher. Simple cause-and-effect conclusions

   are not possible if an experiment has _____ variables.

4. The extraneous variable that is never controlled by a quasi-

   experimental design is _____.

5. Your text described three approaches to strengthening a cause-and-effect conclusion using quasi-experimental designs. They were

   _____ , _____ , and _____.

6. What four potential problems can occur in a random assignment design?

---

[5]The numbers in this problem were chosen to illustrate various points about decision making. We don't know what actual data on this problem would show, but a social worker friend of ours noted that such data can be obtained from Web sites maintained by state health departments (see vital statistics) and departments that provide human services, such as foster care.

7. Match the term with the definition.

   1. differential attrition
   2. diffusion of treatment
   3. selection

   a. groups that differ on variables other than the IV even before the experiment begins
   b. participants in Group J who begin the experiment do not complete it because Treatment J is so harsh
   c. participants in Group J learn the techniques that are taught to participants in Group K

8. Your chapter ended by distinguishing two categories of designs, _____ designs and _____ designs.

Thinking Critically About Research _____

1. In your own words, outline a model experiment that compares two groups.
2. Identify the DV, IV and its levels, and a potential extraneous variable in each of the two scenarios.
   a. Nick gathered data from drivers of convertibles and drivers of sedans of the same make and age at a mall parking lot. Each driver filled out a questionnaire that measured need for stimulation.
   b. Nicole randomly assigned fourth-grade school children to the standard spelling lesson or a spelling lesson based on jokes. The next day she tested each child individually, working with half of them before recess and half of them after recess. For the test, she asked each child to spell *monkey, elephant,* and *giraffe,* which were three of the words that were on the spelling list the day before.
3. Compile the following scores into a stem-and-leaf display. Use Table 7.6 as a model.

13	27	16	10	24	14	14	32	19	19
20	12	26	13	22	15	17	12		

4. What procedures does the text suggest that can address the extraneous variable of differential attrition?
5. What procedures does the text suggest that can address the extraneous variable of diffusion of treatment?
6. Distinguish between between-subjects designs and within-subjects designs.

7. Using either the random numbers table in the back of the book, or the "slips in a container" method, randomly assign the optimism scores in Table 7.12 to two groups of 20. Calculate the two means and compare them to the means of 13.75 and 14.25 for the two samples that are shown in Table 7.14.

Answers to Chapter Review

1. random assignment; quasi-experimental; random assignment
2. stem; leaf
3. dependent; independent; extraneous or confounded
4. selection
5. statistical techniques; literature review; gather more data
6. not applicable for some variables; may not work if samples are small; differential attrition; diffusion of treatment
7. 1. b; 2. c; 3. a
8. between-subjects; within-subjects

Answers to Thinking Critically About Research

1. Your answer should include a comparison of two groups that have had the same experience except for one difference.
2. a. DV—need for stimulation, IV—automobile style, levels of the IV—convertible, sedan, extraneous variable—selection;
   b. DV—spelling score; IV—type of spelling lesson; levels of the IV—standard, joke based, extraneous variable—diffusion of treatment
3.
30–34	2
25–29	7, 6
20–24	4, 0, 2
15–19	6, 9, 9, 5, 7
10–14	3, 0, 4, 4, 2, 3, 2
4. reduce dropout rate to about zero; show that the dropouts are quite similar to participants who stayed
5. conduct the experiment quickly; ask participants not to reveal the procedures to others; hide the true nature of the experiment until after the debriefing session
6. In a between-subjects design, there is no logical reason to pair or match two scores that are in different groups. In a within-subjects design, scores are paired or matched for some reason independent of their value.

7. It is not the numbers you get that make your answer correct but the procedures. Did you follow those in the right panel of Table 7.13?

Know for Sure

8

Design II: Within-Subjects Designs and Pretests

OVERVIEW

The previous chapter introduced many experimental design concepts. This chapter completes our introduction to basic design concepts by focusing on within-subjects designs and the use of pretests. Five experimental designs are outlined, five additional extraneous variables are explained, and three techniques that prevent extraneous variables from becoming confounded with the IV are illustrated. Between-subjects designs and within-subjects designs are compared and external validity is addressed fully. Finally, the relationships between eight extraneous variables and six experimental designs are charted.

OBJECTIVES

After studying this chapter and working through, the exercises, you should be able to:

1. Define *within-subjects design*
2. Write interpretations of within-subjects experiments
3. Diagram the one-group, two-treatment design and the one-group, pretest–posttest design
4. Define or describe the extraneous variables of testing, instrument change, history, maturation, and regression
5. Diagram the quasi-experimental two-group, pretest–posttest design and the random two-group, pretest–posttest design
6. Explain how random assignment, counterbalancing, and matching control extraneous variables
7. Apply simple counterbalancing and block counterbalancing to the levels of an independent variable
8. Compare between-subjects and within-subjects designs on the number of participants, statistical sensitivity, and carryover effects
9. Distinguish between internal validity and external validity
10. Identify three threats to external validity and explain why they are threats
11. Diagram the Solomon four-group design
12. List eight extraneous variables

233

Let's retreat from the 21st century back through the 20th century and into the 19th century. We stop at 1885 and pick up a newly published book on memory, *Über das Gedachtnis (Concerning Memory)*, a book that will influence psychologists well into the 20th century. Indeed, some of the facts in that book are reported in psychology textbooks today. The researcher's name was Hermann Ebbinghaus.

What kind of design did Ebbinghaus use that had such a lasting impact? Did he use random assignment? No, he didn't. Was it a study with thousands of participants, thus guaranteeing the reliability of the results? No, it wasn't. Ebbinghaus's results were based on a sample with one participant—himself. Of course, with just one participant all of Ebbinghaus's comparisons were within-subjects design comparisons. This chapter focuses on within-subjects designs and pretests, both of which are quite popular among psychology researchers.

Chapter 7 covered the quasi-experimental design and the random assignment design. Both of these between-subjects designs had two separate groups of participants that were compared to each other. Between-subjects designs require data from at least two participants if you are to compare the two conditions. As stated, in this chapter we cover within-subjects designs. For many within-subjects designs, participants serve in every condition of the experiment. Thus, within-subjects designs require data from only one participant to have a comparison of the two conditions, although for some within-subjects designs the participants are *similar* rather than the same.[1]

Within-subjects designs have a number of advantages. A major advantage is that they control for the extraneous variable of selection. In within-subjects designs, participants who supply scores for one level of the independent variable are the same participants who supply scores for the other levels. Thus, potential extraneous variables such as age, gender, socioeconomic status, experience, and so forth are exactly the same for every level of the IV.

A second advantage of within-subjects designs is that they are often more economical. More economical means that you can devote fewer resources to a within-subjects design than you would to a between-subjects design that investigates the same variables. For students, fewer resources mean spending less time to complete a project and for researchers, more economical means that more data can be gathered for the same budgeted cost.

We begin our explanation of within-subjects designs with an experiment on cognitive processing. Because participation provides experience that enhances analytical skills, we want you to participate in this within-subjects experiment. This exercise is derived from Craik and Lockhart's (1972) theory of how memory is affected by the depth of cognitive processing.

---

[1]Participants are *similar* rather than the same when matched participants are used.

A WITHIN-SUBJECTS EXPERIMENT ON COGNITIVE PROCESSING

The next few sections are organized around a specific within-subjects experiment on cognitive processing. In this first section, you act as a participant; afterward you act as a researcher who conducts a statistical analysis of the data. Before a final conclusion can be written, however, the experiment must be analyzed for extraneous variables. Our first Stop & Think problem in the section on extraneous variables (p. 242) asks you to identify uncontrolled extraneous variables. Before you begin, you may want to review the explanation of extraneous variables in chapter 2.

To participate in this experiment, you must be able to time a 2-minute interval. A watch or clock that signals seconds is ideal, but one with only a minute hand will work if the face is marked with minute intervals. Before you read any further, get a timer and a pen or pencil.

Tables 8.1, 8.2, and 8.3 are for data collection. For this experiment, there are two different lists of 20 words. After you work with a list, you are to recall as many of the words as you can. Please follow the directions exactly rather than trying to find a way to increase your score.

Ready? If so, look at **Table 8.1** and begin.

TABLE 8.1	Counting Letters

Directions: *Read this paragraph before looking at any of the words below.* Your task is to read words and count letters. Read the first word on the list. Count the number of letters in the word and write that number on the line to the right of the word. Read the second word. Count letters. Continue until you reach the end of the list. When you write the number of letters in the last word, turn *immediately* to the top half of Table 8.2. Record the time on your watch or clock in the place provided. During the 2 minutes that follow, write all the words that you can recall. The order of the words is not important. Do not glance back at the words on this list once you have counted the letters in the last word.

speech	_____	knife	_____
clip	_____	bear	_____
brush	_____	glove	_____
fence	_____	miner	_____
monk	_____	rock	_____
robber	_____	pool	_____
mast	_____	boat	_____
grin	_____	singer	_____
flour	_____	roach	_____
sonnet	_____	drill	_____

Turn to **Table 8.2** and write your start time at the top and then as many words as you can recall.

| TABLE 8.2 | Worksheet for Words Recalled |

First List

Words recalled   Start time _____

At the end of 2 minutes, look at **Table 8.3** and follow the instructions there.

Second List

Words recalled   Start time _____

At the end of 2 minutes, go to the next page and continue reading the text.

TABLE 8.3	Writing Associates

Directionst: *Read this paragraph before looking at any of the words below.* Read the first word on the list. Note the first word that you think of after reading the word on the list. Write that associated word on the line to the right. Read the second word and again, write the first word that you think of. Continue until you reach the end of the list. When you finish with the last word, turn *immediately* to the bottom half of Table 8.2. Note the time and write it in the place provided. During the 2 minutes that follow, write all the words that you can recall. The order of the words is not important. Do not glance back at the words on this list once you have written an associate to the last word.

copper	_____		sheep	_____
pond	_____		lamp	_____
cheek	_____		daisy	_____
flame	_____		clove	_____
cart	_____		week	_____
fiddle	_____		pail	_____
twig	_____		wool	_____
claw	_____		cherry	_____
honey	_____		brake	_____
chapel	_____		trout	_____

Turn back to Table 8.2, write your start time halfway down the page, and then write as many words as you can recall.

You just participated in the data collection portion of this experiment.[2] The first step in analyzing the data is to check the words that you wrote to be sure they were on the lists you studied. Mark through any words you wrote that aren't on the study lists. Count the number of words on your first list and the number on your second list. For most students, the number of words recalled after writing associates is greater than the number recalled after counting letters. So that you will have more than just your own scores to analyze, we had other students do what you have done. **Table 8.4** shows the scores from one class of 28 students.

Identify the IV, its levels, and the DV in the cognitive processing experiment.

STOP & Think

_____

[2]If you haven't yet done the task, it isn't too late to participate. Go to Table 8.1.

TABLE 8.4	Recall Scores of 28 Participants in the Cognitive Processing Experiment		
Count letters	*Write associates*	*Count letters*	*Write associates*
7	9	6	11
8	10	3	11
3	7	8	13
12	11	3	7
5	13	3	5
14	10	10	13
6	12	6	10
8	8	4	8
5	8	2	6
7	14	8	15
9	9	3	5
2	7	5	9
4	12	7	7
10	12	6	13

In the cognitive processing experiment, the independent variable is the kind of cognitive processing. There are two levels of cognitive processing: counting letters and writing associates. The dependent variable is memory for words as measured by the number of words recalled.

ANALYZING THE COGNITIVE PROCESSING EXPERIMENT

We follow once again our recommended steps for data analysis

- Examine the data.
- Create graphs.
- Calculate descriptive and inferential statistics.
- Articulate a conclusion.

Study the scores in Table 8.4. Just a glance at those numbers shows that for most participants their score after writing associates is greater than their score after counting letters. The next step is to create graphs that display the data. As we did for the exercise–tiredness experiment in chapter 7, we began with a rough-draft stem-and-leaf display, which is shown in **Table 8.5.** This time, because the dependent variable had only 14 values (3 to 15), we did not use class intervals but instead listed every value down the middle of the display. The participants' scores are represented with tally marks beside the corresponding DV value.

	TABLE 8.5	Stem-and-Leaf Display of Scores in Table 8.4

Count	Words recalled	Associate
	15	/
/	14	/
	13	////
/	12	///
	11	///
//	10	///
/	9	///
////	8	///
///	7	////
////	6	/
///	5	//
//	4	
HH	3	
//	2	

What can be determined from Table 8.5? The bulk of the scores after letter-counting are in the 3–8 range; after writing associates most of the scores are higher (the 7–13 range). The scores on the left appear to be somewhat positively skewed.

The next step is to construct boxplots of the data. Boxplots, which were explained in chapter 5, present measures of central tendency and variability with one graph.

Using the data in Table 8.5, find the mean and median, the 25th and 75th percentiles, and the maximum and minimum score for each group.

STOP
& *Think*

The recall scores after counting letters results in a mean of 6.21 words, a median of 6 words, and 25th and 75th percentiles of 3 and 8 words. The minimum is 2 and the maximum, 14. For the scores after writing associates, the mean is 9.82 words, the median is 10 words, and 25th and 75th percentiles are 7 and 12 words. The minimum is 5 and the maximum, 15. Using this information, we constructed **Figure 8.1**, which shows boxplots of the scores of the two groups.

The other descriptive statistic we calculated was d, the effect size index. Calculating d requires the standard deviation of the difference scores, SD', which is 2.96.[3] Thus,

$$d = \frac{M_1 - M_2}{SD'} = \frac{6.21 - 9.82}{2.96} = -1.22$$

[3]The formula for SD' is on pages 188 and 189.

FIGURE 8.1
Boxplots of the
two conditions in
the cognitive
processing
experiment.

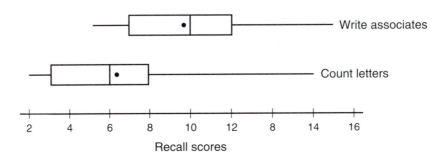

An effect size index of $d = 1.22$ shows that writing associates produces a very large effect on memory as compared to counting letters.

The inferential statistic we thought most informative and appropriate for this experiment was a confidence interval (CI). We chose 99% CI rather than 95% because the two sets of scores showed so little overlap in the stem-and-leaf display. If it had turned out that a 99% interval included zero, we would have "fallen back" to a 95% interval. Following the procedures outlined in chapter 6, we found the 99% CI around the mean difference of 3.61 words to be 2.06 to 5.16 words. Output of an SPSS analysis of the data in Table 8.4 is shown in **Table 8.6.**

A confidence interval gives a particular amount of confidence about the true difference between the two conditions in the experiment. In this case, we are 99% confident that the recall after writing associates is greater than the recall after counting letters and that the difference is between 2.06 and 5.16 words.

TABLE 8.6   SPSS Output for Data in Table 8.4

Paired-Samples Statistics

	Mean	N	Std. deviation	Std. error mean
Count	6.21	28	3.023	0.571
Write	9.82	28	2.776	0.525

Paired-Samples Test

	Paired differences					t	df	Sig. (2-tailed)
				99% confidence interval of the difference				
	Mean	Std. deviation	Std. error mean	Lower	Upper			
Count and Write	−3.607	2.961	0.560	−5.157	−2.057	−6.447	27	.000

As you know, a confidence interval about a mean difference also provides a test of the null hypothesis that the difference in the two population means is zero. Because zero is not in the 99% confidence interval of 2.06 to 5.16, the null hypothesis can be rejected for $\alpha = .01$. Thus, writing associates to words produces significantly better memory than does counting the letters in the words, $p < .01$.

To write a meaningful conclusion for any experiment, background is very helpful; here is some background information on the memory experiment. The memory experiment was designed to compare two kinds of cognitive processing. The cognitive processing that occurs when you write an associate to a word involves the meaning of the word. Attending to the meaning of a word is considered *deep cognitive processing.* On the other hand, the cognitive processing that occurs when you determine the number of letters in words is considered *shallow cognitive processing* because you do not attend to meaning. The idea that the **level of processing** (or depth of processing) helps determine memory was introduced by Craik and Lockhart (1972). With this background information, we are ready to write a tentative conclusion.

> Studying a list of 20 words using deep processing (writing associates to the words) produced recall scores ($M = 9.82$ words, $SD = 2.78$ words) that were significantly greater ($p < .01$) than the recall scores ($M = 6.21$ words, $SD = 3.02$ words) produced by shallow processing (counting the letters in the words). The 99% confidence interval about the mean difference of 3.61 words was 2.06 to 5.16 words. The effect size index, $d = 1.22$, shows that the difference produced by these two levels of cognitive processing was very large. In percentage terms, the mean recall score for deep processing was 58% greater than the mean recall score for shallow processing.

ONE-GROUP TWO-TREATMENT DESIGN

The cognitive processing experiment is an example of a **one-group two-treatment design.** Each participant contributed data to both conditions of the independent variable, which was cognitive processing method. A diagram of a one-group two-treatment design is shown in **Table 8.7.**

TABLE 8.7	Diagram for One-Group Experiments in Which Participants Receive Two Different Treatments

T_1	T_2
O_1	O_2
Time $\longrightarrow$	

Where: T = treatment

O = observations that constitute the dependent variable

level of processing Theory that the depth of processing during learning determines later recall.

one-group two-treatment design One group of participants is measured in one condition and then in a second condition.

Stacking the treatment symbol (*T*) and the traditional DV symbol for observation (*O*) over the same place on the time scale indicates that the treatment takes place at the same time that the DV score is obtained.

EXTRANEOUS VARIABLES IN THE COGNITIVE PROCESSING EXPERIMENT

As you know, an important analysis of any experimental design involves detecting any uncontrolled extraneous variables. Undetected extraneous variables that are confounded with the IV threaten the internal validity of an experiment.

List or describe any uncontrolled extraneous variables in the cognitive processing experiment that you can think of.

The first extraneous variable we discuss is a very important one, but one that is overlooked by many who have not taken a course in research design. The extraneous variable is the order of testing. The recall scores for shallow processing were always obtained first; recall scores for deep processing were obtained last. Thus, it is reasonable to attribute the difference between the two means to the order of testing rather than to depth of processing. A conclusion based on order is that the first effort to recall words produces low scores, but a second effort produces higher scores.

Testing

The name that psychologists use for the extraneous variable of order is *testing.* Testing is an extraneous variable that must always be controlled or accounted for whenever participants take the same or a similar test more than once.

Recognizing that an experiment has an extraneous variable is an important first step in the analysis; explaining how it could affect the difference in scores is the second step. In this case, there are several plausible hypotheses why scores could be affected by the order of conditions. First, when people practice a task, they get better. Thus, better recall after deep processing could be due to practice on a similar task. Second, there is usually some amount of uncertainty and nervousness the first time people perform a task. The second time they are more comfortable. Thus, improved scores might be the result of increased familiarity with the situation. Finally, the poor performance on the first task might have created the determination to do better on the second task. That is, motivation would be expected to be higher on the second task than it was on the first task.

testing An extraneous variable; change in a participant's score is the result of earlier participation in another part of the experiment.

Now that you've read of one extraneous variable, can you identify others that you did not include when we posed this problem earlier?

STOP
& *Think*

Instrument Change

The two lists that the participants recalled were different lists of words. Using different lists creates another potential extraneous variable. Unless we know before the experiment starts that the two lists are equally difficult, the experiment is open to the charge that the recall scores were lower for the first list because that list was more difficult and not because the list was studied using shallow processing.

An experiment whose DV scores come from two different tests or from the same test given at two different times is subject to the extraneous variable of **instrument change.** *Instrument* refers to whatever method is used to measure behavior or cognitive processes in an experiment. An instrument might be a list of words, a questionnaire, or a mechanical device such as a stopwatch or electroencephalograph. An instrument might be the observer who records behavior. Thus, instrument change refers to the situation in which a difference is due to a change in the measuring device and not to a change in behavior or cognitive processes. Usually, an instrument is used to measure the dependent variable, but instruments are also used to assign participants to the independent variable.

Change in *instrument change* can also refer to a change in the instrument itself over time. For example, physical equipment may wear out over the course of the experiment. Or, a psychological test may no longer measure the same thing it did when it was published due to changes in the meanings of words or changes in attitudes toward the test. Instrument change can be a problem in lengthy experiments or when comparing older studies to more recent studies. Instrument change is also referred to as *instrument decay* and as *instrumentation*.

History

The amount of time you spent processing the two lists was different. Because it takes less time to count letters and write a one-digit number than it takes to think of an associate and write a word, the superior scores after deep processing may be due to processing time rather than to the level of processing.

More generally, whenever events in two or more conditions of a study differ, the events may be an extraneous variable. If events differ, psychologists refer to this extraneous variable as **history.** Sometimes an extraneous variable of history is built into the experiment, as it was with the cognitive processing experiment. Sometimes, however, an unexpected event occurs during a study that affects one group but not the other. For example, a loud noise or a nauseous participant during testing creates a

instrument change An extraneous variable; a change in a measuring instrument (human judge, survey, or machine) during the course of an experiment.

history An extraneous variable; events that occur during one treatment but not other treatments that affect the dependent variable.

distracting event. If the distraction occurs for one group but not for the other, the extraneous variable of history, and not the IV, may cause differences in the DV.

Review of Three Extraneous Variables

In chapter 7, we discussed three extraneous variables. Let's analyze the cognitive processing experiment with those three extraneous variables in mind.

Selection   Selection is an uncontrolled extraneous variable if the participants who contribute scores to one condition of the IV are different from the participants who contribute to other conditions (other than the IV difference). One of the best features of a within-subjects design is that the *same* participants contribute to all conditions. Thus, for within-subjects designs that occur in a short time frame, selection is a controlled extraneous variable.

Differential Attrition   Differential attrition occurs if you lose more scores from one level of the IV than from others *and* the loss has a differential effect on the DV. Differential attrition is not a problem for the cognitive processing experiment because there was no attrition at all. Like selection, differential attrition is usually not a problem for experiments with short time frames. In some within-subjects experiments attrition does occur. Participants complete one part of the experiment but not another part. The problem of differential attrition in within-subjects designs is easily solved—the participant is dropped from the analysis and this action noted in the Method section of the writeup.

Diffusion of Treatment   Diffusion of treatment occurs when the participants or conditions of one level of the IV influence in some way the participants or conditions at other levels of the IV. Again, a logical analysis of the procedures of the cognitive processing experiment shows that diffusion of treatment was not a problem. Although it is conceivable that counting letters has an effect on writing associates and that this effect influences recollection of the second list, such "diffusion" does not seem very plausible.

INTERPRETATION OF THE COGNITIVE PROCESSING EXPERIMENT

The search for extraneous variables in the cognitive processing experiment revealed three (testing, instrument change, and history) that prevent us from concluding that the experiment shows that deep cognitive processing of words produces significantly better recall than shallow cognitive processing. In the face of uncontrolled extraneous variables, what should you do? There are two alternatives. One is to learn from mistakes and return to data gathering using a better design. (We discuss two better designs later in this chapter.) The other alternative is to write a conclusion that acknowledges the role that the three extraneous variables might play. Here is our final interpretation of the cognitive processing experiment, which embraces the second alternative. We begin by repeating our conclusion from page 241, which is the first paragraph the follows. We end with an additional paragraph that acknowledges the effect of the uncontrolled extraneous variables.

> Studying a list of 20 words using deep processing (writing associates to the words) produced recall scores ($M = 9.82$ words, $SD = 2.78$ words) that were significantly greater ($p < .01$) than the recall scores ($M = 6.21$ words, $SD = 3.02$ words) produced by shallow processing (counting the letters in the words). The 99% confidence interval about the mean difference of 3.61 words was 2.06 to 5.16 words. In addition, the effect size index, $d = 1.22$, shows that the difference produced by these two kinds of cognitive processing was very large. Put into percentage terms, the mean recall score for deep processing was 58% greater than the mean recall score for shallow processing.
>
> Besides level of processing, three other variables might have contributed to the difference observed. The time the participants spent processing words was greater in the deep processing condition. In addition, both testing order and word lists were confounded with conditions. In summary, the results indicate that memory may depend on depth of processing, but additional research is needed to eliminate explanations based on confounded variables.

ADDITIONAL EXTRANEOUS VARIABLES

Including chapter 7, we have discussed six extraneous variables so far:

- Selection
- Differential attrition
- Diffusion of treatments
- Testing
- Instrument change
- History

The addition of two more extraneous variables completes our list for this textbook. These two are most easily explained with studies that use the one-group pretest–posttest design.

ONE-GROUP PRETEST-POSTTEST DESIGN

A second one-group design is more common than the one-group two-treatment design. In the **one-group pretest–posttest design,** diagrammed in **Table 8.8,** participants are first measured on the DV (the pretest) and then the situation of the participants is changed in some way (a treatment). Finally, the participants are measured a second time on the DV (the posttest). The participants' condition at the time of the pretest is one level of the IV, and the condition at the time of the posttest is the other level.

We use a fairly common situation to illustrate the one-group pretest–posttest design: People with symptoms of depression register as clients at a mental health clinic. Their initial examination includes a test for depression, the Beck Depression Inventory (DBI). Over the next 10 weeks, the clients participate in cognitive therapy sessions. After 10 weeks, they are tested again with the BDI. This experiment is a one-group pretest–posttest design that assesses the effect of cognitive therapy.

Analyzing the data from a one-group pretest–posttest design follows the same pattern as the one you saw for the cognitive processing experiment, a one-group two-treatment design. However, rather than using the names of the two treatments as the levels of the IV, the labels are *pretest* and *posttest*. If the posttest is significantly different from the pretest, the intervening treatment may be responsible.

Maturation

Maturation is a concept that refers to biological and psychological changes that occur over time. When used to describe an extraneous variable, **maturation** refers to both long-term changes such as biological maturation and to short-term changes such as fatigue.

Normal aging can be a maturational extraneous variable in longitudinal studies of children who are assessed over a long period. Consider, for example, a school-based program to improve children's self-esteem. The children's self-esteem is measured in the fall, the program is implemented during the school year, and the children are retested in the spring. Suppose the mean self-esteem score is higher in the spring. Is the program responsible? Perhaps. But another explanation is maturation. Over the course of a school year, children mature. In general, the longer they

**one group pretest–
posttest design** One
group of participants
receives a pretest, a
treatment, and a posttest.

maturation An
extraneous variable; long-
term or short-term changes
in participants that affect
the dependent variable.

TABLE 8.8	Diagram for a One-Group Pretest–posttest Design

$$O_1 \qquad T \qquad O_2$$

Time ⟶

Where: T = treatment

O = observations that constitute the dependent variable

are with the same group of peers, the more comfortable they become and their self-esteem increases. Thus, maturation or the special program or the combination of the two are reasonable explanations for the increase in self-esteem.

As for the temporary, short-term form of maturation, there are many experiments in which participants work for 30 minutes on a task. For some tasks, participants might not be as sharp during the last few minutes as they were in the start. For other tasks, however, the reverse might be true; participants are uncertain and apprehensive at the start, but engaged and confident at the end. These changes in the participants over the course of a session are maturation changes and they can affect DV scores. Tiredness, boredom, or inattention are examples of short-term maturational changes. The usual solution is to provide rest periods.

Maturation may be at work in the depression–cognitive therapy experiment. Over a 10-week period, depression scores may normally improve or they may normally get worse. Improved scores that are due to maturation might be mistakenly attributed to therapy that is actually ineffective. If depression gets worse over 10 weeks due to maturation, effective therapy might go undetected.

For the cognitive processing experiment, maturation is not an extraneous variable. The first half of the experiment lasted less than 5 minutes. It seems unlikely that participants became so engaged or tired or bored that their response during the second half of the experiment was affected.

Regression

Regression (or *regression to the mean*) is a phenomenon that can occur when participants are tested a second time. Regression is most pronounced for participants who made the highest scores or the lowest scores on the first test. Specifically, the phenomenon of regression is that high-scoring participants generally score lower when tested a second time and low-scoring participants generally score higher on a second test. Thus, both groups regress toward the mean that is established when all participants are retested.

Figure 8.2 illustrates the concept of regression. The results of the first test are shown in the upper panel. Those who scored extremely low or extremely high are circled. Their results in the second test are shown in the lower panel. The mean score of those who scored low on the first test is greater on the second test, which moves them as a group closer to the mean. Likewise, the mean score of those who scored high on the first test is lower on the second test. These changes occur unseen. Retesting the whole group a second time would show the same distribution of scores as that pictured for the first test.

regression An extraneous variable; upon retesting, extreme scores produce a mean that is closer to the population mean.

FIGURE 8.2
Illustration of
regression.

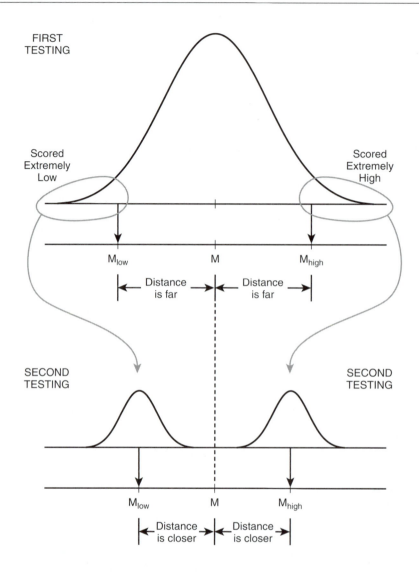

Sometimes the first test is only implied rather than being actually administered. For example, clients who seek therapy and sports figures who appear on the cover of *Sports Illustrated* represent extreme cases. People who seek therapy for depression are at a low point in their lives. Those chosen to be the cover of a magazine such as *Sports Illustrated* are usually selected for outstanding athletic performance. In either case, we can expect regression toward the mean. That is, depressed clients become less depressed and outstanding athletes fail to repeat their best performances. A common observation about Nobel Prize winners is that they seldom continue to create additional ideas of Nobel Prize quality. Regression seems to be at work in these cases as well.

TABLE 8.9	Extraneous Variables and Their Definitions

Extraneous variable	Definition
Selection	Participants in the different conditions are not equivalent before the treatment is administered.
Differential attrition	A differential loss of participants from the conditions that biases the DV scores.
Diffusion of treatment	The conditions intended for only one group of participants are experienced by other groups.
Testing	Change in a participant's score is the result of having taken the same or a similar test earlier.
Instrument change	A change in a measuring instrument (human judge, survey, or machine) during the course of an experiment.
History	Events that affect the DV that occur during one treatment but not other treatments.
Maturation	Either long-term or short-term changes in participants that affect the DV.
Regression	Extreme scores upon retesting produce a mean that is closer to the population mean.

Note: The words *treatments* and *conditions* are used interchangeably.

Regression certainly would be suspected in the depression–cognitive therapy experiment. The pretest probably shows that the clients are at or near the extreme end of the distribution of BDI scores. The mean of the retest 10 weeks later will be expected to regress toward the center of the distribution. Is regression an extraneous variable in the cognitive processing experiment? No; because there was no selection of extreme scores, there is no opportunity for subsequent scores to regress toward the mean.

Close the book and write from memory the eight extraneous variables discussed in this text.

This completes our discussion of extraneous variables. **Table 8.9** provides a list of the eight and gives their definitions.

ASSESSING ONE-GROUP DESIGNS

An assessment of one-group designs is easily made: They are poor designs. Except for selection, one-group designs might harbor any (or all) of the other extraneous variables—testing, instrument change, history, maturation, regression, differential attrition, and diffusion of treatment. Thus, as a stand-alone experiment, one-group designs are almost worthless if you want to draw cause-and-effect conclusions. Some researchers do not even call one-group designs *experiments* (Campbell & Stanley, 1966). One-group designs may be valuable, however, in the early stages of research on a particular IV. At first, researchers may just want to know if the IV *might* have an effect on the DV. Data can be gathered by the researcher or from an archival source. If no effect shows up in the initial research, the variable is not investigated further. If the IV does appear to have an effect, further research is conducted, using a better design such as a two-group design.

TWO-GROUP DESIGNS

An effective solution to the many problems inherent in one-group designs is to use a comparison group (or control group). The comparison group's experience is the same as that of the experimental group except for the treatments that make up the independent variable. The two-group designs that we illustrate are logical extensions of the one-group pretest–posttest design.

Quasi-Experimental Two-Group Pretest–Posttest Design

The **quasi-experimental two-group pretest–posttest design** has elements of both the one-group pretest–posttest design that is diagrammed in Table 8.8 and the quasi-experimental design that is discussed in chapter 7 (Table 7.9). **Table 8.10** shows a diagram of a generic quasi-experimental two-group pretest–posttest design. Each of the two groups is pretested, receives a treatment, and then takes a posttest. The effect of the treatment is expected to show up in the *difference* between the pretest and the posttest.

TABLE 8.10	Generic Notation for the Quasi-Experimental Two-Group Pretest–Posttest Design for Two Treatments		
Method of assignment	Dependent variable	Independent variable	Dependent variable
NR	O_1	T_1	O_2
NR	O_1	T_2	O_2
Time $\longrightarrow$			

Where: NR = assignment to treatments is nonrandom

T_1 and T_2 = two treatment levels of the independent variable

O = observations that constitute the dependent variable

quasi two-group pretest–posttest design Participants are not randomly assigned to two groups; each group is given a pretest and a posttest; one group receives a treatment between the tests.

To illustrate the quasi-experimental two-group pretest–posttest design, let's return to our example of the experiment that attempted to assess the value of cognitive therapy for clients with depression. In that one-group pretest–posttest design experiment, clients completed the BDI, participated in 10 weeks of cognitive therapy, and took the BDI a second time. If improvement were evident, it could be attributed to

1. Cognitive therapy, the IV in the experiment
2. Maturation, the improvement that often occurs when people are ill
3. Regression, the movement of scores toward the mean when a low-scoring group is tested a second time
4. History, the effect of events outside the experiment in the lives of the participants

With these possible explanations in mind, let's consider an experiment that uses a quasi-experimental two-group pretest–posttest design to determine the value of cognitive therapy for depression. The first task is to answer the question of who might serve as a comparison group. One solution that is often available to researchers is to use clients who have been put on a waiting list because no therapist at the clinic has an opening when they first seek help. In this case, the two groups are best identified as *therapy* and *wait-listed*. Examine **Table 8.11**, which converts the generic Table 8.10 into one specific to the depression–cognitive therapy study.

Our next step is to discuss how well the quasi-experimental two-group pretest–posttest design controls for the eight extraneous variables in Table 8.9. But first we want to give you a chance to do the analysis for yourself.

Consider the quasi-experimental two-group pretest–posttest design experiment on cognitive therapy. For each of the eight extraneous variables in Table 8.9, determine how well the design controls it.

STOP & *Think*

TABLE 8.11	Notation for the Quasi-Experimental Two-Group Pretest–Posttest Design for Two Treatments for the Depression–Cognitive Therapy Experiment

Method of assignment	Dependent variable	Independent variable	Dependent variable
Therapist available	BDI_1	Cognitive therapy	BDI_2
No therapist available	BDI_1	No therapy at clinic	BDI_2

Time ──────────────────────────────────────→

Selection   Selection appears to be fairly well controlled. Although the two groups might not be equal in depression to begin with, the effect of the treatment is found in the *difference* between the pretest and the post-test. The fact that the two groups might not be equal in the beginning is not really a problem.

Differential Attrition   Differential attrition could be a problem in this study. Of course, if the dropout rates are comparable, differential attrition is unlikely. However, if the dropout rate is higher for one group, further analysis is in order. Suppose the group with the higher dropout rate was the therapy group and that the dropouts were those with the greatest depression. If so, the scores of the therapy group would improve. In this case, the improvement in the therapy group's performance on the BDI should be attributed to differential attrition and not to therapy.

Diffusion of Treatment   Diffusion of treatment also could be a problem in this study. Clients on the waiting list might seek other sources of therapy. They might find another therapist, or they might seek therapy in less formal ways, such as from a pastor, friend, or family member. Also, they might obtain prescription medicine from a physician.

Testing   Testing and order effects are nicely controlled by the quasi-experimental two-group pretest–posttest design. Whatever the effects of taking the BDI the second time, these effects will show up in both groups, leaving the difference between the two groups unaffected.

Instrument Change   Instrument change, like testing, is well controlled by this design and for the same reason: The effect of any instrument change will not appear in the difference between the two groups.

History   History might be a problem for this particular experiment. Although large public events, such as a war or economic change, will be the same for all participants, their individual histories will surely differ. If the sample size is large, then we would expect that the ups and downs of individual histories will balance out; if the sample size is small, we don't have that assurance.

Maturation   Maturation may be well controlled because whatever maturation occurs in the therapy group can be expected to occur in the wait-listed group. However, if the mean ages of the two groups differ, maturation may be a problem because younger clients exhibit maturational change faster than older clients. To resolve this question, means and standard deviations of the ages of the two groups are needed.

Regression   Although regression to the mean can be expected for clients who seek therapy, there is no reason to expect that regression should occur more in one group than in the other. Thus, the quasi-experimental two-group pretest–posttest design controls for regression.

Data from a quasi-experimental two-group pretest–posttest design can be analyzed in one of two ways. One is fairly simple and easy to understand; the other is more complicated. For the simpler analysis, subtract the pretest score from the posttest score (or vice versa) for each participant. The result is a set of difference scores for the therapy group and a set of difference scores for the wait-listed group. The two sets of difference scores are then analyzed as two independent groups. From this point on, the analyses are the same as those used for the exercise–tiredness experiment in chapter 7. Unfortunately, the simpler, easy-to-understand way has some problems associated with it.[4]

The more complicated way to analyze data from a quasi-experimental two-group pretest–posttest design is to use a statistical technique called the *analysis of covariance (ANCOVA)*. ANCOVA statistically adjusts the posttest scores to reflect the information in the pretest scores, and it does this without creating the reliability problem that goes with difference scores. ANCOVA is usually covered in advanced courses. One other two-group design deserves attention. It is the random two-group pretest–posttest design.

Random Two-Group Pretest–Posttest Design

The **random two-group pretest–posttest design** is diagrammed in Table 8.12. As you can see, the only difference between it and the design you just studied is that the participants are randomly assigned to the two conditions. As we described earlier, random assignment is better if it is feasible. If random assignment were used for the depression–cognitive therapy experiment, the concerns raised earlier about maturation would

TABLE 8.12	Generic Notation for the Random Two-Group Pretest–Posttest Design for Two Treatments		
Method of assignment	Dependent variable	Independent variable	Dependent variable
R	O_1	T_1	O_2
R	O_1	T_2	O_2
Time ⟶			

Where: R = assignment to treatments is random

T_1 and T_2 = two treatment levels of the independent variable

O = observations that constitute the dependent variable

random two-group pretest–posttest design Participants are randomly assigned to two groups; each group is given a pretest and a posttest; one group receives a treatment between the tests.

---

[4]See Pedhazur and Schmelkin (1991) for a discussion of problems associated with difference scores.

be eliminated. With random assignment, the average age of the participants in the two groups would be approximately equal. Any maturational changes would be expected to occur equally in the two groups.

Table 8.13 shows a matrix of the six experimental designs and the eight extraneous variables we described in chapters 7 and 8. This table is a modification of one that appeared in Campbell and Stanley (1966). It is worth studying.

In the Know

In 1957, Donald T. Campbell published an article in the *Psychological Bulletin* that provided a catalog of experimental designs and their ability to control various extraneous variables. Research methods courses since then have typically included modified versions of his catalog. Campbell (1916–1996) was a social psychologist who advocated testing the outcome of governmental social programs designed to help those in need. To assess outcomes, Campbell argued that extraneous variables must be identified and eliminated (or at least reduced). Campbell is credited with popularizing the term *quasi-experimental* (Campbell & Stanley, 1966).

CONTROLLING THE EFFECTS OF EXTRANEOUS VARIABLES

As you can see in Table 8.13, there is no design that assures you that your experiment is free from all extraneous variables. Fortunately, there are techniques that can be used in specific instances that balance out the effects of extraneous variables, leaving you with a relatively pure comparison of the levels of the IV. We describe three different techniques that researchers use to control extraneous variables.

Random Assignment

In chapter 7 we described and explained random assignment, which is a very important technique for controlling extraneous variables. Our discussion and the problems you worked all focused on the random assignment of participants so that the extraneous variable selection is controlled. However, random assignment can be used to ensure equality of other extraneous variables as well.

Counterbalancing

counterbalancing A technique that orders the levels of an extraneous variable so that their effects balance out over the different levels of the independent variable.

Counterbalancing is a powerful, popular technique that can be used in several different kinds of circumstances. It is often used to control for

TABLE 8.13 Control of Extraneous Variables by Different Research Designs

Design	Extraneous Variables							
	Selection	Differential attrition	Diffusion of treatments	Testing	Instrument change	History	Maturation	Regression
Quasi-experimental	Not controlled	Not controlled	Not controlled	Controlled	??	??	??	Not controlled
Random assignment	Controlled	Not controlled	Not controlled	Controlled	Controlled	Not controlled	Controlled	Controlled
One-group two-treatment	Controlled	Controlled	Not controlled	Not controlled	??	Not controlled	Not controlled	Controlled
One-group pretest–posttest	Controlled	Controlled	Controlled	Not controlled	Not controlled	Not controlled	Not controlled	Not controlled
Quasi-experimental two-group pretest–posttest	Controlled	Not controlled	Not controlled	Controlled	??	??	??	??
Random two-group pretest–posttest	Controlled	Not controlled	Not controlled	Controlled	Controlled	??	Controlled	Controlled

Note: Use of double question marks (??) means the procedures must be studied to determine if this extraneous variable is present.

changes that occur over time and is especially useful for within-subjects designs. These changes might be in the participant, researcher, or experimental situation. Like most other methods of controlling extraneous variables, counterbalancing does not eliminate a variable but evens it out. That is, counterbalancing distributes the effect of an extraneous variable so that, on average, each level of the IV is affected the same way.

There are many variations of counterbalancing, but we cover only the simple and intermediate types. You can learn of the more complex versions in an advanced course in research design or, if you need the information for a project, you can study it for yourself (see Kantowitz, Roediger, & Elmes, 2005). Unfortunately, different writers use different terminology to describe different variations of counterbalancing, so be alert in your reading.

Gathering data for an experiment over time is common and often necessary. As time passes, however, changes in variables other than the IV are also common. For example, over the course of one 30-minute experimental session, a participant may change from uncertain to confident, or from engaged to tired. Over the course of 30 experimental sessions, a researcher may change from nervous to comfortable, or from attentive to bored. Over those same 30 sessions, the equipment may change, the kinds of participants available for study may change, and the events of history outside the experiment may change. Counterbalancing is a technique that prevents any of these changes from affecting *differences* among the levels of the IV. Best of all, even if the researcher has not anticipated the change, counterbalancing still works.

To illustrate, imagine an experiment on vigilance in which a participant spends 30 minutes monitoring a display of dials that are constantly changing. The participant's task is to record every deviation from normal on any one of the dials. The DV is the time required to detect the deviation. Over the course of the session, levels of the IV are changed by the researcher. The particular IV for the experiment might be contrast differences of the dial against the background, or color, or brightness differences. Regardless of the IV, fatigue will probably reduce vigilance over the 30-minute period, and detection time will increase.

Figure 8.3 illustrates a hypothetical increase in detection time that is due to increasing fatigue over the 30-minute period. By studying Figure 8.3, you can see that if one level of the IV was administered during the first 15 minutes and a second level during the second 15 minutes, there would be bias favoring shorter detection times for the first level of the IV. Counterbalancing addresses this problem and solves it.

The notation to express counterbalancing is a sequence of letters such as *a*, *b*, and *c*. Each letter stands for one level of the IV. The order of the letters indicates the order of the treatments. If there are two treatments, *a* and *b* are used; if three treatments, *a*, *b*, and *c*.

**simple counter-
balancing** The effects of an extraneous variable are balanced within the scores of one participant.

Simple Counterbalancing   **Simple counterbalancing** is used when participants are tested more than once for every level of the independent

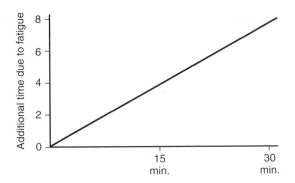

FIGURE 8.3
Hypothetical increase in detection time due to fatigue and extraneous variable.

variable. Such repeated testing is common in experiments that investigate sensation and perception. Let's apply simple counterbalancing to our vigilance experiment, which requires repeated testing. If the experiment has an IV with two levels (*a* and *b*), a counterbalanced order of treatments is:

a b b a

If the IV is contrast, *a* might be *high* and *b low*. **Figure 8.4** shows the application of this sequence to the curve in Figure 8.3. You can see that on the first presentation of the IV (*a*), the average effect is to increase time by 1 unit. On the second presentation of the IV (*b*), fatigue increases the time by 3 units and on the third presentation (*b*), detection time is increased by 5 units. On the last presentation of the IV (*a*), fatigue adds 7 units to the time required to note that a dial in the bank deviated from normal. The average increase for level *a* is 4 units [(1 + 7)/2 = 4 units]. The average increase for level *b* is also 4 units [(3 + 5)/2 = 4 units]. Thus, the effect of fatigue is to increase the time required, but this increase falls equally on both levels of the IV. As a result of counterbalancing, the *absolute difference* in the mean detection time for high contrast and low contrast is not affected by fatigue.

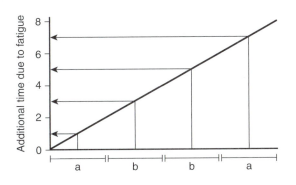

FIGURE 8.4
Application of simple counterbalancing to fatigue problem in the vigilance experiment.

The extension of simple counterbalancing to more than two conditions is straightforward. For three levels of the IV, the sequence is:

a b c c b a

The technique of simple counterbalancing also can be used when testing a participant more than two times on each level of the IV. The following sequences illustrate four tests for two conditions and four tests for three conditions:

a b b a a b b a
a b c c b a a b c c b a

Block Counterbalancing   Block counterbalancing is another versatile counterbalancing technique. It is useful when participants are tested only once on each level of the IV rather than several times as in an *a b b a a b b a* sequence. For instance, if a participant is to read three different scenarios (*a*, *b*, and *c*) and make a moral judgment about each one, it doesn't make sense to present the same scenario a second time. In other experiments, the time required to administer each treatment is such that more than one set of treatments is not feasible. **Block counterbalancing** is used to control sequence effects when a participant experiences each level of the IV only once.

Let's return to the cognitive processing experiment which had a flaw that can now be corrected using block counterbalancing. One of the major complaints about that experiment was that the order of testing was confounded with treatments. Some students, upon first reading (or recognizing) the order problem, come up with the solution: "Just have half the participants do it one order and the other half do it in the reverse order." A diagram of this solution using the *a b* terminology gives:

Order 1   *a b*
Order 2   *b a*

If *a* = shallow processing and *b* = deep processing, order of testing is nicely balanced. Shallow processing occurs first for half of the participants and deep processing occurs first for the other half. Of course, shallow and deep both occur second for half of the participants as well.

A block counterbalanced design is a "square" design. The number of orders is equal to the number of treatments. Block counterbalancing, like simple counterbalancing, distributes changes that occur over time in such a way that differences among levels of the IV are not affected.

Table 8.14 illustrates a block counterbalanced design for an IV with three levels. If being tested first is an advantage, then all three treatments get that advantage because each was presented first one time. If being tested first is a disadvantage, each treatment suffers the disadvantage

block counterbalancing
The effects of an extraneous variable are balanced using several participants.

TABLE 8.14	Block Counterbalancing for an IV With Three Levels		
Order 1	*a*	*b*	*c*
Order 2	*b*	*c*	*a*
Order 3	*c*	*a*	*b*
Time ———————————————————→			

once. In a similar way, you can see that the effects of being tested second and being tested third fall equally on the three treatments.

In the cognitive processing experiment, we identified three extraneous variables that were confounded with the IV (levels of processing). The three were order of testing, different lists, and different processing times. As you saw above, block counterbalancing solves the order of testing problem. Can it also solve the different lists problem? What about the problem of different processing times? Can it solve that one too? After all, we did describe counterbalancing as a versatile technique.

At first glance, it appears that block counterbalancing is a simple solution to the different lists problem. If we designate the two lists 1 and 2, then half the deep processing trials present list 1 and half use list 2. Similarly, for shallow processing, half the trials use list 2 and half use list 1. The next question is whether we can counterbalance both the order of testing *and* the different lists? Unfortunately, this is impossible using only two groups.

Use the designations *deep*$_1$, *deep*$_2$, *shallow*$_1$, and *shallow*$_2$ to indicate the two levels of the IV and the two lists. Prove to yourself that you cannot achieve block counterbalancing of both the levels of the IV and the lists with just two groups of participants.

STOP
& *Think*

Fortunately, a modification of block counterbalancing solves the problem revealed in the Stop & Think feature. The solution is to divide the participants into four groups. Here's our answer to the problem of counterbalancing both order of treatments and two different lists.

Group 1	*deep*$_1$	*shallow*$_2$
Group 2	*shallow*$_1$	*deep*$_2$
Group 3	*deep*$_2$	*shallow*$_1$
Group 4	*shallow*$_2$	*deep*$_1$

Again, you can see that the effects of order of presentation are balanced between the two conditions of the experiment. Deep processing and shallow processing both appear first an equal number of times. Also, the effects of the two different lists are balanced; assessment of the deep condition is based on both the 1 list and the 2 list and the shallow condition is too.

There was one other extraneous variable in the cognitive processing experiment—processing time. Participants studied the deep processing list longer than they studied the shallow processing list. Can counterbalancing solve this problem? No, it cannot. The way to ensure equal times for the two conditions is to pace the participants so that they are forced to spend equal time on each word.

One characteristic of block counterbalancing deserves additional attention. Although block counterbalancing balances out overall order effects, it does not control for **carryover effects.** Look back at Table 8.14. Suppose that *a* was strenuous exercise, *b* was moderate exercise, and *c* was no exercise. If *a* is strenuous exercise, then any carryover effect will fall on *b* twice. (See order 1 and order 3.) The carryover effect of strenuous exercise never falls on *c*, the no-exercise condition. Thus, if there is a carryover effect of *a* that is different from *b*, block counterbalancing will not create the kind of equality that we strive for. More complicated versions of block counterbalancing such as complete counterbalancing, Latin Squares, and Greco-Latin Squares are used to control carryover effects (see Kirk, 1995).

Finally, you may have noted that our graphs and our explanations indicate that the extraneous variable has a linear effect. What if the effect is not linear, but curved in some fashion? Fortunately, counterbalancing still achieves much of what we have claimed for it, even though the perfect equality of our examples is compromised somewhat when the relationship is not linear.

Matching

Matching is a third technique that researchers use to balance out extraneous variables. Like counterbalancing, matching does not remove the effects of the extraneous variable, but distributes its effects equally across the levels of the IV. To use matching a researcher assembles a group of participants and then divides them into sets. Each member of a set is like the other members of that set on some extraneous variable that is related to the DV. Each member of a set supplies data for one level of the IV. Thus, the number of participants in a set is equal to the number of levels of the IV. As with all experiments, the mean scores of the different levels of the IV are compared. Differences among the means on the DV cannot be attributed to the extraneous variable because matching created group equality or near equality of the levels on the extraneous variable.

We illustrate matching using the data in **Table 7.12**. For purposes of illustration, suppose that the DV is to be the number of logic puzzles solved in 20 minutes. To create two samples that are the same in ability to solve logic puzzles, we match participants on a variable related to ability to solve logic puzzles. Our related variable is college grade point average (GPA). In chapter 6 we used random assignment to accomplish this same task of creating two (nearly) equal groups. The outcome of the random assignment in Table 7.14 was two groups with mean GPAs of 2.89 and 2.91.

To match participants, sort the data in Table 7.12 for GPAs from high to low. The result is **Table 8.15.** The GPAs range from 4.0 at the

carryover effect Occurs when the degree of responsiveness to a treatment depends on which other treatment preceded it.

matching Creating groups of participants who have similar scores on a variable correlated with the dependent variable.

| TABLE 8.15 | | | Forty College Students and Three Variables, Sorted by GPA | | | | |

Student ID no.	Gender	GPA	Optimism score	Student ID no.	Gender	GPA	Optimism score
12	female	4.0	15	23	female	2.9	9
24	female	3.8	15	32	male	2.9	18
8	female	3.7	15	3	female	2.8	8
33	male	3.6	20	6	female	2.8	19
36	male	3.6	14	9	female	2.8	16
5	female	3.5	14	18	female	2.7	12
22	female	3.5	11	40	male	2.7	11
30	male	3.4	23	16	female	2.6	7
10	female	3.3	21	21	female	2.6	13
39	male	3.3	17	38	male	2.6	18
2	female	3.2	17	19	female	2.5	11
20	female	3.2	13	35	male	2.5	17
37	male	3.2	5	14	female	2.4	16
26	male	3.1	15	25	male	2.3	14
34	male	3.1	14	29	male	2.3	8
7	female	3.0	10	11	female	2.2	12
17	female	3.0	20	27	male	2.2	13
28	male	3.0	14	4	female	2.1	13
1	female	2.9	10	31	male	2.0	10
13	female	2.9	18	15	female	1.8	14

top to 1.8 at the bottom. The next step creates sets of two participants, matched for GPA. Each set has two members because the IV has two levels. In Table 8.15 the first two students constitute a set, the second two are a set, and so on. One member of a set is assigned to Group 1 and the other to Group 2. We assigned members by alternately placing the first or the second member of the set into Group 1. Another procedure is to randomly assign one of each pair to Group 1. **Table 8.16** shows two groups, matched for GPA. Not surprisingly, the mean GPA of the two groups is exactly the same, 2.90. The standard deviations are similar, 0.54 and 0.51.

Of course, matching guarantees that the means will be the same or almost the same. Your question now might be, "Why not use matching rather than random assignment all the time?" The answer is that although matching guarantees equality on the matched variable, it carries with it no assurance about other variables. Random assignment, on the other hand, assures us of approximately equal samples on all variables. In addition, researchers do not always have a list of their participants before the study, much less a list that includes scores on a variable highly correlated with the DV.

TABLE 8.16	Two Groups of Students Matched for GPA (Data From Table 8.15)

	Group 1	Group 2
	4.0	3.8
	3.6	3.7
	3.6	3.5
	3.4	3.5
	3.3	3.3
	3.2	3.2
	3.2	3.1
	3.0	3.1
	3.0	3.0
	2.9	2.9
	2.9	2.9
	2.8	2.8
	2.8	2.7
	2.6	2.7
	2.6	2.6
	2.5	2.5
	2.4	2.3
	2.2	2.3
	2.2	2.1
	1.8	2.0
M	2.90	2.90
SD	0.54	0.51

BETWEEN-SUBJECTS AND WITHIN-SUBJECTS DESIGNS COMPARED

For many research problems it is possible to choose either a between-subjects design such as those discussed in chapter 7 or a within-subjects design as described in this chapter. Picking a design that provides answers to a research question is governed heavily by the particulars of the research question, but here are three considerations.

Number of Participants

The number of participants required for a within-subjects design is less than the number required for a between-subjects design, except when matching is used. When matching is used, the number of participants is equal for the two different designs. However, in within-subjects designs where participants provide data for every level of the IV, only half as many are needed for a within-subjects design as for a between-subjects design when the IV has two levels. As the number of levels of the IV increases, the proportion of participants required decreases. If the IV has three levels, only one third of the participants are needed, and so forth. Fewer participants may mean less paperwork, fewer debriefings, and quicker data gathering. Some of this efficiency for the researcher comes at a cost to the participants. For their part, they spend more time participating in a within-subjects experiment than they do in a between-subjects experiment. If the time they are required to spend is too great, attrition might become a problem for the researcher.

Statistical Sensitivity

A test with greater **statistical sensitivity** is more likely to detect a false null hypothesis than one with less statistical sensitivity. Statistical tests on data from within-subjects designs are more sensitive to the differences in the levels of the IV than statistical tests on data from between-subjects designs. In a between-subjects design, individual differences produce scores that are variable and the variability may obscure the effect of the IV. When individual differences are great, the effect of the IV has to be large if it is to be detected over the "noise" of the individual differences. The statistical tests for within-subjects design data, however, remove the effects of the individual differences from the scores. The result is that the effect of the IV has less noise to compete with. Because there is less noise, within-subjects designs are more likely to detect differences among the levels of the IV. This issue of sensitivity was discussed in chapter 6 under a different name: *sample variability*. The section on power in that chapter (page 194) explained that reducing sample variability allows better detection of differences in the populations. Thus, another way to express the increased sensitivity of within-subjects designs is to say that within-subjects designs are more powerful than between-subjects designs.

Carryover Effects

A carryover effect occurs if the administration of a level of the IV has an effect on participants that influences their response to the next level of the IV. Carryover effects can be a problem for within-subjects designs but not for between-subjects designs. As mentioned earlier, counterbalancing can equalize the effects of order, but carryover effects remain. Fortunately for many IVs, carryover effects are not a problem. For example, in experiments that have participants make perceptual judgments, carryover effects do not typically occur. Most perceptual judgments are not affected by previous judgments. The usual solution when carryover effects are recognized as a problem is to use a between-subjects design.

EXTERNAL VALIDITY

To complete these two chapters that introduce you to research design, we return to two central concepts that were introduced in chapter 2, internal and external validity. A measurement is valid if it measures what it claims

statistical sensitivity
The degree to which a statistical test can detect a false null hypothesis.

to measure. In an experiment, the researcher typically makes two claims about what is being measured. One claim is about the IV and the DV. Researchers claim to be measuring the effect that changes in the IV have on the DV. If the claim is true, the experiment has **internal validity.** If an experiment has internal validity, it is the IV and not an extraneous variable that is responsible for changes in the DV. An internally valid experiment has no uncontrolled extraneous variables.

A second claim of researchers, either expressed or implied, involves generalization. After determining the results for a sample, researchers generalize their conclusions to a population. Generalization is a goal that characterizes all research. This second claim, that the results of the experiment can be generalized to some larger, untested, unmeasured group, is a claim of **external validity.** Thus, the results of an externally valid experiment can be generalized to some larger group, some additional situations, or some other time.

Every experiment should be examined for threats to both internal and external validity. This chapter and the previous one included extensive explanations of eight threats to internal validity, which are listed in Table 8.13. In this section we discuss four threats to external validity and the techniques that researchers use to counter those threats.

Biased Sampling

Every research sample is a sample of some larger population of participants (or subjects), situations, and times. The population might be sophomores, schizophrenics, or Hispanics. It might be another interesting group such as cities, cats, or archival records. The situation might be a college campus, a factory, or a deserted island. The time might be a day of the week, the past, or a particular time in the future. Of course, every particular experiment is limited and specific. Only certain sophomores, cities, or Sundays are in the experiment. Thus, asking "How representative is the sample?" is always a fair question. *Sample* can refer to the participants, situations, or times. If the researcher's goal is to generalize to a population and the sample is not representative, then the generalization will not be accurate.

The elegant response to the threat of biased sampling is to use a **random sample.** In a random sample, every member of the population had an equal chance of being selected for the sample. Random samples, especially large ones, are known to represent the population they come from quite accurately.

Unfortunately, obtaining a random sample is not easy, and in many cases it is impossible. Obtaining a random sample requires that every member of the population be identified. As a practical matter, it is impossible to identify all sophomores, schizophrenics, or cats. For some populations, however, every member can be identified. Cities and archival records are two examples.

internal validity
No extraneous variables are confounded with the independent variable.

external validity Results can be generalized to other populations, situations, or conditions.

random sample A sample from a population obtained by applying a random sampling technique.

In fact, random samples are rare in published research. For example, of 76 samples reported in 2004–2005 issues of the *Journal of Counseling and Clinical Psychology,* only five (7%) used a random sample (and these were from a restricted population). The rest of the samples (93%) were nonrandom. Sometimes students are surprised to find that so few studies use random samples. Let's explore the justifications that researchers have for not using random samples.

Often, the goal of the researcher is to investigate a psychological process rather than to determine characteristics of the population. Researchers who study sensory and perceptual processes, learning, memory, and other areas focus on the process that is involved and not on whether the participants are representative of some larger population. These researchers are quite willing to assume that if they can explain the process, another researcher can determine if it applies more widely.

In many cases, there is no logical or empirical reason to believe that the sample is *not* representative of the population. Again, researchers who study sensory and perceptual processes, learning, and memory in college sophomores have no reason to think that their participants are different in kind from other humans. As a result, they generalize even though they do not have a random sample.

Probably the most convincing evidence of the generality of a finding is a replication. When an independent researcher repeats procedures and gets essentially the same results, everyone's confidence in the external validity of the original finding goes up.

Reactivity

When psychologists perform an experiment, they do so in a particular setting. Sometimes the setting itself has an effect of its own on the DV, over and above the effect of the IV. If it is the setting that is producing the results, the experiment lacks external validity. This is the problem of **reactivity,** which is sometimes referred to as participant reactivity. Thus, reactivity occurs when a participant's response is influenced by the particular setting in which the data are gathered. The problem of reactivity is sometimes described as being due to the *demand characteristics* of the situation. That is, the situation "demands" a particular response from the participant.

Perhaps the most famous case of reactivity occurred in the early days of I/O psychology.[5] From 1927 to 1932 the Western Electric Company conducted studies on a group of workers at its Hawthorne Works, a manufacturing facility near Chicago. Western Electric manufactured telephones and related equipment for the only telephone company in America, AT&T. For these studies, a group of workers who assembled

---

[5]Industrial/organizational psychology. I/O psychology specializes in applications of psychological facts and principles to problems in organizations.

reactivity Participants' dependent variable scores are affected by the situation in which data are gathered.

electrical relays was separated from the others. A variety of changes in their daily schedules followed, one at a time. Five-minute rest periods were provided, first in the afternoon, and then in the morning as well. The rests were increased to 10 minutes. The company provided snacks during the rest periods. Quitting time was changed to 30 minutes earlier. Rest periods (and snacks) were taken away. The rest periods were reinstituted. With *every* change, production increased. Finally, those conducting the study concluded that it was the special attention paid to the workers, rather than the schedule changes, that increased output. Today we refer to the **Hawthorne effect** as a change in performance that is due to being in an experiment rather than to a planned manipulation by the researcher. The Hawthorne effect is a case of reactivity (see Mayo, 1946). The Hawthorne studies were conducted in a special setting. In one sense, however, anytime participants know they are in a psychological study they may act differently.

Pretest Sensitization

Pretest sensitization occurs when participants respond to a treatment differently if they experience a pretest before the treatment. You can imagine that a participant who is administered a pretest on racial attitudes and then shown a video clip might be much more prone to attend to the racial elements of the clip, as compared to a participant who was not pretested. As a result, pretested participants might respond to the clip differently than unpretested participants.

   If pretest sensitization is known to be a problem or reasonably appears to be a problem, researchers may turn to a fairly expensive solution, the **Solomon four-group design.** This design is diagrammed in **Table 8.17** for an IV with two levels. This Solomon four-group design experiment has one IV with two levels, T_1 and T_2, but there are four groups of participants. Assignment to groups in the Solomon four-group design

Hawthorne effect A performance change when participants know they are being observed.

pretest sensitization Participants' scores are affected by a previous pretest.

Solomon four-group design Four groups are used to assess the independent variable and pretest sensitization.

| TABLE 8.17 | Notation for the Solomon Four-Group Design for Two Treatments |

Group	Method of assignment	Dependent variable	Independent variable	Dependent variable
A	R/NR	O_1	T_1	O_2
B	R/NR		T_1	O_1
C	R/NR	O_1	T_2	O_2
D	R/NR		T_2	O_1

Time ⟶

Where: R/NR = assignment to treatments—either random or nonrandom

   T_1 and T_2 = two treatment levels of the independent variable

   O = observations that constitute the dependent variable

might be random (if that is feasible) or nonrandom. In the Solomon four-group design, half the participants receive a pretest before they receive a treatment (Groups A and C), but half do not (Groups B and D).

To determine if pretest sensitization occurred in the T_1 treatment, compare the O_2 mean of Group A to the O_1 mean of Group B. If there was no pretest sensitization, the means will be about the same. In a similar way, the design reveals any pretest sensitization in the T_2 treatment when the O_2 mean of Group C and the O_1 mean of Group D are compared.

The Solomon four-group design is not popular because it requires nearly twice the resources just to be able to detect pretest sensitization. A search for "Solomon four group" in PsycINFO on March 9, 2006, found only 115 studies since 1964. In the early stages of a research program, researchers usually choose a design that devotes its resources to controlling extraneous variables. Once internal validity is ensured, researchers turn to establishing external validity. If there is a question about pretest sensitivity, the Solomon four-group design can answer the question.

Multiple Treatments

Pretests are not the only things that occur before a treatment is administered. For within-subjects designs with multiple treatments, treatments occur before other treatments are administered. Thus, when there are multiple treatments, there may be a question of how well the results apply to those who have not experienced previous treatments.[6] Counterbalancing assures you that the effects of order (experience) are distributed evenly, but it does not assure you that the results would be the same if there were no previous treatments.

WHICH IS MORE IMPORTANT, INTERNAL OR EXTERNAL VALIDITY?

Which is more important, internal or external validity?

STOP
& *Think*

Most researchers reason that internal validity is more important than external validity. If you have internal validity, you know that the IV (and not some extraneous variable) caused the changes in the DV. If you have external validity, you know not only that the IV caused changes in the DV but also that this relationship is true in some context wider than that of the specific experiment. Thus, according to most researchers, you cannot have external validity without first having internal validity. Once internal validity is secured, the question of external validity is appropriate. The relative importance of internal and external validity is a topic on which not all researchers agree (Mook, 2003).

---

[6]Some researchers consider multiple treatments a threat to external validity that is separate from pretest sensitization.

CONCLUSION

In this chapter and in chapter 7, our principal goal has been to explain the experiment, an invention of science that helps reveal cause-and-effect relationships. Experiments consist of conditions that are compared. Particularly elegant experiments have conditions that are similar, but differ in only one way.

In planning experiments, researchers make many choices such as the kind of design, assignment of participants to groups, and statistical analyses. Researchers make these choices on the basis of both practical considerations and how well the design controls extraneous variables for their particular project. Uncontrolled extraneous variables have the unfortunate effect of reducing the similarity between the conditions of the experiment. The more dissimilar the conditions, the weaker the evidence for a cause-and-effect relationship. An experiment in which extraneous variables are controlled has internal validity, which is a goal of researchers. **Figure 8.5** shows two researchers straining to keep extraneous variables (gremlins) out of their experiment.

FIGURE 8.5   Maintaining a research clean room.

In addition to internal validity, researchers strive for external validity. Experiments with external validity produce conclusions that are true for other populations, situations, and times. As you study methods of research, analyze the research of others, and perhaps conduct studies of your own, we are sure that your efforts will prepare you not only for future courses and research, but also for decision making in your world outside academics.

Chapter Review _____

1. Whereas chapter 7 focused on between-subjects designs, this
   chapter focused on _____ designs.
2. When the effect of counting letters was compared to the effect of writing associates, the result was that recall was better after

   _____.

3. The two one-group designs that were explained in this chapter are the _____ and _____.
4. Match the extraneous variables to the descriptions.

   1. maturation
   2. regression
   3. differential attrition
   4. diffusion of treatment
   5. history
   6. instrument change
   7. testing
   8. selection

   a. During the experiment the air conditioning failed while the experimental group worked, but it was fixed for the control group's session.
   b. The two groups were different even before the IV was introduced.
   c. As the judges got more experience with verbal insults, they noted more and more of them.
   d. The participants became progressively less attentive as the experiment progressed.
   e. The participants who did not return for retesting were the depressed ones who were in the treatment group.
   f. Because they remembered their pretest answers, the participants used the same answers on the posttest.
   g. Almost all of the participants who scored poorly on the first test did better on the second test.
   h. The participants in the morning class explained to those in the afternoon class that there would be a surprise memory test.

5. The two two-group designs that are explained in this chapter are

   the _____ and the _____.

6. Depth perception was measured for the left eye (*L*) and the right eye (*R*). If half the participants were measured for *L* and then for *R* and the other half were measured for *R* and then for *L*, _____ counterbalancing occurred. If each participant was measured first for *L*, then for *R*, then *R*, and finally *L*, _____ counterbalancing was used.

7. List the three techniques that were described to control extraneous variables.

8. The text discussed a problem that is not fixed by either simple counterbalancing or block counterbalancing. The problem is

_____.

9. Three differences that distinguish between-subjects designs from within-subjects designs are _____, _____, and _____.

10. An internally valid study is characterized by _____. If a study is externally valid, the results can be _____.

11. List the four threats to external validity that the text discussed.

12. Selection and testing affect _____ validity. Reactivity and pretest sensitization affect _____ validity.

13. The design that pretests two of the four groups is called the _____ four-group design.

Thinking Critically About Research

1. Explain how to create three groups that are matched for their optimism score using the participants in Table 8.15. What are the scores of the three participants in the lowest-scoring group?

2. For each of the experiments that follow, identify its design and then identify an extraneous variable that is not controlled or that might not be controlled.

    a. Devin had participants work a simple jigsaw puzzle. She then randomly assigned them to one of two conditions. In one condition, Devin encouraged participants while they worked a second jigsaw puzzle. In the other condition, the participants worked the second puzzle in silence. The time required to work the puzzles was recorded for each individual.

    b. Tilly noted the number of students who arrived late for his anthropology class on days when a video was scheduled and on days when no video was scheduled.

c. In the 8 a.m. General Psychology class, students were given a test on operant conditioning. A lecture on operant conditioning followed. The class ended with the students taking the same test on operant conditioning. The 3 p.m. General Psychology class followed an identical schedule except that a demonstration covered the same information as discussed in the lecture.

d. Terry had 6-year-old day-camp children judge 30 pictures of faces as happy or sad. The children then watched a long video clip about a boy with a disability. Afterward, the children again rated the 30 pictures. The DV was the difference in the number of faces judged as sad before and after the video clip.

e. Richard used four classes of fifth-grade students to evaluate a new method of teaching spelling. On Monday, two classes took a 50-word spelling test. One of the classes studied the list Tuesday through Thursday using the new method; the other class did not study the list. Both classes took the spelling test on Friday. The third class studied the list Tuesday through Thursday using the new method and took their first test on Friday. The fourth class simply took the test on Friday, not having studied the words during the week.

f. Khiela's participants filled out an anxiety questionnaire and then joined a yoga class. After attending five yoga classes, they filled out the anxiety questionnaire again.

3. Suppose you wanted to find the effect that color has on a baby's heart rate. You have an awake 2-month-old child, large towels that are red (R), blue (B), and yellow (Y), a way to measure heart rate, and time to take 12 measurements. Write out a counterbalanced order for presentation of 12 stimuli.

Answers to Chapter Review

1. within-subjects
2. writing associates
3. one-group two-treatment design; one-group pretest–posttest design
4. 1. d; 2. g; 3. e; 4. h; 5. a; 6. c; 7. f; 8. b
5. quasi-experimental two-group pretest–posttest design; random two-group pretest–posttest design
6. block; simple
7. randomization, counterbalancing, matching
8. carryover effects
9. number of participants required; statistical sensitivity; carryover effects
10. no uncontrolled extraneous variables; generalized to a population

11. biased sampling, reactivity, pretest sensitivity, multiple treatments

12. internal; external

13. Solomon

Answers to Thinking Critically About Research

1. Order the list of optimism scores from low to high (or vice versa). The three scores in the lowest-scoring group are 5, 7, and 8.

2. a. random two-group pretest–posttest design; extraneous variable: history

   b. one-group two-treatment design; extraneous variables: differential attrition and perhaps instrument change, if the videos are mostly scheduled early or late in the observation period

   c. quasi-experimental two-group pretest–posttest design; extraneous variable: selection

   d. one-group pretest–posttest design; extraneous variables: history, maturation, testing

   e. Solomon four-group design; extraneous variables: selection, diffusion of treatment, and perhaps, differential attrition

   f. one-group pretest–posttest design; extraneous variables: history and perhaps testing. Regression could be an extraneous variable, depending on how participants were recruited.

3. R, B, Y, Y, B, R, R, B, Y, Y, B, R

Know for Sure

Complex Designs

OVERVIEW

Experiments that have more than two groups (multilevel designs) or more than one independent variable (factorial designs) are topics of this chapter. The statistical tests for such designs (one-way ANOVA, factorial ANOVA, Tukey HSD tests, and the effect size index, d), are explained. Two kinds of multilevel designs, between-subjects and within-subjects, are discussed, as well as factorial designs, which permit the detection of interactions between variables. Finally, interpreting the interaction is emphasized.

OBJECTIVES

After studying this chapter and working through the exercises, you should be able to:

1. Distinguish between multilevel experiments and factorial experiments
2. For multilevel experiments, distinguish between between-subjects designs and within-subjects designs
3. Examine the procedures of complex experiments to detect extraneous variables
4. Analyze data from multilevel experiments with a one-way ANOVA and data from factorial experiments with a factorial ANOVA
5. Calculate and interpret Tukey HSD tests for multilevel experiments and factorial experiments
6. Calculate d for multilevel experiments and factorial experiments
7. Name the two variances in F ratios
8. Interpret factorial notation
9. Define *interaction* and *main effect* in factorial designs
10. Interpret the interactions and main effects of between-subjects factorial ANOVAs

O n the morning of July 9, Brad Walker, age 12, awoke with severe stomach cramps. He vomited, had diarrhea, and his temperature was 103 degrees Fahrenheit. His mother rushed him to a family practice medical clinic. Dr. James Taylor, MD, age 63, immediately recognized the symptoms of acute appendicitis. He sent Brad to the hospital where he met him and performed an emergency appendectomy.

The laboratory report on the appendix showed no pathology. It was later determined that Brad's symptoms were caused by a bacterium, *Yersinia enterocolitica,* which mimics the symptoms of acute appendicitis. Twenty-nine other cases of yersiniosis had been reported to health officials by other physicians in the metropolitan area. Dr. Taylor's diagnosis was mistaken and the appendectomy was not necessary.

Having read the scenario, please make a judgment about Dr. Taylor. On a scale of 1–7 with 1 being *blameless* and 7 being *totally to blame,* how much blame do you think that Dr. Taylor deserves for the unnecessary operation? Write your answer.

In a study by undergraduate student Didi Harrison, the average blame score assigned by college students was almost 4 on the 1–7 scale (reported by McKenna, 1995). In Harrison's experiment, however, half the college students saw a slightly different version of the scenario. In the other version, Dr. Taylor was "age 28." For this younger Dr. Taylor, the average blame score was only about 2 on the 7-point scale. The difference in the two means is statistically significant. The conclusion from this experiment so far is that people are more forgiving of a mistake by a young physician than they are of a mistake by an older physician.

Would you agree with the conclusion above, or do you think "it depends"? If you think it depends, then identify one or more things (variables) that affect the conclusion.

Harrison thought that a variable that would affect forgiveness was the age of those who were judging Dr. Taylor. As a result, her experiment included not only traditional college students, ages 18–22, but also residents of a retirement apartment complex whose ages ranged from 64 to 87 years. Half of the retirees read the scenario you read; half read the scenario in which the physician was 28 years old. For the retirees, the effect of the age of the physician was *reversed.* The average blame score for the older physician was just over 2 and the average blame score for the younger physician was 5! Thus, the blame that people ascribe to a physician who performs an unnecessary appendectomy depends not only on the age of the physician but also on the age of the participants who assign the blame.

Was "age of the participants" on your list of variables that might affect the outcome of the Harrison experiment? What about Brad's age? If Brad had been 18 or 20 years old, perhaps the college-age participants would identify with him and be less forgiving of a young doctor who performs an unnecessary operation. Do the names Brad Walker and Dr. James Taylor have any effect on the blame ratings? Perhaps. Although the names in a research scenario may appear to be of no consequence, different names produce effects of their own. For example, Bruning, Polinko, Zerbst, and Buckingham (2000) showed that college students predicted different outcomes for job success, depending on the name in the scenario.

Perhaps the "it depends" variables that we've described do not include one you listed for our Stop & Think problem, but yours could be a perfectly good answer. Of course, the way we worded the problem, any answer will do, but if you can give a reason or cite a study that supports your answer, your grade from us would be an A.

The experiment that investigated the effect of physician age and participant age is an example of a factorial design, which we cover in the last section of this chapter. Factorial designs are probably the most popular research designs in psychology. They are popular because they are efficient and because they yield information about *interactions,* information that can only be found with factorial experiments. Multilevel experiments are simpler than factorial experiments, so we begin with them.

MULTILEVEL EXPERIMENTS

Multilevel experiments have one IV just like the basic experiments described in chapters 7 and 8, but multilevel experiments have three or more levels of the IV rather than two. Multilevel experiments are quite common. An analysis of 50 consecutive articles published in 2006 in *Psychological Science* revealed that more than two-thirds of the IVs had three or more levels.

Multilevel experiments can be either between-subjects designs or within-subjects designs. In between-subjects designs, the participants provide data for just one treatment and they are not matched in any way with another participant. Within-subjects designs are characterized by participants who contribute data to every treatment condition or are part of a matched set of participants each of whom contributes data to one treatment condition. We have examples of both between-subjects and within-subjects designs in the pages that follow.

Between-Subjects Multilevel Experiments

Table 9.1 shows the notation for a between-subjects experiment with one IV that has three levels. Experiments with three or more levels are a little more complicated than the two-group experiment outlined in Table 7.9. Note that the method of assignment of participants to treatments in Table 9.1 might be random or nonrandom. As is always the case, statements

| TABLE 9.1 | Notation for a Between-Subjects Experiment With One IV That Has Three Levels |

Method of assignment	Independent variable	Dependent variable
R/NR	T_1	O
R/NR	T_2	O
R/NR	T_3	O

Time ⟶

Where: R/NR = assignment to treatments can be random or nonrandom

T_1, T_2, and T_3 = three treatment levels of the independent variable

O = observations that constitute the dependent variable

of cause and effect are generally not warranted if assignment is nonrandom. For experiments with *more* than three treatments, you can probably imagine an expanded Table 9.1; additional rows represent additional treatments.

An Experiment on Improving Communication Skills

We illustrate a between-subjects multilevel design with data based on an experiment by Morin and Latham (2000). Morin and Latham's study is a contribution to positive psychology, a subfield of psychology that investigates variables that improve human well-being. In their study, they investigated the effects of goal setting, visualization, and encouragement on becoming a better communicator. Our description covers only a portion of their research.

The participants in the Morin and Latham experiment were supervisors at a large mill that processes trees into paper. The management at the paper mill recognized the importance of good communication skills, so they required supervisors to attend one-day workshops in which 10 specific communication behaviors were taught. Examples of the behaviors included praise others for their suggestions, focus on the topic at hand, and thank others for their efforts. After the supervisors completed the workshop, they were randomly assigned to one of three treatments. In one treatment condition, the supervisors set specific communication *goals* for themselves and participated in a follow-up exercise about twice a week. In a second condition, and again about twice a week, the supervisors *visualized* imaginary scenarios in which they used the 10 communication skills. In the third condition, the supervisors received *encouragement* to apply the communication skills they had been taught. Thus, the IV was the follow-up treatment and the three levels were goal setting, visualization, and receiving encouragement. The dependent variable was the supervisors' communication *self-efficacy*. Self-efficacy is a person's view of his or her own ability to carry out a specific task. To measure communication self-efficacy, the researchers had the participants judge how well they communicated with others by having them rate the frequency that they practiced the 10 specific behaviors that were taught in the workshop. Obviously, a better dependent variable would be the supervisors' actual communication skills rather than their *report* of their communication skills. In this case, and in many other situations, measuring the most desirable dependent variable directly is difficult or impossible. Morin and Latham used the supervisors' self-report as a practical index of their actual communication skills.

Table 9.2 shows data that are consistent with the findings of Morin and Latham (2000). Look at the means and standard deviations.

What is your preliminary interpretation of the data in Table 9.2?

TABLE 9.2	Self-Efficacy Communication Scores of Supervisors One Month After Their Participation in One of Three Treatments Administered Following a Communications Workshop

		Follow-Up Treatment	
	Goals	*Visualization*	*Encouragement*
	126	125	123
	121	136	130
	131	130	127
	115	138	133
	134	144	117
	129	121	125
	118	131	120
	124	133	125
	137	141	136
	123	128	114
	128	145	122
	126	122	128
		135	133
		144	117
		122	
M	126.00	133.00	125.00
SD	6.37	8.35	6.65
N	12	15	14

Source: Based on Morin and Latham, (2000).

A preliminary interpretation of the data in Table 9.2 is that visualization of workshop skills produces higher communication self-efficacy scores than does goal setting or receiving encouragement. Confirmation of this conclusion depends on two additional analyses, one statistical and one conceptual.

One-Way ANOVA　The most common way to analyze data from multi-level experiments (and factorial experiments as well) is with an **analysis of variance (ANOVA).** Could the differences in means in Table 9.2 be the result of chance, or can chance be ruled out as an explanation for the differences? This question is a null hypothesis statistical testing (NHST) question. The NHST technique that is appropriate for these data is a **one-way ANOVA.** A one-way ANOVA is like an unpaired t test except that the number of levels of the IV can be two or *more*.

The null hypothesis of a one-way ANOVA is that all the samples are from populations with identical means. The outcome of a one-way ANOVA is a statistic called F. (ANOVAs are sometimes referred to as F tests.) The probability associated with the F value leads to a familiar decision: if $p < \alpha$, reject H_0; if $p > \alpha$, retain H_0. Typically, $\alpha = .05$. Probabilities for F values might come from a table of F values or from a computer program that analyzes data.

Analysis of variance works by partitioning variances. The total variability in the data, as measured by the variance, is divided into a portion that is due to known causes and a portion that is left over. The leftover portion is referred to as the **residual variance** (and also *error variance* and *within-groups* variance). In the case of a between-subjects multilevel experiment, a one-way ANOVA divides the total variance into a portion due to the IV and the residual portion. The F value in a one-way ANOVA is the ratio of the variance due to the IV divided by the residual variance.

$$F = \frac{\text{Variance due to the IV}}{\text{Residual variance}}$$

analysis of variance (ANOVA)　NHST technique that partitions total variance into components associated with specific effects, such as main effects (means) and interactions.

one-way ANOVA　NHST technique for between-subjects multilevel experiments.

residual variance　The variance in an ANOVA that remains after the variance that is associated with known causes is removed.

Every F value is accompanied by two degrees of freedom, one associated with the variance in the numerator and one with the variance in the denominator. These degrees of freedom (df) for an F are part of the printout of computer software programs such as SPSS.

SPSS Analysis　The task of calculating F values is most efficiently done by statistical software such as SPSS. **Table 9.3** shows a portion of the SPSS output for the data in Table 9.2. The upper panel shows descriptive statistics for the three treatments—means, standard deviations, standard errors, and 95% confidence intervals about the means. The middle panel of Table 9.3 is an ANOVA summary table. The F value for the ANOVA is 5.207, which has a probability of .01. A written expression of an F value typically includes its df and probability. Thus, for the Morin and Latham (2000) experiment,

| TABLE 9.3 | SPSS Output for the Data in Table 9.2, the Morin and Latham (2000) Experiment |

Descriptives

commun_score

	N	M	SD	Std. error	95% confidence interval for mean	
					Lower limit	Upper limit
Goals	12	126.0000	6.36753	1.83815	121.9543	130.0457
Visualization	15	133.0000	8.34951	2.15583	128.3762	137.6238
Encouragement	14	125.0000	6.64484	1.77591	121.1634	128.8366
Total	41	128.2195	7.97343	1.24524	125.7028	130.7362

ANOVA Summary Table

commun_score

	Sum of squares	df	Mean square	F	Sig.
Between-groups	547.024	2	273.512	5.207	.010
Within-groups	1996.000	38	52.526		
Total	2543.024	40			

Tukey HSD Tests

Dependent variable: commun_score Tukey HSD

Test_Time	Test_Time	Mean Difference	Std. Error	Sig.
Goal	viz	−7.00000*	2.80695	.044
	enc	1.00000	2.85115	.935
Visualization	goal	7.00000*	2.80695	.044
	enc	8.00000*	2.69326	.014
Encouragement	goal	−1.00000	2.85115	.935
	viz	−8.00000*	2.69326	.014

*p < .05.

$F(2, 38) = 5.21, p = .01$. This means that there is a probability of only .01 of obtaining the results that were observed, if the null hypothesis is true. Because .01 < .05, reject the null hypothesis that the three groups are all samples from the same population and conclude that one or more of the samples came from a population with a different mean. The question "Which one is different?" is answered by conducting additional tests on the data.

Conducting additional tests after finding a significant F with ANOVA is a complex topic that falls outside the scope of the usual introductory research methods course. Intermediate statistics textbooks such as Howell (2007, chapter 12) cover many aspects of this topic. Our solution to this complexity is to explain just one test, the Tukey Honestly Significant Difference (HSD) test. It is a popular, versatile test that gives answers to many of the questions that researchers have.

The Tukey HSD Test   The Tukey HSD test allows you to separately test all pairs of means in an experiment. Each test determines if two means are significantly different from each other. The formula for a Tukey HSD test is

$$ \text{HSD} = \frac{M_1 - M_2}{SE_{M_1 - M_2}} $$

By looking at the formula, you can see that the HSD test is much like a t test. In both cases, a difference between two means is divided by a standard error.[1] SPSS calculates the difference between all pairs of sample means and provides the probability for each difference. This probability is the probability of a difference as large as or larger than the one observed, if the samples come from identical populations.

For the data in Table 9.2, there are three pairs of means to test: goals $v.$ visualization, goals $v.$ encouragement, and visualization $v.$ encouragement. The lower panel in Table 9.3 shows Tukey HSD output for SPSS. The panel appears to show the results for six HSD tests, but each test is printed twice. The group that practiced visualization (middle row) had significantly higher communication scores than the goal-setting group ($p = .044$) and significantly higher scores than the encouragement group ($p = .014$). The goal-setting group and the encouragement group were not significantly different ($p = .935$).

An Effect Size Index   An effect size index answers the question, "How much effect does the IV have on the DV scores?" There are a number of indexes for one-way ANOVA experiments, but d often works well for interpreting ANOVA experiments (Howell, 2004, pp. 385–386). The statistic d, which is described in chapter 5, indicates the size of the effect an IV has on a DV. When used with ANOVA, two levels of the IV are tested at a time. Each d is a measure of the amount of difference in the DV that the two levels of the IV produce. The formula for d for a between-subjects multilevel experiment is

$$ d = \frac{M_1 - M_2}{\sqrt{MS_{\text{residual}}}} $$

Where: M_1 and M_2 are the means of two levels of the IV

$\sqrt{MS_{\text{residual}}}$ is the denominator of the F ratio

---

[1]Additional explanations for the Tukey HSD text are available in Spatz (2008), Pagano (2007), and Gravetter and Wallnau (2007).

You can use the sample means from SPSS output to calculate $M_1 - M_2$. The number in the denominator, $MS_{residual}$ is found in the ANOVA summary table of SPSS output where it is called the mean square for within groups ($MS_{within\ groups}$). Note that you have to take the square root of $MS_{within\ groups}$ to satisfy the formula for d.

For experiments with three conditions, such as the one with three follow-up treatments on communication, there are three different pairs of means and therefore three d values. The three d values for that experiment are:

$$\text{viz } v. \text{ goal} \qquad d = \frac{133.00 - 126.00}{\sqrt{52.526}} = 0.97$$

$$\text{viz } v. \text{ enc} \qquad d = \frac{133.00 - 125.00}{\sqrt{52.526}} = 1.10$$

$$\text{goal } v. \text{ enc} \qquad d = \frac{126.00 - 125.00}{\sqrt{52.526}} = 0.14$$

The interpretation of d values is explained on pages 147–148. The difference between follow-up treatment of visualization and goal setting is quite large ($d = 1.10$) as is the difference between visualization and encouragement ($d = 0.97$). The difference between goal setting and encouragement was less than 0.20, a value that is considered small.

Looking for Extraneous Variables

Before concluding that it was the follow-up exercises that produced the significant differences in communication skills shown in Table 9.3, a search for extraneous variables is required. Fortunately, all the information about extraneous variables in chapters 7 and 8 applies to multi-level designs. Look back at Table 8.13 in the previous chapter. Because Morin and Latham's procedure used random assignment, you can use the random assignment line in Table 8.13. In that table you can see that the extraneous variables of selection, testing, instrument change, maturation, and regression are normally controlled in a random assignment experiment. To determine if any of the remaining three extraneous variables (differential attrition, diffusion of treatment, or history) might be responsible for the differences observed, we examined the procedure section of the published article.

Differential Attrition Morin and Latham (2000) reported that 51 supervisors completed the workshops and volunteered for the experiment but that complete measures at the end of the experiment were available for only 41 of the supervisors. Thus, the potential for differential attrition was present. Although Morin and Latham do not tell us what groups the

10 participants who failed to complete the experiment were assigned to, they do tell us that among the final groups, there were no statistically significant differences in the age of the participants or in their years of service at the organization. Also, it is difficult to imagine that the treatments used in this experiment would lead to differential dropout rates. Thus, we do not have any evidence that differential attrition produced the differences in communication skills.

Diffusion of Treatment   Diffusion of treatment occurs when the condition that produces changed performance (either for better or for worse) is experienced by other groups, thus diminishing the true difference between groups. Morin and Latham (2000) asked the participants in both the goal-setting group and the encouragement group if they engaged in any visualization activity that was related to communication. All reported that they did not. Thus, diffusion of treatment does not appear to be operating in this experiment.

History   The extraneous variable of history occurs when the participants' experiences other than the IV are not the same and those experiences influence the DV. Unfortunately, detecting the effects of history in a published report is usually difficult. The potential for history problems is greatest when the treatments are administered sequentially, but in the Morin and Latham experiment the three treatments were administered simultaneously. Sometimes, events outside the experiment may affect different groups differently, but because the time that the data were gathered was not part of the report, an analysis based on outside events is not possible. To sum up our analysis, there is no evidence that the extraneous variable of history influenced the results.

Researchers must determine whether or not extraneous variables could be responsible for producing the effects observed in an experiment. If an extraneous variable is discovered that might be responsible, researchers either describe it in their report or redesign the study and gather new data. If no extraneous variables are detected, the report typically does not mention an unsuccessful search for extraneous variables.

Interpretation of the Communication Skills Experiment   During the month after a workshop on communication skills, three groups of supervisors at a paper mill participated in follow-up activities. Based on Tukey HSD tests ($\alpha = .05$), the mean self-efficacy score of those who visualized scenarios in which they practiced specific communication behaviors ($M = 133.00$, $SD = 8.35$, $N = 15$) was significantly higher than that of a group who engaged in goal setting ($M = 126.00$, $SD = 6.37$, $N = 12$) or a group who received encouragement to practice the communication skills ($M = 125.00$, $SD = 6.65$, $N = 14$). The mean scores of the goal-setting group and the encouragement group were not significantly different. Thus, the visualization activity was more effective in increasing communication self-efficacy than the goal-setting activity or receiving encouragement. The effect size indexes, *d*, revealed that visualization had a large effect on self-efficacy scores.

Within-Subjects Multilevel Experiments[2]

The most common within-subjects design is a repeated-measures design in which each participant provides data for every treatment condition. Thus, the DV is repeatedly obtained from each participant, but the conditions differ each time. Because each participant receives all the treatments, the experiment occurs *within one subject.* Other within-subjects designs use different participants in each treatment, but the participants are grouped into sets on the basis of similarity. A set might have similar GPA averages or be of the same socioeconomic status. Sets might be siblings or members of the same family. (See chapter 8 for other examples of variables that researchers use to form groups that are similar.)

We illustrate a within-subjects multilevel experiment with a **repeated-measures design,** which is perhaps the most common type of within-subjects design. **Table 9.4** shows a repeated-measures experiment that has an IV with three levels, T_1, T_2, and T_3. (A matched-participants design would be like Table 9.4 except the *participants* column would be replaced with a column indicating why scores in each row are grouped together—GPA, family name, and so forth.)

TABLE 9.4	Notation for a Within-Subjects Experiment With One IV That Has Three Levels		
	Independent Variable		
Participants	T_1	T_2	T_3
1	O	O	O
2	O	O	O
etc.	etc.	etc.	etc.
N	M_{T_1}	M_{T_2}	M_{T_3}

Where: T_1, T_2, and T_3 = three treatment levels of the independent variable

O = observations that constitute the dependent variable
M_{T_1}, M_{T_2}, M_{T_3} = means of Treatments 1, 2, and 3

repeated-measures design Within-subjects design in which the participants contribute dependent variable scores to every level of the independent variable.

[2]Synonymous terms for within-subjects multilevel designs include *correlated samples, related samples, dependent samples,* and *split plot.*

An Intervention Experiment

An **intervention** usually refers to a planned effort to confront a psychological problem and solve it. Studies designed to assess the effectiveness of an intervention often use a repeated-measures design. Typically, there is a pretest of the participants that reveals the extent of their problem, an intervention to treat the problem, a posttest to show the immediate effect of the program, and a follow-up test some months later to determine the program's long-term effect. Each participant contributes a score to the pretest, posttest, and follow-up, making this a repeated-measures design.

To illustrate, we turned to the topic of intervention programs designed to treat eating disorders. Stice and Shaw's (2004) meta-analysis summarizes the outcome of 60 studies. The data in Table 9.5 produce results that are consistent with their findings. Begin your analysis of this problem by studying the scores of the 10 participants in **Table 9.5.**

After studying Table 9.5, write a preliminary interpretation.

Probably the first two steps in analyzing a table with numbers are to read the title to determine what the numbers stand for and to figure out whether large numbers are good or bad. Often (as is the case in Table 9.5), the title of the table gives the information you need to start your analysis. Larger numbers indicate a more severe eating disorder. The general picture

| TABLE 9.5 | Eating Disorder Scores Consistent With Stice and Shaw's (2004) Meta-Analysis of Intervention Programs for Eating Disorders. The Larger the Score, the More Severe the Eating Disorder |

	Test Time		
Participant	Pretest	Posttest	Follow-Up
1	48	29	29
2	53	33	40
3	45	45	47
4	52	38	48
5	58	49	44
6	40	46	53
7	46	40	39
8	41	32	33
9	57	42	41
10	50	36	36
M	49.00	39.00	41.00
SD	6.16	6.58	7.27

intervention A treatment designed to correct or prevent a problem or psychological disorder.

of the data in Table 9.5 is encouraging. The pretest mean of 49.00 is reduced to 39.00 as a result of the intervention. The follow-up data, however, show some loss of the gains achieved. As with the preliminary analysis of the Morin and Latham data, the changes in the means might or might not be statistically significant. NHST is in order.

Because there are more than two levels of the IV, ANOVA is required for these data. The ANOVA technique that is appropriate for within-subjects multilevel experiments is **repeated-measures ANOVA.** A repeated-measures ANOVA is appropriate for all types of within-subjects designs. The two-group counterpart of a repeated-measures ANOVA is the paired t test.

The null hypothesis of a repeated-measures ANOVA is that the populations the samples come from all have identical means. As with all ANOVAs, the outcome of a repeated-measures ANOVA is an F value that has a probability attached to it. By now, you are on familiar ground: If $p < \alpha$, reject H_0; if $p > \alpha$, retain H_0. Once again, we turn to SPSS for data analysis.

SPSS Analysis Table 9.6 shows some of the SPSS output for the data in Table 9.5. The upper panel of Table 9.6 shows means, standard deviations, and N for the pretest, posttest, and follow-up scores. The lower panel shows

TABLE 9.6	SPSS Output for the Data in Table 9.5

Descriptive Statistics			
	Mean	Std. deviation	N
Pretest	49.0000	6.16441	10
Posttest	39.0000	6.58281	10
Follow-up	41.0000	7.27247	10

Tests of Within-Subjects Effects						
Source		Type III sum of squares	df	Mean square	F	Sig.
Testtime	Sphericity Assumed	560.000	2	280.000	9.208	.002
	Greenhouse-Geisser	560.000	1.348	415.540	9.208	.007
	Huynh-Feldt	560.000	1.500	373.401	9.208	.005
	Lower-bound	560.000	1.000	560.000	9.208	.014
Error (testtime)	Sphericity Assumed	547.333	18	30.407		
	Greenhouse-Geisser	547.333	12.129	45.127		
	Huynh-Feldt	547.333	13.498	40.551		
	Lower-bound	547.333	9.000	60.815		

repeated-measures ANOVA NHST technique for within-subjects multilevel experiments.

the repeated-measures F value (9.208) and four different probability figures. The probability figure on the top line (.002) is appropriate if the population data meet the assumption of sphericity.[3] It is common for researchers to assume sphericity and use that probability figure. Thus, because .002 < .05, reject the null hypothesis and conclude that the pretest, posttest, and follow-up scores do not have a common population mean.

For repeated-measures ANOVAs, the basic SPSS program does not calculate Tukey HSD probabilities, but its output provides you with the elements you need to find them. With HSD values in hand, you can find probabilities in **Table C.5** in appendix C. The formula for HSD is

$$HSD = \frac{M_1 - M_2}{SE_{M_1 - M_2}}$$

Where: M_1 and M_2 are the means of two levels of the IV

$SE_{M_1 - M_2}$ is the standard error of the difference

The elements needed to calculate $SE_{M_1 - M_2}$ are $MS_{residual}$ and N, the number of scores in one treatment. The formula is

$$SE_{M_1 - M_2} = \sqrt{\frac{MS_{residual}}{N}}$$

From the SPSS output in Table 9.6, $MS_{residual}$ is 30.407, which is shown by SPSS as MS_{error}. For the scores in Table 9.5, $SE_{M_1 - M_2} = \sqrt{30.407/10} = 1.744$. Thus,

$HSD_{pre\text{-}post}$ $\quad$ $HSD = \dfrac{49.00 - 39.00}{1.744} = 5.73$ $\qquad p < .01$

$HSD_{pre\text{-}followup}$ $\quad$ $HSD = \dfrac{49.00 - 41.00}{1.744} = 4.59$ $\qquad p < .05$

$HSD_{post\text{-}followup}$ $\quad$ $HSD = \dfrac{39.00 - 41.00}{1.744} = -1.15$ $\qquad p > .05$

To interpret HSD values, use **Table C.5** in appendix C. Critical values for $\alpha = .05$ are on page --; those for $\alpha = .01$ are on page --. The critical value is at the intersection of the df for the $MS_{residual}$ and the number of levels of the IV in the ANOVA. If the calculated HSD is equal to or greater than the critical value, reject H_0. If the calculated HSD is smaller, retain H_0. The probability figures to the right of the HSD values above were determined from Table C.5.

---

[3]For a technical explanation of sphericity, see Keselman (2005).

Effect Size Index   The formula for d for repeated-measures ANOVA is identical to that for between-subjects ANOVA. Thus, using the output from Table 9.6,

$$d_{\text{pre-post}} = \frac{M_1 - M_2}{\sqrt{MS_{\text{residual}}}} = \frac{49.00 - 39.00}{\sqrt{30.407}} = 1.81$$

$$d_{\text{pre-followup}} = \frac{M_1 - M_2}{\sqrt{MS_{\text{residual}}}} = \frac{49.00 - 41.00}{\sqrt{30.407}} = 1.45$$

$$d_{\text{post-followup}} = \frac{M_1 - M_2}{\sqrt{MS_{\text{residual}}}} = \frac{39.00 - 41.00}{\sqrt{30.407}} = -0.36$$

The usual next step is to search for extraneous variables, but because the data in Table 9.5 are based on a meta-analysis of 60 separate experiments, there is no procedure section to examine for uncontrolled extraneous variables. Thus, we proceed directly to an interpretation.

Interpretation of the Eating Disorder Data   Data based on Stice and Shaw's (2004) meta-analysis of intervention programs for eating disorders were analyzed with a repeated-measures ANOVA on pretest, posttest, and follow-up scores. The immediate effect of an intervention was to significantly reduce the severity of eating disorders compared to the pretest scores (HSD = 5.73; $p < .01$). This reduction in severity continued to be apparent at the time follow-up measurements were made (HSD = 4.59; $p < .05$). The size of the effect of the intervention was huge at the time of the posttest ($d = 1.81$) and still very large at the time of the follow-up measurements ($d = 1.45$). The effect size of the posttest–follow-up comparison was just less than medium ($d = 0.36$), but the difference was not statistically significant (HSD = 1.15; $p > .05$). In summary, the intervention worked, both in the short term and in the long term.

FACTORIAL EXPERIMENTS

The word *factor* is a synonym for *independent variable*. Researchers routinely use the two terms interchangeably. **Factorial designs** (experiments) have more than one IV and each IV can have two or more levels. Like all the designs covered in this textbook, a factorial design has one DV. Factorial designs that have two factors produce three separate conclusions. One conclusion is about the effect of the two factors acting together on the DV. This joint effect of the two variables is the **interaction.** In addition, each factor by itself may have an effect on the DV. The effect of a factor acting by itself on the DV is a **main effect.** A main effect is much like a one-way ANOVA of data from a multilevel experiment.

factorial design
Research design with two or more independent variables. Each level of an independent variable occurs with every level of the other independent variable(s).

interaction   NHST technique that determines if the effect of one independent variable on the dependent variable depends on the level of a second independent variable.

main effect   A factorial ANOVA NHST technique that determines if the sample means of an independent variable could have come from populations with identical means.

Factorial designs are very popular with researchers because they can more than double the number of conclusions that two multilevel experiments provide and for less than twice the work. However, analyzing and interpreting data from factorial experiments is somewhat more complex than for two multilevel experiments. Our advice: Learn to interpret factorial designs so you can take advantage of their benefits.

In the Know

Factorial experiments allow researchers to discover the joint effects of two or more variables on a dependent variable. For the many people who are convinced that "everything is related to everything else" (Brewer, 1982), factorial experiments provide the means to discover these relationships.

Factorial Notation

Factorial designs are identified by a notation that tells how many factors there are and how many levels each factor has. In this notation, $\times$ is pronounced *by*. Three examples are:

2×2

3×4

$2 \times 3 \times 5$

The number of numerals tells you the number of factors. Thus, for the three examples, the first two have two factors and the third has three factors. The number itself tells you the number of levels of that IV. Thus, for the second example (3×4), one IV has three levels and the other has four levels.

Table 9.7 shows a generic 2×2 factorial design. The factor labeled A has two levels, A_1 and A_2. The other factor, B, has two levels as well, B_1 and B_2. The scores on the dependent variable are the O's in the cells. Note that there is a margin mean for all the B_1 scores (M_{B_1}) and a margin mean for all the B_2 scores (M_{B_2}). Likewise, there are margin means for the A_1 column and the A_2 column.

Factorial designs are classified as between-subjects designs, within-subjects designs, or mixed designs. In the case of Table 9.7, if both factor A and factor B are between-subjects, the design is a **between-subjects factorial design.** If both factor A and factor B are within-subjects variables, the design is a **within-subjects factorial design.** If one factor is between-subjects and the other is within-subjects, the design is a **mixed-factorial design.** As an example, an experiment in which males and females take a

between-subjects factorial design   Factorial experiment in which every independent variable is a between-subjects variable.

within-subjects factorial design   Factorial experiment in which every independent variable is a within-subjects variable.

mixed-factorial design   Factorial design in which one or more independent variables are between-subjects variables and one or more are within-subjects variables.

TABLE 9.7	Illustration of a Generic 2 × 2 Factorial Design		
	Independent variable A		*Margin means*
	A_1	A_2	
	O	O	
	O	O	
	.	.	
B_1	.	.	M_{B_1}
	.	.	
	O	O	
	Cell mean	Cell mean	
Independent variable B			
	O	O	
	O	O	
	.	.	
B_2	.	.	M_{B_2}
	.	.	
	O	O	
	Cell mean	Cell mean	
Margin means	M_{A_1}	M_{A_2}	

Note: One factor, *A*, has two levels and the other factor, *B*, also has two levels. The *O*s are the participants' scores on the DV.

pretest, experience treatment, and complete a posttest and follow-up six months later is a 2 × 3 mixed-factorial design. Gender is a between-subjects factor and the time of testing is a repeated-measures factor.

For this introduction to factorial designs, we provide examples of between-subjects factorial designs but leave within-subjects and mixed designs to a later course or to your own efforts.

Interpretation of Factorial Experiments

A factorial ANOVA provides *F* values for the interaction and for each of the main effects. In many cases, a conclusion about a main effect can be arrived at directly from the *F* value. However, when the interaction is statistically significant, interpretation of the main effects may require considerations other than the *F* value from ANOVA, as explained below. Thus, we recommend that you attend to the interaction first and then to main effects.

The Interaction   A factorial experiment reveals an interaction when the effect that one IV has on the DV changes if a different level of the other IV is administered. To detect the effect of an interaction, examine the cell means. (There are four cell means in Table 9.7.) If the changes that occur in the means of one row of a factorial table are similar to the changes found in the other row(s), the two factors are *not* interacting. However, if the changes in one row are greater, lesser, or reversed from those in another row, there *is* an interaction. Of course, the changes that we are describing are subject to sampling fluctuation, so a statistical test is required to determine if the changes observed are different enough to make the interaction statistically significant. Several examples and more explanation of interactions follow.

Main Effects   A main effect determines the likelihood that the margin means of an IV came from populations with identical means. In Table 9.7, a test of the two means M_{A_1} and M_{A_2} is a main effect, as is a test of the means M_{B_1} and M_{B_2}. Each main effect in a factorial experiment is just like a one-way ANOVA for a multilevel experiment. The number of main effects in a factorial design is equal to the number of IVs and has nothing to do with the number of levels of the IV. If the interaction is *not* significant, the interpretation of main effects is just like that for one-way ANOVAs. However, if the interaction *is* significant, the interpretation of the main effects depends on the nature of the interaction. We illustrate some of the issues but a warning is in order: The explanations in the examples that follow are abstract. Factors are labeled *A* and *B* and the four examples are W, X, Y, and Z. Just attend to the text, tables, and figures until you understand. We explain using examples in the sections that follow.

Table 9.8 shows four 2 × 2 factorial experiments, W to Z. The numbers in the cells are cell means; the numbers outside the 2 × 2 box are

TABLE 9.8	Four Different 2 × 2 Factorial Designs

EXAMPLE **W**

	A_1	A_2	MARGIN M
B_1	20	30	25
B_2	30	20	25
MARGIN M	25	25	

EXAMPLE **X**

	A_1	A_2	MARGIN M
B_1	20	30	25
B_2	30	40	35
MARGIN M	25	35	

EXAMPLE **Y**

	A_1	A_2	MARGIN M
B_1	20	30	25
B_2	20	20	20
MARGIN M	20	25	

EXAMPLE **Z**

	A_1	A_2	MARGIN M
B_1	10	20	15
B_2	30	50	40
MARGIN M	20	35	

NOTE: THE NUMBERS IN THE CELLS ARE CELL MEANS; MARGIN MEANS ARE AT THE EDGES.

margin means. To interpret a factorial ANOVA, look first for an interaction and then examine the margin means for main effects. Our interpretations are based on the means only. A final interpretation requires an NHST technique to rule out the possibility that chance could produce the differences that are apparent in the means.

Example W In example W of Table 9.8, look at the B_1 row. The effect of changing from A_1 to A_2 is to *increase* the mean score by 10 points (from 20 to 30). To determine if there is an interaction, see if this same change occurs in row B_2. In B_2 the effect of changing from A_1 to A_2 is to *decrease* the mean score by 10 points (from 30 to 20). Thus, in example W, based on the means, there may be an interaction. The effect of changing from one level of the IV to another depends on which level of the second IV is being considered.

The effect of the interaction in example W is obvious when the data are graphed. **Figure 9.1** shows the two ways to graph interactions—a line graph and a histogram. Look at the W panel in Figure 9.1. The characteristic of a line graph that indicates an interaction is that the lines are *not parallel*. In the W panel, the lines are so unparallel that they cross each other. Interactions such as this are often referred to as *crossed interactions*. In histograms the characteristic that indicates an interaction is that the step from one bar to the next for one level of an IV is not equal to the step from one bar to the next for the other level of the IV. Indeed, in panel W, the steps are reversed because the step in the A_1 column rises and the step in the A_2 column falls.

To interpret a main effect of an IV, examine the margin means for that variable. In example W in Table 9.8, the margin mean of A_1 is 25 and the margin mean of A_2 is also 25. A straightforward interpretation is that IV A has no effect on the DV. That is, regardless of the level of A, the mean DV score is 25. However, because of the significant interaction, we know that A does have an effect on the DV, but that the effect depends on which level of factor B is being administered.

The margin mean of B_1 and the margin mean of B_2 are also equal to each other. Factor B appears from the margin means to have no effect on the DV, but again, we know that this is not true; the effect of changing from B_1 to B_2 does have an effect but the effect depends on the level of A that is being administered.

In factorial experiments with crossed interactions, F values for the main effects cannot be interpreted at face value. Most researchers recommend that F values for main effects *not* be interpreted in factorial ANOVAs that have a crossed interaction that is statistically significant. Certainly, any interpretation *requires* a reference to the interaction.

Example X In example X of Table 9.8, look at row B_1. The effect of changing from A_1 to A_2 is to increase the mean score by 10 points. Now,

FIGURE 9.1
Line graphs and histograms of the cell means of examples W, X, Y, and Z in Table 9.8.

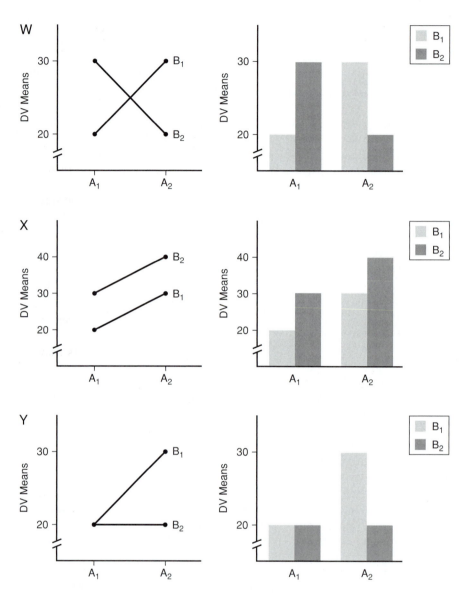

look at row B_2. The change from A_1 to A_2 is exactly the same—an increase of 10 points. Thus, the data in example X show *no* interaction. The effect of changing from A_1 to A_2 does *not* depend on which level of IV B is examined.

Look at the X panel in Figure 9.1. The line graph of the cell means shows parallel lines. Parallel lines in a factorial ANOVA are a sign that there is no interaction. The histogram in the X panel shows a step up of 10 points for A_1 and an identical step up of 10 points for A_2. Equal steps in a histogram are seen when there is no interaction. Both graphs in panel X are characteristic of factorial data that do not have an interaction.

To interpret the main effects in example X in Table 9.8, look at the mean of the A_1 column (25) and the mean of the A_2 column (35). These two means are different, so our interpretation is that the main effect for factor A may be significant. Likewise, the two means of 25 and 35 for factor B lead to the interpretation that the main effect for IV B may be significant. (Our use of *may* is just a reminder that differences in means may be due to a treatment or may be due to sampling fluctuation.) When the interaction is not significant, interpretation of a main effect proceeds as if the experiment was a multilevel experiment with just one IV. In summary, the data in example X show that both main effects may be significant, but that the interaction is not.

Analyze the data in example Y in Table 9.8. Follow the order that we used in our analysis of examples W and X. Write your answer.

Example Y In example Y, row B_1, the change from A_1 to A_2 is an increase of 10 points, but the change in row B_2 is zero. Thus, there is an interaction in example Y data. As for main effects, both factor A and factor B have margin means of 20 and 25. Thus, each of the two main effects may be significant. However, because there is an interaction, the interpretation that factor A or B, acting alone, produces change in the DV is questionable.

Look at the Y panel in Figure 9.1. The lines in the line graph of the cell means are not parallel and the steps in the histogram are not equal. Both graphs indicate an interaction. One feature that stands out in the example Y data table and in both graphs in panel Y is that one cell mean of the four is quite different from the others. The A_2B_1 cell mean is 30 but all the other cell means are 20. The data in this one cell are producing both the interaction and the significant main effects. In the case of actual factorial data with one cell that is quite different from the rest, researchers focus their attention on explaining how the two IVs interact to produce a different cell mean.

Using the data in example Z in Table 9.8, draw a line graph and a histogram. Is the interaction significant? What about factor A? What about factor B?

Example Z A line graph and a histogram of the data in example Z in Table 9.8 appear in **Figure 9.2.** The lines are not parallel and the steps are not equal so there is an interaction. The interaction in example Z is sometimes referred to as an *uncrossed interaction* for a reason that is apparent in the line graph. Many researchers argue that when an interaction is uncrossed, a straightforward interpretation of the main effects is warranted and meaningful (see Howell, 2004, p. 432). Other terms for *crossed* and *uncrossed* are *disordinal* and *ordinal,* respectively.

FIGURE 9.2
Line graph and
histogram of
data in example Z
of Table 9.8.

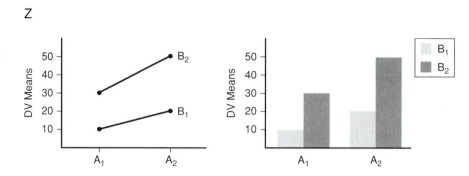

To determine the main effects in example Z, look at the margin means
of Table 9.8. The main effect of factor A is that there is an increase from
A_1 (20) to A_2 (35). Is this pattern the same for both the B_1 row and the
B_2 row? Yes. The B_1 row shows an increase (10 to 20) as does the B_2 row
(30 to 50). Thus, for significant main effects that are accompanied by an
uncrossed interaction, straightforward interpretations of the main effects
seem warranted. Factor A appears significant as does Factor B.

> ### In the Know
> Whether these interactions and main effects would be statistically
> significant for actual sets of 2 × 2 data depends on how variable
> the scores within the cells are. By adjusting the scores within a cell
> to create large or small standard deviations, different patterns of
> significance or nonsignificance emerge.

Our explanation of 2 × 2 factorials used a generic terminology of
A and B for IVs and subscripts of 1 and 2 for the levels of an IV. When
you are explaining actual experiments, always use the names of the IVs
and their levels rather than a generic indicator. You will probably agree
that identifying the levels of the conditions in the Morin and Latham
experiment as goals, visualization, and encouragement is much more
informative than A_1, A_2, and A_3. This is a version of the point we made
about the terms *experimental group* and *control group,* which are fine for
textbook explanations of the general case, but poor choices when talking
about an actual experiment.

For the Harrison experiment at the beginning of the chapter that included the scenario
about Dr. Taylor and the unnecessary appendectomy, construct a table that identifies the
two IVs and their levels. Write the name of the DV in the cells. Use Table 9.7 as a model.

The Harrison 2 × 2 Blame Experiment

Table 9.9 is our version of the answer to the Stop & Think problem, but we also included DV scores that are based on the actual experiment. In addition, cell means and margin means are shown. One of the factors is the age of the doctor in the scenario. The two levels are age 28 and age 63. The other factor is the age of the participants. Our choice of adjectives for the participants is young (college age) and old (retirement apartment residents). By the way, it is just as correct to organize the table with the age of the participants at the top and the age of the doctor on the side.

TABLE 9.9	Harrison's 2 × 2 Factorial Experiment on Blame for an Unnecessary Operation

1 = blameless; 7 = totally to blame

Scenario Doctor

		Age 28	Age 63	
		1	2	
		3	5	
		2	3	
		1	7	
	Young	3	5	
		3	1	
		2	3	
		1	1	
		3	6	
		2	4	
		$M_{cell} = 2.1$	$M_{cell} = 3.7$	$M_{young} = 2.90$
Participants				
		3	2	
		4	3	
		1	1	
		7	1	
	Old	6	3	
		6	2	
		5	2	
		7	1	
		4	2	
		7	3	
		$M_{cell} = 5.0$	$M_{cell} = 2.0$	$M_{old} = 3.50$
		$M_{28} = 3.55$	$M_{63} = 2.85$	Grand $M = 3.20$

Examine the means of the Harrison blame experiment in Table 9.9. Write an analysis using terms specific to the experiment.

Our analysis of the Harrison blame experiment begins with the interaction and proceeds to the main effects.

Interaction   Among the young participants, the effect of changing the doctor's age from 28 to 63 was to increase the blame score by an average of 1.6 points. Among the old participants, the effect of this same change was to decrease the blame score by an average of 3.0 points. Thus, the data reveal a crossed interaction. If you are uncertain about this conclusion, you might construct a graph of the cell means.

Main Effects   For the age of the participants factor, the two means are 2.90 and 3.50. Because there is a difference, the main effect for age of the participants may be significant. In a similar way, the two means of 3.55 and 2.85 for the age of the doctor factor are different, perhaps producing a difference that may be significant.

SPSS Analysis   Like all ANOVAs, a factorial ANOVA divides the total variance into the variance associated with known causes and the variance that is left over (residual variance). For between-subjects factorial ANOVAs, the three known causes are the interaction, the main effect for A, and the main effect for B. The three F values for a between-subjects factorial ANOVA are three ratios of identified variance divided by the residual variance. Thus,

$$F = \frac{\text{Variance due to the interaction}}{\text{Residual variance}}$$

$$F = \frac{\text{Variance due to } A}{\text{Residual variance}}$$

$$F = \frac{\text{Variance due to } B}{\text{Residual variance}}$$

Table 9.10 shows the SPSS output for the data in Table 9.9. The top panel shows the four cell means, the four margin means, and the grand mean along with their standard deviations and N values. The lower panel shows a summary table of factorial ANOVA tests. The two main effects are doc_age, $F(1, 36) = 2.028, p = .163$ and sub_age, $F(1, 36) = 1.490, p = .230$. Neither of these main effects are significant. The interaction doc_age*sub_age, $F(1, 36) = 21.890, p < .001$ is statistically significant.

Interpretation of the Unnecessary Appendectomy Experiment   In a 2×2 factorial design, traditional-age undergraduates (young) and retirement-age apartment dwellers (old) read a scenario about a misdiagnosis and

TABLE 9.10	SPSS Output for the 2 × 2 ANOVA of the Harrison Blame Experiment (Table 9.9)

Descriptive Statistics

Dependent variable: blame

doc_age	sub_age	Mean	Std. Deviation	N
28.00	young	2.1000	0.87560	10
	old	5.0000	2.00000	10
	Total	3.5500	2.11449	20
63.00	young	3.7000	2.05751	10
	old	2.0000	0.81650	10
	Total	2.8500	1.75544	20
Total	young	2.9000	1.74416	20
	old	3.5000	2.13985	20
	Total	3.2000	1.95067	40

Tests of Between-Subjects Effects

Dependent variable: blame

Source	Type III sum of squares	df	Mean square	F	Sig.
Corrected model	61.400[a]	3	20.467	8.469	.000
Intercept	409.600	1	409.600	169.490	.000
doc_age	4.900	1	4.900	2.028	.163
sub_age	3.600	1	3.600	1.490	.230
doc_age*sub_age	52.900	1	52.900	21.890	.000
Error	87.000	36	2.417		
Total	558.000	40			
Corrected total	148.400	39			

[a]R squared = .414 (adjusted R squared = .365).

unnecessary appendectomy performed by a doctor who was described as either 28 years old or 63 years old. The dependent variable was the amount of blame assigned to the doctor. The interaction was statistically significant with $F(1, 36) = 21.89$, $p < .001$. The young participants assigned greater blame to the 63-year-old doctor, whereas the old participants assigned greater blame to the 28-year-old doctor. The main effects of the age of the participants and the age of the doctor were not significant.

Factors That Affect Life Satisfaction

Having examined a 2 × 2 factorial with a significant interaction, we now turn to a 2 × 2 factorial experiment with a nonsignificant interaction. When the interaction is not significant, each IV can be interpreted separately, just as if the factor had been analyzed with a *t* test or one-way ANOVA. Diener, Oishi, and Lucas (2003) in an *Annual Review* article identified some of the factors that affect subjective well-being. Subjective well-being is a broad concept that includes both happiness and life satisfaction.

In the Know

The *"Annual Review"* where Diener, Oishi, and Lucas published their conclusions is the *Annual Review of Psychology*. The authors of chapters in the *Annual Review* are experts who review many articles about one particular area or subarea. About 20 different topics are covered in each volume. Besides the *Annual Review of Psychology*, there are annual reviews published in 28 other disciplines and subdisciplines. If you are interested in a topic that has been covered recently in an *Annual Review*, you are in luck. The chapter will be an up-to-date source of the results and theories on your topic.

Life satisfaction, which is an important component of subjective well-being, can be measured using the short, five-item questionnaire in Table 9.11. You can ensure a greater degree of your own engagement in this chapter if you will stop reading and fill out the Satisfaction With Life Scale (SWLS) in **Table 9.11.**

The SWLS was developed and tested by Diener, Emmons, Larsen, and Griffin and published in 1985. Two important questions about life satisfaction are, "Who has it?" and "Can it be acquired?" Two answers to the question "Who has it?" are contained in the 2 × 2 factorial data in Table 9.12. The two factors in the experiment are gender and personality type. The two levels of gender are the ones you are familiar with. The two levels of personality type are extraverts and introverts. Extraverts are outgoing, talkative, and social. Introverts are reserved, serious, and organized. As you probably know, personality tests permit the classification of people as extraverts or introverts.

The scores for the 23 people in **Table 9.12** were created so that conclusions from them would match those in the *Annual Review* chapter. Thus, the data in Table 9.12 reveal whether gender or personality type or both are related to a person's satisfaction in life. In addition, they show whether an interaction between the two variables affects SWLS scores.

 Calculate appropriate descriptive statistics for the data in Table 9.12 and write a preliminary interpretation.

TABLE 9.11	The Satisfaction With Life Scale (SWLS)

Instructions: Five statements with which you may agree or disagree are shown below. Using the scale that follows, indicate your agreement with each item by placing the appropriate number on the line preceding that item. Please be open and honest in your responding.

> 1 = Strongly disagree
> 2 = Disagree
> 3 = Slightly disagree
> 4 = Neither agree nor disagree
> 5 = Slightly agree
> 6 = Agree
> 7 = Strongly Agree

_____ 1. In most ways my life is close to my ideal.

_____ 2. The conditions of my life are excellent.

_____ 3. I am satisfied with my life.

_____ 4. So far I have gotten the important things I want in life.

_____ 5. If I could live my life over, I would change almost nothing.

Scoring instructions: Add the numbers in the blanks to determine your score.

TABLE 9.12	Life Satisfaction Scores for Women and Men Who Are Extraverts or Introverts

		Women	Men
		33	32
		31	27
	Extraverts	30	23
		26	22
		25	16
		23	
Personality type			
		26	26
		25	25
	Introverts	23	23
		21	21
		19	19
		18	18

Note: High scores indicate greater satisfaction.

| TABLE 9.13 | Cell Means and Margin Means for the Data in Table 9.12 | | |

| | Gender | | |
Personality	Men	Women	Margin M
Extraverts	28	24	26
Introverts	22	22	22
Margin M	25	23	Grand M = 24

Our calculation of the cell means and the margin means appears in **Table 9.13.**

Preliminary Interpretation   Based on the cell means in Table 9.13, the interaction may be significant. Whereas the men and women who were introverts had identical means (22), the men who were extraverts had a mean life satisfaction score (28) that was greater than that of extraverted women (24). As for main effects, the margin means show that men scored higher than women (25 and 23) and that extraverts scored higher than introverts (26 and 22). Thus, both main effects may be significant. Of course, if the interaction is significant, any significant main effects will have to be interpreted with care. Note that one cell mean (28) is larger than the others (24, 22, and 22).

The pattern of cell means and margin means in Table 9.13 is typical of factorial experiments. The margin means for the levels of an IV are not the same and the pattern of cell means do not produce parallel lines exactly (or exactly equal steps in a histogram). What determines whether or not the interaction or either main effect is significant is the *variability* of the numbers in the cells. The greater the variability, the smaller the chance that the effects will be statistically significant. A factorial ANOVA assesses the variability within each cell and yields an *F* value for the interaction and an *F* value for each main effect.

> *In the Know*
>
> The margin means in a 2 × 2 factorial experiment provide direct evidence about the relative size of the *F* values for the main effects in a factorial ANOVA. The greater the difference between means, the larger the *F* value. Thus, the larger difference between the two personality types (26 and 22) will produce an *F* value that is larger than the *F* value for the gender main effect (25 and 23).

SPSS Analysis and Calculation of *d*   The SPSS output of the analysis of the 2 × 2 factorial experiment in Table 9.12 is shown in **Table 9.14.** The upper panel shows cell means, margin means, and the grand mean as well as the standard deviations and Ns. The lower panel is a summary table of factorial ANOVA tests. Gender, $F(1, 19) = 1.349$, $p = .260$, is not significant; personality, $F(1, 19) = 5.395$, $p = .031$, is significant; the interaction of gender and personality, $F(1, 19) = 1.349$, $p = .260$, is not significant. When the interaction is not significant and one or more main effects are significant, calculate *d* using the same procedures you used for multilevel

TABLE 9.14	SPSS Output of the Factorial ANOVA of the SWLS Scores in Table 9.12

Descriptive Statistics				
Dependent variable: Satisfaction_score				
Personality	Gender	Mean	Std. deviation	N
Extravert	Female	28.0000	3.89872	6
	Male	24.0000	5.95819	5
	Total	26.1818	5.11504	11
Introvert	Female	22.0000	3.22490	6
	Male	22.0000	3.22490	6
	Total	22.0000	3.07482	12
Total	Female	25.0000	4.63191	12
	Male	22.9091	4.52669	11
	Total	24.0000	4.60237	23

Tests of Between-Subjects Effects

Dependent variable: Satisfaction_score

Source	Type III Sum of Squares	df	Mean square	F	Sig.
Corrected model	144.000[a]	3	48.000	2.832	.066
Intercept	13165.714	1	13165.714	776.859	.000
Personality	91.429	1	91.429	5.395	.031
Gender	22.857	1	22.857	1.349	.260
Personality gender	22.857	1	22.857	1.349	.260
Error	322.000	19	16.947		
Total	13714.000	23			
Corrected total	466.000	22			

[a]R squared = .309 (adjusted R squared = .200).

experiments. The means in the numerator of the formula are margin means. In Table 9.12, the difference between extraverts and introverts produces a d value of 0.97, which is a large effect size.

Interpretation of the Life Satisfaction Experiment   An analysis of 2×2 factorial data that were based on the conclusions of Diener et al. (2003) showed a relationship between personality type and satisfaction in life. Extraverts had significantly higher life satisfaction scores than introverts, $F(1, 19) = 5.40, p = .031$. The effect that personality had on the scores was quite large, $d = 0.97$. Neither the difference between the genders nor the interaction of the two variables was significant.

Note that none of the participants in the experiment were randomly assigned to the gender condition or the personality type. Because there was no random assignment (nor could there be), it would not be correct to conclude that personality type causes or produces a person's satisfaction in life. The correct wording is that personality type is related to satisfaction in life. Knowing that there is a relationship allows you to predict outcomes but not to draw cause-and-effect conclusions.

Acquiring a Better Life Satisfaction Score   What was your score on the SWLS questionnaire in Table 9.11? Pavot and Diener (1993) report that for American college students, the mean was about 24 and the standard deviation was about 6. They also report descriptive statistics for a variety of samples, including nuns, prison inmates, abused women, college students from five countries, and other cross-cultural samples. Is a person's life satisfaction score fixed or can it be changed? If yours could be changed, what would you have to do to change it? One of the implications of the experiment you just analyzed is that there *may* be a causal link between personality type and life satisfaction. Although a nonrandom assignment experiment cannot establish a causal link, the data in Table 9.12 don't contradict such a link.

One way to help establish a causal link between personality type and life satisfaction is to directly manipulate personality type and see if there is an effect on SWLS. Changed SWLS scores would add support to the causal link hypothesis. In fact, there is evidence that personality type can be adjusted. As one example, Fleeson, Malanos, and Achille (2002) had students *act* extraverted during a group discussion. They were instructed to act bold and be talkative, energetic, and adventurous. The result was that they reported much more positive emotions, regardless of whether their previously recorded personality type was introverted or extraverted. Other research supports the idea that the behavior you exhibit is a strong determinant of the way you feel. However, the effect of these improved positive emotions on SWLS scores has yet to be researched. Thus, a definitive answer to the question "Can higher SWLS scores be acquired?" awaits further research.

In the Know

Two of our examples in this chapter are from the field of positive psychology (Morin and Latham's study of visualization and the SWLS study). Positive psychology is a growing subfield within psychology. A recent issue of the journal *Psychological Science in the Public Interest* (Diener & Seligman, 2004) was devoted to the idea of using the findings from positive psychology to guide public policy decisions, much as economic analyses guide current policy decisions.

Additional Considerations With Factorial ANOVA

We've indicated that factorial ANOVA is a versatile technique. It can be used to control nuisance variables and to investigate more than two factors.

Using a Factorial Design to Control Nuisance Variables   **Nuisance variables** are variables that increase the variability of the DV scores. The problem with nuisance variables is that they make detection of the effect of the IV more difficult. Nuisance variables are like noise when you are trying to detect a signal; the signal is there, but it may be obscured if the noise is too loud.

You will recall that ANOVA works by assigning portions of the total variance to known causes. For a factorial design, the three known causes are the interaction and the two main effects. By treating a nuisance variable as one of the factors in a factorial ANOVA, the variance that it causes can be removed from the experiment. When a nuisance variable is not treated as a factor, it contributes to the residual variance. As residual variance increases, *F* values become smaller and less likely to be significant. Thus, by incorporating a nuisance variable into the design of an experiment, variability (noise) is reduced and the IV (signal) is easier to detect.

In chapter 7 we described a hypothetical experiment that compared two study techniques, mental summaries and do your best. The DV was a recall score for a 12-page article on dinosaurs. Suppose that the participants included both men and women. As you may know, women score slightly higher than men on tests of verbal ability. Because the focus of this experiment is the two study techniques, gender is a nuisance variable that just adds variability to the DV scores. Using a factorial ANOVA, the variability in the scores that is due to gender can be removed. The result is that the analysis is better able to detect the effect of the study techniques.

More Complex Factorials   Our explanations of factorial designs covered a 2 × 2 design with an interaction and a 2 × 2 design without an interaction. As we indicated earlier, factorial designs can be more complex than the two examples we covered.

nuisance variable A factor that causes the dependent variable scores to be more variable.

For a 3 × 4 factorial, how many IVs are there? How many levels does each IV have? For a 2 × 2 × 3 factorial, how many IVs are there? How many levels does each IV have?

A 3 × 4 factorial has two IVs; the first IV has three levels and the second IV has four levels. A 2 × 2 × 3 factorial has three IVs; each of the first two IVs has two levels, and the third has three levels.

Let's consider the 3 × 4 factorial design, which has two main effects and one interaction. The interpretation of the interaction is like that for a 2 × 2 design. The effect of one IV on the DV depends on which level of the other IV is being considered. Sound familiar?

As for the main effects, they are more complex in the same way that a multilevel experiment is more complex than an experiment with two levels. A significant main effect for the 3-level IV in a 3 × 4 factorial means that there is only a small probability that the three sample means came from populations with identical means. Like tests after the *F* test for a one-way ANOVA, tests subsequent to the *F* test for main effects determine which means are significantly different from others. One such test is Tukey HSD tests, which are conducted in much the same way as those for a one-way ANOVA (see Spatz, 2005, pp. 277–279 for details). One caution is in order about Tukey HSD tests on factorial data. Tukey HSD tests and several other tests of margin means are *not* appropriate if the interaction in a factorial ANOVA is significant.

Whereas a 3 × 4 factorial is somewhat more complex than a 2 × 2 factorial, complexity increases exponentially as IVs are added. Consider a three-factor ANOVA such as a 2 × 2 × 3. The three factors can be labeled *A, B,* and *C.* **Figure 9.3** provides a picture of this design. The data for three-way factorial designs are usually presented as a series of two-way factorial designs. **Table 9.15** shows cell means for a 2 × 2 × 3 design as two 2 × 3 tables of cell means. All the scores in the A_1 treatment are in the left panel and all the scores in the A_2 treatment condition are in the right panel.

A three-factor ANOVA has three main effects and four interactions. There is a main effect for each of the *A, B,* and *C* factors. Three of the

FIGURE 9.3
Three-dimensional representation of a 2 × 2 × 3 factorial design.

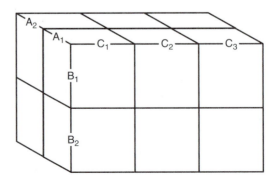

TABLE 9.15	Cell Means From a 2 × 2 × 3 Factorial Shown as Two 2 × 3 Tables

A_1

	C_1	C_2	C_3
B_1	10	20	30
B_2	10	20	30

A_2

	C_1	C_2	C_3
B_1	30	20	10
B_2	30	20	10

interactions are two-way interactions (A × B, A × C, and B × C) and one is a three-way interaction (A × B × C). As with all factorial designs, the interpretation of main effects may not be straightforward if any of the interactions are significant. Higher order factorial designs are usually covered in intermediate or advanced research methods courses.

In the Know

Among psychologists, analysis of variance is probably the most popular statistical technique. It is also used in many other fields. Analysis of variance was conceived of by Ronald A. Fisher (1890–1962) who was head of the Statistics Department at Rothamsted Experiment Station, an agricultural research institute in Harpenden, England, near London. The motivation for much of Fisher's statistical work was his passion for solving problems of genetics and evolution. About half of his 300+ publications were in genetics and about half in statistics. Fisher and his wife Ruth Eileen recognized the importance of genetics in human history and they were committed practitioners, too; they raised eight children. After his work at the agricultural experiment station, Fisher finished his career as a professor, receiving many honors in several countries. He became Sir Ronald A. Fisher when the United Kingdom knighted him in 1952.

Although there are many even more complex designs and statistical techniques to analyze them with, you'll probably be pleased to know that the trend among researchers in recent years is to use "minimally sufficient designs." This phrase was part of the recommendations of the American Psychological Association Task Force on Statistical Inference in 1996 (APA, n.d.).

The next chapter is an introduction to a number of designs that are less complex than those in this chapter. Sample sizes are usually smaller and random assignment is generally not possible. However, the topics investigated with these designs are among the most interesting in psychology.

Chapter Review

1. Experiments called _____ were explained in the first part of this chapter; _____ experiments were covered in the second part.
2. The two kinds of multilevel experiments that were discussed were _____ multilevel experiments and _____ multilevel experiments.
3. A multilevel experiment can be analyzed with a(n) _____ ANOVA; a factorial experiment requires a(n) _____ ANOVA.
4. To determine if one treatment is significantly different from another in a multilevel experiment, use a(n) _____ test.
5. The size of the difference between two means can be measured with _____ , an effect size index.
6. A 2 × 2 factorial ANOVA produces a total of _____ F values. One of the F values tests the _____ and the other two test the _____ .
7. List the eight extraneous variables that were considered when experiments were analyzed.
8. For a one-way ANOVA, F is a ratio of two sources of variance. The two sources are _____ and _____ .
9. The text discussed _____ and _____ , two characteristics of factorial designs that make them attractive to researchers.
10. A 2 × 4 × 6 factorial experiment has _____ independent variables. The number of IVs with three levels is _____ .

Thinking Critically About Research

1. The numbers in the 2 × 2 factorial matrix are cell means but one cell entry is missing. What number should be put into the empty cell so that
   a. there is no indication of a main effect of A
   b. there is no indication of a main effect of B
   c. there is no indication of an interaction effect

$$
\begin{array}{c|c|c|}
 & \multicolumn{2}{c}{A} \\
\hline
\multirow{2}{*}{B} & 20 & 50 \\
\hline
 & 40 & \\
\hline
\end{array}
$$

2. The numbers in the 2 × 2 factorial matrices are cell means. Match the boldfaced letter with the description.

1. there is a main effect for A but not for B; no interaction
2. there is a main effect for B but not for A; no interaction
3. there is a main effect for A and for B; no interaction
4. no main effect for A or B; interaction is present

W

	A	
B	25	25
	10	10

X

	A	
B	5	15
	5	15

Y

	A	
B	5	20
	20	5

Z

	A	
B	5	10
	15	20

3. Participants learned a list of words and recalled them 20 minutes later. Words were learned while sitting on the beach or underwater (using scuba gear). The words were recalled in either the same place or the other place. The four group means are shown in the cells of the 2 × 2 matrix. Write an interpretation of the interaction. (Based on Godden & Baddeley, 1975.)

		Words learned	
		On land	Underwater
Words recalled	On land	14	9
	Underwater	9	11

4. In a sentence or two describe the results of intervention programs on eating disorders.

Answers to Chapter Review

1. Multilevel; factorial
2. between-subjects; within-subjects
3. one-way; factorial
4. Tukey HSD test
5. *d*

6. three; interaction; main effects

7. selection, differential attrition, diffusion of treatment, testing, instrument change, history, maturation, regression

8. variance due to the IV; variance that is residual

9. efficiency; capability to assess interactions

10. three; zero

Answers to Thinking Critically About Research

1. a. 10; b. 30; c. 70

2. 1. X; 2. W; 3. Z; 4. Y

3. The effect on memory of learning on land or underwater depends on where recall takes place. Recalling in the same place where learning took place leads to good recall; recalling in a place different from learning leads to poor recall.

4. Interventions reduce the severity of eating disorders. Participants are significantly improved immediately after the intervention and also at the follow-up time.

Know for Sure

analysis of variance (ANOVA),   278

between-subjects factorial design,   288

factorial design,   287

interaction,   287, 289

intervention,   284

main effect,   287, 290

mixed-factorial design,   288

multilevel experiments,   275

nuisance variable,   303

one-way ANOVA,   278

repeated-measures ANOVA,   285

repeated-measures design,   283

residual variance,   278

Tukey HSD,   280, 304

within-subjects factorial design,   288

10

Observational, Qualitative, and Small-*N* Research

OVERVIEW

This chapter describes several different methods and sources that psychologists use to gather data. Naturalistic observation, participant observation, interviews, focus groups, and small-*N* research are covered as well as archives and oral history. Techniques of analyzing qualitative data are addressed and small-*N* techniques such as AB and ABA designs are explained. For all methods, topics central to conducting the research (participants, apparatus, procedure, results, and ethics) are discussed.

OBJECTIVES

After studying this chapter and working through the exercises, you should be able to:

1. Distinguish between naturalistic and participant observation
2. Describe differences among structured interviews, unstructured interviews, focus groups, and oral history research
3. Distinguish between quantitative and qualitative data
4. Find and use paper and electronic archives
5. Describe archival research
6. Distinguish between baseline and intervention
7. Describe the advantage of an ABA design over an AB design
8. Use the *Ethics Code* as a guide for observational, qualitative, and small-*N* research

Observational research, qualitative research, and small-*N* research are examples of the many ways that psychologists use to investigate a wide variety of topics. We know much more today about chimpanzees, psychiatric inmates, racial identity, Holocaust survivors, cholera, and the recovery of names after a stroke as a result of studies that used observational methods, qualitative analyses, and small-*N* research. What you've learned about controlling extraneous variables, analyzing data, and telling the story remains important for researchers who use the approaches described in the chapter. However, the typical researchers who use these approaches spend most of their time outside the lab or classroom. Our first example concerns chimpanzees that were studied by naturalistic observation, one example of observational research.

NATURALISTIC OBSERVATION

In 1960, Jane Goodall began studying chimpanzees in what is now the country of Tanzania in East Africa. Because of her young age (26) and relative inexperience, the authorities insisted that her mother accompany her. Her study area was near a small stream, the Gombe, which flows into Lake Tanganyika. In 1960 little was known about the behavior of chimpanzees in their natural environment and only one person (Nissen, 1931) had ever conducted similar research. Goodall's research continues today and is the longest-running naturalistic observation in history. Her route to Gombe began when she met Louis Leakey in Nairobi, Kenya, in 1957. Shortly afterward, he hired Goodall as an assistant secretary, a job in which she excelled. He later helped her obtain the research position at Gombe. Today, Leakey is widely known for his physical anthropology research on the remains of prehistoric human beings.

Goodall set up camp at Gombe and began to look for chimpanzees. At first, she could not observe them because they disappeared into the forest at her approach. Her solution was to watch them with binoculars from a nearby mountain peak. One day, weeks later, she spotted four chimpanzees far off and decided to approach them. After a 10-minute walk, she was very near. For the first time, they did not flee from her. Of the original group she had spotted, only two males remained, David Graybeard and Goliath, names she had given them while watching from the mountain. She observed close by for more than 10 minutes. When David Graybeard stood, Goodall's late afternoon shadow covered him, inspiring the title of her book *In the Shadow of Man* (Goodall, 1971).

Goodall's persistence paid off. One day she observed David Graybeard eating a wild piglet. Previously, scientists had believed that chimpanzees were exclusively vegetarian. Later observations revealed that chimpanzees not only ate meat but actively hunted animals to eat. Another exciting early discovery was that chimpanzees made and used tools. Goodall observed several chimpanzees "fishing" for termites in their mounds. The chimpanzees selected and modified grass stems and then inserted them into holes they made in a termite mound with their fingers. The termites, in turn, grasped the stem with their mandibles (jaws) and did not let go. The chimpanzees pulled out the tool, ate the termites, and reinserted it to catch more. As needed, chimpanzees altered their grass stems or discarded them for new ones. Some chimpanzees even selected three or four stems at a time, to have spares handy. This observation of simple tool making and tool using by a nonhuman species was a new finding that shocked the scientific community. Before her discovery, only humans were thought to be toolmakers and tool users. Goodall's naturalistic observations of chimpanzees shattered the then-current notions of human distinctiveness.

Definition of Naturalistic Observation

When researchers observe an individual or group in their natural habitat while limiting their own effect on the individual or group, they are using **naturalistic observation.** The goal of naturalistic observation is to discover behaviors that occur naturally in a particular environment. Goodall's work at Gombe qualifies as naturalistic observation because she observed the chimpanzees while limiting the effects of her presence. After the chimpanzees were accustomed to Goodall's presence, she could observe their usual behavior. Using naturalistic observation, Goodall discovered previously unknown facts about chimpanzees. Lab studies or zoo studies could not have produced data similar to hers. Of course, humans can be studied by naturalistic observation, too.

Examples of Naturalistic Observation Using Humans

Amato (1989) observed caretakers of children in public places in California and Nebraska. He found that 43% of the children he observed had male caretakers. Males were more involved with their children in recreational settings such as playgrounds, but in restaurants, females were more involved. When taking care of older children, boys, and mixed-sex pairs, however, males were more likely to be the caretakers. Amato created a naturalistic observation framework that he considered "sensitive enough to test a variety of hypotheses about male involvement with children" (p. 981). Naturalistic observation research such as Amato's can be conducted easily in public places and can yield surprisingly large amounts of data.

Graham and Wells (2001) conducted a naturalistic observation study of bar patrons by recording late-night aggressive behavior in a Canadian tavern. They used naturalistic observation and interviews in their research. In the naturalistic observation portion of their research, 117 aggressive incidents were observed during the 93 nights of the study. Most of the observation periods were weekend nights between midnight and 2:30 a.m.;

naturalistic observation
Individuals or groups are systematically observed in their natural habitat.

the patrons were unaware that research was being conducted. The researchers documented patterns of aggressive behavior in this particular bar. For example, they found that nearly 75% of the incidents involved males only. Also, moderate or higher levels of physical aggression were observed in 67% of the incidents. About 33% of the incidents occurred outside the bar's premises. Graham and Wells identified several triggers for aggression in bars, including problems with bar staff, rowdy behavior, and interpersonal relationship problems. Studies such as this might be helpful to bar managers who want to reduce aggressive incidents in their establishments.

Naturalistic observation relies on one or more observers entering a specific research environment, observing behavior, and recording it in a reliable manner. In naturalistic observation, researchers take great care not to alter or influence the behaviors they are observing. Because data collection takes place where the behaviors typically occur, naturalistic observation studies tend to be generalizable to other populations. That is, naturalistic observation studies often have high external validity. Chimpanzees in other natural situations are likely to behave the same as chimpanzees at Gombe. Caretakers in other parts of the United States will probably behave like those that Amato observed in California and Nebraska in 1989. Bar patrons throughout the Western world are likely similar to bar patrons in Canada. Naturalistic observation results can be generalized if observers do not alter the behaviors of those being studied. Observers must attend to issues of internal validity, too. Consistency of observations is paramount, as is sampling. When conducting naturalistic observation, observers must take care that their observations are unbiased. They should also address the question of whether their samples are typical of the population. We now look at the details of conducting naturalistic observation research.

Conducting Naturalistic Observation Research

Participants   Either humans or animals can be the subjects of naturalistic observation. The methodological issues are availability of participants, respect for their privacy, and whether observations are conducted from an open or concealed position. Participants can be found in a wide variety of locations other than African jungles, bars, or urban public places. However, some places are unusable. Privacy concerns limit the use of naturalistic observation to places that are generally accessible to the public. Privacy (and the law, as well) prevents researchers from peering into their neighbors' windows. Conducting naturalistic observation in public restrooms is ill advised. Researchers also have to decide whether or not to conduct their observations openly. Both open and concealed strategies are used in animal and human naturalistic observation research. Observing from a hidden position is often preferable because it allows researchers to begin data collection immediately. Being hidden, researchers are confident that those observed are not acting differently because they are being observed. Thus, studies with hidden observers reduce or eliminate **reactivity,** the participant's response to being observed. At times, however, researchers cannot hide. In those cases, they must collect data over a long enough period to assess whether their presence is affecting the behavior of those observed.

Apparatus   The apparatus for naturalistic observation can be extremely simple or very complex. Sometimes a pad, pencil, and stopwatch will suffice. Moving to the complex end of the spectrum, observers might use video cameras, motion detectors, infrared detectors for observations in darkness, or other aids. Regardless of the apparatus used, the task is to reliably record the behavior of the participants.

Procedure   Procedures for conducting naturalistic observations vary widely. The key is to find and record behaviors in psychologically interesting situations. Suppose we wanted to naturalistically observe a second-grade classroom. Ideally, observing the students through one-way mirrors built into a wall of their classroom, or observing them via video cameras (which are standard features in many classrooms) minimizes reactivity. Using either of those methods allows data collection to begin immediately. If there are no one-way mirrors or video cameras, data can still be collected, although additional time may be needed. Observers can enter the room daily and sit in the same place. After a time, the second graders pay less and less attention to the researcher and eventually begin to act as they did before. When observers are confident that the second graders are acting as their usual selves, data collection begins.

Results   Naturalistic observations may produce either quantitative or qualitative data. Often observations are coded into numerical form such as counting the number of times a behavior occurs and analyzed quantitatively. Naturalistic observation data can be qualitative as well; most qualitative methods involve observing and reobserving recorded observations and then identifying emergent commonalities and themes. Afterward, researchers summarize the commonalities and themes as results.

Ethics   As with any research method, ethics must always be considered in planning, conducting, and reporting naturalistic observation research. Section 8.05 (see appendix B) of the *Ethical Principles of Psychologists and Code of Conduct* (APA, 2002) specifically excludes naturalistic observation from the requirement of informed consent. However, researchers must still protect participants' "risk of criminal or civil liability or damage [to] their financial standing, employability, or reputation, and confidentiality" (p. 11). For animals, parts of Section 8.09 apply. Thus, researchers

reactivity   Participants' dependent variable scores are affected by the situation in which data are gathered.

conducting naturalistic observations on animals should not cause animals pain or stress. An important ethical issue in animal naturalistic observation research is whether or not the researcher should intervene to prevent harm or death to that animal by other agents in the natural environment. The answer is *no,* researchers should not intervene.

Jury deliberations are an example of a situation in which naturalistic observation cannot be used. They are private and only members of the jury can observe and report on those deliberations. However, a juror who observes the jury's proceedings and then reports them is engaging in participant observation, our next topic.

PARTICIPANT OBSERVATION

Picture this: In the early 1970s a psychologist recruits you to participate in an experiment. You are to present yourself to a mental hospital, use a pseudonym (a false name), and state that you are hearing voices (a symptom typical of schizophrenia). If you are admitted to the hospital, you are to act completely normal and give the actual details of your life (other than your real name), and no longer report hearing voices. You agree to participate, and to your great surprise, when you go to the mental hospital you are admitted quickly. Your diagnosis is schizophrenia. Once in the hospital, you act normally. In addition, you go out of your way to be friendly and cooperative with the staff. You accept the medication they give you, but you secretly dispose of it afterward (as do many of the other patients, you discover). The only strange thing you do is to take notes about your experiences. At first, you take notes covertly, but soon you realize that you may take them openly. No one on the staff is really watching you (or the other patients) closely. Some of the patients, however, ask you why you are there. They are convinced that you don't belong in a mental hospital. The staff, on the other hand, believes that you belong there. They see your note taking as a symptom of schizophrenia.

Rosenhan (1973) conducted the study just described to find out if the staff at mental hospitals could reliably distinguish between normal and abnormal behavior. The hospitals ranged from large to small, rural to urban, research to private, and old to new. He discovered that, regardless of type of hospital, the staff did not distinguish real patients from pseudopatients. (A pseudopatient is a person playing the role of a patient. In reality, pseudopatients were confederates of the experimenter. None had a prior history of psychopathology.) Pseudopatients were admitted and hospitalized from 7 to 52 days, with an average hospitalization of 19 days. All were discharged, but not because they were cured. They were labeled *schizophrenic in remission* (not cured, but asymptomatic).

Rosenhan (1973) argued that labeling is a very powerful determinant of perception in a mental health setting. Time and time again, the pseudopatients' normal behaviors were interpreted as symptoms of schizophrenia and not as indicators of normal behavior. Once admitted, the pseudopatients (and real patients, too, presumably) could do little to convince the hospital staff to change their diagnosis. Another finding was that the pseudopatients and staff had very little interaction with each other despite their close proximity. Rosenhan's experiment is an example of participant observation, and the effect of his research was profound. Today, procedures for admission to mental health hospitals are much more stringent and the definition of schizophrenia is more complex.

Definition of Participant Observation

The **participant observation** technique that Rosenhan used differs from naturalistic observation in that the observer is not only part of the observed environment but also a participant in the situation being studied. Participant observation has a greater potential for researcher bias, and that problem must be addressed in the design of the research. Typically, participant observation is used when naturalistic observation would be impractical or impossible.

Examples of Participant Observation

Barber-Parker (2002) used participant observation to study nurses' integration of teaching with bedside care. The data were collected in three phases; the first phase was a participant observation of one nurse, which served as a pilot study. When Barber-Parker was satisfied that there were no methodological problems, she observed the remaining two nurses one at a time; the nurses knew they were being observed. The researcher found that teaching took place concurrently with the nurses' other duties such as administering medication and not at a separate time. Teaching was brief and repetitive and was directed primarily to patients and only secondarily to family members.

Participant observation can take place in unusual circumstances, including jail. Elizabeth Morgan, a psychologist and surgeon, was jailed for civil contempt in a custody battle with her ex-husband over her daughter (Morgan, 1996). She was incarcerated for more than 2 years because she refused to divulge the location of their daughter. The details of the custody battle included two Acts of Congress and were described by Groner (1992). During her time in prison, Morgan kept a diary that eventually ran to 250,000 words.[1] She described her diary as a "naïve and observational record" (p. 90) that was not kept for research purposes. After leaving prison, Morgan searched her diary for instances of dissociation by

participant observation
Study of naturally occurring situations by researchers who are participants in the situation.

---

[1]This textbook has about 135,000 words.

inmates and employees. (Dissociative disorders involve the presence of multiple personalities and severe memory problems.) She found 40 such instances. She grouped these into five categories: named alters (multiple personalities with their own names that take control of a person), trances or sudden switches in personality, flashbacks, switches to childlike speech, and deliberate use of dissociation. However, she did not diagnose any of the women (neither inmates nor employees) as being psychotic. Nor did she believe that illegal drug use, which was common, was associated with the dissociation she observed. She concluded that the inmates' dissociative behaviors contributed to prison employees' absenteeism. Morgan's study illustrates how participant observation can take place in unusual circumstances.

> ### In the Know
> The story of Dr. Morgan was the subject of a 1992 made-for-television movie: *A Mother's Right: The Elizabeth Morgan Story.*

Conducting Participant Observation Research

Participants   Unlike naturalistic observation, only humans can be the objects of participant observation research. (We do not regard efforts to communicate with animals using symbols as participant observation.)

Apparatus   Most important in the choice of apparatus is whether or not the participants know they are under observation. If they are unaware, data collection requires subtle methods. In such situations, researchers are limited to covert data collection techniques. For example, some cell phones allow note taking and could be used surreptitiously. If participants know they are being observed, then recording equipment can be used openly.

Procedure   The contexts of participant observation can vary widely. Rosenhan's (1973) pseudopatients secured admission to different types of mental hospitals. Barber-Parker (2002) used the hospital in which she worked as her research setting. Morgan (1996) used her involuntary incarceration as an opportunity to conduct participant observation research. Entry into the group to be observed can be more problematic in participant observation than with naturalistic observation. For groups that are difficult to enter, such as motorcycle gangs, the success of the research depends on becoming a member. Once entry is secured, observations start. As in naturalistic observation, researchers conducting participant observations have to deal with reactivity if the participants know they are under observation. In those situations, researchers must ensure that their presence is not affecting the behavior of the observed. When participants are unaware that they are being observed, reactivity is less of an issue.

Results   In participant observation research, the data are handled in ways similar to those in naturalistic observation. The data that are generated can be quantitative, qualitative, or both.

Ethics   Ethical issues can loom large in participant observation research. For his dissertation research, Quinn (1987) joined a motorcycle gang but eventually had to remove himself because of his potential involvement in criminal activities if he remained in the gang. Researchers cannot use participant observation methods as an excuse for engaging in unethical or criminal activity. Also, participant observers may or may not have a commitment to the group they join. In the example above, Rosenhan's (1973) pseudopatients were not committed to the groups they were observing. On the other hand, Barber-Parker (2002) did have a commitment to the nurses that she was observing. In participant observation, researchers must first decide what their relationship will be to the group under observation. Issues such as commitment and whether or not the participants will know that they are under observation should be approved by an IRB before a participant observation project begins. Now we turn our attention to research involving qualitative research, a rapidly developing field within psychology.

QUALITATIVE RESEARCH

Qualitative research is characterized by results that are presented in narrative form rather than quantitative form. Often, qualitative research is conducted in a naturalistic setting using interviews. In this chapter we cover interviews, focus groups, and oral history. However, qualitative research includes other methods such as ethnography, action research, and content analysis. For more comprehensive accounts of qualitative research, see Patton (2005), Silverman (2004), Michell (2004), or Berg (2001).

The first two sections that follow explain structured and unstructured interviews. They are followed by three other variations of interviews: focus groups, oral history, and archival research.

One of the more influential studies of structured interviews in America was by Clark and Clark (1940). Their work was cited by the United States Supreme Court in the 1954 landmark case of *Brown v. Board of Educ.*, a case that led to the desegregation of public schools in America. Their technique was to interview African American and white children with the aid of two dolls, one with African American features and one with Caucasian features. Children of both races were much more likely to label

qualitative research
Studies characterized by narrative results.

the Caucasian featured doll as "nice" and the African American featured doll as "bad." African American children interviewed after looking at black or white dolls preponderantly identified themselves as black. Much of the data the Clarks collected came from structured interviews of children after they viewed the dolls. The following section explains structured and unstructured interviews. Interviews are a commonly used method of research.

Definition of Interviews

The interview technique involves orally asking questions and recording the answers. Interviews can result in qualitative or quantitative data or a mixture of the two. In this section we focus on interviews that produced qualitative data. Interviews allow researchers to interact with participants and to explore psychologically interesting questions thoroughly. However, interviews take more time than other methods. Successful interviewing requires preparation and practice. If the questions are created in advance and the same questions are asked of each participant, the interviews are **structured interviews.** If the questions vary as a result of the interviewee's responses, the interviews are **unstructured interviews.**

Examples of Structured Interviews

Unusual groups are a fruitful source for interview research. Campbell and Jones (2002) interviewed 10 world-class male wheelchair basketball players. The interviews focused on the sources of stress (both general and competition related) experienced by these athletes. The interviews began with an introduction that set the context: the athletes' experiences in their sport. The interview then moved to questions designed to help the athletes recall their wheelchair basketball experiences. Questions about both general and competition-related stress followed. The interview ended with questions about the interview itself. Interviews lasted as long as 150 minutes. All were tape recorded and transcribed. Each interviewee later verified the transcript for accuracy. The transcripts were analyzed with a technique called inductive content analysis.[2] In this type of analysis, researchers independently read raw data transcripts searching for uniformities that are grouped into emergent themes. In the Campbell and Jones study, seven steps were used in data analysis:

1. listening to the tapes and reading the transcripts for familiarization
2. identifying quotations and paraphrasing to yield the raw data
3. writing down each raw datum on a separate card

structured interviews
Interviews that are based on prepared questions that are the same for each interviewee.

unstructured interviews
Interviews based on questions that vary among interviewees.

---

[2]See Patton (2005) for description of the details of inductive content analysis.

4. grouping the raw data into higher and lower level themes

5. checking for bias in the themes by comparing to other readers

6. rereading the transcripts to ensure all themes had been captured

7. computing a frequency analysis

This analysis led to 156 raw data themes that were condensed into 10 higher level themes related to stress: pre-event concerns, negative match preparations, on-court concerns, postmatch performance concerns, negative aspects of match events, poor interaction and communication, negative coaching issues, relationship issues, demands of wheelchair basketball, and lack of disability awareness. Campbell and Jones (2002) found that many aspects of wheelchair basketball competition were stressful and that some of those stresses could come from competition whereas others came from the outside. Most of the stresses came from basketball but two nonbasketball themes were also stressful—cost of the wheelchair and the public's lack of disability awareness.

Researchers can also recruit interviewees from a larger established group. Sidebotham (2001) interviewed 16 parents (15 mothers and 1 father) at a meeting of parents involved in the Avon Longitudinal Study of Parents and Children, a large-scale longitudinal study. Sidebotham was interested in their perceptions of parenting. He first used two parents in a pilot study to refine his interview technique and questions. The interviews with the parents lasted from 30 to 90 minutes. Sidebotham used a multistage analysis. The first stage eventually yielded eight categories related to parenting:

1. family in society

2. parental attitudes toward children

3. society's attitudes toward children

4. parental and societal responsibilities toward childrearing

5. parental perception of dangers to children

6. family stresses

7. attitudes toward violence

8. child abuse

These categories yielded four higher order themes: family stresses, time pressures, financial stresses, and cultural expectations and guilt. Parents found parenting stressful due to intrinsic stressors such as children's health and time pressures, negative attitudes about parenting, and lack of community support. Sidebotham (2001, p. 480) concluded, "First, our culture imposes particular pressures on families; secondly, there are increasing expectations felt by parents; and thirdly, there are increasing restrictions on children and their families."

Examples of Unstructured Interviews

Prisoners of war (POWs) are another uncommon group. The United States Navy (Nice, Garland, Hilton, Baggett, & Mitchell, 1996) conducted a 20-year study of 138 Vietnam-era prisoners of war (VPOWs) and found that their incidence of posttraumatic stress disorder (PTSD) was indistinguishable from that of the general population. In contrast, POWs from earlier wars exhibited high levels of PTSD. To resolve conflicting research reports on POWs, Henman (2001) interviewed 50 VPOWs using the unstructured interview technique. Henman's VPOWs were older, more educated, and better prepared for possible captivity by their training than previously studied groups of POWs. Her interviews with the VPOWs uncovered a frequent and effective use of humor, which is a way of coping with stress. One example of humor was that of one prisoner, Gerald Venanzi, who invented an imaginary motorcycle and an imaginary chimpanzee cellmate. So effective were these devices that even the Vietnamese guards and the camp commandment bought into the story. The commandant went so far as to ask the prisoner to evict the chimp before assigning a new cellmate! Henman concluded that the use of humor by the VPOWs she interviewed had been a major factor in their later adjustment.

Johnson (1998) conducted unstructured interviews with 10 psychiatric patients (5 males and 5 females) who had been restrained for therapeutic reasons. (Therapeutic restraint is belting a patient to a bed to prevent self-injury.) Johnson began each interview by asking patients to recall the experience of restraint. After that opening question, she allowed the patients to speak their minds. Following the interviews, verbatim transcripts were examined for emerging themes. Two specific themes, power and powerlessness, were selected for further analysis. Patients under restraint did not feel safe and protected, nor did they see being restrained as a form of therapy. Instead, they saw restraint as the consequence of rule breaking or disobedience.

Focus Groups

Focus groups are a kind of small-group interview. Typically, researchers recruit participants, convene a meeting, and conduct structured or unstructured interviews with the whole group. Besides colleges and universities, marketers and manufacturers often use focus group interviews to test consumer reactions to products and advertisements. Focus groups can also be considered collaborative research because the groups often develop a group identity and the members provide information not easily obtained from single-person interviews. Two differences between focus groups and other interviews are the number of interviewees and the social nature of the setting.

Examples of Focus Group Interviews

Focus group interviews take advantage of the social nature of groups. Jackson and Cram (2003) conducted six focus group interviews with 16- to 18-year-old female students in New Zealand. The groups ranged in size from 4 to 12, but most consisted of 6 to 8 students. The interviews explored the sexual double standard, the idea that some behaviors are acceptable for males but not for females. Jackson conducted all of the interviews. Because she was only a few years older than the women interviewed and had a youthful appearance, the participants felt comfortable talking with her. Each focus group session lasted 2 hours. The researchers made transcripts of all the sessions and conducted a multistage qualitative analysis to find patterns related to the women's perceptions of their sexuality. The data that emerged centered around three themes: (1) challenging the language of the double standard, (2) articulating sexual desire, and (3) exploring the role of sex in adolescence that is created by peers, the media, and other social sources. The women possessed a sophisticated understanding of their own sexuality, saw themselves as actors, and had created ways of viewing themselves outside the double standard.

In another study, Fallis and Opotow (2003) used student interviewers to gather information on class cutting by high school students in large urban schools in the northeastern United States. Over a 4-year period, they conducted eight focus groups that involved 160 students. Previous research had shown that class cutting was common and that schools treated it as an individual issue of minor importance. The main reason the students gave for cutting class was boredom. Fallis and Opotow discovered that to students *boredom* meant something different from its dictionary definition. For students who cut class, the structure of the curriculum, unengaged teachers, staff turnover, and lack of resources were the major reasons for class cutting. Fallis and Opotow suggest that class cutting can be reduced by changing the curriculum, including students in decision making, and having administrators relate to staff in more constructive ways.

Oral History

Oral history is a research method that allows researchers to investigate events, facts, and relationships that happened in the past. To conduct an oral history, researchers personally interview someone about past events or analyze video or audio recordings of such interviews. Oral histories can investigate how individuals reacted to specific historical events. Oral histories rely on participants' memories of events and, thus, are a form of retrospective research using interview techniques.

focus group interviews A small group of participants interact with each other and an interviewer who poses questions.

oral history Participants describe in person or in recorded interviews historical events they experienced.

Oral History Examples

Survivors of the Holocaust, a major historical event, have been extensively interviewed and many of those interviews are archived. (Archives and archival methods are discussed in the section that follows.) Suedfeld, Krell, Wiebe, and Steel (1997) analyzed 30 video-recorded interviews of five male and five female Holocaust survivors. Data from the interviews were analyzed quantitatively and qualitatively. The interviews included the Ways of Coping Scale (Folkman, Lazarus, Dunkel-Schetter, DeLongis, Gruen, and 1986); those data constituted the quantitative portion of the study. The interviews were also analyzed qualitatively for memory content differences for pre-Holocaust, early Holocaust, late Holocaust, and post-Holocaust events. All of the survivors were living normal lives when interviewed and saw themselves as successful problem solvers. They all downplayed the role of emotional strategies in their survival.

A less dramatic story is that of the sale of medicinal pharmaceuticals containing opium after the passage of the Dangerous Drugs Act of 1920 in Great Britain. The Dangerous Drugs Act specified that only pharmacists could dispense opiate drugs such as raw opium, cocaine, morphine, or heroin.[3] Anderson and Berridge (2000) collected oral histories of 50 retired pharmacists who first began working between 1920 and 1978. Most interviewees stated that the Dangerous Drugs Act of 1920 had little effect on the dispensing of opium. Especially in rural areas, pharmacists sold prepared products containing opium or the ingredients for home remedies that contained opium. One such preparation was "Infant's Thunder" that was used to put babies to sleep! The main finding of this oral history study was that the passage of the Dangerous Drug Act, as well as later drug-prohibiting regulations, did little to prevent the continuing sale of such drugs.

Conducting Qualitative Research

Participants   All interview methods require the presence of a willing interviewee. In focus group interviews, a group of interviewees is used. In oral history interviews, the interviewees may be present or they may have been previously recorded.

Apparatus   Recording interviews is a common and useful practice. Recording allows researchers to analyze the data multiple times. In interviews about sensitive issues, audio recording is preferable to video recording because interviewees feel less self-conscious.

Procedure   Establishing rapport with interviewees is essential for the success of any of these techniques. In both of the focus group interviews

---

[3]Before 1920 in Great Britain, such drugs could be obtained over the counter.

described above, the researchers successfully established rapport by having the focus group conducted by a youthful female researcher (Jackson & Cram, 2003) or fellow students (Fallis & Opotow, 2003). Another important procedural issue to decide is what kind of interview to conduct—structured or unstructured. Nearly all interviews are transcribed after they are recorded and the transcripts become the raw material for later analyses.

Results   When interviews are analyzed qualitatively researchers read the transcripts several times. From these readings, commonalities and themes emerge. Researchers then summarize the commonalities and themes as results. When interviews are analyzed quantitatively, scores are derived either from coded observations or from the answers to specific questions. Those scores are then treated as typical quantitative data.

Ethics   Obtaining truly informed consent is an important ethical issue when using interview techniques. Interviewees must know beforehand that the conversations with researchers are for research. Interviewing people without first explaining the purpose, telling them they will be recorded, revealing all of the other requirements of informed consent, and obtaining their permission is unethical (see chapter 3).

Our last category of qualitative research is archival research. We begin with a historical example from the field of public health.

Archival Research

One of the most famous cases of archival research involved a public water pump on Broad Street in the Soho section of London. During the summer of 1854, hundreds of people in London died of cholera. (Cholera is an intestinal disease that causes vomiting, diarrhea, and death.) At that time, most doctors thought that cholera was caused by bad air. Dr. John Snow, however, believed that water from the Broad Street pump was the source of the cholera epidemic. (During the 19th century many London residents drew water from public wells.) Snow obtained the records of recent cholera deaths from the office of the Register of Deaths. He mapped the addresses of those who died and found that most of the cholera deaths had occurred near the Broad Street water pump (see **Figure 10.1**). When he investigated further, he discovered that people hauling water from the Broad Street pump to more distant locations had died as well. Armed with his data, Snow persuaded the Board of Guardians of St. James Parish to remove the pump handle of the Broad Street pump. In the days that followed, cholera deaths dropped dramatically. Snow's theory of how cholera was transmitted in water turned out to be correct. A later excavation of the Broad Street pump revealed that a nearby sewer line sometimes overflowed its contents into the pump's water supply and contaminated it (Tuthill, 2003).

FIGURE 10.1   Snow's map of cholera cases in London.
From http://www.ph.ucla.edu/epi/snow.html

Definition of Archives

archive   A secure repository of records such as print, audio, video, or electronic material that might be cataloged for access.

An **archive** is any collection of records. Traditional archives include library records, courthouse records, and business records. Most archives are valuable, so pains are taken to keep them safe. Natural disasters and wars can destroy archives and cause the loss of priceless information. Archival data are collected for a variety of reasons. Because these archives are usually printed or handwritten, they are called *paper archives*.

With the advent of computers and the Internet, many archives now exist only in electronic form; they are called *electronic archives*. In the next chapter we explain how to use a well-known electronic archive, PsycINFO, which lists more than 2 million records from the 1800s until today.

> ## In the Know
>
> The library at Alexandria, Egypt, was the greatest archive in the ancient world. The fire that consumed it deprived historians of priceless records.

Examples of Archival Research

Archives often span many years, which enables researchers to study behaviors that develop over decades. Mullen's (2001) **archival research** used several paper archives spanning 150 years to investigate ethnophaulisms, which are words that are used as slurs to describe immigrant groups. The archives he examined included 40 years of data from U.S. immigration quotas records, 30 years of naturalization records, and 150 years of data on words used to describe 19 European ethnic immigrant groups (Allen, 1983).[4] All archives indicated that "smaller, less familiar, and more foreign immigrant groups tend to be cognitively represented in a simplistic and negative manner" (Allen, 1983, p. 472).

Using electronic archives obtained from litigation, Lê Cook, Wayne, Keithly, and Connolly (2003) examined more than 5 million online documents related to internal research conducted by tobacco companies over a 35-year period.[5] From that large body of documents, the researchers found 239 that dealt with research on smokers' psychological needs and market segmentation.[6] The 239 documents were selected by a computerized, index-based word search for terms related to psychological needs, segmentation, and personality. At least two researchers performed independent

---

[4]The European groups were: Belgians, Dutch, English, French, German, Greek, Hungarian, Irish, Italian, Norwegian, Polish, Portuguese, Russian, Scot, Spanish, Swede, Swiss, Turk, and Welsh.

[5]Tobacco companies Phillip Morris, RJ Reynolds, Brown & Williamson Tobacco Company, and Lorillard were sued by state attorneys general that resulted in the 1998 Master Settlement. The database for the Lê Cook et al. study can be accessed at http://tobaccodocuments.org.

[6]In the cigarette industry, market segmentation is accomplished by tailoring brands and advertising to specific groups of smokers. Brand marketing and advertising target different groups of smokers. Thus, one brand may appeal to young rural males and another brand may appeal to young urban women.

archival research
Analysis of records that were obtained from archives.

searches until the results were consistent. The 239 documents were cataloged and placed online as another, smaller archive.[7]

Archival data are nearly always plagued by inconsistencies and incompleteness. Lê Cook et al. (2003) noted that the research methods used for internal, industrial research are sometimes not explicitly stated, and peer review is not as stringent as in research published in journals. Also, the different tobacco companies conducted research under conditions that were not always consistent so the results may not be directly comparable. Finally, unreleased documents or documents missed in the computer search may exist. Nevertheless, the researchers concluded that the tobacco companies did use sophisticated market research to segment smokers and then market cigarettes and other tobacco products accordingly. Such research is not illegal or unethical in general. However, the researchers questioned whether such methods are ethical in industries in which the products cause addiction and preventable deaths.

Conducting Archival Research

Participants   In archival research, there are no live participants as there are in other types of research. Instead, the archives consist of records already collected from "participants" in the past. In the Mullen (2001) study, some of the records were 150 years old.

Apparatus   Paper archives come in many forms. They might be the correspondence in a box in a library. Such an example is the correspondence between Ivan Pavlov and Robert M. Yerkes at the Yale University Library (Wight, 1993). Paper archives may also be collections of public or private records such as those found in libraries, courthouses, or businesses. Finding and gaining access to the archives is the first step in archival research with paper archives. Once access is obtained, the archives must be searched, the necessary materials identified, and data collected.

Electronic archives, too, may be public or restricted. Public archives are available to all. Restricted archives may require subscription or payment. As illustrated in the tobacco company archival research, successful use of electronic archives requires knowledge and expertise of computer searches.

Procedure   Regardless of the type of archive, the procedures for data collection from the archive are similar. Records on the topic must be

---

[7]The archive is available at http://tobaccodocuments.org/product_design/?field_id=9&field_value=Behavior+Targeting.

identified, categorized, and converted into data that are then analyzed with quantitative or qualitative methods.

Results   Conclusions from archival research are subject to the limitations that surround the original records. Nearly always, the original records were collected for reasons other than those of the archival researcher. For example, many tobacco companies originally conducted research to help them sell cigarettes to particular market segments (young people, women, and particular ethnic groups) but publicly denied doing so. Lê Cook et al. (2003) used the archived data to demonstrate that the tobacco companies had lied about their practices. Another methodological limitation is that we can only study data already archived and cannot collect new data from the "participants" in the archive.

Ethics   Because archival data have already been collected, many of the ethical issues of informed consent do not apply. However, the confidentiality of participants must still be protected. Depending on the archive, personal information about the people who provided the data may or may not be available. Researchers and their IRBs should determine how to handle privacy issues before accessing archives. In electronic archives, this problem can be solved by careful selection of archival fields. To avoid privacy concerns, researchers might choose not to access fields such as names, addresses, or telephone numbers. Some archives may be covered by copyright law; researchers may have to obtain permission of the copyright holder to gain access to the archives and publish the results. Naturally, such permission should be secured before accessing the archives.

SMALL-*N* RESEARCH

Earlier, we introduced Hermann Ebbinghaus and his $N = 1$ research. As we circle back to him, he is about to get the idea that leads to his fame. At the moment he is delighted with his purchase of Fechner's *Elemente der Psychophysik (Elements of Psychophysics)* from a secondhand bookstore in Paris.[8] Once in the street, he begins thumbing its pages. After a few near collisions with passersby, he stops for coffee in a small bistro and begins to read more closely. Soon, it hits him. Why not study memory using psychophysical methods? But how, he wonders. He spends the next 7 years inventing ways to study memory using only himself as the research participant.

---

[8]Most authors write that the bookstore was in Paris. Some say it was in London.

In the Know

The practice of conducting scientific research on oneself has a long history. Hendricks (1996) documents examples that go back as far as Newton, who drank mixtures containing lead and other heavy metals. Later, medical researchers in the 19th century such as Lazear allowed themselves to be bitten by mosquitoes to prove that the insects were the disease vector for yellow fever. In 1984, Marshall ingested a bacterium to prove that it was the cause of gastric ulcers. In 2005, Marshall and Warren shared the Nobel Prize in medicine for their discovery of the bacterium. Ebbinghaus, thus, was part of a scientific tradition when he began to test his own memory. Other early psychologists followed this tradition, as exemplified by Cannon and Washburn's (1912) study on hunger and stomach contractions, in which Washburn swallowed and retained a balloon that measured contractions.

Ebbinghaus published his results in 1885. His book *Über das Gedächtnis (Concerning Memory)* caused an immediate sensation among the members of the young science of psychology. The book made him famous. Ebbinghaus single-handedly created a new field within psychology, the empirical study of memory. Until then, psychologists believed that the so-called higher mental processes such as memory, thinking, and other cognitive topics beyond simple perception were scientifically inaccessible. With a single book, Ebbinghaus demonstrated that memory could be part of scientific psychology. Scientific study of other higher mental processes followed. One of Ebbinghaus's findings was that memory rapidly declines shortly after learning and then declines much more slowly as time passes. **Figure 10.2** shows his classic curve of forgetting. Interestingly, Ebbinghaus's

FIGURE 10.2
Ebbinghaus's curve
of forgetting.

work is one of the few examples of 19th-century psychological research that is still reported in textbooks.

Definition of Small–N Research

Small-N research is conducted in many areas of psychology, especially in clinical psychology and in Skinnerian behavior analysis. The number of participants varies from 1 (the smallest N) to larger numbers of participants. Dukes (1965) notes that small-N research is most appropriate for situations involving low variability between subjects or when the opportunity to research a specific situation is limited. We cover three small-N designs in this chapter: the case study design, the AB design (intervention-only design), and the ABA design (reversal design).

Case Study

The simplest type of small-N research is the case study or case history. In a **case study,** a researcher closely studies a single person or a single group. Usually, the researcher does not attempt any experimental manipulations.

Fabrega (2004) presents case studies of two men who committed homicides. Both were "residents of a medium-large American city and one can assume that they understood and knew its culture of law" (p. 182). Both men were eventually convicted of first-degree murder. One man, referred to as Mr. H, killed his wife of 8 years by stabbing her following her announced decision to divorce him, take their two children, and make him leave their home. The other man, Mr. A, was an avowed racist who killed four men of another race after an altercation at his apartment with a maintenance worker of another race. He told the maintenance worker, "You're a dead man" (p. 181) just before retrieving his gun and loading it. Not finding the worker when he returned, he instead killed another maintenance worker and later three patrons at nearby fast-food restaurants. All of the victims were of a different race than the killer and he spared potential victims of his own race at both homicide locations. During the shootings, witnesses described Mr. A as, "calm, controlled, and methodical" (p. 192).

Mr. A had a long history of contact with mental health professionals. He had been diagnosed as schizophrenic and had been given haloperidol (an antipsychotic drug), but refused to continue the drug treatment and had been dropped from therapy. Fabrega (2004) analyzed the cultural differences surrounding both killers, closely examining their respective lives, culture, clinical histories, events precipitating the homicides, and events during the day of the homicides. Fabrega concluded that determinations of guilt depend on factors beyond factual ones and include the emotional, political, and historical implications that have been presented

case study Study of a single person or group without altering the situation.

to juries and to the media. As we pointed out in chapter 1, juries do not make decisions scientifically (Devine, Clayton, Dunford, Seying, & Pryce, 2001). Fabrega, (2004), too, concludes that scientific formulations alone cannot totally account for society's decisions about homicide. Culture, in many ways and both directly and indirectly, affects society's decisions, too. Both of the cases, although quite different, reveal the complex interaction of law, psychiatry, and culture.

AB Designs (Intervention Only)

In small-*N* research, the letter *A* is used to designate the original situation, the situation before the application of a treatment. The original situation is referred to as the **baseline.** The letter *B* is use to designate the situation after the researcher applies a treatment. This new situation is often referred to as the **intervention.** Thus, an **AB design** has a baseline period of data gathering followed by an intervention.

DeDe, Parris, and Waters (2003) used an AB design to assess whether an anomic 49-year-old man (LN) could learn to name items after being trained to use both written and tactile cues. (Anomia is the inability to name objects. In this case the anomia was caused by a stroke.) LN was a college-educated former vice president of a chain of restaurants who had suffered a stroke 4 years before the study. He was highly motivated to speak well again, but previous therapies had been ineffective. LN could comprehend spoken language, but when it came to speech production, he was unable to make the sound, although he could often name the first letter of the word. His reading and writing were also impaired, but not as severely as his speaking.

Given the specifics of LN's anomia, the researchers focused their treatment on naming of objects in pictures. LN was presented with two sets of pictures. One set was the treatment pictures, and the words for each picture in that set started with *d, f, t,* and either *k* or hard *c* phonemes. The other set was the control pictures, and they all started with *b, p, s,* and *g* phonemes. The study lasted 16 weeks. The first 3 weeks established the baseline (A) and the last 13 weeks were the treatment (B). During the baseline period, pictures were presented and LN attempted to name the objects. The treatment was a three-step hierarchical cueing strategy. The first step was a general prompt such as "Can you write the word?". The second step was a set of tactile cues associated with the first sound of the words. (For example, the letter *c* was associated with the therapist's finger placed on LN's neck.) In the final step, the experimenter said the initial sound of the word. If none of the cues were sufficient, the experimenter said the entire word. **Figure 10.3** shows the results. During the baseline (A), the mean percentage correct was 4.2% for the control pictures and 6.8% for the treatment pictures. At the end of treatment, the mean percentage correct for control pictures was 12.1% and

baseline   The situation before a treatment is applied.

intervention   A treatment designed to correct or prevent a problem or psychological disorder.

AB design   Design with a baseline (A) followed by a treatment (B).

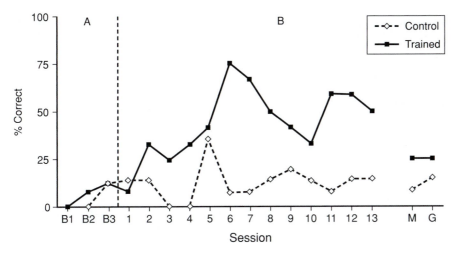

FIGURE 10.3

Percentage of control and trained items named accurately at baseline (B1–B3), during end of session probes (1–13), and in posttreatment assessment of maintenance (M) and generalization (G).

Source: From Teaching self cues: A treatment approach for verbal naming. *Aphasiology,* 2003, by kind permission of Psychology Press, www.psypress.co.uk/journals.asp, 2006.

55.5% for the treatment pictures. The intervention improved LN's ability to name pictures.

Of course, every conclusion should be subjected to an extraneous variables analysis. A characteristic of the AB design that helps alleviate many concerns is the stable baseline. If baseline measures stay the same for several periods of observation, you can almost rule out testing, instrument decay, maturation, and regression because these extraneous variables typically have their effects gradually. Any effect of these variables would not be expected to show up suddenly halfway into several sessions of data collection. Selection and differential attrition are controlled by having the same participants in each condition. This leaves diffusion of treatment and history to be examined. If they can be eliminated, the intervention remains as the only cause for the improvement in LN's anomia. A design that goes a long way toward eliminating the extraneous variables of diffusion of treatment and history is the ABA design.

ABA Designs (Reversal Designs)

In an **ABA design,** the baseline (A) is followed by an intervention (B). The intervention is then removed, which creates the A condition again. If the DV scores in the second A condition revert to baseline levels, you have some assurance that the change that accompanied B was not due to

ABA design Design with a baseline (A), followed by a treatment (B), and then restoration of the original condition (A).

the extraneous variables of testing, instrument change, history, maturation, or regression. Such extraneous variables might have produced the
change seen at B, but their effects would not be expected to reverse
later.

Serbin, Tonick, and Sternglanz (1977) used an ABA reversal design to
study whether levels of cooperative cross-sex play among 4 to 5-year-olds
could be increased by a simple verbal intervention. They used two preschool classes from a private cooperative nursery school, after getting
permission from parents and the school. Data were gathered from Class
1 using an ABA design and from Class 2 using an AAABA design. The
length of the study was 10 weeks. In the AAABA design (also known as a
time-lagged reversal design), the baseline period extended over 6 weeks,
the time required to complete the ABA design for Class 1. Adding the
AAABA group helps control for history and makes for a methodologically
stronger design. In both classes, teachers provided the intervention during the B phase. The intervention was comments such as, "I like the tower
John and Kathy are building with the blocks" (p. 926) that teachers made
when they observed children engaging in cooperative cross-sex play. The
results were dramatic and similar in both classes. **Figure 10.4** shows the
results. The intervention raised the level of cooperative cross-sex play significantly in both classes. In the reversal phase (the final A), cooperative
sex play returned to baseline levels for both classes. Thus, verbal interventions increase cross-sex play, but the effect of a weeklong intervention
dissipates rapidly.

STOP & Think   How does the AAABA class control for the extraneous variable of history in the Serbin,
et al. (1977) research?

FIGURE 10.4
Average rates of
cooperative
opposite-sex play
during baseline,
treatment, and
reversal periods.
Each child was
observed an
average of 40 times
per phase.

Source: From Serbin, L.
A., Tonick, I. J., and
Sternglanz, S. H. *Child
Development,* Blackwell
Publishing.

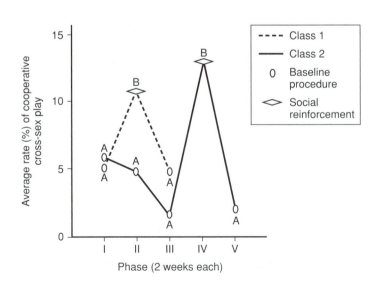

By delaying the intervention for the second class, Serbin, Tonick, and Sternglanz (1977) could see the effect of the intervention at two different times. The fact that the intervention worked twice at two different times makes the extraneous variable of history an unlikely explanation for the change.

Conducting Small-*N* Research

Small-*N* designs more complex than those we discussed exist. Kennedy (2004) covers recent innovations, including brief experimental designs and nonconcurrent multiple baseline designs. Onghena (2005) and Saville and Buskist (2003) provide a more extensive introduction to small-*N* designs.

Participants   Humans or animals can be used in small-*N* research. Humans are the typical participants in case studies. AB designs and ABA designs are conducted with both human and animal subjects. Although only a few participants are used, many data points are collected from each participant or animal subject.

Apparatus   The apparatus for small-*N* research ranges from a pad and a pencil to complex electronic and recording equipment.

Procedure   Case studies are methodologically simpler than AB or ABA designs. ABA designs (and other designs beyond ABA) provide more methodological rigor than AB designs because researchers are better able to eliminate extraneous variables. If possible, use an ABA design. However, if ethical considerations do not allow an ABA sequence, then a case study or AB design is better than not conducting the research at all.

Results   Results from small-*N* research may be quantitative, qualitative, or both. Results from case studies and AB designs cannot yield cause-and-effect conclusions. ABA designs, however, control many extraneous variables. If behavior changes each time the intervention is introduced and then withdrawn (as in an ABABA design), a powerful argument can be made that the intervention is producing the change. That is, an up-and-down behavior pattern cannot be explained by the extraneous variables of maturation, testing, instrument change, or regression, which produce linear effects. An up-and-down pattern also makes history (outside events) an unlikely explanation. (These extraneous variables are discussed in chapters 7 and 8.)

Ethics   Privacy concerns are probably the most important ethical concern of small-*N* research. When reporting small-*N* research, psychologists must be extremely careful not to identify their participants. For that reason pseudonyms (or false names) are often used to report the data from small-N studies.

Another ethical concern involves informed consent and communication with participants. Because most small-N research involves close and extended contact between researchers and participants, a personal relationship is more likely to develop than in other types of psychological research. The perils of relationship and role confusion in small-N research were evident after Bailey (2003) published a book about transsexuals. After its publication, several of the transsexuals studied accused Bailey of failing to inform them that their interactions with him constituted research. One "participant" claimed that she and Bailey had sex during the time he later claimed he had been observing her as part of his research.

Still another ethical concern involves the interventions in AB and ABA designs. Researchers must monitor interventions carefully to be sure that they are not causing harm to their participants. If the interventions are harmful, the experiment must be stopped immediately.

SUMMARY

This chapter covers research methods that many psychologists use. All of these methods involve collecting data from human or animal participants or collecting data from archives where others have deposited data. The chapter began with naturalistic observation and participant observation, two closely related research methods. In naturalistic observation, researchers take advantage of naturally occurring situations to collect data. In participant observation, researchers insert themselves into naturally occurring situations, participate in those situations, and collect data. The essence of qualitative research is the detailed description of events and their interpretation. Interview research can utilize structured or unstructured interview forms, both of which are usually conducted one-to-one between a researcher and an interviewee. Structured interviews produce responses to the same questions from every participant, whereas unstructured interviews allow for individual variations among the questions. For the popular focus group interview method, a small group of participants is assembled and asked to respond to questions. With oral history methods, people who have experienced psychologically interesting events recall their experiences and observations. With archival research, researchers use data deposited by others to find relationships. In small-N research the number of participants may be as few as one. Case studies examine closely people or groups and attempt to generalize the observations to others. Typically, case studies extend the interview process over a long period; a case study may last weeks or years. With AB and ABA designs, a baseline or initial condition (A) is altered by an intervention (B). In ABA designs, the effect of the intervention is revealed by removing the intervention to observe if the behavior returns to its baseline level.

Unlike the methods described in previous chapters, researchers using observational, qualitative, and small-N methods often sacrifice some degree of control over extraneous variables. In return, however, they gain external validity and access to many kinds of psychological data that cannot be studied using more controlled methods. In fact, it would be impossible to replicate exactly much of the research discussed in this chapter or to conduct it as a laboratory experiment. Observational, qualitative, and small-N research occupy an important niche in the complete collection of psychological research methods. As always, researchers must be mindful of the ethical consequences of their research, especially when they are applying or manipulating interventions.

In the next two chapters, we turn from research design to research practice. Chapters 11 and 12 guide you in a stepwise fashion through the process of research—from getting an idea to presenting reports of your research.

Chapter Review

1. Several types of research described in this chapter can yield qualitative data. List three of them.

2. What is the longest running example of naturalistic observation?

   _____

3. Goodall's research became well known when she discovered that chimpanzees:

   a. made simple tools

   b. hunted other animals

   c. could only be observed from afar

   d. both a and b

4. Two places identified in the text where naturalistic observation is

   not possible are _____ and _____.

5. What happened to Rosenhan's pseudopatients when they reported to a mental hospital and claimed to be hearing voices?

6. The principal difference between participant observation and

   naturalistic observation is _____.

7. Which interview technique poses the same questions to every interviewee?
   a. structured
   b. unstructured
   c. focus group
   d. oral history

8. Which interview technique assembles a small group and asks questions of them all?
   a. structured
   b. unstructured
   c. focus group
   d. oral history

9. The research method that investigates events in the past by interviewing people who lived through those events is:
   a. structured interview
   b. unstructured interview
   c. focus group
   d. oral history

10. Where might you find a paper archive?

11. What are two limitations of archival data?

12. Three categories of small-*N* research discussed in the text were
    _____ , _____ , and _____ .

13. May researchers reveal the names of their participants?

Thinking Critically About Research _____

1. Provide a scenario where observational research could be conducted only by using participant observation.

2. Match the situation with the most appropriate interview method.

   1. A fast-food restaurant selects new menu items.   a. structured
   2. A fast-food restaurant hires a new manager.   b. unstructured
   3. Ask people about their favorite fast-food restaurant.   c. focus group

3. Briefly describe an archival research question that could be answered by a trip to city hall or the county courthouse.

4. Match the situation with the appropriate small-*N* method.

1. Studying the effect of eating high-fat food   a. case study
2. Describing the success of a fast-food   b. AB design
   entrepreneur   c. ABA design
3. Weight loss through education of fast-food patrons

Answers to Chapter Review

1. Correct choices include: interviews, both structured and unstructured; focus group interviews, oral histories, case studies, and archival research
2. Jane Goodall's Gombe chimpanzee project, which began in 1960
3. d. both a and b
4. jury deliberations; bathrooms. Naturalistic observation should not be conducted in any place that society deems private.
5. They were admitted with a diagnosis of schizophrenia.
6. In participant observation, a research is both researcher and participant. In naturalistic observation, the researcher does not become part of the situation under observation.
7. a. structured
8. c. focus group
9. d. oral history
10. libraries, courthouses, and businesses are three places.
11. Archives may not have the data desired, and data they have might be missed.
12. case studies (or case histories); AB designs (or interventions); ABA designs (or reversals)
13. No.

Answers to Thinking Critically About Research

1. Any scenario in which the researcher must hold membership to be able to collect data will fit. Examples might include jury members, prize winners, and disaster survivors.
2. 1. c; 2. a; 3. b
3. Any question that can be answered by the types of records available will work. Examples include: births by decade (courthouse), early

settlers in a locality (library), and change in consumer spending for goods and services (business).

4. 1. c; 2. a; 3. b

Know for Sure _____

11

Planning Research

OVERVIEW

This chapter focuses on what must be done to produce a prospectus, which is a detailed plan for the research project. Topics such as getting an idea, doing a literature search using PsycINFO, and contacting other researchers are covered. Advice is offered for organizing the materials associated with a research project and for writing the prospectus.

OBJECTIVES

After studying this chapter and working through the exercises, you should be able to:

1. Think up research ideas
2. Access and search the scientific literature
3. Conduct your own personal research project
4. Organize the materials for your research project
5. Write a prospectus, or research plan
6. Join the international community of scholars interested in topics similar to yours

- How do you get a research idea?
- What should you do after you think of a research idea?
- Where do you find previous research?
- What is the scientific literature?
- How can you conduct your own research project?
- Why is being organized so important?
- What is a prospectus and how do you write one?
- How do you join the international community of scholars who are investigating similar ideas?

We answer these questions in this chapter. After reading it, you will be ready to embark on your personal research project. By now, you should be ready to conduct research of your own, but where do you start? Of course, you can't just go out and collect data aimlessly and hope that something good will happen. Conducting research that way is a recipe for disaster. There is a better way to conduct research, and planning is the key. In this chapter, we show you how to think of a research idea and then develop a plan (a *prospectus*) to turn the idea into a legitimate scientific research project.

GETTING AN IDEA

Although it appears that getting an idea for a research project is difficult, the truth is that getting an idea is difficult only early in your research career. Soon, you will think of research ideas all the time. The hard part will be picking just one! For the present, however, you may be struggling to find that one idea. What should you do? Here are four suggestions.

Read

To get ideas, you should read and read and read. What should you be reading? You can start with a general psychology text. If you don't have one, you can probably borrow one from a professor. First, review the table of contents. What chapters do you remember as particularly interesting? Choose one of those chapters to read. Pay attention to specific articles cited in the chapter; you may wish to look them up later. (We explain how to find them in this chapter.) Other sources of reading materials are professional journals, popular magazines, and newspapers. When you find an article that makes you stop and think, note it for later. You might even copy it for later reference. Whatever you read, the trick is to read it without thinking about getting an idea. You are simply preparing yourself for an idea that will inevitably come along later.

Observe

Another way to get a research idea is to observe the behavior of others around you. Suppose that you notice that some shoppers in the checkout line use coupons, but many do not. That observation could be the beginning of a research project. Now, more questions come easily. Who else uses coupons? How do they obtain them? What kinds of items do they buy? Are the items bought by coupon users different from those who do not use coupons? In what other ways do the two groups differ?

You might notice women in a restaurant showing each other pictures of their children. Do you ever notice men doing the same thing? Maybe you could ask parents, both mothers and fathers, how many pictures of their children they carry with them in their wallets or purses. Do you think women have more pictures in their purses than men have in their wallets?

Or, you might be walking along a campus path and see a brand-new pencil that somebody accidentally dropped. Would you pick it up? Would you have picked up a half-length, chewed-up pencil with a broken point? What would your fellow students do if they found either pencil? Again, your research project might develop from such a simple event. In case you are wondering, all of these examples came from projects conducted by students.

Relax

If you read enough and if you look at the world with the innate curiosity you had as a child, an idea will come. Ideas often come unexpectedly, so you need to be ready for them. Carry a pen and pad or a PDA (personal digital assistant) with you so you can write down the idea when it arrives. The idea might come to you while you are walking or jogging, or while you are just kicked back in your room. It might come while you are showering! Unfortunately, ideas can leave just as quickly as they arrive, so capture them while you can.

Feel Good About Your Topic

Find a topic interesting to you. Nothing is deadlier to the success of a research project than an unmotivated researcher. If you cannot get enthusiastic about your project, you should probably look for another one. When someone asks you about your project and you just go on and on about it, you have probably found the perfect project for you. Don't worry if no one else seems to share your enthusiasm about your project. What really matters is how you feel about your topic. Rest assured that somewhere in the world other people are just as enthused about your topic as you are. Near the end of this chapter we will tell you how to find those people and communicate with them.

After a few days, you should have a list of potential research ideas. Once you have that list, you are ready for the next steps. Taken together, those steps yield your prospectus, or your research plan. Choose one of the ideas on your list. Review the literature concerning your research idea. You will find research that others have conducted related to your idea. More than likely, you will also find people who are interested in your topic. Thanks to the Internet, you can communicate with them via e-mail. Later in this chapter, we show you how to find other researchers' e-mail addresses so you can contact them about your similar research interests.

THE PROSPECTUS

All good research starts with a plan. Another name for a research plan is **prospectus,** a Latin word that means "look ahead." When you write your prospectus, you are looking ahead, explaining how you will conduct your research project. A prospectus, which is sometimes called a *protocol,* does more than tell others about your plan. A prospectus is a way to clarify your own thinking. By the time you have written the final draft of your prospectus, you will understand your research project so well that you can easily explain it to others.

In this chapter you learn how to create a prospectus for your project. There are prospectus examples on the Web page for this chapter. You can use those examples as a model for your own. In all likelihood, you will need to write plans like this one in later undergraduate courses, in graduate school, or on the job. The best way to know if you understand something is to explain it to someone else. Thus, your prospectus is both the means for you to understand exactly how you intend to approach your research question and how to explain to others what you intend to do and why. As Ludy Benjamin, a longtime teacher and director of many student research projects, says, you know your prospectus is ready when you can explain your project to your mother (personal communication, April 12, 2002).

AN EXAMPLE LITERATURE SEARCH

In chapter 8, we described Craik and Lockhart's (1972) concept of levels of processing. Their research used words and showed that deep processing produced better recall than shallow processing. If you engaged in the exercise on page 235, you experienced a task similar to that of Craik and Lockhart's original participants.

Shortly after Craik and Lockhart's original study, Bower and Karlin (1974) used faces instead of words as stimuli in their depth of processing research. They found that deep processing led to better memory for faces,

prospectus   A detailed plan for a research project; sometimes referred to as a *protocol.*

just as Craik and Lockhart found that deep processing led to better memory for words. In this chapter, we use Bower and Karlin's research as a starting point. The task is to see how others since 1974 have investigated topics that involve faces and depth of processing. For this task, we find the **citations** of all of those studies, select those that interest us, download the abstracts of those studies, print hard copies, organize the materials we collect, and propose eight new research projects. Finally, we put all of those tasks together when we show you how to write a prospectus.

The terms *scientific literature, psychological literature,* or just plain **literature** refer to published research found in books, journals (both print and electronic), dissertations, and other reports. Every academic discipline has its own literature. As a budding psychologist, you must learn how to access that body of information. Naturally, you cannot hope to read or know all of the literature of your discipline, but you must know how to search and find the literature on a specific topic. Learning how to conduct a literature search will help you not only in psychology but also in any other academic discipline or career where information is archived.

ADVANTAGES OF A LITERATURE SEARCH

Scientists don't conduct a research project immediately after they get an idea. One reason is that someone else may have already had the same idea and already published on it. Another reason is that reading the literature may improve the idea. Literature searches also show who else is interested in similar ideas, and they reveal the history of research about the topic.

Answer May Already Be Known

By consulting the literature, scientists may find the answer to their research question without having to conduct their own research project. Building on the work of others is one of the benefits of science's practice of publishing research. Your ability to find answers directly from the literature is a valuable skill that you can take to graduate school or to a career.

Your Own Research Is Improved

By reading the literature, scientists refine and sharpen their ideas. By knowing the research others have published, they can design better and more important research projects. Previous projects often provide examples of materials, control procedures, statistical tests, and background information that are helpful to your research.

Connects You With Others

Reading the literature is also an avenue to the worldwide community of those interested in the same topic. As part of your project, you can explore

citation The author(s), publication date, title, journal or publisher, and pages of an article or book.

literature The entire collection of published research in a scientific discipline.

and enter that community. Technology has made the process of joining scientific communities easier and has removed many geographical barriers. It is exciting to find others who are interested in the same ideas that you are.

Shows the History of Topics

By reading the literature, scientists learn the history of their topic. A literature search tells them how popular a topic is, when research on that topic began, and how the topic developed. They also can determine how their own research question fits into that history.

Replicates Previous Work

As noted in chapter 1, science is a self-correcting system. The mechanism that fixes science's errors is **replication.** When scientists replicate the work of others, they intentionally repeat the original work. If they obtain the results found by the original researcher, confidence in the original conclusions increases. Sometimes, however, the original results are not obtained the second time. In those cases, confidence in the original conclusions is suspended. The discrepancy between the original work and its replication usually produces further research that may resolve the discrepancy. (See p. 6 for a dramatic example of replication failure in chemistry, cold fusion.) Conducting a replication is a worthwhile research project for beginners, both for reasons of training and scientific confirmation.

You Reap the Benefits

If you conduct a thorough literature search, you will be ready to take the next steps in planning your research project. The good news is that it is easier to conduct a literature search today than ever before. Why? The answer is the Internet or the World Wide Web, the creation of large electronic databases, and the tools necessary to search them. A **database** is a collection of information that is organized so that it can be searched for specific items. A telephone book or box of recipe cards are examples of paper databases. More commonly, a database is a computerized collection of information that can be searched, browsed, and sorted.

ACCESSING THE SCIENTIFIC LITERATURE IN PSYCHOLOGY

The scientific literature in psychology consists of articles in professional journals and books. In all science, more than one million scientific articles are published each year as are thousands of books. That is a lot of information. Until 1985, the journal *Psychological Abstracts* was the main source psychologists used to search their literature. The *Psychological Abstracts* are

replication   Repeating an experiment with the same procedures or with planned changes in the procedures to confirm the original results.

database   An organized collection of information.

paper journal issues that contain information about research findings in psychology. The information includes author(s), title, date of publication, an **abstract** (summary), and other information. A search for a single topic could take hours, and all information had to be copied by hand or photocopied. Thanks to electronic abstracting services, finding and reproducing material on your topic of interest is now fairly easy. Most psychologists use PsycINFO, a searchable, electronic database maintained by the American Psychological Association. Today, PsycINFO has replaced the *Psychological Abstracts* for most researchers.

PsycINFO

PsycINFO provides abstracts and other information on articles published in almost 2,000 journals. The oldest item in PsycINFO is Pinel's (1806) book *A Treatise on Insanity*. The first journal articles listed are the contents of the first volume of the *American Journal of Psychology,* a journal first published in 1887 and still published today. PsycINFO also gives information about books, chapters in books, dissertations, and technical reports in psychology and related disciplines. In short, PsycINFO gives you access to nearly everything ever published in psychology. Other similar electronic resources are PsycARTICLES, PsycBOOKS, PsycCRITIQUES, and PsycEXTRA. These databases list articles in APA journals, review books, and publish less formal publications such as reports and conference papers. Ask your local librarian if you have access to PsycINFO or the other databases provided by the American Psychological Association. If you cannot access these databases locally, visit the American Psychological Association's Web page (http://www.apa.org/psycinfo/products/) where you will find access options for institutions and individuals.

PsycINFO's Structure

Depending on the age and type of item, PsycINFO **records** contain some or all of the **fields** listed below. A database record contains all of the information for a particular search item. Database fields are individual items of information that collectively make up a record. The more commonly used fields are marked with an asterisk (*).

> **Title*:** title of the article.
>
> **Journal*:** title of the journal in which the article appears.
>
> **Publication Date*:** year the work was published.
>
> **Author(s)*:** author or authors of the work.
>
> **Abstract*:** short summary of the article or book.
>
> **ISSN:** number used by librarians to track serials (journals).

abstract   Short summary of a research article or the contents of a book.

record   All database fields about an item such as an article or book.

field   A place in a database to store a particular type of information.

Accession Number: number used by PsycINFO to catalog the record.

Language: language used in the article or book.

Document Type*: type of publication, such as journal article, book, chapter, or other.

Source Details*: for journals, this field gives the volume numbers, issue number, and page numbers.

Class Descriptors: terms used to classify the citation into its superordinate (more general) category. These descriptors may be hyperlinked (depending on the vendor) to other citations with the same descriptor.

Major Descriptors: specific to PsycINFO, these terms classify the citation with other closely related areas of psychology. These terms can be used to search for similar citations.

Minor Descriptors: specific to PsycINFO, these terms classify the citation with other more distantly related areas of psychology. These terms may be hyperlinked (depending on the vendor) to similar citations.

Identifier: brief statement about the contents of the article or book.

Content Type*: brief description of the type of article, such as empirical article or literature review.

Population Group: population studied, such as human or animal.

Age Group: age of the population studied, such as adulthood or adolescent.

Author Affiliation*: institution where the first author was employed when the citation was published. Newer records may contain e-mail addresses.

Special Features: other distinguishing characteristics of the citation. "References" is the most common entry here.

PsycINFO has a very useful tool called the **thesaurus.** If you don't know what search term to use, start with the thesaurus. Type in your search term and it will tell you what word or words PsycINFO uses to classify a particular topic. The thesaurus also tells you when that term was first used, gives you narrower terms to search on, and explodes a topic. Exploding creates a new search that finds the original search term plus narrower terms related to it. Talk to your local librarian for more information on how to use PsycINFO's thesaurus.

PsycINFO Search Example

We describe a search we conducted using PsycINFO. When you duplicate this search on your own, your results will not be exactly the same as ours

thesaurus A tool that provides words or phrases that are similar to the target word or phrase.

because of new citations added to the PsycINFO database since we conducted our search. To provide material for an illustration, we returned to a topic in chapter 8, depth of processing and memory. Using PsycINFO's advanced search, we typed in two terms: "depth of processing" and "face." (We use quotes here to illustrate the exact search terms we typed. In PsycINFO, you would type the word(s) without quotes.) We chose those **search terms** after looking at the title of Bower and Karlin's 1974 article. We searched for "face" instead of "faces" because "face" will find both words but "faces" will not. We searched for "depth of processing" because Bower and Karlin used that combination of words in their title. PsycINFO returned 16 **hits** for these two terms combined. A search for "depth of processing" alone produced 296 hits, whereas a search for "face" alone yielded 32,411 hits. Notice how searching for both terms simultaneously drastically reduced the number of hits.

You may conduct the same searches on PsycINFO now to find the number of hits at present. Enter your hits below:

Conduct a PsycINFO search and enter your results in the spaces provided:

Search term	Our hits	Your hits
depth of processing	296	————
face	32,411	————
face and depth of processing	16	————

Finding 16 hits is a fortunate result because 16 is a small number of abstracts to read. We are satisfied when our initial combination of search terms gives us around 20 to 100 hits. Getting many more than 100 hits usually means that you should refine your search by adding more terms. Just think how long it would take you to look through all 296 citations for "depth of processing." We'll bet you do not even want to think about how long it would take to look at 32,411 hits! Combining the two search terms resulted in a manageable task. For searches of heavily researched areas, you may have to type in three or more terms to end up with a manageable number of abstracts. PsycINFO also allows you to perform other search operations. By using the **operators** found in PsycINFO, you can refine your search efficiently. You may use *OR, AND, PRE/n, W/n,* and *AND NOT* as operators. Your local librarian can help you learn how to use these operators. Or, you may read the "Help" sections that PsycINFO provides to learn how to use the operators yourself.[1]

search term Word or phrase used in a search engine to find a record or URL.

hit A record that matches a set of search criteria.

operator Terms that aid searching; *OR, AND, PRE/n, W/n,* and *AND NOT* are PsycINFO examples.

---

[1]*PRE/n* allows you to search for terms previous to another. *W/n* allows you to search for terms within a few words of another. In both operators, *n* is the number of words previous or within.

Citation List and How It Was Culled

PsycINFO returned 16 hits in our search of "depth of processing" and "face." **Table 11.1** shows the 16 citations in reverse order of publication date by default. The reverse chronological order provides a picture of the research community's interest in a topic. PsycINFO can also sort the hits by author, source, or relevance, if desired. Each box in Table 11.1 shows one of the 16

TABLE 11.1	Our List of Hits Showing Raw PsycINFO Format and Our Comments

1. Online versus face-to-face conversation: An examination of relational and discourse variables. Mallen, Michael J.; Day, Susan X.; Green, Melinda A.; *Psychotherapy: Theory, Research, Practice, Training, Vol 40*(1–2), Spr–Sum 2003. pp. 155–163. [Peer Reviewed Journal]
   Cited References (26)
   Notes: Check Library's catalog for availability

   We culled this article after reading its abstract. Its topics were related to conversations, emotional disclosure, and interpersonal communication, not memory.

2. Hemispheric encoding asymmetry is more apparent than real. Miller, Michael B.; Kingstone, Alan; Gazzaniga, Michael S.; *Journal of Cognitive Neuroscience, Vol 14*(5), Jul 2002. pp. 702–708. [Peer Reviewed Journal]
   Cited References (24) Times Cited in this Database (6)
   Notes: Check Library's catalog for availability
   Linked Full Text

   We culled this article. Although its topic was memory, the main focus of the article was hemispheric specialization (a physiological topic).

3. Encoding activity and face recognition. Coin, Christian; Tiberghien, Guy; *Memory, Vol 5*(5), Sep 1997. pp. 545–568. [Peer Reviewed Journal]
   Times Cited in this Database (2)
   Notes: Check Library's catalog for availability
   Linked Full Text

   We kept this article. Its topics were memory and faces.

4. How wearing eyeglasses affects facial recognition. Terry, Roger L.; *Current Psychology: Developmental,* *Learning, Personality, Social, Vol 12*(2), Sum 1993. pp. 151–162. [Peer Reviewed Journal]
   Notes: Check Library's catalog for availability

   We kept this article. It looked at how wearing eyeglasses affected memory for faces.

5. Cross-racial facial identification: A social cognitive integration. Anthony, Tara; Copper, Carolyn; Mullen, Brian; *Personality & Social Psychology Bulletin, Vol 18*(3), Jun 1992. pp. 296–301. [Peer Reviewed Journal]
   Times Cited in this Database (26)
   Notes: Check Library's catalog for availability

   Here was another keeper. This meta-analysis looked at how the race affected memory for faces. Finding racial and ethnic variables in memory for faces was an unexpected finding for us, but we wanted to know more.

6. Depth of processing approach to face recognition: A test of two theories. Bloom, Lance C.; Mudd, Samuel A.; *Journal of Experimental Psychology: Learning, Memory, & Cognition, Vol 17*(3), May 1991. pp. 556–565. [Peer Reviewed Journal]
   Times Cited in this Database (2)
   Notes: This title is held locally

   This article looked at two theories of how memory for faces might work. We kept it.

7. Deep—deeper—deepest? Encoding strategies and the recognition of human faces. Sporer, Siegfried L.; *Journal of Experimental Psychology: Learning, Memory, & Cognition, Vol 17*(2), Mar 1991. pp. 323–333. [Peer Reviewed Journal]
   Times Cited in this Database (8)

(continued)

TABLE 11.1 (continued)

Notes: This title is held locally

This article also tested theoretical issues surrounding memory for faces, so we kept it.

8. Techniques for cognitive training of memory in age-associated memory impairment. Yesavage, Jerome A.; *Archives of Gerontology & Geriatrics, Suppl 1, 1989.* pp. 185–190. [Peer Reviewed Journal]
   Notes: Check Library's catalog for availability

We culled this article. Its main topic was training older adults mnemonic memory aids and their efficacy.

9. Meta-analysis of facial identification studies. Shapiro, Peter N.; Penrod, Steven; *Psychological Bulletin, Vol 100(2),* Sep 1986. pp. 139–156. [Peer Reviewed Journal]
   Times Cited in this Database (54)
   Notes: This title is held locally

Another meta-analytic article; we kept this one because it looked at factors leading to improved memory for faces.

10. Effect of depth of processing on recognition memory for normal and inverted photographs of faces. McKelvie, Stuart J.; *Perceptual & Motor Skills, Vol 60(2),* Apr 1985. pp. 503–508. [Peer Reviewed Journal]
    Times Cited in this Database (1)
    Notes: This title is held locally

This one was a tough call, but we ultimately culled it because its main focus was the variable of upside-down faces, not depth of processing.

11. Effect of schema-incongruent information on memory for stereotypical attributes. O'Sullivan, Chris S.; Durso, Francis T.; *Journal of Personality & Social Psychology, Vol 47(1),* Jul 1984. pp. 55–70. [Peer Reviewed Journal]
    Times Cited in this Database (20)
    Notes: This title is held locally

We culled this one because its main topics were stereotypes and social perception, not memory for faces per se.

12. Depth of processing, context, and face recognition. Baddeley, Alan D.; Woodhead, Muriel; *Canadian Journal of Psychology, Vol 36(2),* Jun 1982. pp. 148–164. [Peer Reviewed Journal]

Times Cited in this Database (4)
Notes: Check Library's catalog for availability

This article was an easy call. We kept it because looked at whether or not additional context cues improved memory for faces (they did).

13. Depth of processing in response to own—and other—race faces. Chance, June E.; Goldstein, Alvin G.; *Personality & Social Psychology Bulletin, Vol 7(3),* Sep 1981. pp. 475–480. [Peer Reviewed Journal]
    Times Cited in this Database (9)
    Notes: Check Library's catalog for availability

We kept this one. We had not anticipated finding ethnic and racial effects in facial recognition, but when we did, we wanted to know more.

14. Depth of processing and anxiety in facial recognition. Mueller, John H.; Bailis, Karen L.; Goldstein, Alvin G.; *British Journal of Psychology, Vol 70(4),* Nov 1979. pp. 511–515. [Peer Reviewed Journal]
    Times Cited in this Database (2)
    Notes: Check Library's catalog for availability
    Linked Full Text

We culled this one because its main focus was anxiety.

15. Recognition memory for typical and unusual faces. Light, Leah L.; Kayra-Stuart, Fortunee; Hollander, Steven; *Journal of Experimental Psychology: Human Learning & Memory, Vol 5(3),* May 1979. pp. 212–228. [Peer Reviewed Journal]
    Times Cited in this Database (34)
    Notes: This title is held locally

This was another easy-to-keep article. It looked at memory for typical versus unusual faces.

16. Depth of processing pictures of faces and recognition memory. Bower, Gordon H.; Karlin, Martin B.; *Journal of Experimental Psychology, Vol 103(4),* Oct 1974. pp. 751–757. [Journal]
    Times Cited in this Database (24)
    Notes: Check Library's catalog for availability

This was the easiest call of all. This article was the one that began the entire line of investigation in depth of processing and memory for faces.

Source: PsycINFO citations reprinted with permission of the American Psychological Association, © APA.

citations plus our notes about culling the citation. Culled citations are removed from further consideration.

Each journal citation may show the title, author(s), journal, volume and issue number, page numbers, type of journal, number of references, whether the journal is in your local library, or whether the article is available in full-text format. References to books show author(s), title, and publisher. In PsycINFO, clicking on the title will take you to another page that shows more information about that citation. PsycINFO does not format the citations in APA style.

The next step is to look at each citation to be sure it is relevant to the topic of depth of processing and memory for faces. Reading the abstract usually gives you enough information to decide whether to keep or discard a citation. Our rule of thumb for our search was to keep any article we might ever need in researching the topic. Better to have an article on hand and not need it, than to not have an article and wish we did. We culled 6 citations. So, of the 16 citations returned by PsycINFO, we kept 10.

Organizing the Abstracts and Articles

The next step is to print the abstracts and obtain the articles. The abstracts can be printed from PsycINFO. It turned out that one citation (#3) we wanted was for a full-text[2] article, so we printed it directly from PsycINFO. Five others were already in our local library, so we found and copied them too. The remaining four articles were ordered using interlibrary loan.[3] When all 10 articles were in hard-copy form, they were three-hole punched and placed alphabetically by first author in a loose-leaf notebook. Psychologists typically refer to research by the author's name and date of publication. So, article #7 would be referred to in conversation as "Sporer, 1991."

Figure 11.1 shows the abstracts of the 10 articles as single pages as they would print out from PsycINFO arranged in alphabetical order by first author. Behind each abstract is the article itself. So, we literally have our work at hand.

In the Know

When discussing research literature, psychologists use the author(s)' last name(s) and the date of publication as a kind of shorthand to identify the article.

---

[2]Full-text articles are becoming more common. Unlike abstracts, they provide an electronic version of the entire article.

[3]Ask your local librarian about the interlibrary loan policy on your campus.

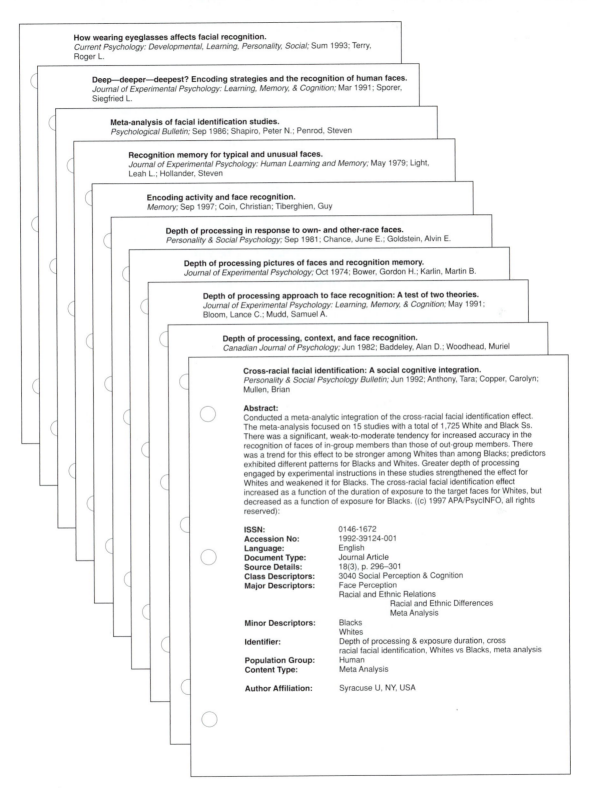

How wearing eyeglasses affects facial recognition.
Current Psychology: Developmental, Learning, Personality, Social; Sum 1993; Terry, Roger L.

Deep—deeper—deepest? Encoding strategies and the recognition of human faces.
Journal of Experimental Psychology: Learning, Memory, & Cognition; Mar 1991; Sporer, Siegfried L.

Meta-analysis of facial identification studies.
Psychological Bulletin; Sep 1986; Shapiro, Peter N.; Penrod, Steven

Recognition memory for typical and unusual faces.
Journal of Experimental Psychology: Human Learning and Memory; May 1979; Light, Leah L.; Hollander, Steven

Encoding activity and face recognition.
Memory; Sep 1997; Coin, Christian; Tiberghien, Guy

Depth of processing in response to own- and other-race faces.
Personality & Social Psychology; Sep 1981; Chance, June E.; Goldstein, Alvin E.

Depth of processing pictures of faces and recognition memory.
Journal of Experimental Psychology; Oct 1974; Bower, Gordon H.; Karlin, Martin B.

Depth of processing approach to face recognition: A test of two theories.
Journal of Experimental Psychology: Learning, Memory, & Cognition; May 1991; Bloom, Lance C.; Mudd, Samuel A.

Depth of processing, context, and face recognition.
Canadian Journal of Psychology; Jun 1982; Baddeley, Alan D.; Woodhead, Muriel

Cross-racial facial identification: A social cognitive integration.
Personality & Social Psychology Bulletin; Jun 1992; Anthony, Tara; Copper, Carolyn; Mullen, Brian

Abstract:
Conducted a meta-analytic integration of the cross-racial facial identification effect. The meta-analysis focused on 15 studies with a total of 1,725 White and Black Ss. There was a significant, weak-to-moderate tendency for increased accuracy in the recognition of faces of in-group members than those of out-group members. There was a trend for this effect to be stronger among Whites than among Blacks; predictors exhibited different patterns for Blacks and Whites. Greater depth of processing engaged by experimental instructions in these studies strengthened the effect for Whites and weakened it for Blacks. The cross-racial facial identification effect increased as a function of the duration of exposure to the target faces for Whites, but decreased as a function of exposure for Blacks. ((c) 1997 APA/PsycINFO, all rights reserved):

ISSN:	0146-1672
Accession No:	1992-39124-001
Language:	English
Document Type:	Journal Article
Source Details:	18(3), p. 296–301
Class Descriptors:	3040 Social Perception & Cognition
Major Descriptors:	Face Perception
	Racial and Ethnic Relations
	Racial and Ethnic Differences
	Meta Analysis
Minor Descriptors:	Blacks
	Whites
Identifier:	Depth of processing & exposure duration, cross racial facial identification, Whites vs Blacks, meta analysis
Population Group:	Human
Content Type:	Meta Analysis
Author Affiliation:	Syracuse U, NY, USA

FIGURE 11.1   Facsimile of pages from PsycINFO.

BRAINSTORMING FOR IDEAS

Our initial search of the literature was over. The next task was to generate ideas for an experiment. To do this, we assembled a group of 15 undergraduates who acted as a focus group. Their task was to brainstorm for ideas. After examining the loose-leaf notebook, the group came up with ideas. Brainstorming rules about "newborn" ideas were followed, which means that no criticism of others' ideas was allowed and every idea was written down. Most members of the focus group thought up experiments about faces, and a few thought up experiments on depth of processing. Of course, the ideas were only first-draft, sketchy ideas. They would have to be refined considerably before they became research projects. **Table 11.2** shows the eight ideas generated. This list was generated with great excitement in less than 10 minutes. The group (which was actually a research

TABLE 11.2	Focus-Group-Generated Research Ideas

Eyewitness and facial recognition by race
> Inspired by Anthony, Copper, and Mullen (1992), several students wished to investigate the effect of cross-racial facial identification.

The effect of emotion or trauma on recall of faces
> One student wondered how emotion or trauma might affect facial recognition and depth of processing. She speculated that under high levels of emotion, facial recognition would be better under both shallow and deep processing.

Matching adult faces to childhood photographs
> A mother wondered whether strangers could match photos of children's faces with their corresponding adult faces.

Recognizing strangers who are regularly seen in a variety of settings
> People seen in particular contexts are easily recognized. However, recognizing the same people outside their usual context is more difficult. Does level of processing make a difference?

Memory for faces by attractiveness and gender
> Some wondered if attractive people are more easily recognized and whether there is a gender effect.

Recognizing passersby riding in automobiles
> In many rural areas, drivers wave at other drivers who are traveling the oncoming lane. One student commented that this characteristic made for a field experiment in which drivers categorized themselves as wavers and nonwavers.

Recognizing familiar people in unfamiliar automobiles
> In small towns, residents learn to associate autos with their owners. One student proposed that people drive around in their own cars and later in rental cars and to count the number of waves they received from other drivers.

Effect of frequency and duration of exposure on facial recognition memory
> A student wondered whether frequency of exposure to the same face or the length of time a face was seen would affect recognition in both shallow and deep processing.

methods class) then asked if they could have similar focus group meetings for each of their individual research projects, a clear indication that research can be fun! The students in the focus group learned that there is no shortage of research ideas. Indeed, the opposite is true. Getting a research idea is not a problem; the problem is picking just one to explore further.

OTHER SOURCES OF INFORMATION

Besides PsycINFO, there are other sources of information. We describe two paper sources and list other electronic databases.

Annual Review of Psychology

Every year the *Annual Review of Psychology* publishes a volume with chapters that explain the recent research in 20 to 25 different areas of psychology. Over a number of years, most areas of psychology are covered. The *Annual Review of Psychology* is available online at http://annualreviews.org/. This Web site provides abstracts (freely available) and full-text articles from 1984 to the present. Access to the full-text articles requires an institutional subscription. Articles in the *Annual Review* summarize and synthesize interesting areas of research in psychology. A search for "depth of processing" and "face" yielded 96 hits. None of those hits, however, were directly related to our interest in the combined topics.

Psychological Bulletin

The APA journal, *Psychological Bulletin,* publishes "evaluative and integrative reviews and interpretations of issues in scientific psychology." *Psychological Bulletin* does not publish original research. Notice that one of the articles that we found in the PsycINFO search was from *Psychological Bulletin* (Shapiro & Penrod, 1986; our citation #9). That article summarized 128 studies that used eyewitness identification and facial recognition. Anyone reading that article would get a quick lesson about the previous research in those two topics. Use *Psychological Bulletin* as another source for learning about previous research within a given field or area in psychology. Access *Psychological Bulletin* at http://www.apa.org/journals/bul/description.html.

Other Databases

There are other databases that may contain information useful to psychology students. One such database is Medline, which is run by the National Library of Medicine. Medline has information on diseases, hospitals, and physicians, and it also contains a medical dictionary. Another useful database is CINAHL (published by the National League of Nursing and the American Nurses Association. CINAHL covers nursing and related topics such as biomedicine and consumer health. Finally, JSTOR (a not-for-profit organization) provides a collection of databases in both multidisciplinary and discipline-specific formats. Depending on your local library, you may have access to all, some, or none of these databases. Consult your librarian to see if you may access these or other databases.

> ### In the Know
> A recent student project revealed that the topic of access to handicapped restrooms resulted in very few hits in PsycINFO. However, a search in CINAHL found a larger number of hits using the indexed item "toilet facilities." In PsycINFO, the only similar indexed item was "toilet training." Sometimes you have to match the topic to the database.

MAKING PERSONAL CONTACT

Personal contact is the most powerful way that humans influence each other. In research, personal contact with a mentor, fellow researchers, or mentees produces ideas, direction, and often, excitement. You are lucky if there are others nearby who share your research interests. Otherwise, you can find people with similar research interests through the use of modern technology. Thanks to the Internet, you can easily send messages to the authors of articles and books on your topic. If you know the author's name and institution, you can usually find an e-mail address. Here is how you can find e-mail addresses and then contact the authors.

First, check PsycINFO for the institution of the first author. For more recent citations, PsycINFO shows the e-mail address. Otherwise, go to the institution's Web page. If you do not know the **URL** (uniform resource locator, or the Web address) of the institution, use a **search engine** to find it. Type the name of the institution into the search engine. When the list of hits is displayed, look for one that ends with *.edu*. (This tactic works in the United States, but foreign schools may not use the *.edu* extension.) Now click on that URL and see if it takes you to the home page of the institution. If it does not, look on the page displayed to see if there is a link to the institution's home page. If not, go back to the list of hits from the search engine and try again.

Once you locate the institution's home page, look for a search window or a link to a directory. Now search for the person you are looking for. Often, the person's e-mail address will be displayed for you. If there are no directories or search fields, look for a link to a school or department. If one exists, click on it and look for links to faculty, students, or staff. See if you can find your author. Most of the time you will. If not, don't give up. Go back to your search engine and perform a search for the person's name. See what turns up. Do any of the hits look promising?

To illustrate a search for an e-mail address, we chose the article by Coin and Tiberghien (1997) (citation #3 in Table 11.1). We picked this

URL Uniform resource locator; a Web address that consists of a protocol such as *http* or *ftp* and a domain name.

search engine Computer program that allows users to search a database or the World Wide Web.

particular article because it looked difficult. According to PsycINFO, the first author, Christian Coin, was from *Université Claude Bernard* in Lyon, France. Using a search engine, we found that the URL for the school was http://www.univ-lyon1.fr/ucbl/. Naturally, that page was in French! We could not find a directory, nor could we find a link for the *Institut des Sciences Cognitives* which was Coin's academic unit listed in PsycINFO. Using "Christian Coin" in a search engine did not pan out either, even when combined with "Claude Bernard," his institution. At this point we switched tactics and searched for the second author "Guy Tiberghien." We were successful. We found a page with his e-mail address on it. Tiberghien's address was tiberghien@isc.cnrs.fr. Based on his e-mail address we tried the following server: http://www.isc.cnrs.fr.

Can you see how we deduced the name of the server from the e-mail address?

The mail server's name was *isc.cnrs.fr,* so by adding *www* to it, we got *www.isc.cnrs.fr.* That URL turned out to be the home page of the *Institut des Sciences Cognitives.* The *Institut*'s page had a directory, listed in French as *"membres,"* but Christian Coin was not listed. We inferred that Coin might have been a student when he published the article in 1997, and had since moved away. We e-mailed Guy Tiberghien and he replied a few days later and provided Coin's e-mail address, which was cio-amberieu@ac-lyon.fr. Using his e-mail address to once again deduce a Web home page, we found http://www.ac-lyon.fr, and that turned out to be the *Academie de Lyon* in Lyon, France, *naturellement.*

As noted, we picked this citation because it was not in the United States and not in English. Still, in less than 10 minutes, we discovered that one of the authors was still at the same university and we found his and his co-author's e-mail address. Not bad detective work, if we say so ourselves. Fortunately, PsycINFO is now providing e-mail addresses for authors, making the job of communicating with the authors of recent articles much easier.

THE RESEARCH COMMUNITY

Today's technology gives you an easy way to enter and join the virtual community of researchers in psychology (and other disciplines). Many students correspond with researchers after conducting searches such as the one just described. Usually, students receive warm and enthusiastic replies to the e-mail they send to working researchers. For example, one of our students recently read an article about paranoia and how it affects political decision making. Using PsycINFO, she found a questionnaire developed by a researcher in Australia. She e-mailed him and received a prompt reply and now has his permission to use his questionnaire in a study of her own.

If you think about it, it is not hard to imagine why students get that kind of reception. If someone wrote you out of the blue and asked about the very topic you were working on, how would you feel? If you are like most, you would feel flattered by the attention. So, make contact with other researchers, either personally or by e-mail.

Notice how far we have come in this chapter. We started with one reference (Bower & Karlin, 1974). We searched PsycINFO using two terms (*face* and *depth of processing*), found 16 hits, and culled them to 10. We obtained the articles and put them in a binder in alphabetical order by first author. Along the way, we learned a lot about our topic. The next step is to flesh out the idea into a full-fledged prospectus.

Think of the process we described as a model you might follow. Notice how we found information about our research idea and then organized that information. Getting your material organized is helpful for writing a prospectus. We also learned a lot along the way.

FURTHER DEVELOPMENT OF THE PROSPECTUS

Once you have found an idea for research, searched the literature, selected and acquired the relevant materials, and decided on a topic, you are ready to write your prospectus. Although this may seem like a lot of work before you begin your prospectus, writing is much easier when you prepare first.

The prospectus contains most of the sections of an empirical article except for those sections that cannot be written until the data are collected. A prospectus consists of title page, Introduction section, Method section (including proposed statistical analyses), Expected Results section, and References list. Because the prospectus is a plan for future action, the Method and Expected Results sections should be written in the future tense. The prospectus often serves as the document you submit to an IRB, so it should address ethical issues.

Write the Method Section First

At this point (provided you have an idea), you are ready to write your prospectus. We recommend that you write the **Method section** first because all the other sections depend on the Method section. The articles you cite in the Introduction section depend on how you plan to conduct your project. The Expected Results section depends on the statistical analyses you will perform. An explicit Method section acts as the skeleton for the rest of the prospectus.

Most often, the Method section consists of three subsections: Participants, Apparatus or Materials, and Procedure. In the Participants subsection, describe who the participants will be and how you will recruit them. If you plan to offer incentives to obtain participants, mention the incentives. Will your participants have certain demographic characteristics? For instance, will you need only traditional college students or only nontraditional college students? Will your project require specialized

Method section
Research report section that describes how the research was conducted.

demographics, such as participants over the age of 65 or native Spanish speakers? Whatever your project requires in terms of participants, the Participants subsection describes them and how you plan to select and recruit them. Attend to the ethical treatment of the participants. How will you obtain informed consent? Can you dispense with informed consent because you are conducting anonymous surveys or making naturalistic observations? Where and when will you debrief them? The Participants subsection is the place to deal with these and other ethical issues.

The second subsection, Apparatus or Materials, lists and describes all of the apparatus or materials you need to conduct your project. Test instruments and questionnaires are identified and described here. Will you use recording devices such as digital video cameras, audio tape recorders, or film cameras? Will your study take place in a laboratory, classroom, or outdoors? Will you have to build any specialized apparatus? If so, you should describe the construction details. Ordinary items such as tables and chairs only need mention, not detailed description.

The Procedure subsection is very important. In it, provide a verbal or graphic timeline that shows the order of events in your project. Design information such as the IV, DV, assignment of participants, statistical analyses, and the step-by-step particulars of your project are described in this subsection. The Procedure subsection should be detailed enough so that a reader could replicate your project. Once you can put this subsection on paper, you will know that your project is beginning to take shape.

What do you believe the data will show? Using the statistical techniques you listed in the Procedure subsection, describe the expected outcomes. Include graphs of your expected results; they will serve as a template for your actual results and also help others understand your project.

Compose the Introduction

The *Publication Manual of the American Psychological Association* (APA, 2001) states that the **Introduction** should accomplish three goals: introduce the problem, develop the background, and state the purpose and rationale of your project. Let's look at each of these in turn.

Introducing the problem is really telling the story of your interest in your research topic. How did you and your topic find each other? Do you believe others will find your topic important? Why? What is the theoretical background of your topic and how will your project relate or contribute to that theory? Telling this story is not always easy. Write it down and show it to others. If they understand it, you are well on your way. If they do not understand, incorporate the answers you give to their questions into your rewrite.

The second thing the *Publication Manual* tells you is to develop the background. The notebook you created during your literature search really helps at this point. Read the articles in your notebook. Which articles are most relevant to your project? Show the connection between the

Introduction section Research report section that introduces the background and purpose of the research.

previous research and your project. Did you find any controversies? Are there differences of opinion about your topic in the literature? If so, describe these differences in this part of the Introduction section.

The third goal of the introduction is to briefly describe your research plan. Give an overview of the Method section that you wrote. In this part of the Introduction section, briefly describe your hypotheses, the independent and dependent variables, your expected results, and your interpretation of the expected results. The Introduction section should provide a fairly complete picture of your proposed work.

List the References

The last section of a prospectus, **References,** is a list of articles and books cited in other sections. This list is arranged alphabetically by the first author's last name. Writing a citation in APA format is best learned by finding a matching example in one of the two APA publications on APA style. One of the publications is the *Publication Manual of the American Psychological Association* (APA, 2001) and the other is *Concise Rules of APA Style* (APA, 2005). We cover referencing in more detail in chapter 12.

With a prospectus in hand and IRB approval (if needed), you are ready to conduct research. For most students, the fun is doing the research itself. Your directions are in your prospectus; they help make you confident as you start conducting your research. The next chapter tells you how.

Chapter Review ⎯⎯⎯⎯⎯⎯⎯⎯⎯⎯⎯⎯⎯⎯⎯⎯⎯

1. Your text suggests ⎯⎯⎯⎯, ⎯⎯⎯⎯, ⎯⎯⎯⎯, and ⎯⎯⎯⎯, as ways to generate an initial research idea.

2. *Research plan* and *protocol* are other names for ⎯⎯⎯⎯.

3. Why should you conduct a literature search before you conduct an experiment?

4. ⎯⎯⎯⎯ contributes directly to the self-correcting nature of science.

5. Current book reviews can be found online in ⎯⎯⎯⎯.

6. The part of a research report that summarizes the article is called the ⎯⎯⎯⎯.

7. Why will *face* yield more hits from PsycINFO than *faces* will?

8. The text suggests that you organize your collection of citations by with a(n) ⎯⎯⎯⎯.

9. ⎯⎯⎯⎯ articles are found in the *Annual Review of Psychology* and *Psychological Bulletin*.

references List of sources cited in a manuscript.

10. The _____ section of the prospectus should be written before the other sections.

11. The usual subsections of the Method section of a prospectus are _____, _____, and _____.

12. In the Introduction section, you should _____, _____, and _____.

Thinking Critically About Research _____

1. Think about a situation in which you usually find yourself, such as eating at a restaurant, studying at the library, or interacting with your friends. Come up with a research idea based on that situation.

2. What does the "scientific literature" consist of?

3. Find e-mail addresses for the following people. Describe how you found them.
   a. the president of the American Psychological Association
   b. the lead author of a PsycINFO journal article published in 2005–2006
   c. the lead author of a PsycINFO journal article published in 1990

4. Find a recent review article on the topic of couple therapy.

5. After you get a research idea, why should you write the Method section first?

Answers to Chapter Review _____

1. read, observe, relax, and feel good about your topic

2. prospectus

3. The answer to many research problems you think of may already be known.

4. Replication

5. PsycCRITIQUES

6. abstract

7. *Face* yields more hits because *face* also picks up *faces*. However, *faces* will not pick up *face*.

8. notebook, organizing the abstracts and articles alphabetically by first author

9. Review (articles that summarize a particular area of psychology)

10. Method

11. Participants, Apparatus or Materials, and Procedure

12. introduce the problem; develop the background; briefly describe the research plan

Answers to Thinking Critically About Research

1. Obviously, lots of research ideas could emerge from those situations. That's the point! Here are some sample possibilities:

   Restaurant: Tipping behavior and variables that affect tips.

   Library: Are males or females more likely to use library computers to play games?

   Friends: Friends make a great population for testing preliminary ideas.

2. The scientific literature consists of books, journals, dissertations, reports, and other published sources of scientific studies.

3. President of APA: look it up on the APA Web site: http://www.apa.org.

   PsycINFO 2005–2006: the lead author's e-mail should be listed.

   PsycINFO 1990: you will have to try a search engine or the search at the lead author's 1990 institution. Good luck!

4. There are several ways to answer this question. The 2006 edition of *Annual Review of Psychology* just happens to have such a review: "Current Status and Future Directions in Couple Therapy." Another way to find such an article is to use PsycINFO and limit the search. We found 82 such articles when we searched "couple therapy" and limited the results to Document Type "Review" and the Publication Type "Peer Reviewed Journal."

5. The Method section should be written first because all the other sections depend on it and because doing so will crystallize your idea further.

Know for Sure

abstract,   345

citation,   343

database,   344

field,   345

hit,   347

Introduction
   section,   357

literature,   343

Method section,   356

operator,   347

prospectus,   342

record,   345

References
   section,   358

replication,   344

search engine,   354

search term,   347

thesaurus,   346

URL,   354

12

Conducting and Reporting Research

OVERVIEW

This chapter identifies similarities between conducting research and throwing a big party. Many of the logistical details of conducting and reporting research are covered. Several lists of helpful hints are included as well. The chapter also gives advice on how to present completed research in the form of APA-style research reports, make oral presentations to professional audiences, conduct poster and e-poster sessions, and give speeches to general audiences.

OBJECTIVES

After studying this chapter and working through the exercises, you should be able to:

1. Describe a pilot study and list the advantages of conducting one
2. Identify several logistical details related to conducting a research project
3. List some guidelines of data collection
4. Debrief participants
5. Discuss storing raw data, sharing it, and leaving a data trail
6. List steps to follow when interpreting data
7. Use a prospectus to guide the writing of an APA-style research report
8. List in order the sections of an APA-style research report
9. List some helpful hints for writing research reports
10. Make oral presentations about research to peers
11. Prepare and present posters about research to peers
12. Give speeches about research to general audiences

A BIG PARTY

The research process is a lot like having a big party. A successful party includes

- planning
- preparation
- the party itself
- publicity

The planning phase includes creating a guest list, choosing a menu and beverages, setting a date and time, and finding a place to hold the party. The preparation phase is logistical. **Logistics** is the planning and implementing of all the details up to the time the guests arrive. Logistics include such things as scheduling a date and time, sending invitations, buying and preparing food (or hiring a caterer), and preparing the party location. The party itself comes next. Guests arrive, food and drinks are served, people have a good time, and the party ends. After the party, someone cleans up. A few parties are reported on later (think of the society pages in newspapers). Who came, what they wore, what foods were served, and much more may appear in the newspaper.

Let's look more closely at how research is similar to a party. Research requires:

- planning
- preparation
- data collection
- publication

The planning phase for research includes getting an idea, reading the literature, considering ethical issues, choosing variables, refining the design, and selecting the appropriate statistical analyses. Like a party, the preparation phase involves logistics too. Research logistics require plans for such things as preparing measurements, setting the date and time for data collection, selecting participants, and preparing the research site. Data collection and the party are similar. During data collection, researchers and participants get together and interact. After data collection, researchers stay behind and handle details such as analyzing, interpreting, and publishing the data. Successful researchers are like successful party givers—both plan, prepare, meet people, and report on their success. If you can give a good party, then you possess many of the skills needed to conduct high-quality research.

logistics Planning and handling of all the details of a process or operation.

PRELIMINARY STEPS IN RESEARCH

We expect that you have already read chapter 11, Planning Research, where you studied the steps required to begin a research project. Those steps include getting an idea for research, reviewing the literature using PsycINFO and other sources, and creating a prospectus for the research project. In chapter 3 we discussed the institutional review board (IRB) and its role as you plan research. In this chapter we outline the remaining steps in a research project. We begin with advice on conducting the research, then describe how to write a research report, and finish with how to report research (or tell the story) in a variety of settings. If you are conducting your own research or planning to do so later, chapter 11 and this chapter will be especially useful.

Describe a prospectus and its sections and the role of the IRB.

As stated in chapter 11, The prospectus includes the following sections: title page, Introduction section, Method section, Expected Results section, and Reference section. A final report includes these additional sections: Abstract, Discussion, and Author notes. Of course, everything in the prospectus is subject to editing. Many psychological research proposals are first submitted to an IRB. The IRB reviews the proposal for ethical and related methodological issues. The IRB may recommend changes to the proposal, and if it does, the researcher must resubmit the proposal until the IRB gives its approval. Once the IRB has approved a project, researchers may collect data.

In this section, we cover some preliminary but necessary steps in the research process that follow IRB approval. Logistical issues related to data collection must be resolved before data collection begins. In addition, many research projects incorporate a pilot study before collecting data for the research project itself.

Prepare to Collect Data

Collecting data is one of the most important parts of any research project. The logistics of data collection include recruiting participants, scheduling data collection times, treating participants appropriately, and handling and storing the collected data. Most of the logistical issues should have been anticipated during the planning phase of research and addressed in the prospectus. However, no one can anticipate all possible logistical issues. One way to detect them is by conducting a pilot study.

Conduct a Pilot Study

A **pilot study** is a brief and limited version of the planned research. The goal of a pilot study is to refine the procedures of the research project. A pilot study is similar to a shakedown cruise of a new ship. In a shakedown cruise, the ship is put to sea for a short cruise to find out if all the systems work. No sailor would consider a long trip on a new ship without first checking whether the ship is seaworthy. Similarly, many research projects benefit from a pilot study to determine their seaworthiness. The primary goal of a pilot study is not to collect research data, but to check out research procedures so that adjustments can be made before the actual data are collected. A secondary goal is to determine if the planned statistical analyses work. Problems that show up in the pilot study are fixed by changing the data collection procedures or the statistical analyses.

Here are three examples of how pilot studies helped reveal unanticipated problems in a research proposal. A student researcher built a maze for rats that had vertical, sliding doors that prevented rats from retracing their steps. Before she collected data, however, she conducted a pilot study with two rats. She soon discovered a major problem: She had not accounted for the rats' tails! The problem was that the doors descended all the way to the floor and struck the rats' tails. Rather quickly, the two rats in the pilot study refused to enter new sections of the maze. She solved the problem by installing small wooden blocks at the bottom of the slides so that the doors no longer struck the rats' tails. A second pilot study with two more rats confirmed the success of her solution. The doors did not hit the rats' tails and they readily entered the next section of the maze.

Here is another example. A doctoral student (English, 2002) investigating the dream content of women in the first stages of menopause wanted to pilot test her data collection procedures. She recruited a small sample using the community snowball technique. In community snowball sampling, researchers find a few participants and then ask them to identify others who share the characteristic under study, in this case, being in the early stages of menopause. English administered her dream content questionnaire to the pilot sample. An additional variable, subjective sleep quality, was added. She conducted her dissertation research with the new variable using a larger sample.

Another researcher's pilot study revealed that going door-to-door to recruit participants in a college residence hall to individually administer a questionnaire took too much time. He changed his procedure to recruit participants at a weekly residence hall meeting, distributing the questionnaire in a group setting instead of individually.

pilot study   A preliminary, abbreviated experiment to evaluate aspects of a planned experiment.

What would have happened if these three researchers had not conducted these two pilot studies?

The student's maze learning study might have failed entirely. Rats fearful of entering the next section of the maze are very slow learners. The doctoral student benefited too. The adjustments she made led to a methodologically stronger procedure. The last researcher saved much time and effort by changing his original plans.

After conducting a pilot study, some final adjustments to the data collection procedure or to the apparatus are usually necessary. Just like planning for a party, the planning for data collection may go on until the very last minute. Once data collection begins, however, the same research methodology should be used for all participants. No further changes should be made.

COLLECTING DATA

Collecting data is exciting. Data collection marks the end of the planning and the beginning of the party! Just as a party has guests, data collection has research participants. As the researcher, you must act as the host for your participants as you interact with them. When you meet your participants, you must be ready for them, so here are some recommendations.

Schedule Participants

There are many ways to collect data from participants. If you are collecting observational data from animals or humans, you may not actually meet or interact with them. If you are conducting research with animals in a laboratory setting, you must follow established guidelines for handling them. If you are collecting data from human participants face-to-face, you must be practiced and ready. If you meet them one by one and collect data, you will have prepared a place to meet, set a time for them to arrive, and will have all your materials ready. If you meet them as a group in a place where they normally meet (such as at a classroom or in their residence hall), you will take whatever you need with you. There are so many ways to collect data from human participants face-to-face that the best we can do is provide you with some overall guidelines.

Follow Data Collection Guidelines

Collecting data is more than getting numbers or words from participants. The following sections discuss some of the commonsense guidelines that should be followed.

Be Ready to Collect Data   The first step in collecting data is to have an IRB-approved prospectus. Attending to logistical details follows. Do you need to schedule or reserve a room for data collection? Should you post a sign outside the door to prevent interruptions? Do you have all the materials you will need for data collection? For example, if you collect data on a bubble form that will be machine scanned, do you have extra #2 pencils? In short, before you can collect data, you must be ready for your participants (your party guests) before they arrive.

Be on Time　If you scheduled arrival times for participants, be there before the appointment time. Arriving tardy is a sign of disrespect; furthermore, participants will not take you or your study seriously. Help participants be there at the appointed time. Perhaps a reminder call or e-mail the night before will help.

Treat All Participants the Same　Unlike a party, you will not have guests of honor or celebrities who deserve special attention. All of your participants must be treated alike. Your research design should include procedures that help you treat all the participants the same. For instance, if all participants receive complex instructions before providing data, you should ensure that all participants get exactly the same instructions. A simple way to accomplish this is to read written instructions (instead of telling them items as you think of them). Another way is to videotape a presentation of the instructions and play the tape for each participant. Similarly, instructions may be presented on a computer screen. Of course, treating all participants the same means more than just providing instructions. All details of the research and all interactions with participants should be the same within each treatment condition. If your prospectus calls for you to treat participants differently because they are in different groups, do so. But be sure to treat everyone in the same group the same. Our best advice is to respect your participants and to convey this respect to them.

Keep Data Confidential　Maintaining the participants' privacy is a major ethical issue; privacy is one of the general principles of the *Ethics Code*. Psychologists do not violate privacy or confidentiality. At times, maintaining privacy requires a deliberate effort. For example, two friends might serve as participants in your research project. One might ask you about the data you collected from the other. As a researcher, you cannot reveal that information. To do so would be a breach of ethics on your part. The solution to this problem is to prepare ahead of time. Practice saying, "I'm sorry, but for ethical reasons I can't tell you that information." Of course, you cannot reveal data to anyone else either. That includes parents, relatives, school officials, and others. You may reveal individual data to other researchers, provided they have a research-based reason to know and they agree to maintain confidentiality. However, you may not reveal individual data to other researchers who want to know for nonresearch reasons. For example, if a fellow student finds a participant attractive and wants to know information about the participant that was obtained as part of your research, you must not reveal those data. You may, of course, reveal averaged data to anyone as long as individual participants' scores cannot be identified.

Three student researchers conducted a study on self-esteem. Later, one of the men took a human sexuality class and learned that there is a high inverse correlation between self-esteem and sexuality in college females (Walker-Hill, 2000). He retrieved the data that he and his fellow students had collected so he could identify female participants with low self-esteem to ask out for a date. Should he have looked at the data again for that purpose?

Using the data collected for such a personal purpose is a serious violation of confidentiality. Furthermore, such behavior could result in consequences such as suspension or expulsion from school.

PROJECT ETIQUETTE AND RESPONSIBILITIES

After the data are collected, there are a number of things yet to do. Some are required by the *Ethics Code,* and others ensure that future research by other psychologists will continue to be well received.

Communicate With Participants

Throughout the research process, communication with participants is important. In the early stages of research, communication is necessary to recruit participants and to get them to the research site. During the data collection phase, participants must know exactly what is being asked of them. After data collection, researchers still have communication responsibilities to their participants. Most research involving human participants requires that participants be debriefed or at least be given an opportunity to be debriefed.

Debrief Participants

The American Psychological Association's *Ethical Principles of Psychologists and Code of Conduct* (APA, 2002) requires researchers to **debrief** (give information to) participants about their own performance if they wish to know. *Debriefing* is a term borrowed from the intelligence community. It refers to the practice of asking agents about their experiences in the field shortly after they return home. Similarly, researchers ask participants about their experiences in the research they just completed.

Debriefing is a reciprocal process. The researchers obtained data because participants volunteered to participate. The participants are entitled to know their own performance. How debriefing is accomplished is

debriefing Explaining to participants the nature, results, and conclusions of the research they participated in and correcting any misconceptions.

up to the researchers. In every case, however, researchers should reveal any deceptions in the research. They should ask if the participants have any questions about the research and answer them. If the data are not yet known or analyzed, researchers should tell participants how they may obtain that information later, which might be by postal mail, e-mail, or posted on a Web page. Researchers' responsibilities to their participants do not end when data collection ends.

Clean Up and Write Thank–You Notes

If your research involved setting up an area for data collection or setting up equipment not normally in that area, you will have to return that area to its original condition and return equipment. Or, if your research involved help from others or permission to use space or equipment, you should thank those who made your research possible. As an example, some of our students conducted a perception experiment in the library. They secured permission from the librarian to use the staff lounge for one week. They moved in the necessary equipment and rearranged the furniture. During that week, several hundred students came to the lounge to participate in the research. The librarians did not have to relinquish their space, but they did so to support the research. After the data were collected, the student researchers moved out their equipment, put back the furniture, and cleaned the lounge. Later, they sent a thank-you note to the librarian.

Handle and Store Data

All materials used in data collection and the data themselves should be kept and stored. Hard copy and software files used to analyze the data should also be kept. Ideally, these materials should be available to you and others for years. As a practical matter, research materials should be kept at least for 5 years. Materials that lead to published research should be kept for 10 years. In most cases, the person responsible for these research materials should be the first author or the principal investigator. Often, in the case of student research, the instructor supervising the research keeps the materials. The rules of confidentiality still apply, so data storage must be secure. Only the original researchers should have access to these records.

Another issue with published research is the mailing of reprints or the e-mailing of electronic copies of manuscripts. **Reprints** are copies of articles printed by the publishers of the journal in which the article appears, whereas **manuscripts** are typewritten reports or electronic files of a research project. Readers of published research often want their own copy of the article. Published articles usually include a footnote stating to whom reprint requests should be directed. Readers request reprints of the article by mail or by e-mail from the author designated. Because of the Internet, many readers now ask for an electronic version of the article. The designated author handles these requests too.

reprints Facsimile reproductions of published articles provided by the publisher.

manuscript A typewritten report or an electronic file of a research project.

Share Research Data for Verification

Some readers of your research may request your data so they can reanalyze it. The *Ethics Code* covers such requests. Standard 8.14 (APA, 2002) states (in part):

> [P]sychologists do not withhold the data on which their conclusions are based from other competent professionals who seek to verify the substantive claims through reanalysis and who intend to use such data only for that purpose.

Standard 8.14 also covers details such as who pays for reproduction and mailing (the person requesting does). Sieber (1991) discusses issues in data sharing in the social sciences, including responding to requests for research data.

Other researchers ask to reanalyze data for a number of reasons. One reason is that they believe the original analysis was mathematically incorrect. Published research in psychology does not include the **raw data**—data that have not been calculated or analyzed. Thus, researchers who believe an analysis is mathematically incorrect cannot perform a reanalysis without the raw data. Another reason for a request for raw data occurs when other researchers wish to reanalyze data using a different statistical test.

In chapter 1, we described science as a self-correcting system of knowledge managed by peers and checked by peer review. Requesting raw data is a mechanism for self-correction. It helps ensure that those who conduct research do so with care, and it provides a way to identify and correct erroneous conclusions (and those who make them). Unfortunately, actual efforts to obtain data for re-analysis have been disappointing. For example, Wicherts, Borsboom, Kats, and Molenaar (2006) were able to obtain only 25.7% of the 249 data sets they requested. Nevertheless, members of the research community expect you to keep the data you collect. You don't want to respond to requests by saying, "I lost my data," or, "I didn't know I was supposed to keep the data." Wicherts, et al. recommended that journals require electronic copies of the raw data and that these be available on a Web page. Keeping the records of research is important.

Part of your research planning must include provisions for storing the data you collect. It should be stored in a safe place, and it should be easily accessible in case of reanalysis requests. If you ever receive a request from a peer for your raw data, you should:

- Contact your instructor immediately.
- Respond in writing, by letter or by e-mail.
- Communicate precisely with the requestor about the nature of the request.

raw data Research project data before calculation or analysis.

- Decide in advance what both parties will do in the event that a discrepancy is discovered. You should be able to review the reanalysis, for instance.
- Correct any mistakes discovered, preferably by issuing an **erratum** (a correction).

ANALYZING DATA

As we have emphasized throughout this text, you should select statistical tests you will use *before* the data are collected or as part of the prospectus. Not doing so can lead to serious trouble. For example, if an analysis of variance (ANOVA) was selected for the statistical analysis but the data collected were yes–no responses, the data and the analysis are mismatched. ANOVAs require scaled data. Yes–no data are frequency counts of categorical data and should be analyzed with a chi-square test or other nonparametric statistic.

Using the data actually collected is the key to a proper analysis. What we mean is that you must be careful in transferring data from the collection format to the analysis method. Most data analysis is conducted with computer-based statistical software. Be sure you transfer the data accurately from data collection forms to the software input. You may have collected the data perfectly, but if you make mistakes inputting the data to the statistical software, your research will become invalid.

In the Know

GIGO stands for "garbage in, garbage out." GIGO refers to the fact that computers act on the data you input without checking it for you. Your output will be garbage if you do not accurately enter the data you collected. Careful data entry is necessary for an accurate analysis.

Prepare Data

Before raw data are entered into a statistics program, they should be organized. The details of this organization will vary depending on the type of research conducted, but the general suggestions we give below usually apply. These suggestions also make data entry, which is a tedious process at best, a little easier.

Raw data collected during research take many forms. For example, returned questionnaires constitute raw data. In a naturalistic observation study, the raw data may be tally marks that indicate the different behaviors observed. A data file in a computer program could be the raw data. Regardless of the form of the raw data, the first task in data analysis is to convert it into a form amenable to statistical analysis.

erratum An error; *Errata* is the plural form.

Leave a trail that shows how the raw data were converted into a computer data file. For questionnaire studies, write an identification number on each questionnaire as you enter its data into the statistics software. As part of that participant's record, reenter the identification number as another variable. Having an identification number for each participant in the statistical software file ensures that you can trace back from the software to the raw data so that the data entry process can be verified.

Conduct a preliminary check of the data before conducting any analyses. An easy method is to compute descriptive statistics for all variables using your statistics software. Look at the ranges. Do any of the variables show an impossible range? For example, if a variable has Likert scale values of 1 to 5 and the range for that variable is 1 to 50, you know you have at least one error. Find the error and correct it. Recompute the descriptive statistics until all easy-to-detect errors are corrected. Next, examine a printout of the data. Compare the printout to your raw data. It is easier to catch and correct errors on paper than it is on the computer screen. Once you are satisfied that the raw data are entered correctly, analysis can continue.

Graph Data

Examine your scores by graphing them. How do your data look? Are there obvious variations between groups? Do the graphed means correspond to the calculated means? A good graph presents your data visually and succinctly; it allows you to see the data all at once.

Most graphs are created with statistical software packages that include 3-D tools and shading. Be careful. Those tools can lead to graphical overkill and actually make your graph less understandable. Avoid the temptation to add computer-graphic elements such as shading and color. Tufte (2001) calls such additions that hinder interpretation "chartjunk." He advises that you keep your graphs simple and elegant. Here are some rules to follow for making graphs that are based on the recommendations of Pittenger (1995) and Cleveland and McGill (1985):

- It is tempting to crowd as much data as possible on one graph. Better to make more graphs, each with its own story to tell. A simple graph depicting one dependent variable is clearer than a graph that shows multiple dependent variables.

- Line graphs are the easiest to read and to interpret. However, line graphs are not appropriate for categorical, qualitative, or dichotomous data. Use bar graphs instead.

- Use pie charts sparingly because they require that users interpret both angles and areas displayed, a more difficult task than interpreting the two-dimensional position of a point in a scatterplot (Pittenger, 1995). However, flat pie charts are useful for conveying information about proportions and can be very clear.

After preparing your graphs, show them to friends and colleagues. What kind of response do you get? The first time they ooh or ahh at your graphed data is a Kodak moment! They understood what your graph means.

Interpret Data

As we have stressed throughout, data do not speak for themselves, it is the researcher who speaks for the data. Data interpretation is a complex process, not just a single step near the end of data analysis. The task is to tell a story that the data support. Recall how you became interested in the research topic in the first place. Reread the literature about your topic. Look at your graphs and your results. What kind of story do they support? Can you tell the story aloud or in writing? Let's look at some specific steps in data interpretation.

Compare Results to Hypotheses   In NHST research hypotheses are generated. How did those hypotheses fare? Were you able to reject any null hypotheses? If yes, what are the alternative hypotheses? If none were rejected, what does that mean? These are the types of questions you should ask as you begin to interpret your data.

Separate Statistically Significant Results From Nonsignificant Results For research using NHST tests, separate statistically significant results from nonsignificant results. For the significant results, the null hypothesis is rejected. The story the data support must be made with the significant results. Can the story you want to tell emerge from those results?

Order Correlations   In correlational research, order the correlations numerically from high to low (meaning from +1.00 to −1.00). Keep in mind that the sign of the correlation indicates the direction of the relationship only. Now look at the absolute value of the correlations (the numerical part only). Use Hemphill's (2003) suggested empirical cut-off values for interpreting the strength of correlations (see p. 179). Be sure to interpret the sign of the correlation correctly!

Tell a Story   Regardless of the topic, area, or design, data interpretation is the climax of research. All of the effort expended during the research is directed toward the goal of interpreting the data obtained. In the next two sections, we give you more help with interpretation as we discuss writing the report of your research.

PREPARING TO WRITE

Writing the report is the step in the research process that follows data analysis and interpretation. Don't begin to write before you complete the earlier, necessary steps. Writing is easier when you are prepared.

Use Your Prospectus as a Guide

The prospectus you wrote serves as a guide in writing your final report. As described in chapter 11, the prospectus is a plan written mostly in the future tense. Your final report is an account of how you executed your plan and what results you obtained. The Introduction, Method, and Results sections of the final report should be written in the past tense.

Are there any differences between what you planned to do and what you did? Your report tells what actually happened, and not what you planned. For instance, your prospectus may have stated you planned to recruit 100 participants, but you actually recruited only 74. Or, your prospectus might have stated you were going to observe a naturalistic situation during morning hours only. However, as a result of a pilot study, you made observations in the afternoon as well. Look at your prospectus and compare what it said to what actually happened during the research. Report what actually happened.

Organize Results and References

After you have spent time understanding the results of your research, you are ready to write the Results section. A good strategy is to talk to colleagues and teachers about your results. Explain to them what the results and graphs show. Their responses give clues as to the clarity of your explanation. Talk about your results to friends and family. Can you explain to them what you did and why? When you can explain your research to others, you are better prepared to write.

We suggested that you make a notebook in which your PsycINFO abstracts and articles were organized alphabetically by first author. We believe that is a good way to organize your references, but other ways may work better for you. The key is to organize the references so you can find them quickly and easily. There are two main ways to organize references: paper methods and computer methods.

Paper methods organize references through physical manipulation of pieces of paper. The notebook we suggested is an example of a paper method. The notebook serves as a place for all the references you found concerning your project. Another paper method is to use index cards and a box. With this method, you transfer information about each reference to an index card and then file it in the box. Each method has its advantages and disadvantages. We like the notebook method because it minimizes the amount of writing necessary. If you use cards, you must hand write the information on each card, which takes a lot of time.

Today, many researchers use computers to store and organize their references. Computers allow you to browse and search through your references easily. They also allow you to sort (reorganize) them. Products such as Manuscript Manager and Endnote are specifically designed to handle manuscript references. They convert references to APA style directly. Databases such as FileMaker Pro or Access, spreadsheets such as Excel, and word processors such as Word or WordPerfect can be adapted to manage the referencing process. For these more general computer applications, users must create or purchase templates that convert references to APA style. Of course, users with advanced computer skills can create custom templates themselves. Regardless of whether you choose to organize with paper or computer, referencing will be easier if you make it an ongoing task rather than a step at the end. If you keep track of your references from the very beginning of the research project, the task will not be so difficult at the end.

THE *APA PUBLICATION MANUAL*

The *Publication Manual of the American Psychological Association, 5th edition* (APA, 2001) (*APA Publication Manual* henceforth) tells writers nearly all they need to know about the mechanics of writing research reports. The style of writing the *APA Publication Manual* promotes is extremely popular and has spread far beyond its original audience of psychologists to many disciplines; it has become one of the most commonly used scientific style manuals in the world. An abbreviated, pocket-sized publication, *Concise Rules of APA Style* (APA, 2005), gives tips on writing and the most widely encountered style rules.

APA style is a form of scientific writing and, as such, is different from other types of writing. Ideally, scientific writing is clear, concise, and efficient. A playwright, for instance, might mention the shotgun over the mantle three times in the first act. A scientific writer would mention it only once. Scientific readers are a homogeneously educated and motivated group. Playwrights, on the other hand, write for a much more diverse audience, so they use repetition to make all of their audience understand that the shotgun over the mantle will have an important role later in the play.

In the Know

The *APA Publication Manual* evolved from a few pages in the 1929 *Psychological Bulletin* to a 439-page guidebook in 2001 that covers practically every aspect of psychological writing. The *APA Publication Manual* is not the only style manual. Many biology journals use the AIBS (American Institute of Biological Sciences) manual, English departments use MLA (Modern Language Association) style, and other manuals also exist. However, APA style has become very popular and is used by journals as diverse as *The Journal of Men's Studies, The International Journal of Agriculture and Rural Development,* and *The Journal of Excellence in Higher Education.* A Google search for "instructions to authors" and "APA" produced over 17,000 hits, which is further electronic testament to the popularity of APA style.

The audience is not the only difference between scientific writing and other writing. The economics of publishing scientific articles also plays a big role. More than one million scientific manuscripts are published each year, and nearly all are read first by unpaid volunteers (mostly professors) who pass judgment on the quality of the research and its report. In fact, one of the primary reasons for APA style and other similar scientific writing styles is to make the lives of those volunteer readers easier. Without all of that "free" labor, it would cost much, much more to publish scientific articles. Standard styles (such as APA's) make it easier to read articles because readers do not have to decipher a different style for each article. Readers and editors already know what the structure of the article will be and that makes reading easier.

Another economic factor is the cost of publishing. Scientific publishing is a labor-intensive business. Reviewers and editors work for free or for token payments. Producing the scientific literature is a costly enterprise that would be much more costly without the donated time and labor of individual scientists.

In the Know

A debate about the future of scientific publishing is now raging. The debate centers on using the Internet as the primary medium for publishing scientific articles. In psychology, Stevan Harnad edits *Psycoloquy,* which is an example of the electronic publishing of scientific articles. In existence since 1990, *Psycoloquy* offers free, online access to its articles. Long established, for-profit publishers are on the other side of this debate as they seek to protect the high prices they have set for their journals. At stake here is the future of scientific publication.

WRITING

When it comes to writing a report of the research, our party metaphor breaks down. Very few party hosts report what happened at their parties in printed publications. But nearly all psychologists report what happened in their research and, of course, students report to their instructors. In this section we cover some concepts that will help you become a better writer of research reports. Practice helps! The more you write, the easier writing becomes.

Know Your Audience

Research reports are written for an audience of peers. Your peers, in this context, are others who share your interest in psychological research and who share your experience. However, you will sometimes write for other audiences, including the general public. At the end of this chapter we tell how to write and speak to the general public about your results.

Break the Job Into Smaller Tasks

Big jobs of any kind often appear difficult just because of their size. To students, writing a research report usually appears to be a big job too. Fortunately, the individual sections of research reports serve as convenient, smaller working units. Each section can be written individually and then combined at the end to create a finished report. Let's look at the sections of a research report more closely and see how this idea of breaking down the job of writing into smaller tasks works in practice.

Sections in Your Research Report

A typical research report has the following major components:

- Title page
- Abstract
- Introduction section
- Method section
- Results section
- Discussion section
- References list

The title page shows the title, author(s), and affiliation(s). The title page is the only page that identifies authors, which allows journals to use blind reviews (authors are not identified). The abstract is a summary (120 words maximum) of your entire research report. The abstract is the most important part of the report because it appears in databases such as PsycINFO. Many more people read abstracts than ever read the corresponding published articles. The Introduction section tells why you picked the research problem, gives your hypotheses, and reviews research that is similar to yours. The Method section is usually composed of three subsections: Participants (or Subjects when using animals), Apparatus or Materials, and Procedure. The Results section presents the analysis of the data. The Discussion section focuses on interpretation and whether the results support the hypotheses. The Discussion section also gives an opportunity to speculate as to why the data turned out as they did and to make predictions about future data collection. The Reference section lists all the literature you cited in the research report. We return to *each of these sections* in more detail later. For another description of what should go into the Method, Results, and Discussion sections, see Wilkinson and the Task Force on Statistical Inference (1999). Research reports also may include an author note and one or more appendices. The author note is where you mention

title page   First page of a manuscript; includes title, author(s), affiliation(s), and running head.

financial support, help from others, and possible conflicts of interest. An appendix (or several appendices) includes supplementary material such as stimulus materials or an author-constructed questionnaire.

Method Section   We emphasized the importance of the Method section to the rest of the research report when we discussed the prospectus. The Method section is written first because all of the other sections depend on it. Writing a research report is easier when you start with the Method section.

Reread the Method section in your prospectus. Note the changes that occurred during data collection. Look at the subsections. In the Participants subsection, who actually participated? Make any changes necessary to the number of participants and their demographic characteristics. In the Apparatus or Materials subsection, did you change any of your plans? If so, revise that subsection. In the Procedure subsection, does your procedure describe the actual conduct of the research? Incorporate the changes into a new Method section and you have completed the first step in writing your research report.

Results Section   You should have already made graphs, looked carefully at your significant and nonsignificant results, compared those results to your hypotheses, and put any correlations in numerical order. Writing the **Results section** is fairly straightforward if you have taken these steps. Write about the results objectively and clearly. The Results section is not the place to dismiss or argue about the meaning of your results. Instead, it is the place to present the results plainly so that others can understand them. You will use the results later to support your conclusion. To do so, you must show the reader what your results were and provide the reader with information about the magnitude of your results. As mentioned previously, one way to show the magnitude of your results is to use an effect size index. The *APA Publication Manual* states, "For the reader to fully understand the importance of your findings, it is *almost always* (emphasis added) necessary to include some index of effect size or strength of relationship in your Results section" (p. 25).

Tables and Figures   Tables and figures may be placed anywhere in a research report, but they are often most appropriate in the Results section. A **table** shows numerical results displayed in tabular form, whereas a **figure** is a graphical depiction such as a chart, photograph, drawing, and so on. The *APA Publication Manual* recommends that tables be used for "crucial data that are directly related to the content of your article and to trim text that would otherwise be dense with numbers" (p. 147).

According to the *APA Publication Manual,* a figure is any "chart, graph, photograph, drawing, or other depiction" (p. 176). Figures should be used to display global patterns of results, statistical interactions, nonlinear

Results section   Research report section that summarizes and analyzes data and statistics.

table   Numerical results displayed in tabular form.

figure   A graphical depiction such as a chart, photograph, drawing, or similar materials.

relationships, and conceptual details that are difficult to capture using words. Computer software may be used to prepare figures for publication or they can be prepared by hand. Regardless of how figures are prepared they should be **camera ready.**

In the Know

CRC (camera-ready copy) is material ready to be photographed and prepared for printing. CRC needs no additional work prior to printing. See http://cpc.cadmus.com/white_papers/detail.asp?wpID=B68B316A-3B66-4B91-8494-492AA4486CFF for information about the details of preparing camera-ready copy.

Introduction   When you wrote your prospectus, you composed a substantial introduction to your research problem and its related literature. Look at your Introduction section again. Does it still read well? Now that you have actually collected and analyzed data, do you need to make changes to the Introduction section? Have you read additional literature about your problem since you wrote the prospectus? Rewrite the introduction and incorporate the changes that occurred since you wrote your prospectus.

Discussion Section   For many students (and for many working researchers too!) writing the **Discussion section** is the most difficult part of preparing a research report. Unlike other sections, the Discussion section leaves you "free to examine, interpret, and qualify the results, as well as to draw inferences from them" (*APA Publication Manual,* p. 26). Being free really means that you are on your own. In the other sections, you are always constrained by some kind of template. Much of the Introduction section, for example, is based on the previous literature. Similarly, the Results section came directly from data collection. In the Discussion section, you may have to leave familiar surroundings (such as your procedure and results) and generalize your research to a broader context.

Fortunately, the *APA Publication Manual* has some specific advice for writing the Discussion section. First, tell what happened during your research. Did the results support your hypotheses? Tell how your results compared to those of others you cited in the Introduction. What, if anything, went wrong during your research? You may briefly comment on how or why things went wrong and what you could do to fix such problems in the future. You may speculate about data or theory, provided you do so briefly and indicate clearly that you are speculating. Are there any practical applications of the research? If so, what are they?

camera ready   Materials that do not require further editing or typesetting before publication.

Discussion section   Research report section that evaluates and interprets results.

Abstract   Write the abstract last. As stated in chapter 11, the abstract is a short summary (120 words or less) of your research report. The *APA Publication Manual* (pp. 12–14) notes that a well-written abstract is accurate, self-contained, concise and specific, nonevaluative, coherent, and readable. Do not include anything in the abstract that is not in the rest of the report. Summarize your rationale for the research, how you did it, what you found, and what the results mean. The abstract should be completely self-contained, which means that you should not abbreviate (except for common measurements), you should use complete names for key concepts in the research, and you should include key terms from the research. Those key terms aid readers who use electronic search tools. To save space in the abstract, you may use abbreviations and digits to express numbers. Use the active voice while omitting the words "I" and "we." The goal of the abstract is to summarize your research report, not to evaluate it. Conclusions should be described in the present tense, as should current results. Independent and dependent variables as well as historical results should be described in the past tense.

Reference List   The APA Publication Manual shows 95 different reference types that include all kinds of paper publications as well as electronic sources. In addition, the APA Web home page includes a link to a page showing APA style for electronic references: http://www.apastyle.org/elecref.html. The basic structure for APA-style references (*APA Publication Manual*, p. 223) for periodicals, nonperiodicals, and electronic sources, respectively, is reproduced in **Table 12.1.** All other types of references are variations on these four basic styles.

Citations (In-Text)   All the research listed in the references must also be cited in the text of your research report. Within the text of research reports, APA style uses the author-date method of citation. Unlike traditional footnotes, citations in the text allow readers to continue to read without shifting their attention to the bottom of the page. Readers can choose to flip to the references list if they want to see all bibliographic information, or they can just read on. Here are the examples from the APA Publication Manual (pp. 207–208) of how to write one-author citations within the text:

Walker (2000) compared reaction times

In a recent study of reaction times (Walker, 2000)

In 2000 Walker compared reaction times

In a recent study of reaction times, Walker (2000) described the method. . . . Walker also found

TABLE 12.1	Basic APA Reference Style

For periodicals, the basic structure is:

> Author, A. A., Author, B. B., & Author, C. C. (1994). Title of article.
> *Title of Periodical, xx,* xxx–xxx.

(Note that the title of the periodical and its volume number are italicized, but the page numbers are not.)

For nonperiodicals (books, reports, manuals, and audiovisuals), the basic structure is:

> Author, A. A. (1994). *Title of work.* Location: Publisher.

(Note that the title of the work is italicized. The location is the city where the work was published and the publisher is the company that published it.)

For electronic periodicals published online, the basic structure is:

> Author, A. A., Author, B. B., & Author, C. C. (2000). Title of article.
> *Title of Periodical, xx,* xxx–xxx. Retrieved month, day, year, from source.

(The source is the URL.)

For online documents (Web pages), the basic structure is:

> Author, A. A. (2000). *Title of work.* Retrieved month, day, year, from source.

(The source is the URL.)

Note: xx = volume number
  xxx–xxx = beginning and ending page numbers

All other APA-style references derive from these basic structures.

Source: Reprinted with permission of the American Psychological Association, © APA.

Notice that all the citations give the same basic information. Someone named Walker published an article in the year 2000. However, all citations convey the information slightly differently. When writing a research report, you may use any of these forms. The choice is up to you and depends on the clarity of exposition more than anything else. Look at the last example, where discussion of Walker's research is ongoing. The writer did not add the date of publication again because it was easily understood in the context of the previous sentences. Your job is to provide the reader with full bibliographic information in the Reference section while making the research report readable. Do not include any work in the Reference section that is not cited in the text and do not cite any work in the text of the research report that does not appear in References. More concisely, cite every reference and reference every citation. Ensuring this is often the final check of your research report.

Apply These Hints on Writing

Here are some suggestions on the mechanics of writing. These hints apply to writing the prospectus and to the final report.

Time Management   Good writing takes a lot of time. Successful writers schedule daily periods for writing and then stick to that schedule (Cameron, 1999). Of course, you are not a full-time writer (at least, not yet!), but it is still a good idea to manage your writing time. Here are some guidelines.

- Know the deadline.
- Block out time for writing.
- Write often in short chunks of time.

The chunk of time optimal for writing varies from person to person, but a rule of thumb is about 2 hours minimum. Two hours is enough time to get into the writing process. Determine how much time you have to finish the report and allot your time accordingly. It is a good idea to write sooner rather than later, just in case unexpected events occur.

Where to Write   If possible, set up one place for writing and write there only. That way, you can keep all your materials close to your word processor. If you cannot set up a place to write, a reasonable alternative is to organize your materials and put them in a bag or container you can carry around as a kind of portable office. With your portable office you can write anywhere you can find a computer.

Saving What You Write   Another vital detail is to preserve what you write. Back up the files you create. Even if you do not use a computer to write early drafts, you still should keep your handwritten material. Save your electronic work in several places. Save it to your hard drive, save it to floppy disks, rewritable CDs, or flash drives, or e-mail it to yourself. The trick is to make backing up your files part of your writing routine. Imagine how you would feel if you lost your nearly completed manuscript because of a computer problem.

Drafts and Revisions   The *APA Publication Manual*'s outline provides you with the structure for your research report. Suppose you already revised your prospectus based on the outcome of your study. Now what? Let some time pass before you revise what you wrote. Reread the draft aloud. Look and listen for particular problems. The first problem is errors. Thanks to your word processor, you should have already eliminated spelling errors. However, the spell checker does not catch errors such as "an" rather than "and." Correct awkward or unclear phrasings. Look for omissions; add detail or other facts where necessary. Your overall logical structure, too, may need revision: You might need to reorder paragraphs, for instance. Finally, save your changes to a new file with a different (and descriptive) name. That way, you preserve your first draft in case you want to use material from it later.

Check and Edit   Print a draft and get someone else to proofread it. Almost inevitably, he or she will discover errors or make useful suggestions. Make changes and you may have your next draft. Look over this draft carefully and decide if it is ready to give to your "editor." In most cases, your editor will be your instructor.

Most students are shocked when they receive a marked-up research report back from their instructor. Each page may be covered with comments, slashes, and other proofreading marks! What happened to your beautiful report? Veteran writers, however, expect to see their manuscripts come back covered with suggestions. After you get over your initial shock, read the comments and suggestions carefully. Put them next to you, open up yet another draft file (with a new name!) on your word processor and begin to incorporate the editor's suggestions. Depending on your individual situation, you may send this draft back to the editor for another revision. Or, this draft may become the version of your research report that you turn in for a grade.

> ### In the Know
> When we asked our students to record the number of times they revised their research reports, 7 revisions was the mode.

Publishing   Some students wish to submit their research reports to journals, especially undergraduate journals. These journals publish research reports and other articles written by undergraduates. A few undergraduates wish to publish their research reports in regular psychology journals. Consult with your instructor before you send a research report to any psychology journal.

The Review Process   When you send your research report to the journal editor, the editor reads it and decides if it merits review. If it does, the editor sends the research report to (usually) three reviewers.

> ### In the Know
> Reviewers, typically, are researchers who have previously published in that journal. The editor recruits them because of their past success getting published and willingness to review manuscripts. Reviewers do not get paid. Reviewers are another example of peer review and the community of scientists.

The reviewers return the manuscripts to the editor. As you might imagine, the manuscript pages may be covered with comments and suggestions. Many reviewers attach a page or two of additional comments about the manuscript. They also recommend whether or not the manuscript should be published. The usual recommendation categories are: accept as is, accept with minor modifications, accept with major modifications, or reject. The editor has the final say. If the decision is not rejection, you possess three edited manuscripts to help with the next revision. If this revision is accepted, your research report appears in print some months later, to become part of the body of psychological literature. You are a published researcher!

OTHER WAYS TO REPORT YOUR RESEARCH

Writing research reports is a nearly universal requirement for research in psychology. However, there are additional ways to present your results. Oral presentations and posters are methods used to present research results to peers, and speeches can be made to nonpsychologists. Such speeches must be different from those made at professional meetings because the audience does not have the same level of preparation as do your peers.

Oral Presentations to Peers

Giving oral presentations about your research has been the traditional method of presenting research results at professional meetings. One of your authors once attended an oral presentation by a well-known (and now deceased) researcher. In his deep voice, he announced that he was going to read his presentation word-for-word so that he would be sure to state the results accurately. He read the same written report that he later submitted to a journal. He promptly lost his audience. The lesson: What works in writing does not work in an oral presentation; oral presentations have different requirements. Although psychologists often say that they are going to "read a paper" at a professional meeting, almost none actually read their report to the audience. Unlike written research reports, oral presentations can be much more varied. *The APA Publication Manual* (pp. 329–330) recommends that you:

- Concentrate on one or two main points
- Omit most of the procedural details
- State your topic and why you chose it
- Describe how you conducted the research
- Convey your results
- Explain the implications of your research

In addition, it recommends an old adage: "Tell the audience what you are going to say, say it, and then tell them what you said" (p. 329). The audience at an oral presentation does not have the printed research report at hand. You should not expect them to remember details after saying something only once. The *APA Publication Manual* also advises presenters to rehearse their presentations in front of similar audiences before giving the presentation at a scientific meeting. To this we would add that presenters should be especially aware of the time limitations for their presentation.

Typically, oral presentations are assigned a specific period of time within a longer paper session in which several researchers report their results. During rehearsal, presenters should adjust their presentation to fit the allotted time with 2 to 3 minutes to spare. That way any questions from the audience can be answered without running over the time allowed.

Know where your paper session will meet. Have handouts and visual aids (overhead transparencies, slides, or computer-based graphics) prepared. Be at the room about 15 minutes before the paper session begins, and introduce yourself to the session's **moderator.** The moderator runs the session, introduces speakers, and keeps track of the time for each speaker. Near the end of your presentation, the moderator may signal how much time you have left. Do not ask for additional time and do not exceed your allotted time. When you finish your presentation, professional etiquette suggests that you remain to listen to your fellow presenters. (You may leave the session early if you have a compelling reason.) If you plan to leave early, you should inform the moderator of your plans at the beginning of the session.

A major element in your oral presentation will be presenting the results. Here you have several choices: You may use a computer, an overhead projector, a slide projector, or paper handouts. Consult the instructions for oral presentations provided by the group sponsoring the meeting. For example, the American Psychological Association (APA) provides an overhead projector, a screen, and an audio cassette player (for playback only) in all rooms where oral presentations are made. Regardless of the type of equipment used, presenters must present the data clearly so that the audience can comprehend it. Technical difficulties before or during the presentation distract the audience and give you less time to make your presentation.

In the Know

Presenting research at scientific meetings has long been a characteristic of science. Since the founding of the Royal Society in England in 1662, scientists have created thousands of similar organizations that sponsor meetings where their members present research to peers. The American Psychological Association and the Association for Psychological Science meet yearly. Many psychologists present their research at those meetings. Regional psychology groups (Eastern Psychological Association, Midwestern Psychological Association, New England Psychological Association, Southeastern Psychological Association, Southwestern Psychological Association, Rocky Mountain Psychological Association, and Western Psychological Association), state associations, independent groups, and student groups also meet regularly. Scientific meetings and the sharing of results further illustrate the community of science.

moderator Person who introduces speakers and keeps time at scientific meetings.

To present research at a professional meeting, you first submit a proposal. Each association has its own procedures for submission. Look at the group's Web page for instructions on submitting a proposal and the deadline. Your proposal will be reviewed and accepted or rejected. If it is accepted, the group will notify you and put your presentation on the meeting schedule. All that remains is for you to attend the meeting and make your presentation.

At the end of your presentation you may get questions from the audience. Always repeat the question because the rest of the audience may not have heard it and repeating helps you understand the question before you attempt to answer it. If you don't know the answer to a question, just say so.

Oral presentations at meetings remain a major component at scientific gatherings. In recent years, however, poster presentations have become the most common method of presenting research results. The dynamics of presenting a poster are quite different from those of reading a paper.

Posters

Poster sessions usually take place in large rooms equipped with easels and large blank poster boards. Presenters are assigned a poster board, which they use to post materials describing their research. After they post their materials, presenters stand next to their poster and wait for viewers (their audience) to file by. Interested viewers may pause, read the posted materials, and discuss them with the presenter. Poster presenters usually have copies of a complete report to give to those who are interested.

Preparing a poster is different from writing a research report or making an oral presentation. A poster must fit on the poster board assigned. Find out how large the poster boards will be. The information on the poster must be readable from a distance as the audience may be 10 or more feet away from the poster itself. The title of the poster, at least, must be readable from that distance. The APA recommends a 72-point font (1 inch or 2.54 cm) as a minimum for titles, and a 27-point bold font (3/8 inch or 0.95 cm) as a minimum for all characters.

In the Know

Type is measured in points. For most computer software today, 72 points make a character about 1 inch tall. Serif and sans serif ("sans" is French for "without") refer to the presence or absence, respectively, of strokes (serifs) at the edges of printed characters. **Times New Roman** is a common example of a serif font and **Helvetica** is a common example of a sans serif font. Many writers use sans serif fonts for titles and headings and serif fonts for text because serif fonts are more readable. *Use italics sparingly; they are harder to read.*

poster session
Presenting research to peers using a display board.

In oral presentations, time is limited, and in poster presentations space is limited. Information on the poster must be selected carefully. One typical way to organize a poster is to use selected sections from the journal outline: abstract, or Introduction, Method, Results, and Conclusion (or Discussion) sections. Posters should also include the presenter's name and affiliation. References are usually not posted because of space limitations. That information is better conveyed in a handout. **Figure 12.1** shows two four-column formats that Nicol and Pexman (2003) describe as standard layouts.

Figure 12.2 shows three additional sample poster arrangements endorsed by the APA (2004). Other poster arrangements are permissible, if they meet the readability criteria discussed previously.

Presenting the poster is the easiest part! Once the poster is assembled, you stand next to it and wait. The ideal of poster presentations is to draw interested passersby into an oral discussion with you. When that ideal is realized, you may find yourself in a series of animated conversations about your research. Or, you may have brief conversations with passersby who request a copy of the written report.

Electronic Posters (E-Posters)

A recent development in poster presentations is **electronic posters (e-posters).** Some associations now use e-posters, which may consist of a limited number of PowerPoint slides or other similar media. Like regular poster sessions, e-poster presenters stand next to their e-poster. Unlike hard-copy posters, e-posters resemble a short movie. Between viewings, presenters may answer questions or discuss issues concerning the research. A major advantage of e-posters is that, being electronic, they may be posted on the Web, thus increasing their potential audience and making the presentation's lifetime much longer. Presenters of e-posters may interact with their audience in person at the time of the meeting or afterward over the Internet.

Speeches to Nonpsychological Audiences

A nonpsychological group, such as a civic club or a high school class, may invite you to talk about your research. A speech to such groups is different from an oral presentation at a psychological meeting. The audience consists mostly of nonpsychologists, so you should attend to basic issues and avoid psychological jargon. To begin your preparation, consider why you were invited to speak. Research the group that invited you. Who are they? How long have their previous speakers spoken? Does the group expect you to use visual aids? Will they ask questions at the end? Speeches to nonpsychological groups are important to psychology as a whole. By making speeches you are following Miller's (1969) advice to "give psychology away."

If you have already read a paper or presented a poster about the topic of your speech, you are well on your way toward being ready. Simplify your

electronic poster (e-poster) Research report presented on a computer screen.

FIGURE 12.1
Standard layout for a poster.

Source: Reprinted with permission of the American Psychological Association, © APA.

When the authors have the same affiliation, the superscript letters following the names are unnecessary, and a single university is identified.

Thanks for Ruining My Day:
The Effect of Misfortune on Mood
Joanne L. Mytocki[a], Jake Lalonde[b], & Mary Smith[c]
[a]Redhills College, [b]Smithton University, [c]University of the Atlantic

Introduction

Method

Results

Conclusions

Research Questions

References

Acknowledgments

For optimum readability, it is best to present black text on a white background.

The empty space between sections could be a solid color other than white, but patterned backgrounds are distracting.

As an alternative, the title could be printed as a banner across several pieces of paper and reconstructed on the poster board.

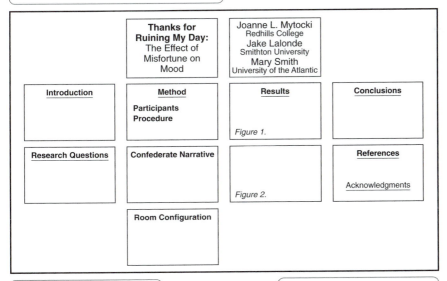

Thanks for Ruining My Day: The Effect of Misfortune on Mood

Joanne L. Mytocki
Redhills College
Jake Lalonde
Smithton University
Mary Smith
University of the Atlantic

Introduction

Method
Participants
Procedure

Results

Conclusions

Figure 1.

Research Questions

Confederate Narrative

References

Acknowledgments

Figure 2.

Room Configuration

Panels can be numbered in the order they should be read.

Each panel should be limited to 16 lines of text.

Panels are usually printed on white 8.5 × 11-in. paper, in landscape orientation, and often each panel is mounted on a piece of stiffer, colored paper.

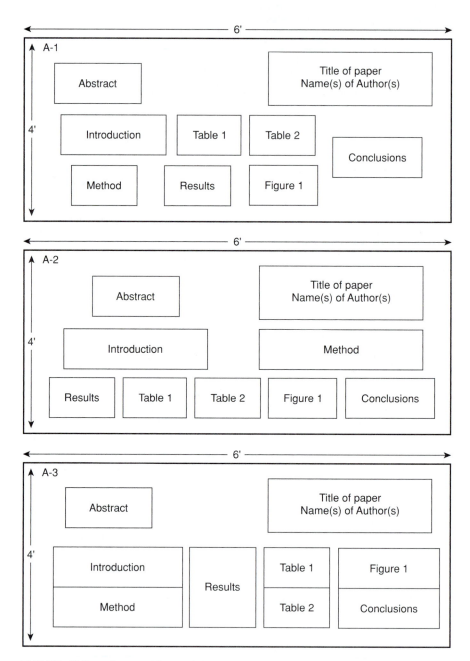

FIGURE 12.2   Three additional formats for a poster presentation.

Source: Reprinted with permission of the American Psychological Association, © APA.

organization. Instead of the APA organization use a simpler organization such as introduction, data, and summary. Simplify the content, but without violating the integrity of your research. Practice your speech to yourself and in front of a practice audience (one person is enough). You should be familiar enough with your speech to speak extemporaneously from an outline of key concepts.

Putting the audience at ease is always a good idea. If you know of a good joke about psychologists, tell it at the beginning of your speech. Another good way to start is to tell how you became interested in your research topic. Quickly move into the introduction. Don't give citations for research. Instead, cover the previous literature globally, but not in detail. Tell how your research fits into the topic and briefly describe your research. Don't dwell on the methodological details. Concentrate on the big picture and how your research fits into it. At the end, ask for questions and answer them. Don't forget to thank your hosts for the opportunity to speak to the group.

SUMMARY

This chapter deserves to be the last chapter because it takes everything you learned in all of the other chapters and puts it to use. Research should be like a party. Parties are fun, but they are also a lot of work for the host. After most parties are over the work stops, but with research, the work continues (the data collection). Researchers must report on their parties. Most often, the reports are to peers, are in writing, and follow APA style. Reports may also be made to peers at meetings in the form of oral presentations or posters, and these reports are sometimes published in journals. Finally, psychologists often report on their research to the general public. Those presentations must be simpler but still accurate. Our hope is that by the time you read these words you will have or will soon host your own party (conduct your own research) and then report on it to your fellow psychologists and to the world. Good luck and have a great time!

Chapter Review

1. Three logistical aspects of collecting data are _____, _____, and _____.
2. What is the primary goal of a pilot study?
3. When should participants be debriefed?
4. List in order the sections of a typical research report in APA style.
5. What section of the research report should you write first? Why?

6. In the _____ section you are "free to examine, interpret, and qualify the results."

7. The abstract should be no longer than _____ words.

8. When should you write the abstract?

9. What does "reading a paper" really mean?

10. Describe the process of presenting a poster of your research project at a scientific meeting.

Thinking Critically About Research

1. What are raw data? What steps should you take before you analyze raw data?

2. Edit the following abstract.

Research has shown that gender and religiosity can affect attitudes to homosexuality. This study set out to test these assumptions and to determine if an attribution of homosexuality to biological or social causes influences perceptions of homosexual people. The participants of the study were 105 students at Southern Arkansas University. The Francis Scale of Attitude towards Christianity (Francis, 1993), a homemade Nature/Nurture Questionnaire, and the Attitudes Toward Lesbians and Gay Men Scale (Herek, 1988) were used. A 2 × 2 × 2 factorial ANOVA showed that the highly religious participants and the supporters of nurture tended to endorse more negative attitudes towards homosexuals. Highly religious students also tended to attribute homosexuality to learned, rather than to biological causes. The study found no significant gender difference in attitudes toward homosexuality. (Courtesy of Elena Yakunina)

3. Describe your responsibilities during a poster presentation.

4. How should a speech to a nonpsychological audience be different from an oral presentation at a scientific meeting?

Answers to Chapter Review

1. Correct answers include: recruiting participants, scheduling data collection times, treating participants correctly, and handling the data properly afterward.

2. to check out research procedures before using them in actual research

3. as soon as possible after the completion of data collection

4. Title page; Abstract; Introduction, Method, Results, and Discussion sections; references list; and if appropriate, appendices and author notes.

5. You should write the Method section first because all the other sections depend on it.

6. Discussion

7. 120

8. last

9. making an oral report to peers in class or at a scientific meeting

10. Set up the poster at the designated time. Stand by your poster during the session and discuss your project or answer questions with people who stop by.

Answers to Thinking Critically About Research _____

1. Raw data may be a pile of questionnaires, the tally marks on a clipboard, or the transcripts of interviews. Raw data must be organized prior to analysis. Adding identification numbers, entering the raw data onto computer analysis software, and checking your organized data prior to analysis are all helpful steps.

2. Here is a revised abstract:

   To test if attributions of homosexuality are made to biological or social causes (nature/nurture) and whether religiosity influences those attributions, 105 male and female students completed the short version of Francis Scale of Attitude Towards Christianity (Francis, 1993), a researcher-constructed Nature/Nurture Questionnaire, and the Attitudes Toward Lesbians and Gay Men Scale (Herek, 1988). A 2 (gender) $\times$ 2 (religiosity) $\times$ 2 (nature/nurture) factorial ANOVA showed that highly religious participants and supporters of nurture endorsed significantly higher negative attitudes toward gay men and lesbians. Highly religious students also attributed homosexuality to learned, rather than to biological causes. The study found no significant gender differences in attitudes toward homosexuality.

3. At poster sessions, authors quickly set up their materials on boards previously assigned to them. Once set up, authors stand by their poster while viewers file by. Some viewers may ask questions or make comments. Other viewers may request a printed copy of the research report that the poster is derived from. After the alloted time passes, authors quickly remove their materials (especially if other sessions are to follow) and leave the area.

4. When giving a speech to a nonpsychological audience, you should avoid jargon, simplify the organization and content of your speech, be prepared to answer questions, and "give psychology away."

Know for Sure

Abstract,   379

appendix,   376

author notes,   376

camera ready,   378

debriefing,   367

Discussion
   section,   378

electronic poster
   (e-poster),   386

erratum,   370

figure,   377

Introduction
   section,   378

logistics,   362

Method section,   379

moderator,   384

pilot study,   364

poster session,   385

raw data,   369

Reference
   section,   379

reprints,   368

Results section,   377

table,   377

title page,   376

manuscript,   368

Appendix A

A Sample Student Manuscript in APA Style

Professors of research methods classes often require their students to conduct a research project, either individually or with a partner or two. In many ways, this text is a handbook of advice for conducting such a project. This appendix focuses on one aspect of the project—the completed manuscript. The heart of this appendix is a sample research manuscript that is annotated with notes about APA style and helpful sections of this textbook. For the course you are taking, your instructor may have somewhat different requirements, which, of course, take precedence over APA-style rules.

Although a single manuscript can illustrate many of the common rules and conventions of APA style, it cannot cover all of them. For questions that remain, consult more comprehensive sources such as the *Concise Rules of APA Style* (APA, 2005), Szuchman (2005), or a Web-based help program. The most detailed authority on form and style is the *Publication Manual of the American Psychological Association* (APA, 2001).

An APA-style research article is characterized by concise, terse prose fitted into a set outline. Particular information is put in particular sections that come in an established order. Like limericks, APA-style research papers have a rigid structure. Limericks have a specified number of lines of limited length and a particular rhyme and meter pattern. Part of the fun of a limerick is the satisfied feeling that occurs when the last line rhymes with the first two and completes a thought that was established earlier. Once you understand the form, reading an APA-style research paper can be quite satisfying too, because everything is in its place and your expectations are met.

One additional comparison may help illustrate APA style. The writing style for scientific research articles (including APA-style articles) is quite *unlike* the style in textbooks, particularly this textbook. In this textbook, our style is to repeat important points; journal writing, however, is not redundant. Our style is to address the reader as *you;* journal writing is in the third person (and sometimes in the first person as well). We use occasional humor, informal language, and contractions; journal writing does not.

One reason for the difference in writing style is the difference in readers. Readers of this textbook are beginning research methods students who are just learning about research. They benefit from a personal approach that includes encouragement and repetition. The readers of scientific research articles are already interested in the topic of the article and they have a good deal of background knowledge about research. The caution that you should take from this discussion is not to use textbook style writing for your research paper. Besides this appendix, we included lots of other advice on writing research reports in chapter 12.

From time to time, we ask our own research methods students to write a letter about their research project experience to the students who will be in the class the next term. The most common theme in the letters is the advice: *Start early.* When is a good time to begin your project? This very moment, now, is not too early. Start a file, either electronic or paper. Make some notes to go in your file. Whatever comes to your mind about the project is worth writing down for starters. If you aren't set on a topic, read the section "Getting an Idea" in chapter 11. If you are part of a group who is doing the project, contact one of your partners—now—or at least soon.

AN ANNOTATED MANUSCRIPT

The manuscript that follows is based on a paper that JoAnna Holt turned in for her research methods course at Hendrix College when she was a junior. The annotations are comments and explanations that we added in the margins of the manuscript to guide you when you prepare your own manuscript. Not all the rules for producing an APA-style manuscript are covered. In addition, there are places where our annotations convey a common practice, but the common practice is not required. For a complete set of rules and suggestions, see the *Publication Manual of the American Psychological Association* (APA, 2001).

The manuscript that follows, like most formal manuscripts, does not have an appendix. However, we encourage you to compile one and, if permitted by your instructor, turn it in with your manuscript. The material that goes into an appendix includes stimulus materials that were used in the study, statistical analysis output, and if feasible, copies of the raw data. By including an appendix, all the immediately relevant material is together in one place. Besides turning in an appendix, we encourage students to keep a file of all the articles they copied, whether or not they were used in the final manuscript.

BACKGROUND INFORMATION

Early in JoAnna's research methods class, the professor required the students to spend time browsing for psychological tests. The purpose of this browsing was to find a test that might serve as the dependent variable for an experiment. JoAnna selected the UCLA Loneliness Test. She had observed that some acquaintances turned to negative comments when they encountered a couple who appeared to be having a good time and JoAnna thought these negative comments might be an expression of loneliness. She also wondered how generalizable her observation was. Was it just her particular acquaintances or was it a more general phenomenon? In developing her idea for the prospectus, she decided that showing pictures to participants was much more practical than presenting actual people.

Finding usable pictures in magazines was not easy. JoAnna wanted pictures of approximately the same size that showed attractive people in a good mood. She also had trouble deciding between gathering data from participants one at a time or from groups that assembled because they had signed up for an experiment. She chose the one-at-a-time method because it gave her more direct control over the final number of participants.

As a way to ensure that participants attended to the pictures, JoAnna had them rate the attractiveness of the people in each picture on a 7-point scale. Using those data later as a way to assess the similarity of the two sets of pictures was an afterthought (and a good one at that). The project was conceived, materials assembled, and data gathered over a period of about 3 weeks. Over the next week, she analyzed the data and wrote the report.

Over the course of her work, JoAnna said that she read some 15–20 abstracts of journal articles. Of the articles, she read five or six articles carefully. She used four of these in her introduction and discussion. (The Russell, Peplau, and Cutrona [1980] reference just indicates where the UCLA Loneliness Scale can be found.)

When we asked JoAnna if she had any advice to research methods students about starting their own experiments, she said, "Pick something that you are interested in. It doesn't have to be complicated." She also affirmed our advice about starting early and said not to worry, "you get more ideas as you go along."

Loneliness Influenced 1

Running Head: LONELINESS INFLUENCED BY PHOTOGRAPHS

Right justify the header, which appears on every page. Use the first two or three words in the title.

Page number is on header line.

Left justify the running head, which is in CAPS. It is a phrase that identifies the title.

Double-space everything. Use margins of at least 1 inch.

Title is centered with important words capitalized. It often includes the variables that are being investigated.

Author(s) and institutional affiliation.

Loneliness Influenced by the Number of People in Photographs

and Relationship Status

JoAnna L. Holt

Hendrix College

Loneliness Influenced 2

Abstract

This study was conducted to determine if looking at photographs of people or the relationship status of the participants affects loneliness. The 60 college-student participants judged the attractiveness of photographs of either individuals or couples and then completed the UCLA Loneliness Scale. They also indicated whether or not they were in a romantic relationship. A *number in photograph × relationship status* factorial ANOVA revealed an interaction. For those in a relationship, pictures of couples increased loneliness and pictures of individuals reduced it. For those not in a relationship, the number in the photograph had little effect. Neither main effect was statistically significant. Loneliness scores can be affected by stimuli that immediately precede testing.

*The abstract begins on a separate page. Center the label, **Abstract**. Abstract should not exceed 120 words.*

Abstract is one paragraph, not indented.

Left justify the text, which leaves the right margin ragged.

The abstract summarizes the Introduction, Method, Results, and Discussion sections. It is nonevaluative and should be accurate, self-contained, concise, and specific.

Loneliness Influenced 3

Degree of Loneliness Influenced by the Number of People
in Photographs

Feelings of loneliness are experienced by everyone at some point in time, and for many, loneliness may not be a fleeting problem. *Loneliness* refers to a feeling of sadness that results from being or feeling alone or abandoned and is often predictive of a person's ability to form relationships with others. Previous research has examined the influence that culture, personality factors, age, and gender have on feelings of loneliness, but there are still many factors that may affect loneliness or certain aspects of loneliness that need to be explored. Lonely people are usually more prone to feelings of pessimism, depression, and anxiety (Stokes, 1985). The things and events that people see and experience on a daily basis may cause variations in feelings of loneliness.

Demographic variables such as age and gender are related to loneliness. Schmitt and Kurdek (1985) examined age and gender differences with the Differential Loneliness Scale. Men were more dissatisfied with family relationships, large group relationships, and friendships than women were. Also, college-age women and elderly women both had feelings of dissatisfaction with romantic/ sexual relationships that were significantly related to feelings of low family social support. The researchers took these results to mean that men may have more difficulty with social and emotional relationships than women and that women may be better able to guard against feelings of loneliness. They also concluded that the elderly are more dissatisfied with friendships and romantic relationships than are college-age people. The overall conclusion was that loneliness is a diverse and subjective experience that varies due to factors such as gender and age. Green, Richardson, Lago, and Schatten-Jones (2001) also investigated the loneliness of college students and elderly adults.

The Introduction section begins on a separate page with the title of the paper centered. The label, Introduction, *does not appear. The introduction presents background details on the research and leads up to the topic being investigated.*

The opening paragraph introduces the topic of the research.

The first line of every paragraph is indented.

Facts are documented by citing a study or studies that support them.

The first time a reference is cited, all the surnames are written. All citations are included in the reference list.

Loneliness Influenced 4

They did not find gender differences among college students on the UCLA Loneliness Scale.

　　There is also research on social variables that influence loneliness. Rook (1987) examined whether feelings of loneliness were more closely related to social support relationships—"problem-focused aid is exchanged" (p. 1134) or to companionship relationships—"shared leisure activities . . . are undertaken primarily for the intrinsic goal of enjoyment" (p. 1134). Two studies involved college-age students and one drew from the community. Rook found that when loneliness was measured with the UCLA Loneliness Scale, social support scores and companionship scores were negatively correlated with loneliness. Rook concluded that people with social support relationships were more lonely than people with companionship relationships.

If you use the exact words from another publication, put them in quotation marks and reference the page number.

A reference that is mentioned again in the same paragraph does not include the date.

　　The social variable that Stokes (1985) studied was the effect that social networks have on loneliness. Stokes found that the density of a person's social network was significantly related to loneliness. The more dense the social network, the less lonely the participants were. Social networks "in which the members are interconnected and are important in each other's lives" (p. 989) were considered dense. Stokes also concluded that it is not the amount of time a person spends with other people that impacts loneliness, but the number of different people in their social networks and how they interact with them. Two people may spend the same amount of time socializing, but if one person spends the majority of the time with one or two people, he or she will be lonelier than another person who spends the majority of time with different groups of people at different times.

Loneliness Influenced 5

When a citation is mentioned again, use only the first author followed by et al. *(which means "and others").*

Toward the end of the introduction, explain how your study is different from others, unless your goal is to replicate a study.

Toward the end of the introduction, identify the variables that you investigated. You may include your hypothesis about the outcome, citing research or reasoning that supports your hypothesis.

Although there is space here for "Method," break the page to avoid a heading with nothing following it.

Green et al. (2001) distinguished between social loneliness (due to lack of a social network with peers) and emotional loneliness (due to lack of a partner). In their college student sample, they found that having a partner was negatively correlated with UCLA Loneliness Scale scores.

In the studies cited above, the variables shown to affect loneliness were relatively stable characteristics such as age, gender, social network density, and having a partner. I think that loneliness also varies with changes in the immediate environment. One goal of this research is to show that loneliness scores are affected by attending to the number of people in a set of photographs.

In this paper I explore the effect of two variables on the UCLA Loneliness Scale scores of college students. One variable is the number of people shown in photographs that are presented to the participants. For this variable, some photographs show one person and others show a male–female couple. The other variable is relationship status which has two levels: in a relationship or not in a relationship.

Based on the research of Green et al. (2001), I hypothesize that students who are not in a relationship will have higher loneliness scores than those who are in a relationship. I also expect that participants who view photographs of couples will have higher loneliness scores than participants who view photographs of individual people because they will be reminded of their lack of a partner or the absence of their partner at the moment.

Loneliness Influenced 6

Method

Participants

The participants were 61 Hendrix College students (32 women and 29 men) who were approached at various locations on campus. The ages of participants ranged from 18 to 23 years, with a mean of 20.2 years. One participant's scores were excluded from the study because of unanswered questions. Thirty-one participants were in a romantic relationship and 29 were not in a romantic relationship.

Procedure

Participants were approached and asked to participate in a survey. Once consent was given, they received a survey from one of two envelopes, chosen haphazardly by the researcher. One envelope had loneliness surveys and copies of photographs of six individuals (three female, three male). The surveys in the other envelope had copies of photographs of six male–female couples. The photographs, cut from magazines, were of people in their 20s. Participants rated the attractiveness of each individual or each couple on a 7-point scale. After viewing the photographs, participants completed the Revised UCLA Loneliness Scale (Russell, Peplau, & Cutrona,1980). Finally, participants provided demographic information and answered whether or not they were in a romantic relationship. Thus, the two independent variables were the number of people in the photographs and the participant's relationship status. The dependent variable was scores on the UCLA Loneliness Scale.

Results

Scores on the Revised UCLA Loneliness Scale were analyzed with a 2 × 2 factorial ANOVA. The scores ranged from 20 to 80,

Method *is centered, singular. Follows the Introduction section without a page break. The Method section provides details of how the study was conducted so that another researcher could replicate the study.*

Second-level headings are flush left, italicized.

Additional second-level headings can be used for topics such as appara-tus *or* materials *if the topic requires a paragraph or more of explanation.*

Results is *centered, plural. Follows the Method section without a page break. The Results section presents analyses of the data and some interpretation.*

Loneliness Influenced 7

Tables and figures are
on separate pages at the
end of the manuscript.

Italicize statistical tests
(F). Include the result
of the test (4.11), df
(1, 56), and p *value*
(.048). Note that the
letters are italicized.

Explain the meaning of
the result using the
terms of the study.

Include effect size
indexes.

Discussion is centered,
singular. Follows the
Results section without
a page break. In the
Discussion section,
evaluate your study.
Explain how the results
supported or failed to
support your hypotheses.
Problems that might
reasonably be expected
to affect the results are
noted, as are any
implications for future
research.

with higher scores representing a higher degree of loneliness. The means, standard deviations, and cell counts are shown in Table 1. A bar graph of the cell means is shown in Figure 1.

The interaction was significant, $F(1, 56) = 4.11$, $p = .048$. The mean loneliness score was about the same regardless of the number in the photographs for those who were not in a relationship (36.82 and 36.44). However, for those participants in a relationship, viewing photographs of one person produced lower loneliness scores ($M = 31.63$) whereas viewing photographs of a couple produced higher loneliness scores ($M = 40.00$). Thus, the effect of the photographs depended on whether or not the participant was in a relationship.

The main effect for photographs did not reach the .05 level of significance, $F(1, 56) = 3.43$, $p = .069$; neither did the main effect of a relationship, $F(1, 56) = 0.14$, $p = .707$. For photographs, the effect size index was $d = 0.52$; for relationships, $d = 0.20$.

The attractiveness ratings of the photographs of the individuals were compared to the ratings of photographs of the couples, $t(58) = 0.20$, $p = .841$, $d = 0.05$. Thus, there was no evidence that the attractiveness of the photographs was different for the two groups.

Discussion

These results show that feelings of loneliness can be altered by a fairly brief experience with photographs. Thus, future research on loneliness should attend to and report the circumstances that immediately precede the administration of a loneliness scale.

The finding that participants who were in relationships were lonelier when they viewed photographs of couples compared to

Loneliness Influenced 8

individuals is surprising, but it is consistent with the research by Stokes (1985). Stokes showed that people with large, interconnected (dense) social networks are less lonely than people with small social networks who don't interact. It can be assumed that many people in romantic relationships spend the majority of their time with their significant other, which suggests that they do not have dense social networks. If this is the case, when participants saw the photographs of couples, they were reminded of the close relationship they have with their significant other, the time they spend together, and the lack of time that they spend with other friends or peers. Reminding the participants of their small social networks could arouse feelings of loneliness.

The other finding, that participants who were not in romantic relationships did not differ in their feelings of loneliness when viewing couples or individuals, was also surprising. This could be explained if both couples and individuals aroused feelings of loneliness in single participants. They could feel lonely when seeing the individuals because they are single and the individuals would remind them of that fact, or they could feel lonely when seeing the couples because they are not in a relationship and want to be.

The results of this study should not be generalized to other populations because of the evidence that loneliness varies across age and culture (Schmitt & Kurdek, 1985). This study might also not be generalized to a larger population because college-age participants usually have not experienced marriage or divorce. However, the finding that participants in romantic relationships were lonelier when seeing couples suggests that marriage would not necessarily cause a change in the outcome.

The Discussion section is the place to note limitations of your study.

There are two factors that could have affected the outcome of the experiment. One factor is that some participants had trouble understanding the wording of a few of the loneliness scale items and asked for clarification of what was being asked. The participants could have answered differently than they had intended to. Another factor is that having participants rate the attractiveness of the people in the photographs could have affected their answers on the loneliness scale. Asking about ideas of attractiveness could lead participants to compare their attractiveness to the photographs, therefore, making them feel either good or bad, and possibly affecting their answers on the loneliness scale.

To test the effect of asking for attractiveness ratings, it would be beneficial to present a slideshow of couples or individuals so that participants spend an adequate amount of time observing but are not being subjected to questions of attractiveness. Also, to help understand why pictures of couples produce higher loneliness scores, participants could provide their thoughts about the photographs or about couples in general.

Loneliness Influenced 10

References

Green, L. R., Richardson, D. S., Lago, T., & Schatten-Jones, E. C. (2001). Network correlates of social and emotional loneliness in young and older adults. *Personality and Social Psychology Bulletin, 27,* 281–288.

Rook, K. S. (1987). Social support versus companionship: Effects on life stress, loneliness, and evaluation by others. *Journal of Personality and Social Psychology, 52,* 1132–1147.

Russell, D., Peplau, L., & Cutrona, C. (1980). The revised UCLA Loneliness Scale: Concurrent and discriminant validity evidence. *Journal of Personality and Social Psychology, 39,* 472–482.

Schmitt, J. P., & Kurdek, L. A. (1985). Age and gender differences in and personality correlates of loneliness in different relationships. *Journal of Personality Assessment, 49,* 485–496.

Stokes, J. P. (1985). The relation of social network and individual difference variables to loneliness. *Journal of Personality and Social Psychology, 48,* 981–990.

References is *centered, plural (if more than one). References begin on a separate page. All citations in the text, and only those citations, are included in the reference list.*

Use hanging indents for each citation.

Note the format of a journal article citation: order of information, punctuation, capitalization, and italics.

Table number is flush left. Tables are numbered consecutively. Use a separate page for each table.

Table 1

UCLA Loneliness Scale scores. Means, Standard Deviations, and N for the Four Groups of Participants

Table title is flush left, italicized.

Use horizontal lines only, not vertical lines.

		Photographs	
		Individual	Couple
	M	31.63	40.00
In a relationship	SD	7.70	8.41
	N	19	12
	M	36.82	36.44
Not in a relationship	SD	9.28	7.60
	N	11	18

Loneliness Influenced 12

Figure Caption

Figure 1, Mean loneliness scores as a function of number of people in photographs and relationship status of participants.

Figure caption is centered. Use plural if there is more than one figure. Include all figure captions on one page.

Figure designation is flush left, italicized.

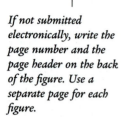

If not submitted electronically, write the page number and the page header on the back of the figure. Use a separate page for each figure.

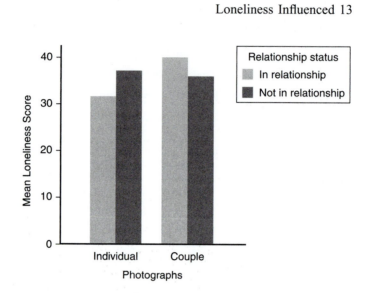

Loneliness Influenced 13

Appendix B

Ethical Principles of Psychologists and Code of Conduct (2002)

CONTENTS

INTRODUCTION AND APPLICABILITY

The American Psychological Association's (APA's) Ethical Principles of Psychologists and Code of Conduct (hereinafter referred to as the Ethics Code) consists of an Introduction, a Preamble, five General Principles (A–E), and specific Ethical Standards. The Introduction discusses the intent, organization, procedural considerations, and scope of application of the Ethics Code. The Preamble and General Principles are aspirational goals to guide psychologists toward the highest ideals of psychology. Although the Preamble and General Principles are not themselves enforceable rules, they should be considered by psychologists in arriving at an ethical course of action. The Ethical Standards set forth enforceable rules for conduct as psychologists. Most of the Ethical Standards are written broadly, in order to apply to psychologists in varied roles, although the application of an Ethical Standard may vary depending on the context. The Ethical Standards are not exhaustive. The fact that a given conduct is not specifically addressed by an Ethical Standard does not mean that it is necessarily either ethical or unethical.

This Ethics Code applies only to psychologists' activities that are part of their scientific, educational, or professional roles as psychologists. Areas covered include but are not limited to the clinical, counseling, and school practice of psychology; research; teaching; supervision of trainees; public service; policy development; social intervention; development of assessment instruments; conducting assessments; educational counseling; organizational consulting; forensic activities; program design and evaluation; and administration. This Ethics Code applies to these activities across a variety of contexts, such as in person, postal, telephone, internet, and other electronic transmissions. These activities shall be distinguished from the purely private conduct of psychologists, which is not within the purview of the Ethics Code.

Membership in the APA commits members and student affiliates to comply with the standards of the APA Ethics Code and to the rules and procedures used to enforce them. Lack of awareness or misunderstanding of an Ethical Standard is not itself a defense to a charge of unethical conduct.

The procedures for filing, investigating, and resolving complaints of unethical conduct are described in the current Rules and Procedures of the APA Ethics Committee. APA may impose sanctions on its members for violations of the standards of the Ethics Code, including termination of APA membership, and may notify other bodies and individuals of its actions. Actions that violate the standards of the Ethics Code may also lead to the imposition of sanctions on psychologists or students whether or not they are APA members by bodies other than APA, including state psychological associations, other professional groups, psychology boards, other state or federal agencies, and payors for health services. In addition, APA may take action against a member after his or her conviction of a felony, expulsion or suspension from an affiliated state psychological association, or suspension or loss of licensure. When the sanction to be imposed by APA is less than expulsion, the 2001 Rules and Procedures do not guarantee an opportunity for an in-person hearing, but generally provide that complaints will be resolved only on the basis of a submitted record.

The Ethics Code is intended to provide guidance for psychologists and standards of professional conduct that can be applied by the APA and by other bodies that choose to adopt them. The Ethics Code is not intended to be a basis of civil liability. Whether a psychologist has violated the Ethics Code standards does not by itself determine whether the psychologist is legally liable in a court action, whether a contract is enforceable, or whether other legal consequences occur.

The modifiers used in some of the standards of this Ethics Code (e.g., *reasonably, appropriate, potentially*) are included in the standards when they would (1) allow professional judgment on the part of psychologists, (2) eliminate injustice or inequality that would occur without the modifier, (3) ensure applicability across the broad range of activities conducted by psychologists, or (4) guard against a set of rigid rules that might be quickly outdated. As used in this Ethics Code, the term *reasonable* means the prevailing professional judgment of psychologists engaged in similar activities in similar circumstances, given the knowledge the psychologist had or should have had at the time.

In the process of making decisions regarding their professional behavior, psychologists must consider this Ethics Code in addition to applicable laws and psychology board regulations. In applying the Ethics Code to their professional work, psychologists may consider other materials and guidelines that have been adopted or endorsed by scientific and professional psychological organizations and the dictates of their own conscience, as well as consult with others within the field. If this Ethics Code establishes a higher standard of conduct than is required by law, psychologists must meet the higher ethical standard. If psychologists' ethical responsibilities conflict with law, regulations, or other governing legal authority, psychologists make known their commitment to this Ethics Code and take steps to resolve the conflict in a responsible manner. If the conflict is unresolvable via such means, psychologists may adhere to the requirements of the law, regulations, or other governing authority in keeping with basic principles of human rights.

PREAMBLE

Psychologists are committed to increasing scientific and professional knowledge of behavior and people's understanding of themselves and others and to the use of such knowledge to improve the condition of individuals, organizations, and society. Psychologists respect and protect civil and human rights and the central importance of freedom of inquiry and expression in research, teaching, and publication. They strive to help the public in developing informed judgments and choices concerning human behavior. In doing so, they perform many roles, such as researcher, educator, diagnostician, therapist, supervisor, consultant, administrator, social interventionist, and expert witness. This Ethics Code provides a common set of principles and standards upon which psychologists build their professional and scientific work.

This Ethics Code is intended to provide specific standards to cover most situations encountered by psychologists. It has as its goals the welfare and protection of the individuals and groups with whom psychologists work and the education of members, students, and the public regarding ethical standards of the discipline.

The development of a dynamic set of ethical standards for psychologists' work-related conduct requires a personal commitment and lifelong effort to act ethically; to encourage ethical behavior by students, supervisees, employees, and colleagues; and to consult with others concerning ethical problems.

GENERAL PRINCIPLES

This section consists of General Principles. General Principles, as opposed to Ethical Standards, are aspirational in nature. Their intent is to guide and inspire psychologists toward the very highest ethical ideals of the profession. General Principles, in contrast to Ethical Standards, do not represent obligations and should not form the basis for imposing sanctions. Relying upon General Principles for either of these reasons distorts both their meaning and purpose.

Principle A: Beneficence and Nonmaleficence

Psychologists strive to benefit those with whom they work and take care to do no harm. In their professional actions, psychologists seek to safeguard the welfare and rights of those with whom they interact professionally and other affected persons, and the welfare of animal subjects of research. When conflicts occur among psychologists' obligations or concerns, they attempt to resolve these conflicts in a responsible fashion that avoids or minimizes harm. Because psychologists' scientific and professional judgments and actions may affect the lives of others, they are alert to and guard against personal, financial, social, organizational, or political factors that might lead to misuse of their influence. Psychologists strive to be aware of the possible effect of their own physical and mental health on their ability to help those with whom they work.

Principle B: Fidelity and Responsibility

Psychologists establish relationships of trust with those with whom they work. They are aware of their professional and scientific responsibilities to society and to the specific communities in which they work. Psychologists uphold professional standards of conduct, clarify their professional roles and obligations, accept appropriate responsibility for their behavior, and seek to manage conflicts of interest that could lead to exploitation or harm. Psychologists consult with, refer to, or cooperate with other professionals and institutions to the extent needed to serve the best interests of those with whom they work. They are concerned about the ethical compliance of their colleagues' scientific and professional conduct. Psychologists strive to contribute a portion of their professional time for little or no compensation or personal advantage.

Principle C: Integrity

Psychologists seek to promote accuracy, honesty, and truthfulness in the science, teaching, and practice of psychology. In these activities psychologists do not steal, cheat, or engage in fraud, subterfuge, or intentional misrepresentation of fact. Psychologists strive to keep their promises and to avoid unwise or unclear commitments. In situations in which deception may be ethically justifiable to maximize benefits and minimize harm, psychologists have a serious obligation to consider the need for, the possible consequences of, and their responsibility to correct any resulting mistrust or other harmful effects that arise from the use of such techniques.

Principle D: Justice

Psychologists recognize that fairness and justice entitle all persons to access to and benefit from the contributions of psychology and to equal quality in the processes, procedures, and services being conducted by psychologists. Psychologists exercise reasonable judgment and take precautions to ensure that their potential biases, the boundaries of their competence, and the limitations of their expertise do not lead to or condone unjust practices.

Principle E: Respect for People's Rights and Dignity

Psychologists respect the dignity and worth of all people, and the rights of individuals to privacy, confidentiality, and self-determination. Psychologists are aware that special safeguards may be necessary to protect the rights and welfare of persons or communities whose vulnerabilities impair autonomous decision making. Psychologists are aware of and respect cultural, individual, and role differences, including those based on age, gender, gender identity, race, ethnicity, culture, national origin, religion, sexual orientation, disability, language, and socioeconomic status and consider these factors when working with members of such groups. Psychologists try to eliminate the effect on their work of biases based on those factors, and they do not knowingly participate in or condone activities of others based upon such prejudices.

Ethical Standards

1. Resolving Ethical Issues

1.01 Misuse of Psychologists' Work
If psychologists learn of misuse or misrepresentation of their work, they take reasonable steps to correct or minimize the misuse or misrepresentation.

1.02 Conflicts Between Ethics and Law, Regulations, or Other Governing Legal Authority
If psychologists' ethical responsibilities conflict with law, regulations, or other governing legal authority, psychologists make known their commitment to the Ethics Code and take steps to resolve the conflict. If the conflict is unresolvable via such means, psychologists may adhere to the requirements of the law, regulations, or other governing legal authority.

1.03 Conflicts Between Ethics and Organizational Demands
If the demands of an organization with which psychologists are affiliated or for whom they are working conflict with this Ethics Code, psychologists clarify the nature of the conflict, make known their commitment to the Ethics Code, and to the extent feasible, resolve the conflict in a way that permits adherence to the Ethics Code.

1.04 Informal Resolution of Ethical Violations
When psychologists believe that there may have been an ethical violation by another psychologist, they attempt to resolve the issue by bringing it to the attention of that individual, if an informal resolution appears appropriate and the intervention does not violate any confidentiality rights that may be involved. (See also Standards 1.02, Conflicts Between

Ethics and Law, Regulations, or Other Governing Legal Authority, and 1.03, Conflicts Between Ethics and Organizational Demands.)

1.05 Reporting Ethical Violations

If an apparent ethical violation has substantially harmed or is likely to substantially harm a person or organization and is not appropriate for informal resolution under Standard 1.04, Informal Resolution of Ethical Violations, or is not resolved properly in that fashion, psychologists take further action appropriate to the situation. Such action might include referral to state or national committees on professional ethics, to state licensing boards, or to the appropriate institutional authorities. This standard does not apply when an intervention would violate confidentiality rights or when psychologists have been retained to review the work of another psychologist whose professional conduct is in question. (See also Standard 1.02, Conflicts Between Ethics and Law, Regulations, or Other Governing Legal Authority.)

1.06 Cooperating With Ethics Committees

Psychologists cooperate in ethics investigations, proceedings, and resulting requirements of the APA or any affiliated state psychological association to which they belong. In doing so, they address any confidentiality issues. Failure to cooperate is itself an ethics violation. However, making a request for deferment of adjudication of an ethics complaint pending the outcome of litigation does not alone constitute noncooperation.

1.07 Improper Complaints

Psychologists do not file or encourage the filing of ethics complaints that are made with reckless disregard for or willful ignorance of facts that would disprove the allegation.

1.08 Unfair Discrimination Against Complainants and Respondents

Psychologists do not deny persons employment, advancement, admissions to academic or other programs, tenure, or promotion, based solely upon their having made or their being the subject of an ethics complaint. This does not preclude taking action based upon the outcome of such proceedings or considering other appropriate information.

2. Competence

2.01 Boundaries of Competence

(a) Psychologists provide services, teach, and conduct research with populations and in areas only within the boundaries of their competence, based on their education, training, supervised experience, consultation, study, or professional experience.

(b) Where scientific or professional knowledge in the discipline of psychology establishes that an understanding of factors associated with age, gender, gender identity, race, ethnicity, culture, national origin, religion, sexual orientation, disability, language, or socioeconomic status is essential for effective implementation of their services or research, psychologists have or obtain the training, experience, consultation, or supervision necessary to ensure the competence of their services, or they make appropriate referrals, except as provided in Standard 2.02, Providing Services in Emergencies.

(c) Psychologists planning to provide services, teach, or conduct research involving populations, areas, techniques, or technologies new to them undertake relevant education, training, supervised experience, consultation, or study.

(d) When psychologists are asked to provide services to individuals for whom appropriate mental health services are not available and for which psychologists have not obtained the competence necessary, psychologists with closely related prior training or experience may provide such services in order to ensure that services are not denied if they make a reasonable effort to obtain the competence required by using relevant research, training, consultation, or study.

(e) In those emerging areas in which generally recognized standards for preparatory training do not yet exist, psychologists nevertheless take reasonable steps to ensure the competence of their work and to protect clients/patients, students, supervisees, research participants, organizational clients, and others from harm.

(f) When assuming forensic roles, psychologists are or become reasonably familiar with the judicial or administrative rules governing their roles.

2.02 Providing Services in Emergencies

In emergencies, when psychologists provide services to individuals for whom other mental health services are not available and for which psychologists have not obtained the necessary training, psychologists may provide such services in order to ensure that services are not denied. The services are discontinued as soon as the emergency has ended or appropriate services are available.

2.03 Maintaining Competence

Psychologists undertake ongoing efforts to develop and maintain their competence.

2.04 Bases for Scientific and Professional Judgments

Psychologists' work is based upon established scientific and professional knowledge of the discipline. (See also Standards 2.01e, Boundaries of Competence, and 10.01b, Informed Consent to Therapy.)

2.05 Delegation of Work to Others

Psychologists who delegate work to employees, supervisees, or research or teaching assistants or who use the services of others, such as interpreters, take reasonable steps to (1) avoid delegating such work to persons who have a multiple relationship with those being served that would likely lead to exploitation or loss of objectivity; (2) authorize only those responsibilities that such persons can be expected to perform competently on the basis of their education, training, or experience, either independently or with the level of supervision being provided; and (3) see that such persons perform these services competently. (See also Standards 2.02, Providing Services in Emergencies; 3.05, Multiple Relationships; 4.01, Maintaining Confidentiality; 9.01, Bases for Assessments; 9.02, Use of Assessments; 9.03, Informed Consent in Assessments; and 9.07, Assessment by Unqualified Persons.)

2.06 Personal Problems and Conflicts

(a) Psychologists refrain from initiating an activity when they know or should know that there is a substantial likelihood that their personal problems will prevent them from performing their work-related activities in a competent manner.

(b) When psychologists become aware of personal problems that may interfere with their performing work-related duties adequately, they take appropriate measures, such as obtaining professional consultation or assistance, and determine whether they should limit, suspend, or terminate their work-related duties. (See also Standard 10.10, Terminating Therapy.)

3.   Human Relations

3.01 Unfair Discrimination

In their work-related activities, psychologists do not engage in unfair discrimination based on age, gender, gender identity, race, ethnicity, culture, national origin, religion, sexual orientation, disability, socioeconomic status, or any basis proscribed by law.

3.02 Sexual Harassment

Psychologists do not engage in sexual harassment. Sexual harassment is sexual solicitation, physical advances, or verbal or nonverbal conduct that is sexual in nature, that occurs in connection with the psychologist's activities or roles as a psychologist, and that either (1) is unwelcome, is offensive, or creates a hostile workplace or educational environment, and the psychologist knows or is told this or (2) is sufficiently severe or intense to be abusive to a reasonable person in the context. Sexual harassment can consist of a single intense or severe act or of multiple persistent or pervasive acts. (See also Standard 1.08, Unfair Discrimination Against Complainants and Respondents.)

3.03 Other Harassment

Psychologists do not knowingly engage in behavior that is harassing or demeaning to persons with whom they interact in their work based on factors such as those persons' age, gender, gender identity, race, ethnicity, culture, national origin, religion, sexual orientation, disability, language, or socioeconomic status.

3.04 Avoiding Harm

Psychologists take reasonable steps to avoid harming their clients/patients, students, supervisees, research participants, organizational clients, and others with whom they work, and to minimize harm where it is foreseeable and unavoidable.

3.05 Multiple Relationships

(a) A multiple relationship occurs when a psychologist is in a professional role with a person and (1) at the same time is in another role with the same person, (2) at the same time is in a relationship with a person closely associated with or related to the person with whom the psychologist has the professional relationship, or (3) promises to enter into another relationship in the future with the person or a person closely associated with or related to the person.

A psychologist refrains from entering into a multiple relationship if the multiple relationship could reasonably be expected to impair the psychologist's objectivity, competence, or effectiveness in performing his or her functions as a psychologist, or otherwise risks exploitation or harm to the person with whom the professional relationship exists.

Multiple relationships that would not reasonably be expected to cause impairment or risk exploitation or harm are not unethical.

(b) If a psychologist finds that, due to unforeseen factors, a potentially harmful multiple relationship has arisen, the psychologist takes reasonable steps to resolve it with due regard for the best interests of the affected person and maximal compliance with the Ethics Code.

(c) When psychologists are required by law, institutional policy, or extraordinary circumstances to serve in more than one role in judicial or administrative proceedings, at the outset they clarify role expectations and the extent of confidentiality and thereafter as changes occur. (See also Standards 3.04, Avoiding Harm, and 3.07, Third-Party Requests for Services.)

3.06 Conflict of Interest

Psychologists refrain from taking on a professional role when personal, scientific, professional, legal, financial, or other interests or relationships could reasonably be expected to (1) impair their objectivity, competence, or effectiveness in performing their functions as psychologists or (2) expose the person or organization with whom the professional relationship exists to harm or exploitation.

3.07 Third-Party Requests for Services

When psychologists agree to provide services to a person or entity at the request of a third party, psychologists attempt to clarify at the outset of the service the nature of the relationship with all individuals or organizations involved. This clarification includes the role of the psychologist (e.g., therapist, consultant, diagnostician, or expert witness), an identification of who is the client, the probable uses of the services provided or the information obtained, and the fact that there may be limits to confidentiality. (See also Standards 3.05, Multiple Relationships, and 4.02, Discussing the Limits of Confidentiality.)

3.08 Exploitative Relationships

Psychologists do not exploit persons over whom they have supervisory, evaluative, or other authority such as clients/patients, students, supervisees, research participants, and employees. (See also Standards 3.05, Multiple Relationships; 6.04, Fees and Financial Arrangements; 6.05, Barter With Clients/Patients; 7.07, Sexual Relationships With Students and Supervisees; 10.05, Sexual Intimacies With Current Therapy Clients/Patients; 10.06, Sexual Intimacies With Relatives or Significant Others of Current Therapy Clients/Patients; 10.07, Therapy With Former Sexual Partners; and 10.08, Sexual Intimacies With Former Therapy Clients/Patients.)

3.09 Cooperation With Other Professionals

When indicated and professionally appropriate, psychologists cooperate with other professionals in order to serve their clients/patients effectively and appropriately. (See also Standard 4.05, Disclosures.)

3.10 Informed Consent

(a) When psychologists conduct research or provide assessment, therapy, counseling, or consulting services in person or via electronic transmission or other forms of communication, they obtain the informed consent of the individual or individuals using language that is reasonably understandable to that person or persons except when conducting such activities without consent is mandated by law or governmental regulation or as otherwise provided in this Ethics Code. (See also Standards 8.02, Informed Consent to Research; 9.03, Informed Consent in Assessments; and 10.01, Informed Consent to Therapy.)

(b) For persons who are legally incapable of giving informed consent, psychologists nevertheless (1) provide an appropriate explanation, (2) seek the individual's assent, (3) consider such persons' preferences and best interests, and (4) obtain appropriate permission from a legally authorized person, if such substitute consent is permitted or required by law. When consent by a legally authorized person is not permitted or required by law, psychologists take reasonable steps to protect the individual's rights and welfare.

(c) When psychological services are court ordered or otherwise mandated, psychologists inform the individual of the nature of the anticipated services, including whether the services are court ordered or mandated and any limits of confidentiality, before proceeding.

(d) Psychologists appropriately document written or oral consent, permission, and assent. (See also Standards 8.02, Informed Consent to Research; 9.03, Informed Consent in Assessments; and 10.01, Informed Consent to Therapy.

3.11 Psychological Services Delivered To or Through Organizations

(a) Psychologists delivering services to or through organizations provide information beforehand to clients and when appropriate those directly affected by the services about (1) the nature and objectives of the services, (2) the intended recipients, (3) which of the individuals are clients, (4) the relationship the psychologist will have with each person and the organization, (5) the probable uses of services provided and information obtained, (6) who will have access to the information, and (7) limits of confidentiality. As soon as feasible, they provide information about the results and conclusions of such services to appropriate persons.

(b) If psychologists will be precluded by law or by organizational roles from providing such information to particular individuals or groups, they so inform those individuals or groups at the outset of the service.

3.12 Interruption of Psychological Services

Unless otherwise covered by contract, psychologists make reasonable efforts to plan for facilitating services in the event that psychological services are interrupted by factors such as the psychologist's illness, death, unavailability, relocation, or retirement or by the client's/patient's relocation or financial limitations. (See also Standard 6.02c, Maintenance, Dissemination, and Disposal of Confidential Records of Professional and Scientific Work.)

4.   Privacy And Confidentiality

4.01 Maintaining Confidentiality

Psychologists have a primary obligation and take reasonable precautions to protect confidential information obtained through or stored in any medium, recognizing that the extent and limits of confidentiality may be regulated by law or established by institutional rules or professional or scientific relationship. (See also Standard 2.05, Delegation of Work to Others.)

4.02 Discussing the Limits of Confidentiality

(a) Psychologists discuss with persons (including, to the extent feasible, persons who are legally incapable of giving informed consent and their legal representatives) and organizations with whom they establish a scientific or professional relationship

(1) the relevant limits of confidentiality and (2) the foreseeable uses of the information generated through their psychological activities. (See also Standard 3.10, Informed Consent.)

(b) Unless it is not feasible or is contraindicated, the discussion of confidentiality occurs at the outset of the relationship and thereafter as new circumstances may warrant.

(c) Psychologists who offer services, products, or information via electronic transmission inform clients/patients of the risks to privacy and limits of confidentiality.

4.03 Recording

Before recording the voices or images of individuals to whom they provide services, psychologists obtain permission from all such persons or their legal representatives. (See also Standards 8.03, Informed Consent for Recording Voices and Images in Research; 8.05, Dispensing With Informed Consent for Research; and 8.07, Deception in Research.)

4.04 Minimizing Intrusions on Privacy

(a) Psychologists include in written and oral reports and consultations, only information germane to the purpose for which the communication is made.

(b) Psychologists discuss confidential information obtained in their work only for appropriate scientific or professional purposes and only with persons clearly concerned with such matters.

4.05 Disclosures

(a) Psychologists may disclose confidential information with the appropriate consent of the organizational client, the individual client/patient, or another legally authorized person on behalf of the client/patient unless prohibited by law.

(b) Psychologists disclose confidential information without the consent of the individual only as mandated by law, or where permitted by law for a valid purpose such as to (1) provide needed professional services; (2) obtain appropriate professional consultations; (3) protect the client/patient, psychologist, or others from harm; or (4) obtain payment for services from a client/patient, in which instance disclosure is limited to the minimum that is necessary to achieve the purpose. (See also Standard 6.04e, Fees and Financial Arrangements.)

4.06 Consultations

When consulting with colleagues, (1) psychologists do not disclose confidential information that reasonably could lead to the identification of a client/patient, research participant, or other person or organization with whom they have a confidential relationship unless they have obtained the prior consent of the person or organization or the disclosure cannot be avoided, and (2) they disclose information only to the extent necessary to achieve the purposes of the consultation. (See also Standard 4.01, Maintaining Confidentiality.)

4.07 Use of Confidential Information for Didactic or Other Purposes
Psychologists do not disclose in their writings, lectures, or other public media, confidential, personally identifiable information concerning their clients/patients, students, research participants, organizational clients, or other recipients of their services that they obtained during the course of their work, unless (1) they take reasonable steps to disguise the person or organization, (2) the person or organization has consented in writing, or (3) there is legal authorization for doing so.

5.   Advertising and Other Public Statements

5.01 Avoidance of False or Deceptive Statements

   (a) Public statements include but are not limited to paid or unpaid advertising, product endorsements, grant applications, licensing applications, other credentialing applications, brochures, printed matter, directory listings, personal resumes or curricula vitae, or comments for use in media such as print or electronic transmission, statements in legal proceedings, lectures and public oral presentations, and published materials. Psychologists do not knowingly make public statements that are false, deceptive, or fraudulent concerning their research, practice, or other work activities or those of persons or organizations with which they are affiliated.

   (b) Psychologists do not make false, deceptive, or fraudulent statements concerning (1) their training, experience, or competence; (2) their academic degrees; (3) their credentials; (4) their institutional or association affiliations; (5) their services; (6) the scientific or clinical basis for, or results or degree of success of, their services; (7) their fees; or (8) their publications or research findings.

   (c) Psychologists claim degrees as credentials for their health services only if those degrees (1) were earned from a regionally accredited educational institution or (2) were the basis for psychology licensure by the state in which they practice.

5.02 Statements by Others

   (a) Psychologists who engage others to create or place public statements that promote their professional practice, products, or activities retain professional responsibility for such statements.

   (b) Psychologists do not compensate employees of press, radio, television, or other communication media in return for publicity in a news item. (See also Standard 1.01, Misuse of Psychologists' Work.)

(c) A paid advertisement relating to psychologists' activities must be identified or clearly recognizable as such.

5.03 Descriptions of Workshops and Non-Degree-Granting Educational Programs

To the degree to which they exercise control, psychologists responsible for announcements, catalogs, brochures, or advertisements describing workshops, seminars, or other non-degree-granting educational programs ensure that they accurately describe the audience for which the program is intended, the educational objectives, the presenters, and the fees involved.

5.04 Media Presentations

When psychologists provide public advice or comment via print, internet, or other electronic transmission, they take precautions to ensure that statements (1) are based on their professional knowledge, training, or experience in accord with appropriate psychological literature and practice; (2) are otherwise consistent with this Ethics Code; and (3) do not indicate that a professional relationship has been established with the recipient. (See also Standard 2.04, Bases for Scientific and Professional Judgments.)

5.05 Testimonials

Psychologists do not solicit testimonials from current therapy clients/patients or other persons who because of their particular circumstances are vulnerable to undue influence.

5.06 In-Person Solicitation

Psychologists do not engage, directly or through agents, in uninvited in-person solicitation of business from actual or potential therapy clients/patients or other persons who because of their particular circumstances are vulnerable to undue influence. However, this prohibition does not preclude (1) attempting to implement appropriate collateral contacts for the purpose of benefiting an already engaged therapy client/patient or (2) providing disaster or community outreach services.

6. Record Keeping and Fees

6.01 Documentation of Professional and Scientific Work and Maintenance of Records

Psychologists create, and to the extent the records are under their control, maintain, disseminate, store, retain, and dispose of records and data relating to their professional and scientific work in order to (1) facilitate provision of services later by them or by other professionals, (2) allow for replication of research design and analyses, (3) meet institutional requirements, (4) ensure accuracy of billing and payments, and (5) ensure compliance with law. (See also Standard 4.01, Maintaining Confidentiality.)

6.02 Maintenance, Dissemination, and Disposal of Confidential Records of Professional and Scientific Work

(a) Psychologists maintain confidentiality in creating, storing, accessing, transferring, and disposing of records under their control, whether these are written, automated, or in any other medium. (See also Standards 4.01, Maintaining Confidentiality, and 6.01, Documentation of Professional and Scientific Work and Maintenance of Records.)

(b) If confidential information concerning recipients of psychological services is entered into databases or systems of records available to persons whose access has not been consented to by the recipient, psychologists use coding or other techniques to avoid the inclusion of personal identifiers.

(c) Psychologists make plans in advance to facilitate the appropriate transfer and to protect the confidentiality of records and data in the event of psychologists' withdrawal from positions or practice. (See also Standards 3.12, Interruption of Psychological Services, and 10.09, Interruption of Therapy.

6.03 Withholding Records for Nonpayment

Psychologists may not withhold records under their control that are requested and needed for a client's/patient's emergency treatment solely because payment has not been received.

6.04 Fees and Financial Arrangements

(a) As early as is feasible in a professional or scientific relationship, psychologists and recipients of psychological services reach an agreement specifying compensation and billing arrangements.

(b) Psychologists' fee practices are consistent with law.

(c) Psychologists do not misrepresent their fees.

(d) If limitations to services can be anticipated because of limitations in financing, this is discussed with the recipient of services as early as is feasible. (See also Standards 10.09, Interruption of Therapy, and 10.10, Terminating Therapy.)

(e) If the recipient of services does not pay for services as agreed, and if psychologists intend to use collection agencies or legal measures to collect the fees, psychologists first inform the person that such measures will be taken and provide that person an opportunity to make prompt payment. (See also Standards 4.05, Disclosures; 6.03, Withholding Records for Nonpayment; and 10.01, Informed Consent to Therapy.)

6.05 Barter With Clients/Patients

Barter is the acceptance of goods, services, or other nonmonetary remuneration from clients/patients in return for psychological services. Psychologists may barter only if (1) it is not clinically contraindicated, and (2) the resulting arrangement is not exploitative. (See also Standards 3.05, Multiple Relationships, and 6.04, Fees and Financial Arrangements.)

6.06 Accuracy in Reports to Payors and Funding Sources

In their reports to payors for services or sources of research funding, psychologists take reasonable steps to ensure the accurate reporting of the nature of the service provided or research conducted, the fees, charges, or payments, and where applicable, the identity of the provider, the findings, and the diagnosis. (See also Standards 4.01, Maintaining Confidentiality; 4.04, Minimizing Intrusions on Privacy; and 4.05, Disclosures.)

6.07 Referrals and Fees

When psychologists pay, receive payment from, or divide fees with another professional, other than in an employer-employee relationship, the payment to each is based on the services provided (clinical, consultative, administrative, or other) and is not based on the referral itself. (See also Standard 3.09, Cooperation With Other Professionals.)

7. Education and Training

7.01 Design of Education and Training Programs

Psychologists responsible for education and training programs take reasonable steps to ensure that the programs are designed to provide the appropriate knowledge and proper experiences, and to meet the requirements for licensure, certification, or other goals for which claims are made by the program. (See also Standard 5.03, Descriptions of Workshops and Non-Degree-Granting Educational Programs.)

7.02 Descriptions of Education and Training Programs

Psychologists responsible for education and training programs take reasonable steps to ensure that there is a current and accurate description of the program content (including participation in required course- or program-related counseling, psychotherapy, experiential groups, consulting projects, or community service), training goals and objectives, stipends and benefits, and requirements that must be met for satisfactory completion of the program. This information must be made readily available to all interested parties.

7.03 Accuracy in Teaching

(a) Psychologists take reasonable steps to ensure that course syllabi are accurate regarding the subject matter to be covered, bases for evaluating progress, and the nature of course experiences. This standard does not preclude an instructor from modifying course content or requirements when the instructor considers it pedagogically necessary or desirable, so long as students are made aware of these modifications in a manner that enables them to fulfill course requirements. (See also Standard 5.01, Avoidance of False or Deceptive Statements.)

(b) When engaged in teaching or training, psychologists present psychological information accurately. (See also Standard 2.03, Maintaining Competence.)

7.04 Student Disclosure of Personal Information

Psychologists do not require students or supervisees to disclose personal information in course- or program-related activities, either orally or in writing, regarding sexual history, history of abuse and neglect, psychological treatment, and relationships with parents, peers, and spouses or significant others except if (1) the program or training facility has clearly identified this requirement in its admissions and program materials or (2) the information is necessary to evaluate or obtain assistance for students whose personal problems could reasonably be judged to be preventing them from performing their training- or professionally related activities in a competent manner or posing a threat to the students or others.

7.05 Mandatory Individual or Group Therapy

(a) When individual or group therapy is a program or course requirement, psychologists responsible for that program allow students in undergraduate and graduate programs the option of selecting such therapy from practitioners unaffiliated with the program. (See also Standard 7.02, Descriptions of Education and Training Programs.)

(b) Faculty who are or are likely to be responsible for evaluating students' academic performance do not themselves provide that therapy. (See also Standard 3.05, Multiple Relationships.)

7.06 Assessing Student and Supervisee Performance

(a) In academic and supervisory relationships, psychologists establish a timely and specific process for providing feedback to students and supervisees. Information regarding the process is provided to the student at the beginning of supervision.

(b) Psychologists evaluate students and supervisees on the basis of their actual performance on relevant and established program requirements.

7.07 Sexual Relationships With Students and Supervisees

Psychologists do not engage in sexual relationships with students or supervisees who are in their department, agency, or training center or over whom psychologists have or are likely to have evaluative authority. (See also Standard 3.05, Multiple Relationships.)

8. Research and Publication

8.01 Institutional Approval

When institutional approval is required, psychologists provide accurate information about their research proposals and obtain approval prior to conducting the research. They conduct the research in accordance with the approved research protocol.

8.02 Informed Consent to Research

(a) When obtaining informed consent as required in Standard 3.10, Informed Consent, psychologists inform participants about (1) the purpose of the research, expected duration, and procedures; (2) their right to decline to participate and to withdraw from the research once participation has begun; (3) the foreseeable consequences of declining or withdrawing; (4) reasonably foreseeable factors that may be expected to influence their willingness to participate such as potential risks, discomfort, or adverse effects; (5) any prospective research benefits; (6) limits of confidentiality; (7) incentives for participation; and (8) whom to contact for questions about the research and research participants' rights. They provide opportunity for the prospective participants to ask questions and receive answers. (See also Standards 8.03, Informed Consent for Recording Voices and Images in Research; 8.05, Dispensing With Informed Consent for Research; and 8.07, Deception in Research.)

(b) Psychologists conducting intervention research involving the use of experimental treatments clarify to participants at the outset of the research (1) the experimental nature of the treatment; (2) the services that will or will not be available to the control group(s) if appropriate; (3) the means by which assignment to treatment and control groups will be made; (4) available treatment alternatives if an individual does not wish to participate in the research or wishes to withdraw once a study has begun; and (5) compensation for or monetary costs of participating including, if appropriate, whether reimbursement from the participant or a third-party payor will be sought. (See also Standard 8.02a, Informed Consent to Research.)

8.03 Informed Consent for Recording Voices and Images in Research

Psychologists obtain informed consent from research participants prior to recording their voices or images for data collection unless (1) the research consists solely of naturalistic observations in public places, and it is not anticipated that the recording will be used in a manner that could cause personal identification or harm, or (2) the research design includes deception, and consent for the use of the recording is obtained during debriefing. (See also Standard 8.07, Deception in Research.)

8.04 Client/Patient, Student, and Subordinate Research Participants

(a) When psychologists conduct research with clients/patients, students, or subordinates as participants, psychologists take steps to protect the prospective participants from adverse consequences of declining or withdrawing from participation.

(b) When research participation is a course requirement or an opportunity for extra credit, the prospective participant is given the choice of equitable alternative activities.

8.05 Dispensing With Informed Consent for Research

Psychologists may dispense with informed consent only (1) where research would not reasonably be assumed to create distress or harm and involves (a) the study of normal educational practices, curricula, or classroom management methods conducted in educational settings; (b) only anonymous questionnaires, naturalistic observations, or archival research for which disclosure of responses would not place participants at risk of criminal or civil liability or damage their financial standing, employability, or reputation, and confidentiality is protected; or (c) the study of factors related to job or organization effectiveness conducted in organizational settings for which there is no risk to participants' employability, and confidentiality is protected or (2) where otherwise permitted by law or federal or institutional regulations.

8.06 Offering Inducements for Research Participation

(a) Psychologists make reasonable efforts to avoid offering excessive or inappropriate financial or other inducements for research participation when such inducements are likely to coerce participation.

(b) When offering professional services as an inducement for research participation, psychologists clarify the nature of the services, as well as the risks, obligations, and limitations. (See also Standard 6.05, Barter With Clients/Patients.)

8.07 Deception in Research

(a) Psychologists do not conduct a study involving deception unless they have determined that the use of deceptive techniques is justified by the study's significant prospective scientific, educational, or applied value and that effective nondeceptive alternative procedures are not feasible.

(b) Psychologists do not deceive prospective participants about research that is reasonably expected to cause physical pain or severe emotional distress.

(c) Psychologists explain any deception that is an integral feature of the design and conduct of an experiment to participants as early as is feasible, preferably at the conclusion of their participation, but no later than at the conclusion of the data collection, and permit participants to withdraw their data. (See also Standard 8.08, Debriefing.)

8.08 Debriefing

(a) Psychologists provide a prompt opportunity for participants to obtain appropriate information about the nature, results, and conclusions of the research, and they take reasonable steps to correct any misconceptions that participants may have of which the psychologists are aware.

(b) If scientific or humane values justify delaying or withholding this information, psychologists take reasonable measures to reduce the risk of harm.

(c) When psychologists become aware that research procedures have harmed a participant, they take reasonable steps to minimize the harm.

8.09 Humane Care and Use of Animals in Research

(a) Psychologists acquire, care for, use, and dispose of animals in compliance with current federal, state, and local laws and regulations, and with professional standards.

(b) Psychologists trained in research methods and experienced in the care of laboratory animals supervise all procedures involving animals and are responsible for ensuring appropriate consideration of their comfort, health, and humane treatment.

(c) Psychologists ensure that all individuals under their supervision who are using animals have received instruction in research methods and in the care, maintenance, and handling of the species being used, to the extent appropriate to their role. (See also Standard 2.05, Delegation of Work to Others.)

(d) Psychologists make reasonable efforts to minimize the discomfort, infection, illness, and pain of animal subjects.

(e) Psychologists use a procedure subjecting animals to pain, stress, or privation only when an alternative procedure is unavailable and the goal is justified by its prospective scientific, educational, or applied value.

(f) Psychologists perform surgical procedures under appropriate anesthesia and follow techniques to avoid infection and minimize pain during and after surgery.

(g) When it is appropriate that an animal's life be terminated, psychologists proceed rapidly, with an effort to minimize pain and in accordance with accepted procedures.

8.10 Reporting Research Results

(a) Psychologists do not fabricate data. (See also Standard 5.01a, Avoidance of False or Deceptive Statements.)

(b) If psychologists discover significant errors in their published data, they take reasonable steps to correct such errors in a correction, retraction, erratum, or other appropriate publication means.

8.11 Plagiarism

Psychologists do not present portions of another's work or data as their own, even if the other work or data source is cited occasionally.

8.12 Publication Credit

(a) Psychologists take responsibility and credit, including authorship credit, only for work they have actually performed or to which they have substantially contributed. (See also Standard 8.12b, Publication Credit.)

(b) Principal authorship and other publication credits accurately reflect the relative scientific or professional contributions of the individuals involved, regardless of their relative status. Mere possession of an institutional position, such as department chair, does not justify authorship credit. Minor contributions to the research or to the writing for publications are acknowledged appropriately, such as in footnotes or in an introductory statement.

(c) Except under exceptional circumstances, a student is listed as principal author on any multiple-authored article that is substantially based on the student's doctoral dissertation. Faculty advisors discuss publication credit with students as early as feasible and throughout the research and publication process as appropriate. (See also Standard 8.12b, Publication Credit.)

8.13 Duplicate Publication of Data

Psychologists do not publish, as original data, data that have been previously published. This does not preclude republishing data when they are accompanied by proper acknowledgment.

8.14 Sharing Research Data for Verification

(a) After research results are published, psychologists do not withhold the data on which their conclusions are based from other competent professionals who seek to verify the substantive claims through reanalysis and who intend to use such data only for that purpose, provided that the confidentiality of the participants can be protected and unless legal rights concerning proprietary data preclude their release. This does not preclude psychologists from requiring that such individuals or groups be responsible for costs associated with the provision of such information.

(b) Psychologists who request data from other psychologists to verify the substantive claims through reanalysis may use shared data only for the declared purpose. Requesting psychologists obtain prior written agreement for all other uses of the data.

8.15 Reviewers

Psychologists who review material submitted for presentation, publication, grant, or research proposal review respect the confidentiality of and the proprietary rights in such information of those who submitted it.

9.   Assessment

9.01 Bases for Assessments

(a) Psychologists base the opinions contained in their recommendations, reports, and diagnostic or evaluative statements, including
forensic testimony, on information and techniques sufficient to
substantiate their findings. (See also Standard 2.04, Bases for
Scientific and Professional Judgments.)

(b) Except as noted in 9.01c, psychologists provide opinions of the
psychological characteristics of individuals only after they have
conducted an examination of the individuals adequate to support their statements or conclusions. When, despite reasonable
efforts, such an examination is not practical, psychologists
document the efforts they made and the result of those efforts,
clarify the probable impact of their limited information on the
reliability and validity of their opinions, and appropriately limit
the nature and extent of their conclusions or recommendations.
(See also Standards 2.01, Boundaries of Competence, and 9.06,
Interpreting Assessment Results.)

(c) When psychologists conduct a record review or provide consultation or supervision and an individual examination is not warranted or necessary for the opinion, psychologists explain this
and the sources of information on which they based their
conclusions and recommendations.

9.02 Use of Assessments

(a) Psychologists administer, adapt, score, interpret, or use assessment techniques, interviews, tests, or instruments in a manner
and for purposes that are appropriate in light of the research on
or evidence of the usefulness and proper application of the
techniques.

(b) Psychologists use assessment instruments whose validity and
reliability have been established for use with members of the
population tested. When such validity or reliability has not been
established, psychologists describe the strengths and limitations
of test results and interpretation.

(c) Psychologists use assessment methods that are appropriate to an
individual's language preference and competence, unless the use
of an alternative language is relevant to the assessment issues.

9.03 Informed Consent in Assessments

(a) Psychologists obtain informed consent for assessments, evaluations, or diagnostic services, as described in Standard 3.10,
Informed Consent, except when (1) testing is mandated by law
or governmental regulations; (2) informed consent is implied

because testing is conducted as a routine educational, institutional, or organizational activity (e.g., when participants voluntarily agree to assessment when applying for a job); or (3) one purpose of the testing is to evaluate decisional capacity. Informed consent includes an explanation of the nature and purpose of the assessment, fees, involvement of third parties, and limits of confidentiality and sufficient opportunity for the client/patient to ask questions and receive answers.

(b) Psychologists inform persons with questionable capacity to consent or for whom testing is mandated by law or governmental regulations about the nature and purpose of the proposed assessment services, using language that is reasonably understandable to the person being assessed.

(c) Psychologists using the services of an interpreter obtain informed consent from the client/patient to use that interpreter, ensure that confidentiality of test results and test security are maintained, and include in their recommendations, reports, and diagnostic or evaluative statements, including forensic testimony, discussion of any limitations on the data obtained. (See also Standards 2.05, Delegation of Work to Others; 4.01, Maintaining Confidentiality; 9.01, Bases for Assessments; 9.06, Interpreting Assessment Results; and 9.07, Assessment by Unqualified Persons.)

9.04 Release of Test Data

(a) The term *test data* refers to raw and scaled scores, client/patient responses to test questions or stimuli, and psychologists' notes and recordings concerning client/patient statements and behavior during an examination. Those portions of test materials that include client/patient responses are included in the definition of *test data*. Pursuant to a client/patient release, psychologists provide test data to the client/patient or other persons identified in the release. Psychologists may refrain from releasing test data to protect a client/patient or others from substantial harm or misuse or misrepresentation of the data or the test, recognizing that in many instances release of confidential information under these circumstances is regulated by law. (See also Standard 9.11, Maintaining Test Security.)

(b) In the absence of a client/patient release, psychologists provide test data only as required by law or court order.

9.05 Test Construction

Psychologists who develop tests and other assessment techniques use appropriate psychometric procedures and current scientific or professional knowledge for test design, standardization, validation, reduction or elimination of bias, and recommendations for use.

9.06 Interpreting Assessment Results

When interpreting assessment results, including automated interpretations, psychologists take into account the purpose of the assessment as well as the various test factors, test-taking abilities, and other characteristics of the person being assessed, such as situational, personal, linguistic, and cultural differences, that might affect psychologists' judgments or reduce the accuracy of their interpretations. They indicate any significant limitations of their interpretations. (See also Standards 2.01b and c, Boundaries of Competence, and 3.01, Unfair Discrimination.)

9.07 Assessment by Unqualified Persons

Psychologists do not promote the use of psychological assessment techniques by unqualified persons, except when such use is conducted for training purposes with appropriate supervision. (See also Standard 2.05, Delegation of Work to Others.)

9.08 Obsolete Tests and Outdated Test Results

(a) Psychologists do not base their assessment or intervention decisions or recommendations on data or test results that are outdated for the current purpose.

(b) Psychologists do not base such decisions or recommendations on tests and measures that are obsolete and not useful for the current purpose.

9.09 Test Scoring and Interpretation Services

(a) Psychologists who offer assessment or scoring services to other professionals accurately describe the purpose, norms, validity, reliability, and applications of the procedures and any special qualifications applicable to their use.

(b) Psychologists select scoring and interpretation services (including automated services) on the basis of evidence of the validity of the program and procedures as well as on other appropriate considerations. (See also Standard 2.01b and c, Boundaries of Competence.)

(c) Psychologists retain responsibility for the appropriate application, interpretation, and use of assessment instruments, whether they score and interpret such tests themselves or use automated or other services.

9.10 Explaining Assessment Results

Regardless of whether the scoring and interpretation are done by psychologists, by employees or assistants, or by automated or other outside services, psychologists take reasonable steps to ensure that explanations of results are given to the individual or designated representative unless the nature of the relationship precludes provision of an explanation of results (such as in some organizational consulting, preemployment or security screenings, and forensic evaluations), and this fact has been clearly explained to the person being assessed in advance.

9.11 Maintaining Test Security

The term *test materials* refers to manuals, instruments, protocols, and test questions or stimuli and does not include *test data* as defined in Standard 9.04, Release of Test Data. Psychologists make reasonable efforts to maintain the integrity and security of test materials and other assessment techniques consistent with law and contractual obligations, and in a manner that permits adherence to this Ethics Code.

10. Therapy

10.01 Informed Consent to Therapy

(a) When obtaining informed consent to therapy as required in Standard 3.10, Informed Consent, psychologists inform clients/patients as early as is feasible in the therapeutic relationship about the nature and anticipated course of therapy, fees, involvement of third parties, and limits of confidentiality and provide sufficient opportunity for the client/patient to ask questions and receive answers. (See also Standards 4.02, Discussing the Limits of Confidentiality, and 6.04, Fees and Financial Arrangements.)

(b) When obtaining informed consent for treatment for which generally recognized techniques and procedures have not been established, psychologists inform their clients/patients of the developing nature of the treatment, the potential risks involved, alternative treatments that may be available, and the voluntary nature of their participation. (See also Standards 2.01e, Boundaries of Competence, and 3.10, Informed Consent.)

(c) When the therapist is a trainee and the legal responsibility for the treatment provided resides with the supervisor, the client/patient, as part of the informed consent procedure, is informed that the therapist is in training and is being supervised and is given the name of the supervisor.

10.02 Therapy Involving Couples or Families

(a) When psychologists agree to provide services to several persons who have a relationship (such as spouses, significant others, or parents and children), they take reasonable steps to clarify at the outset (1) which of the individuals are clients/patients and (2) the relationship the psychologist will have with each person. This clarification includes the psychologist's role and the probable uses of the services provided or the information obtained. (See also Standard 4.02, Discussing the Limits of Confidentiality.)

(b) If it becomes apparent that psychologists may be called on to perform potentially conflicting roles (such as family therapist and then witness for one party in divorce proceedings), psychologists take reasonable steps to clarify and modify, or withdraw from, roles appropriately. (See also Standard 3.05c, Multiple Relationships.)

10.03 Group Therapy

When psychologists provide services to several persons in a group setting, they describe at the outset the roles and responsibilities of all parties and the limits of confidentiality.

10.04 Providing Therapy to Those Served by Others

In deciding whether to offer or provide services to those already receiving mental health services elsewhere, psychologists carefully consider the treatment issues and the potential client's/patient's welfare. Psychologists discuss these issues with the client/patient or another legally authorized person on behalf of the client/patient in order to minimize the risk of confusion and conflict, consult with the other service providers when appropriate, and proceed with caution and sensitivity to the therapeutic issues.

10.05 Sexual Intimacies With Current Therapy Clients/Patients

Psychologists do not engage in sexual intimacies with current therapy clients/patients.

10.06 Sexual Intimacies With Relatives or Significant Others of Current Therapy Clients/Patients

Psychologists do not engage in sexual intimacies with individuals they know to be close relatives, guardians, or significant others of current clients/patients. Psychologists do not terminate therapy to circumvent this standard.

10.07 Therapy With Former Sexual Partners

Psychologists do not accept as therapy clients/patients persons with whom they have engaged in sexual intimacies.

10.08 Sexual Intimacies With Former Therapy Clients/Patients

(a) Psychologists do not engage in sexual intimacies with former clients/patients for at least two years after cessation or termination of therapy.

(b) Psychologists do not engage in sexual intimacies with former clients/patients even after a two-year interval except in the most unusual circumstances. Psychologists who engage in such activity after the two years following cessation or termination of therapy and of having no sexual contact with the former client/patient bear the burden of demonstrating that there has been no exploitation, in light of all relevant factors, including (1) the amount of time that has passed since therapy terminated; (2) the nature, duration, and intensity of the therapy; (3) the circumstances of termination; (4) the client's/patient's personal history; (5) the client's/patient's current mental status; (6) the likelihood of adverse impact on the client/patient; and (7) any statements or actions made by the therapist during the course of therapy suggesting or inviting the possibility of a posttermination sexual or romantic relationship with the client/patient. (See also Standard 3.05, Multiple Relationships.)

10.09 Interruption of Therapy

When entering into employment or contractual relationships, psychologists make reasonable efforts to provide for orderly and appropriate resolution of responsibility for client/patient care in the event that the employment or contractual relationship ends, with paramount consideration given to the welfare of the client/patient. (See also Standard 3.12, Interruption of Psychological Services.)

10.10 Terminating Therapy

(a) Psychologists terminate therapy when it becomes reasonably clear that the client/patient no longer needs the service, is not likely to benefit, or is being harmed by continued service.

(b) Psychologists may terminate therapy when threatened or otherwise endangered by the client/patient or another person with whom the client/patient has a relationship.

(c) Except where precluded by the actions of clients/patients or third-party payors, prior to termination psychologists provide pretermination counseling and suggest alternative service providers as appropriate.

History and Effective Date Footnote

This version of the APA Ethics Code was adopted by the American Psychological Association's Council of Representatives during its meeting, August 21, 2002, and is effective beginning June 1, 2003. Inquiries concerning the substance or interpretation of the APA Ethics Code should be addressed to the Director, Office of Ethics, American Psychological Association, 750 First Street, NE, Washington, DC 20002-4242. The Ethics Code and information regarding the Code can be found on the APA web site, http://www.apa.org/ethics. The standards in this Ethics Code will be used to adjudicate complaints brought concerning alleged conduct occurring on or after the effective date. Complaints regarding conduct occurring prior to the effective date will be adjudicated on the basis of the version of the Ethics Code that was in effect at the time the conduct occurred.

The APA has previously published its Ethics Code as follows:

American Psychological Association. (1953). Ethical standards of psychologists. Washington, DC: Author.

American Psychological Association. (1959). Ethical standards of psychologists. American Psychologist, 14, 279-282.

American Psychological Association. (1963). Ethical standards of psychologists. American Psychologist, 18, 56-60.

American Psychological Association. (1968). Ethical standards of psychologists. American Psychologist, 23, 357-361.

American Psychological Association. (1977, March). Ethical standards of psychologists. APA Monitor, 22-23.

American Psychological Association. (1979). Ethical standards of psychologists. Washington, DC: Author.

American Psychological Association. (1981). Ethical principles of psychologists. American Psychologist, 36, 633-638.

American Psychological Association. (1990). Ethical principles of psychologists (Amended June 2, 1989). American Psychologist, 45, 390-395.

American Psychological Association. (1992). Ethical principles of psychologists and code of conduct. American Psychologist, 47, 1597-1611.

Request copies of the APA's Ethical Principles of Psychologists and Code of Conduct from the APA Order Department, 750 First Street, NE, Washington, DC 20002-4242, or phone (202) 336-5510.

Appendix C

Tables

	TABLE C.1		10,000 Random Digits							
	00—04	05—09	10—14	15—19	20—24	25—29	30—34	35—39	40—44	45—49
00	37643	04920	11761	47606	68076	23570	93403	73916	44349	95097
01	31495	53606	53555	81170	83578	45628	64489	35288	69678	59684
02	29257	64295	96646	75722	31383	74617	10853	51406	72348	22401
03	35743	95232	98326	13521	77188	55176	35440	58031	98200	44620
04	76786	00037	39985	83682	98634	18973	42438	58119	16721	54652
05	69130	35324	06795	26202	32273	42623	50693	67416	81789	43821
06	24940	40415	84364	46839	35231	06360	32127	22459	44717	46019
07	01467	91155	57970	28579	68189	77284	30378	16356	31500	57963
08	90292	41893	91390	54199	38075	69162	65871	61165	31618	41885
09	26574	95962	29695	05502	46889	07341	35955	49269	66309	15131
10	34026	10133	04368	37512	17556	06085	85185	22630	26092	14429
11	56363	52525	06658	80214	94499	91014	14602	42350	35566	31312
12	35143	05678	19748	99327	30213	06964	80261	00262	93269	82375
13	03351	76593	42373	59478	13768	17598	81267	31060	51991	18455
14	78058	30701	41790	89587	55701	93891	58576	53697	02008	07099
15	08281	73780	78627	01078	85016	93844	74662	25322	71121	05391
16	89389	75528	95563	31613	51612	42387	85377	06898	25142	48364
17	04843	02768	97399	63739	86507	49076	93483	47841	22205	01798
18	47995	39479	14791	90202	94851	48706	17364	50917	94877	88244
19	25274	76542	18004	19524	14392	27692	04462	64120	01064	48663
20	17221	71767	36903	79645	12696	79212	37461	23136	67036	84590
21	79554	79509	44638	69022	82050	26014	31933	64655	52905	98780
22	94457	95840	77076	90255	28151	51648	47144	03234	23928	78334
23	50805	39338	62108	78966	12994	33914	27741	35115	23212	59130
24	07122	82178	21957	88723	99597	26425	92386	46358	07934	88506
25	11518	66456	85365	85369	93261	29283	22597	40765	19584	93958
26	15606	66651	98287	81554	29900	37756	23733	00594	01398	75104
27	97887	72853	10880	46765	54235	66568	07786	83348	26243	20897
28	40172	92360	10430	94038	31742	69798	23058	03684	66256	38052
29	36236	82181	52534	70079	42686	35339	66884	13201	92353	79312
30	38868	79725	83555	58949	37102	96275	77702	53851	77544	14386
31	11622	79072	51436	01561	99374	79768	88994	46503	17165	19885
32	74562	23025	35208	26533	87647	79013	42289	69357	91351	14344
33	09235	11793	83574	38184	58634	46599	22997	08255	58671	16617
34	04962	97324	05395	68269	12771	59391	41052	23733	01932	96560
35	11908	08921	68144	02479	78553	15915	00949	85588	62064	96134
36	53150	53425	56536	02299	55351	37713	80569	87338	28490	66667
37	78752	47860	93443	22986	67695	15570	76528	59085	99406	56230
38	76002	87237	78960	95119	80131	95835	84745	95751	24981	83280
39	97533	38935	80997	08883	69970	29688	34503	97349	82793	85923
40	75193	53138	66164	35203	83681	41665	39807	20891	94479	29714
41	21398	70317	49440	43180	61708	73498	87166	85470	86205	00197
42	57385	04319	72355	13143	20094	68022	59415	86375	57683	45447
43	40519	32172	45520	33009	18736	83946	09143	69436	84540	40193
44	16916	29459	61711	73205	04280	68474	33683	59486	94993	96029
45	19805	00240	94528	33342	76965	96089	52521	90871	87150	11678
46	97147	78347	08195	67576	68190	77269	19181	86651	78191	29172
47	72980	28093	27533	21057	09492	28014	30168	09330	41100	56497
48	21591	45517	07115	95688	59693	98571	77391	46166	89051	15247
49	84590	15148	28189	12178	55796	30843	01726	80806	49118	33674

(*continued*)

TABLE C.1	(continued)

	50–54	55–59	60–64	65–69	70–74	75–79	80–84	85–89	90–94	95–99
00	68983	82624	20755	84946	81652	74350	46479	62538	67611	81475
01	74152	20321	06423	22624	93039	87851	40142	04639	35261	48650
02	33361	19206	00213	19033	87523	11519	90195	80463	38897	93122
03	56999	54980	83230	24250	20287	41263	79182	03894	19331	85742
04	75983	65857	53986	13874	24983	64111	76060	25874	09945	04639
05	27303	69990	18300	28655	72916	63311	66887	84146	35357	34769
06	15249	99514	18565	06720	74364	19835	10628	24954	40605	84376
07	28781	84680	16947	55315	61197	79515	06394	61509	76726	85877
08	35279	60786	19578	44133	27007	91481	28964	70830	19305	04134
09	74584	50877	98467	15756	75325	90857	21772	27444	29237	53316
10	38571	78632	33349	92759	06740	34016	04121	76309	97787	37230
11	71320	11895	23062	92279	65962	86489	75702	34193	99847	80396
12	31406	84988	06145	89829	38902	62313	60127	02428	26132	10795
13	89492	57291	28224	96114	32621	23404	46642	94087	25509	79625
14	10963	12431	13479	50711	54977	61687	53480	97237	14572	54280
15	52816	75304	34409	26205	31519	48154	56468	59229	11320	53802
16	12272	64150	76140	65879	82114	75895	04459	95644	52300	75575
17	39251	31470	01118	73662	87034	27405	13612	40450	74385	55948
18	89324	25320	15129	12030	39493	68529	97715	36516	22347	49324
19	57301	21642	25652	53331	87657	80707	45378	05280	85165	56485
20	97188	27053	11246	14692	80885	26694	56166	98947	87291	10964
21	94786	82773	37199	42052	28193	00505	19961	86162	60936	55275
22	40282	66356	06914	25131	44466	63822	37402	22141	20697	31742
23	37959	94325	80293	60657	51919	60021	52368	95161	58285	50010
24	47606	00830	27951	83706	70101	20684	77395	96294	60355	06540
25	89783	31984	32286	66151	28224	94238	66576	98672	88996	88060
26	11888	05696	03236	85614	33800	38096	53115	52332	07609	15725
27	79504	16616	53547	02181	27685	20086	58728	77143	33641	54312
28	56965	29270	05074	04138	95479	81886	68141	85150	93694	30152
29	77560	40462	22907	35776	17460	02124	68176	44070	84120	36078
30	19486	39291	45642	13423	39181	29311	22593	30396	15150	72913
31	36631	69569	89157	02141	02567	25862	38661	52542	69323	48755
32	19128	82860	69474	40009	70997	97042	08413	65788	22953	18548
33	05566	94328	29607	03416	66826	77293	26492	77076	48934	36312
34	91006	63648	76382	86638	37932	25012	18049	97726	89507	49023
35	23524	16086	34719	78915	98950	50715	29559	48146	21974	23550
36	21708	28615	64001	39507	05923	03770	15608	22683	93120	57091
37	14087	09104	08061	55643	09203	32675	52889	60525	30552	21026
38	97104	87334	19526	59872	20351	04008	50581	27339	83299	47514
39	01545	64024	89199	57683	74002	09156	16175	41907	64281	11401
40	35429	13038	04989	53767	19819	63333	44940	67137	17823	92809
41	90977	87863	83486	63263	53343	45656	71813	64619	81136	87300
42	26524	50310	12051	16086	61936	90157	05053	80929	39219	73550
43	77909	45273	47323	18697	82784	16077	26478	47707	64563	49926
44	14505	23190	02847	71600	30914	77258	64095	91412	57393	90007
45	47019	48779	63813	13775	48742	67573	29395	65489	42376	03631
46	63550	53034	70350	46031	63777	27605	29677	58013	86715	29780
47	75408	15246	29466	91941	13545	51335	31637	21615	63725	76932
48	43196	19619	94962	41331	08123	22863	08465	49342	33695	42784
49	79116	81729	63323	01592	98007	70410	09917	76218	45414	40807

(*continued*)

| TABLE C.I | (continued) |

	00—04	05—09	10—14	15—19	20—24	25—29	30—34	35—39	40—44	45—49
50	57141	59665	14081	59312	89685	00644	12099	99327	32959	72175
51	07255	49357	50214	03387	95831	34585	36976	66425	12089	42282
52	33059	84643	07271	75242	10366	19789	92100	89372	83841	73141
53	45078	48698	99939	30158	96883	36982	18254	34023	78718	45106
54	30457	30289	19902	43494	04355	02763	93773	22097	22122	30906
55	16213	80706	50264	38542	64672	74643	72221	17706	91584	45528
56	12075	45627	54285	64664	34451	43557	46372	25639	62776	24855
57	52796	20283	44533	88500	44084	00423	60534	22441	52531	25022
58	60389	84238	45828	85779	05760	92062	00736	18555	34536	28504
59	14056	42083	18507	93210	37171	08269	03627	22194	91187	25155
60	57616	63230	30760	67867	50229	35003	06609	97895	97502	88028
61	57082	07152	62971	34476	13945	21047	26528	22965	89876	17555
62	22722	91342	62648	72630	61937	19843	48012	00208	38876	91746
63	85903	98713	21465	07359	22132	82566	34188	85229	27221	89895
64	14334	37968	69133	51873	77473	03630	13399	24250	73133	14255
65	78344	24115	55715	43761	59506	12318	81733	02136	38879	23503
66	56281	86034	77091	89600	86602	00865	09621	55043	17928	32498
67	23918	90916	34722	25267	94910	25247	21536	14690	08406	78601
68	18144	63164	21663	26007	80836	75625	94138	36553	30535	10787
69	31454	33853	32912	75378	66020	58990	28069	54753	80160	48511
70	42824	77702	32597	18768	47882	69306	05151	62282	71586	90352
71	04104	18179	47016	21287	29302	30733	11634	84095	22053	66095
72	02083	78957	55204	99776	96311	64782	35189	00879	76366	47547
73	78650	39301	71485	43767	75928	70706	91765	88263	15614	92584
74	85993	68630	56425	53192	76378	77425	85480	22103	47068	96891
75	95890	89025	92730	38584	23460	71234	73641	74117	78276	42728
76	28281	83000	77714	03331	54866	40243	33505	80236	87074	33118
77	73833	53316	53933	28636	80163	28265	84564	65207	25793	44328
78	02588	99463	09940	00902	72085	73261	22779	60322	74081	47373
79	48538	71455	77184	40271	01794	35241	49008	71248	96050	66417
80	71169	47877	28856	39066	69428	28387	12067	72669	71173	21406
81	57320	75147	74536	88789	57433	57497	45014	00337	83447	17476
82	83520	95528	13513	43446	04873	36341	29251	17577	62234	35028
83	97643	85893	99585	81546	11938	61886	89579	41139	95109	65772
84	66826	92246	23565	30810	21703	80028	50168	12235	63688	22032
85	84724	07113	46924	91276	45941	58067	16781	22822	49114	74362
86	36610	53024	85027	53325	40944	17152	27902	70110	93405	34556
87	73648	33549	44927	45627	22577	25123	24386	18115	98149	92720
88	89525	39637	65723	08812	90347	71781	63145	01312	64084	49624
89	38092	90788	83780	95934	17687	35733	87897	96468	19461	69182
90	80583	02973	39899	41173	31878	47780	59845	08006	26729	01478
91	04704	16594	34523	10589	29175	27687	15490	65434	47003	01763
92	27648	65023	25497	20688	72596	82289	19225	78989	46373	95147
93	19493	60401	00501	43852	35632	16573	39909	90027	59246	53237
94	23250	54317	40887	92848	12285	53632	37923	51678	76923	71190
95	25068	17041	47486	23820	75289	11651	59608	83353	24573	15554
96	39176	29016	89094	76944	05172	44036	42028	29321	33508	31758
97	29182	78255	53802	77641	27941	14074	02787	50493	90697	86385
98	95475	70405	86523	16996	35202	48974	73262	82302	51793	31562
99	38939	69230	85040	58307	06458	21699	46304	00906	87640	60946

TABLE C.1 (continued)

	50–54	55–59	60–64	65–69	70–74	75–79	80–84	85–89	90–94	95–99
50	39169	55614	77555	69519	12395	50099	70709	12849	59923	78161
51	24447	26015	86761	28930	72171	22539	19631	65306	31399	51199
52	85617	90274	93597	84629	32365	73961	92346	49855	84514	13886
53	93985	28383	03481	57702	27637	20552	66229	57811	67747	34439
54	97454	52036	09300	80422	35301	55706	08560	69293	67553	95155
55	38350	55344	79733	41002	38599	61307	52000	01182	32650	72742
56	32466	33422	81674	87822	74777	33021	88843	76519	05895	68364
57	78663	40916	63853	67142	03532	74121	26213	47783	88410	26787
58	35602	98009	26581	20135	68179	12471	82779	99045	25581	23729
59	27778	77393	36867	88083	92551	81921	86340	84414	36282	50726
60	70129	14167	07819	02760	61634	43348	33171	43696	62842	79366
61	75501	80871	33624	45376	83073	40738	54112	40817	71045	05157
62	37183	37381	21458	65631	68915	91427	71857	35821	13706	64684
63	94060	99242	66947	09413	42386	93122	40766	49195	22802	81876
64	28120	40928	57775	44031	58604	33794	60787	48480	03144	49516
65	74344	47906	48103	87081	97664	50994	41695	03604	90077	23279
66	57622	73242	02372	83648	92858	22636	44996	90999	66221	43294
67	88262	83693	62441	12286	60048	70933	20463	52830	88859	92076
68	48439	03736	74089	93709	95095	70640	50330	13004	31033	50886
69	30609	82300	29897	65714	81743	07954	00443	29878	95899	29450
70	07346	15126	64681	52541	36234	97135	71709	73175	49562	00060
71	86678	54976	62866	54690	75693	21734	76474	04960	77168	33840
72	41759	18312	79049	59649	80591	00639	39336	80825	62234	55953
73	10952	97033	01944	15808	01318	79070	90336	59861	27714	19628
74	30793	69499	39537	12520	34359	72170	02002	36405	13102	25108
75	28868	22657	60964	85551	74816	38792	96910	70176	94050	68089
76	96914	79133	81513	17207	75790	12619	86861	58185	84365	53505
77	20755	48196	78470	00736	76832	11305	59031	84345	17808	16641
78	58326	25849	23827	77159	09120	48377	85258	29716	57251	10694
79	24229	48061	83535	28047	70413	40887	61501	18899	88954	09067
80	12202	15454	84811	23273	80781	13708	70107	87410	11609	44074
81	36228	03696	69288	18959	99990	03213	05444	92643	91827	42243
82	05287	40462	50427	63882	54615	07782	07185	42921	87895	29476
83	38758	58615	40994	81135	78274	55461	30041	84433	38220	41842
84	01737	22846	38565	03102	94541	52201	79940	19034	14387	79362
85	53607	58225	97075	14996	97873	60015	92781	74560	75532	43419
86	86687	17627	24670	66254	61140	92608	99138	92013	94461	37876
87	33611	85106	13522	40353	29750	96833	91327	81522	70026	17830
88	12758	89950	43646	93920	35191	20923	37887	52434	77211	81604
89	09385	09377	36682	66970	88852	67898	53495	35757	89184	93625
90	36809	74319	27682	10289	77752	97447	85977	35921	02687	74368
91	46058	19443	39312	21660	97844	96390	63020	40166	81855	87419
92	44449	79390	57965	99159	30622	71609	69006	18122	23871	39812
93	81328	21741	65849	59162	82265	88052	63152	54057	77485	55601
94	09924	35556	81090	17929	02411	34985	40570	37335	09946	57983
95	62924	76702	78539	69209	69936	37602	53129	51170	85235	70640
96	68016	54321	28398	01980	70888	25459	52440	31019	30341	52749
97	86292	94023	36273	62547	44780	73406	16256	89070	57893	42009
98	81602	01443	32107	31251	82791	59431	92352	04832	76868	27225
99	71794	82510	78274	75598	62846	45667	01175	13902	78822	25456

Source: Generated by the software program, *Mathematica.*

TABLE C.2	*t* Distribution Values			

	Confidence Interval Percents (two-tailed)				
	80%	90%	95%	98%	99%

	α *Level for a Two-Tailed Test*				
	.20	.10	.05	.02	.01

	α *Level for a One-Tailed Test*				
df	.10	.05	.025	.01	.005
1	3.078	6.314	12.706	31.821	63.657
2	1.886	2.920	4.303	6.965	9.925
3	1.638	2.353	3.182	4.541	5.841
4	1.533	2.132	2.776	3.747	4.604
5	1.476	2.015	2.571	3.365	4.032
6	1.440	1.943	2.447	3.143	3.707
7	1.415	1.895	2.365	2.998	3.499
8	1.397	1.860	2.306	2.896	3.355
9	1.383	1.833	2.262	2.821	3.250
10	1.372	1.812	2.228	2.764	3.169
11	1.363	1.796	2.201	2.718	3.106
12	1.356	1.782	2.179	2.681	3.055
13	1.350	1.771	2.160	2.650	3.012
14	1.345	1.761	2.145	2.624	2.977
15	1.341	1.753	2.131	2.602	2.947
16	1.337	1.746	2.120	2.583	2.921
17	1.333	1.740	2.110	2.567	2.898
18	1.330	1.734	2.101	2.552	2.878
19	1.328	1.729	2.093	2.539	2.861
20	1.325	1.725	2.086	2.528	2.845
21	1.323	1.721	2.080	2.518	2.831
22	1.321	1.717	2.074	2.508	2.819
23	1.319	1.714	2.069	2.500	2.807
24	1.318	1.711	2.064	2.492	2.797
25	1.316	1.708	2.060	2.485	2.787
26	1.315	1.706	2.056	2.479	2.779
27	1.314	1.703	2.052	2.473	2.771
28	1.313	1.701	2.048	2.467	2.763
29	1.311	1.699	2.045	2.462	2.756

(*continued*)

TABLE C.2	(continued)				
30	1.310	1.697	2.042	2.457	2.750
32	1.309	1.694	2.037	2.449	2.738
34	1.307	1.691	2.032	2.441	2.728
36	1.306	1.688	2.028	2.434	2.719
38	1.304	1.686	2.024	2.429	2.712
40	1.303	1.684	2.021	2.423	2.704
45	1.301	1.679	2.014	2.412	2.690
50	1.299	1.676	2.009	2.403	2.678
55	1.297	1.673	2.004	2.396	2.668
60	1.296	1.671	2.000	2.390	2.660
65	1.295	1.669	1.997	2.385	2.654
70	1.294	1.667	1.994	2.381	2.648
80	1.292	1.664	1.990	2.374	2.639
90	1.291	1.662	1.987	2.368	2.632
100	1.290	1.660	1.984	2.364	2.626
∞	1.282	1.645	1.960	2.326	2.576

Note: To be statistically significant, the *t* value calculated from the data must be equal to or greater than the value in the table.

Source: Engineering Statistics Handbook, http://www.itl.nist.gov/div898/handbook/eda/section3/eda3672.htm. Values for *t* for 1–100 *df* are at this site.

| TABLE C.3 | Chi-Square Distribution Values | | | | |

			α Levels		
df	.10	.05	.02	.01	.001
1	2.706	3.841	5.024	6.635	10.828
2	4.605	5.991	7.378	9.210	13.816
3	6.251	7.815	9.348	11.345	16.266
4	7.779	9.488	11.143	13.277	18.467
5	9.236	11.070	12.833	15.086	20.515
6	10.645	12.592	14.449	16.812	22.458
7	12.017	14.067	16.013	18.475	24.322
8	13.362	15.507	17.535	20.090	26.125
9	14.684	16.919	19.023	21.666	27.877
10	15.987	18.307	20.483	23.209	29.588
11	17.275	19.675	21.920	24.725	31.264
12	18.549	21.026	23.337	26.217	32.910
13	19.812	22.362	24.736	27.688	34.528
14	21.064	23.685	26.119	29.141	36.123
15	22.307	24.996	27.488	30.578	37.697
16	23.542	26.296	28.845	32.000	39.252
17	24.769	27.587	30.191	33.409	40.790
18	25.989	28.869	31.526	34.805	42.312
19	27.204	30.144	32.852	36.191	43.820
20	28.412	31.410	34.170	37.566	45.315
21	29.615	32.671	35.479	38.932	46.797
22	30.813	33.924	36.781	40.289	48.268
23	32.007	35.172	38.076	41.638	49.728
24	33.196	36.415	39.364	42.980	51.179
25	34.382	37.652	40.646	44.314	52.620
26	35.563	38.885	41.923	45.642	54.052
27	36.741	40.113	43.195	46.963	55.476
28	37.916	41.337	44.461	48.278	56.892
29	39.087	42.557	45.722	49.588	58.301
30	40.256	43.773	46.979	50.892	59.703

Note: To be statistically significant, the χ^2 calculated from the data must be equal to or greater than the value in the table.

Source: Engineering Statistics Handbook, http://www.itl.nist.gov/div898/handbook/eda/section3/eda3674.htm. Values for chi-square for 1–100 *df* are at this site.

TABLE C.4	Critical Values for *r*, the Pearson Product-Moment Correlation Coefficients

	α Levels (two-tailed test)			
	.10	.05	.02	.01
	α Levels (one-tailed test)			
df	.05	.025	.01	.005
1	.988	.997	.9995	.99988
2	.900	.950	.980	.990
3	.805	.878	.934	.959
4	.729	.811	.882	.917
5	.669	.755	.833	.875
6	.621	.707	.789	.834
7	.582	.666	.750	.798
8	.549	.632	.715	.765
9	.521	.602	.685	.735
10	.497	.576	.658	.708
11	.476	.553	.634	.684
12	.457	.532	.612	.661
13	.441	.514	.592	.641
14	.426	.497	.574	.623
15	.412	.482	.558	.606
16	.400	.468	.542	.590
17	.389	.456	.529	.575
18	.378	.444	.515	.561
19	.369	.433	.503	.549
20	.360	.423	.492	.537
21	.352	.413	.482	.526
22	.344	.404	.472	.515
23	.337	.396	.462	.505
24	.330	.388	.453	.496
25	.323	.381	.445	.487
26	.317	.374	.437	.479
27	.311	.367	.430	.471
28	.306	.361	.423	.463
29	.301	.355	.416	.456
30	.296	.349	.409	.449
32	.287	.339	.397	.436

(*continued*)

TABLE C.4	(continued)		
34	.279	.329	.386	.424
36	.271	.320	.376	.413
38	.264	.312	.367	.403
40	.257	.304	.358	.393
45	.243	.288	.338	.372
50	.231	.273	.322	.354
55	.220	.261	.307	.339
60	.211	.250	.295	.325
65	.203	.240	.284	.313
70	.195	.232	.274	.302
80	.183	.217	.257	.283
90	.173	.205	.242	.267
100	.164	.195	.230	.254

Note: To be statistically significant, the *r* obtained from the data must be equal to or greater than the table value.

Source: Calculated from *t* distribution values by Chris Spatz.

TABLE C.5 Critical Values for Tukey HSD Tests

$\alpha = .05$

Number of Levels of the Independent Variable

$df_{residual}$	2	3	4	5	6	7	8	9	10	11	12	13	14	15
1	17.97	26.98	32.82	37.07	40.41	43.12	45.40	47.36	49.07	50.59	51.96	53.20	54.33	55.36
2	6.08	8.33	9.80	10.88	11.74	12.44	13.03	13.54	13.99	14.39	14.75	15.08	15.38	15.65
3	4.50	5.91	6.82	7.50	8.04	8.48	8.85	9.18	9.46	9.72	9.95	10.15	10.35	10.53
4	3.93	5.04	5.76	6.29	6.71	7.05	7.35	7.60	7.33	8.03	8.21	8.37	8.52	8.66
5	3.64	4.60	5.22	5.67	6.03	6.33	6.58	6.80	7.00	7.17	7.32	7.47	7.60	7.72
6	3.46	4.34	4.90	5.31	5.63	5.90	6.12	6.32	6.49	6.65	6.79	6.92	7.03	7.14
7	3.34	4.16	4.68	5.06	5.36	5.61	5.82	6.00	6.16	6.30	6.43	6.55	6.66	6.76
8	3.26	4.04	4.53	4.89	5.17	5.40	5.60	5.77	5.92	6.05	6.18	6.29	6.39	6.48
9	3.20	3.95	4.42	4.76	5.02	5.24	5.43	5.60	5.74	5.87	5.98	6.09	6.19	6.28
10	3.15	3.88	4.33	4.65	4.91	5.12	5.30	5.46	5.60	5.72	5.83	5.94	6.03	6.11
11	3.11	3.82	4.26	4.57	4.82	5.03	5.20	5.35	5.49	5.60	5.71	5.81	5.90	5.98
12	3.08	3.77	4.20	4.51	4.75	4.95	5.12	5.26	5.40	5.51	5.62	5.71	5.79	5.88
13	3.06	3.74	4.15	4.45	4.69	4.88	5.05	5.19	5.32	5.43	5.53	5.63	5.71	5.79
14	3.03	3.70	4.11	4.41	4.64	4.83	4.99	5.13	5.25	5.36	5.46	5.55	5.64	5.71
15	3.01	3.67	4.08	4.37	4.60	4.78	4.94	5.08	5.20	5.31	5.40	5.49	5.57	5.65
16	3.00	3.65	4.05	4.33	4.56	4.74	4.90	5.03	5.15	5.26	5.35	5.44	5.52	5.59
17	2.98	3.63	4.02	4.30	4.52	4.70	4.86	4.99	5.11	5.21	5.31	5.39	5.47	5.54
18	2.97	3.61	4.00	4.28	4.50	4.67	4.82	4.96	5.07	5.17	5.27	5.35	5.43	5.50
19	2.96	3.59	3.98	4.25	4.47	4.64	4.79	4.92	5.04	5.14	5.23	5.32	5.39	5.46
20	2.95	3.58	3.96	4.23	4.44	4.62	4.77	4.90	5.01	5.11	5.20	5.28	5.36	5.43
24	2.92	3.53	3.90	4.17	4.37	4.54	4.68	4.81	4.92	5.01	5.10	5.18	5.25	5.32
30	2.89	3.49	3.84	4.10	4.30	4.46	4.60	4.72	4.82	4.92	5.00	5.08	5.15	5.21
40	2.86	3.44	3.79	4.04	4.23	4.39	4.52	4.64	4.74	4.82	4.90	4.98	5.04	5.11
60	2.83	3.40	3.74	3.98	4.16	4.31	4.44	4.55	4.65	4.73	4.81	4.88	4.94	5.00
120	2.80	3.36	3.69	3.92	4.10	4.24	4.36	4.47	4.56	4.64	4.71	4.78	4.84	4.90
∞	2.77	3.31	3.63	3.86	4.03	4.17	4.29	4.39	4.47	4.55	4.62	4.68	4.74	4.80

(continued)

TABLE C.5 (continued)

$\alpha = .01$

Number of Levels of the Independent Variable

$df_{residual}$	2	3	4	5	6	7	8	9	10	11	12	13	14	15
1	90.03	135.00	164.30	185.60	202.20	215.80	227.20	237.00	245.60	253.20	260.00	266.20	271.80	277.00
2	14.04	19.02	22.29	24.72	26.63	28.20	29.53	30.68	31.69	32.59	33.40	34.13	34.81	35.43
3	8.26	10.62	12.17	13.33	14.24	15.00	15.64	12.60	16.69	17.13	17.53	17.89	18.22	18.52
4	6.51	8.12	9.17	9.96	10.58	11.10	11.55	11.93	12.27	12.57	12.84	13.09	13.32	13.53
5	5.70	6.98	7.80	8.42	8.91	9.32	9.67	9.97	10.24	10.48	10.70	10.89	11.08	11.24
6	5.24	6.33	7.03	7.56	7.97	8.32	8.62	8.87	9.10	9.30	9.48	9.65	9.81	9.95
7	4.95	5.92	6.54	7.00	7.37	7.68	7.94	8.17	8.37	8.55	8.71	8.86	9.00	9.12
8	4.75	5.64	6.20	6.62	6.96	7.24	7.47	7.68	7.86	8.03	8.18	8.31	8.44	8.55
9	4.60	5.43	5.96	6.35	6.66	6.92	7.13	7.32	7.50	7.65	7.78	7.91	8.02	8.13
10	4.48	5.27	5.77	6.14	6.43	6.67	6.88	7.06	7.21	7.36	7.48	7.60	7.71	7.81
11	4.39	5.15	5.62	5.97	6.25	6.48	6.67	6.84	6.99	7.13	7.25	7.36	7.46	7.56
12	4.32	5.05	5.50	5.84	6.10	6.32	6.51	6.67	6.81	6.94	7.06	7.17	7.26	7.36
13	4.26	4.96	5.40	5.73	5.98	6.19	6.37	6.53	6.67	6.79	6.90	7.01	7.10	7.19
14	4.21	4.90	5.32	5.63	5.88	6.08	6.26	6.41	6.54	6.66	6.77	6.87	6.96	7.05
15	4.17	4.84	5.25	5.56	5.80	5.99	6.16	6.31	6.44	6.56	6.66	6.76	6.84	6.93
16	4.13	4.79	5.19	5.49	5.72	5.92	6.08	6.22	6.35	6.46	6.56	6.66	6.74	6.82
17	4.10	4.74	5.14	5.43	5.66	5.85	6.01	6.15	6.27	6.38	6.48	6.57	6.66	6.73
18	4.07	4.70	5.09	5.38	5.60	5.79	5.94	6.08	6.20	6.31	6.41	6.50	6.58	6.66
19	4.05	4.67	5.05	5.33	5.55	5.74	5.89	6.02	6.14	6.25	6.34	6.43	6.51	6.58
20	4.02	4.64	5.02	5.29	5.51	5.69	5.84	5.97	6.09	6.19	6.28	6.37	6.45	6.52
24	3.96	4.55	4.91	5.17	5.37	5.54	5.69	5.81	5.92	6.02	6.11	6.19	6.26	6.33
30	3.89	4.46	4.80	5.05	5.24	5.40	5.54	5.65	5.76	5.85	5.93	6.01	6.08	6.14
40	3.82	4.37	4.70	4.93	5.11	5.26	5.39	5.50	5.60	5.69	5.76	5.84	5.90	5.96
60	3.76	4.28	4.60	4.82	4.99	5.13	5.25	5.36	5.45	5.53	5.60	5.67	5.73	5.78
120	3.70	4.20	3.50	4.71	4.87	5.01	5.12	5.21	5.30	5.38	5.44	5.51	5.56	5.61
∞	3.64	4.12	4.40	4.60	4.76	4.88	4.99	5.08	5.16	5.23	5.29	5.35	5.40	5.45

Note: To be statistically significant, the HSD value calculated from the data must be equal to or greater than the value in the table.

Source: From "Tables of Range and Studentized Range," by H. L. Harter, 1960, *Annals of Mathematical Statistics, 31,* 1122–1147. Copyright © 1960 The Institute of Mathematical Statistics. Reprinted with permisson.

Glossary

AB design Design with a baseline (A) followed by a treatment (B).

ABA design Design with a baseline (A), followed by a treatment (B), and then restoration of the original condition (A).

abstract Short summary of a research article or the contents of a book.

alpha The probability that is the criterion for rejecting the null hypothesis.

alternative hypothesis A hypothesis that two variables are related or that two population means are not equal.

analysis of variance (ANOVA) NHST technique that partitions total variance into components associated with specific effects, such as main effects (means) and interactions.

appendix Supplementary material at the end of an article or book.

archival research Analysis of records that were obtained from archives.

archive A secure repository of records such as print, audio, video, or electronic material that might be cataloged for access.

author notes Notes that identify affiliation(s), financial support, acknowledgments, and possible conflicts of interest.

bar graph A graph of the frequency distribution of nominal or qualitative data.

baseline The situation before a treatment is applied.

between-subjects design Any research design in which participants contribute scores to only one level of the independent variable.

between-subjects factorial design Factorial experiment in which every independent variable is a between-subjects variable.

block counterbalancing The effects of an extraneous variable are balanced using several participants.

boxplot A graph that shows a distribution's range, interquartile range, skew, median, and sometimes other statistics.

camera ready Materials that do not require further editing or typesetting before publication.

carryover effect Occurs when the degree of responsiveness to a treatment depends on which other treatment preceded it.

case study Study of a single person or group without altering the situation.

categorical data Frequency counts of the events observed in designated categories.

ceiling effect Scores clustered near the maximum possible score prevent the detection of variables that raise scores.

central tendency Descriptive statistics that indicate a typical or representative score. Examples are mean, median, and mode.

chi-square test NHST technique that is appropriate for category data.

citation The author(s), publication date, title, journal or publisher, and pages of an article or book.

confederate Member of the research team who appears as a naïve participant but instead play a predetermined role.

confidence interval (CI)   Range of scores that is expected with a specified degree of confidence to capture a parameter.

confidence interval about a mean   A range of scores that is expected with a specified degree of confidence to include the population mean.

confidentiality   Requirement to keep research data about individual participants private.

confounded variable   Variable whose values change in step with changes in the independent variable.

constructivism   Rejects the ideal theory; proposes that science is just one of many approaches to knowledge.

content validity   Determined by the degree to which the test items represent the characteristic tested.

continuous variable   Variable that is theoretically infinitely divisible; for any two values, you can imagine an intermediate value.

control group   Generic name of the group in an experiment that does not receive a treatment.

controlled variable   An extraneous variable that does not vary in step with the independent variable.

convenience sample   A sample that was not obtained randomly from the population.

correlational research   Scientific research that predicts the outcome of one variable based on the scores of one or more other variables.

counterbalancing   A technique that orders the levels of an extraneous variable so that their effects balance out over the different levels of the independent variable.

criterion-related validity   Determined by the degree to which the test correlates with other measures of the same variable.

critical theory   Rejects the ideal theory; uses ethical principles as its main theoretical guide.

critical value   The number from a sampling distribution that determines whether the null hypothesis is rejected.

database   An organized collection of information.

debriefing   Explaining to participants the nature, results, and conclusions of the research they participated in and correcting any misconceptions.

deception   Deliberately misleading participants about any aspect of the research.

degrees of freedom   Concept used by mathematical statisticians to determine the sampling distribution that is appropriate for a set of data.

dependent variable (DV)   Variable that is expected to change as a result of changes in the independent variable.

descriptive statistics   Numbers or graphs that summarize a data set.

design   Part of a research plan that identifies the independent and dependent variables, tells how they are measured, and explains procedures for collecting data.

dichotomous variable   Variable that can have only two values.

differential attrition   An extraneous variable caused by a differential loss of participants from the levels of the independent variable in such a way as to bias the outcome.

diffusion of treatment   An extraneous variable that occurs when the conditions intended for only one group of participants are experienced by other groups.

discrete variable   Variable with a limited number of values; many intermediate values are not possible.

Discussion section   Research report section that evaluates and interprets results.

effect size index   The amount or degree of separation between two distributions.

electronic poster (e-poster)   Research report presented on a computer screen.

empirical frequency polygon   A frequency polygon of observed scores.

empiricism Philosophical and scientific approach to knowledge that uses unbiased observation to discover truths about the world.

erratum An error; *Errata* is the plural form.

error bar A line the length of which indicates degree of variability.

ethical codes Written or widely accepted prescriptions of proper behavior and morality.

experiment A comparison of two or more conditions in search of differences.

experimental group Generic name of the group in an experiment that receives a treatment.

experimental research Scientific research to compare two or more groups that received different treatments.

external validity Results can be generalized to other populations, situations, or conditions.

extraneous variable General term for a variable that varies concomitantly with the independent variable.

factorial design Research design with two or more independent variables. Each level of an independent variable occurs with every level of the other independent variable(s).

falsifiable Karl Popper's criterion for deciding the worth of a scientific theory. Falsifiable theories allow their predictions to be tested.

field A place in a database to store a particular type of information.

figure A graphical depiction such as a chart, photograph, drawing, or similar materials.

floor effect Scores clustered near the minimum possible score prevent the detection of variables that lower scores.

focus group interviews A small group of participants interact with each other and an interviewer who poses questions.

frequency distribution Arrangement of scores from the highest to the lowest with the frequency of each score shown.

frequency polygon A frequency distribution graph of a scaled variable with frequency points connected by lines.

geocentric model Model of the solar system in which the earth was in the center orbited by the sun, moon, the five planets, and surrounded by the stars.

Hawthorne effect A performance change when participants know they are being observed.

heliocentric model Model of the solar system in which the sun is the center and the planets orbit the sun.

histogram A graph of frequencies of a scaled variable constructed with contiguous vertical bars.

history An extraneous variable; events that occur during one treatment but not other treatments that affect the dependent variable.

hit A record that matches a set of search criteria.

ideal theory Traditional theory in physical science that creates generalizable models and laws from observations of the universe.

idealizing theory Modification of the ideal theory that creates models based on a few, core variables.

independent variable (IV) Variable whose values are controlled by the researcher.

inducements Cash, grades, or recognition prizes, to encourage or reward research participation.

inferential statistics Method of reaching conclusions using samples and probability.

informed consent Agreement, usually written, to participate in a study after being informed of the consequences of participation.

institutional review board (IRB) Group that reviews research proposals for ethical propriety.

instrument change An extraneous variable; a change in a measuring instrument (human judge, survey, or machine) during the course of an experiment.

interaction   NHST technique that determines if the effect of one independent variable on the dependent variable depends on the level of a second independent variable.

internal validity   No extraneous variables are confounded with the independent variable.

interobserver reliability   Method of detecting inconsistent measuring by comparing observations of two independent observers.

interquartile range   A range of scores that captures the 50% of a distribution that is between the 25th and 75th percentiles.

interval scale   Scale in which equal differences between measurements indicate equal differences in the thing measured.

intervention   A treatment designed to correct or prevent a problem or psychological disorder.

Introduction section   Research report section that introduces the background and purpose of the research.

law-oriented theory   Modification of the ideal theory that limits the universality of its theoretical constructs.

level of processing   Theory that the depth of processing during learning determines later recall.

levels   Values of the independent variable that the researcher chooses for an experiment.

line graph   A graph that shows the relationship between two variables with lines rather than bars.

literature   The entire collection of published research in a scientific discipline.

logistics   Planning and handling of all the details of a process or operation.

main effect   A factorial ANOVA NHST technique that determines if the sample means of an independent variable could have come from populations with identical means.

manuscript   A typewritten report or an electronic file of a research project.

matching   Creating groups of participants who have similar scores on a variable correlated with the dependent variable.

maturation   An extraneous variable; long-term or short-term changes in participants that affect the dependent variable.

mean   The arithmetic average; the sum of the scores divided by the number of scores.

median   The point that divides a distribution into equal halves; half the scores are above the median and half are below it; 50th percentile.

meta-analysis   A quantitative technique that summarizes the results of many studies of a single topic.

Method section   Research report section that describes how the research was conducted.

mixed-factorial design   Factorial design in which one or more independent variables are between-subjects variables and one or more are within-subjects variables.

mode   The score that occurs most frequently in a distribution.

moderator   Person who introduces speakers and keeps time at scientific meetings.

natural selection   Survival and reproduction of living things best suited to particular environments.

naturalistic observation   Individuals or groups are systematically observed in their natural habitat.

nominal scale   Measurement scale in which numbers or names serve as labels and do not indicate a numerical relationship.

normal curve   A mathematically defined, theoretical distribution with a particular bell shape. An empirical distribution of similar shape.

nuisance variable   A factor that causes the dependent variable scores to be more variable.

null hypothesis   Usually a hypothesis that there is no relationship or that population means are equal.

null hypothesis statistical testing (NHST) An inferential statistics technique that produces accurate probabilities about samples when the null hypothesis is true.

Nuremberg Code Ten recommendations about permissible medical research released after the Nuremberg Doctors' Trial.

one-group pretest–posttest design One group of participants receives a pretest, a treatment, and a posttest.

one-group two-treatment design One group of participants is measured in one condition and then in a second condition.

one-tailed test A statistical test to detect a difference in population means, either positive or negative but not both.

one-way ANOVA NHST technique for between-subjects multilevel experiments.

operational definition Procedures or operations used to measure a variable or establish a condition.

operator Terms that aid searching; *OR, AND, PRE/n, W/n,* and *AND NOT* are PsycINFO examples.

oral history Participants describe in person or in recorded interviews historical events they experienced.

ordinal scale Measurement scale in which numbers indicate rank order, but equal differences between numbers do not indicate equal differences between the thing measured.

outlier A score separated from others and 1.5 (*IQR*) beyond the 25th or 75th percentile.

paradigm A global viewpoint that determines which scientific questions are asked and the methods used to answer them.

participant observation Study of naturally occurring situations by researchers who are participants in the situation.

peer review Formal process in which scientists judge colleagues' work submitted for publication or funding.

phi An effect size index for categorical data.

pilot study A preliminary, abbreviated experiment to evaluate aspects of a planned experiment.

plagiarism The unintentional or intentional use of words or ideas of others without attribution.

population An entire set of scores.

poster session Presenting research to peers using a display board.

power The probability of correctly rejecting a false null hypothesis.

power analysis A statistical analysis that solves for one of the factors involved in rejecting a false null hypothesis with an NHST technique.

pretest sensitization Participants' scores are affected by a previous pretest.

prospectus A detailed plan for a research project; sometimes referred to as a *protocol.*

publish Recording of scientific results, methods, and theories to create a permanent knowledge base of science.

qualitative research Studies characterized by narrative results.

qualitative variable A variable whose values differ in kind rather than in amount.

quantitative research Studies characterized by numerical results.

quantitative variable A variable whose values indicate different numerical amounts.

quasi-experimental design Experimental design in which participants are assigned to levels of the independent variable according to a known characteristic.

quasi two-group pretest–posttest design Participants are not randomly assigned to two groups; each group is given a pretest and a posttest; one group receives a treatment between the tests.

random assignment Procedure that uses chance to assign participants, procedures, or materials to groups.

random assignment design Experimental design in which participants are randomly assigned to levels of the independent variable.

random error Variation in a data set that comes from uncontrolled variables that cannot be specified.

random sample A sample from a population obtained by applying a random sampling technique.

random two-group pretest–posttest design Participants are randomly assigned to two groups; each group is given a pretest and a posttest; one group receives a treatment between the tests.

range The highest score minus the lowest score.

ranked data Each observation is a rank score.

ratio scale Measurement scale with the characteristics of an interval scale plus the characteristic of a true zero; zero means that none of the thing measured is present.

raw data Research project data before calculation or analysis.

reactivity Participants' dependent variable scores are affected by the situation in which data are gathered.

record All database fields about an item such as an article or book.

references List of sources cited in a manuscript.

regression An extraneous variable; upon retesting, extreme scores produce a mean that is closer to the population mean.

rejection region The portion of a sampling distribution that includes sample data that are less probable than alpha (α).

reliability The consistency or dependability of a measure.

repeated-measures ANOVA NHST technique for within-subjects multilevel experiments.

repeated-measures design Within-subjects design in which the participants contribute dependent variable scores to every level of the independent variable.

replication Repeating an experiment with the same procedures or with planned changes in the procedures to confirm the original results.

reprints Facsimile reproductions of published articles provided by the publisher.

research hypothesis The researcher's expectation of what the data will show; often the alternative hypothesis.

research plan A description of the tasks required to complete a research project.

residual variance The variance in an ANOVA that remains after the variance that is associated with known causes is removed.

Results section Research report section that summarizes and analyzes data and statistics.

robust A statistical test that produces reasonably accurate probabilities even when the assumptions the test is based on are not fulfilled.

sample A subset of the population.

sampling distribution A theoretical distribution based on random sampling that shows probabilities of actual sample outcomes.

sampling fluctuation The chance differences between samples and the population the samples are from.

scaled data Numerical measurements that are not ranks.

scatterplot A graph of participants' scores on two variables.

science A method of inquiry that uses unbiased empirical observation, public methods, reproducible results, and theory to reveal universal truths about the universe.

search engine Computer program that allows users to search a database or the World Wide Web.

search term Word or phrase used in a search engine to find a record or URL.

selection An extraneous variable that occurs when participants for the different levels of the independent variable are not equivalent even before the treatment is administered.

sensitivity The ability of a test or measure to make distinctions.

simple counterbalancing The effects of an extraneous variable are balanced within the scores of one participant.

skewed Scores clustered at one end of a distribution.

social loafing Working less as a group member as compared to working alone.

Solomon four-group design Four groups are used to assess the independent variable and pretest sensitization.

split-half reliability Determining reliability by dividing a test in half and correlating the two part scores.

standard deviation A measure of the dispersion of scores around the mean of a distribution.

standard error of the mean Standard deviation of the sampling distribution of the mean.

statistical independence Two variables that, as their own levels change, do not produce changes in the other variable.

statistical sensitivity The degree to which a statistical test can detect a false null hypothesis.

statistically significant Sample data with a probability less than alpha (α).

structured interviews Interviews that are based on prepared questions that are the same for each interviewee.

systematic error Variation in a data set from causes that can be specified.

t distribution Sampling distribution used to determine probabilities for t tests.

table Numerical results displayed in tabular form.

testing An extraneous variable; change in a participant's score is the result of earlier participation in another part of the experiment.

test–retest reliability Determining reliability by administering a test a second time and correlating the two scores.

theoretical frequency polygon A frequency polygon of hypothesized scores.

theory The cognitive frameworks by which scientists understand the phenomena they study and guide them toward future research.

thesaurus A tool that provides words or phrases that are similar to the target word or phrase.

title page First page of a manuscript; includes title, author(s), affiliation(s), and running head.

treatment Values of the independent variable that the researcher chooses for an experiment.

two-tailed test A statistical test to detect a difference in population means, regardless of direction.

Type I error Rejecting the null hypothesis when it is true.

Type II error Retaining the null hypothesis when it is false.

unstructured interviews Interviews based on questions that vary among interviewees.

URL Uniform resource locator; a Web address that consists of a protocol such as *http* or *ftp* and a domain name.

validity The extent to which a test measures what it claims to measure.

within-subjects design A research design in which participants' scores are matched or paired on the basis of a similarity other than the independent or dependent variable.

within-subjects factorial design Factorial experiment in which every independent variable is a within-subjects variable.

z score Score expressed in standard deviation units.

References

ACT (1997). *ACT assessment technical manual.* Iowa City, IA: Author.

Allen, I. L. (1983). *The language of ethnic conflict: Social organization and lexical culture.* New York: Columbia University Press.

Amato, P. R. (1989). Who cares for children in public places: Naturalistic observation of male and female caretakers. *Journal of Marriage and Family, 51,* 981–990.

American Psychiatric Association. (1994). *Diagnostic and statistical manual of mental disorders* (4th ed.). Washington, DC: Author.

American Psychological Association. (n.d.) *Task force on statistical inference initial report.* Retrieved November 8, 2006 from http://www.apa.org/science/tfsi.html

American Psychological Association. (2001). *Publication Manual of the American Psychological Association* (5th ed.). Washington, DC: Author.

American Psychological Association. (2002). *Ethical Principles of Psychologists and Code of Conduct.* Washington, DC: Author.

American Psychological Association (2004). *Poster instructions.* Available from the American Psychological Association, Convention Office, 750 First street, NE, Washington. DC. 20002–4242.

American Psychological Association. (2005). *Concise rules of APA style.* Washington, DC: Author.

American Psychological Association. (n.d.) *Guidelines for ethical conduct in the care and use of animals.* Retrieved September 8, 2006 from http://www.apa.org/science/anguide.html

Anderson, S., & Berridge, V. (2000). Opium in 20th-century Britain: Pharmacists, regulation and the people. *Addiction, 95,* 23–47.

Anthony, T., Copper, C., & Mullen, B. (1992). Cross-racial facial identification: A social cognitive integration. *Personality and Social Psychology Bulletin, 18,* 296–301.

Anthrax vaccinations allowed to resume. (2005, April 8). *The Washington Post,* p. A08.

Aron, A., Aron, E. N., & Coups, E. J. (2006). *Statistics for psychology* (4th ed.). Upper Saddle River, NJ: Prentice Hall.

Babbie, E. (2007). *The practice of social research* (11th ed.). Belmont, CA: Wadsworth.

Baddeley, A. D., & Woodhead, M. (1982). Depth of processing, context, and face recognition. *Canadian Journal of Psychology, 36,* 148–164.

Bailey, J. M. (2003). *The man who would be queen: The science of gender-bending and transsexualism.* Washington, DC: Joseph Henry Press.

Barber-Parker, E. D. (2002). Integrating patient teaching into bedside care: A participant-observation study of hospital nurses. *Patient Education and Counseling, 48,* 107–113.

Baumrind, D. (1964). Some thoughts on ethics of research: After reading Milgram's "Behavioral study of obedience." *American Psychologist, 19,* 421–423.

Beck, A. T., Steer, R. A., & Gabin, M. G. (1988). Psychometric properties of the Beck Depression Inventory: Twenty-five years of evaluuation. *Clinical Psychology Review, 8,* 77–100.

Berg, B. L. (2001). *Qualitative research methods for the social sciences* (4th ed.). Needham Heights, MA: Allyn & Bacon.

Bernstein, I. H. (1988). *Applied multivariate analysis.* New York: Springer-Verlag.

Blewett, D. T., Lucey, P. G., Hawke, B. R., & Jolliff, B. L. (1997). Clementine images of the lunar sample-return stations: Refinement of the FeO and TiO$_2$ mapping techniques. *Journal of Geophysical Research, 102,* 16,319–16,325.

Bloom, L. C., & Mudd, S. A. (1991). Depth of processing approach to face recognition: A test of two theories. *Journal of Experimental Psychology: Learning, Memory, and Cognition, 17,* 556–565.

Boehner, C., & Howe, S. (1996, June). *Statistical graphics in psychological research*. Poster session at annual meeting of American Psychological Society, San Francisco, CA.

Bolton, P. A. (2002, June 10). Scientific ethics. In *Managing science as a public good: Overseeing publicly funded science* (chap. 16). Retrieved November 8, 2006, from www.bccmeteorites.com/Ch%2016%20Scientific%20Ethics%2006.10.02.pdf

Bower, G. H., & Karlin, M. B. (1974). Depth of processing pictures of faces and recognition memory. *Journal of Experimental Psychology, 103,* 751–757.

Brewer, C. L. (1982, August). *Gladly learn and gladly teach*. Paper presented at the annual meeting of the American Psychological Association, Washington, DC.

Broeder, A. (1998). Deception can be acceptable. *American Psychologist, 53,* 805–806.

Brown v. Board of Educ., 347 U.S. 483 (1954).

Bruning, J. K., Polinko, N. K., Zerbst, J. I., & Buckingham, J. T. (2000). The effect on expected job success of the connotative meanings of names and nicknames. *Journal of Social Psychology, 140,* 197–201.

Cameron, J. (1999). *The right to write: An invitation and initiation to the writing life*. Los Angeles: J. P. Tarcher.

Campbell, D. T. (1957). Factors relevant to the validity of experiments in social settings. *Psychological Bulletin, 54,* 297–312.

Campbell, D. T., & Stanley, J. C. (1966). *Experimental and quasi-experimental designs for research*. Chicago: Rand-McNally.

Campbell, E., & Jones, G. (2002). Sources of stress experienced by elite male wheelchair basketball players. *Adapted Physical Activity Quarterly, 19,* 82–100.

Cannon, W. B., & Washburn, A. L. (1912). An explanation of hunger. *American Journal of Physiology, 29,* 441–454.

Chance, J. E., & Goldstein, A. G. (1981). Depth of processing in response to own— and other—race faces. *Personality and Social Psychology Bulletin, 7,* 475–480.

Cipolat, U. (2004). Nuclear weapons exact a terrible price. Retrieved November 8, 2006 from http://www.wagingpeace.org/articles/2004/05/06_cipolat_weapons-price.htm

Clark, K. B., & Clark, M. K. (1940). Skin color as a factor in racial identification of Negro preschool children: A preliminary report. *Journal of Experimental Education, 8,* 161–163.

Cleveland, W. S., & McGill, R. (1985). Graphical perception and graphical methods for analyzing scientific data. *Science, 229,* 828–833.

Cohen, B. C. (n.d.). *The ethics of using medical data from Nazi experiments*. Retrieved November 8, 2006, from http://www.jlaw.com/Articles/NaziMedEx.html

Cohen, J. (1969). *Statistical power analysis for the behavioral sciences*. New York: Academic Press.

Cohen, J. (1992). A power primer. *Psychological Bulletin, 112,* 155–159.

Cohen, R. J., & Swerdlik, M. E. (2005). *Psychological testing and assessment: An introduction to tests and measurement* (6th ed.). New York: McGraw-Hill.

Coin, C., & Tiberghien, G. (1997). Encoding activity and face recognition. *Memory, 5,* 545–568.

Coles, P. (1999). *Einstein and the total eclipse*. Icon Books: Cambridge, UK.

Craik, F. I., & Lockhart, R. S. (1972). Levels of processing: A framework for memory research. *Journal of Verbal Learning and Verbal Behavior, 11,* 671–684.

Cronbach, L. J., & Gleser, G. C. (1965). *Psychological tests and personnel decisions* (2nd ed.). Urbana: University of Illinois Press.

Crook, L. S., & Dean, M. C. (1999a). Logical fallacies and ethical breaches. *Ethics & Behavior, 9,* 61–68.

Crook, L. S., & Dean, M. C. (1999b). "Lost in a shopping mall"—A breach of professional ethics. *Ethics & Behavior, 9,* 39–50.

Cumming, G., & Finch, S. (2005). Inference by eye: Confidence intervals and how to read pictures of data. *American Psychologist, 60,* 170–180.

Darwin, C. (1859). *On the origin of species by means of natural selection*. London: John Murray.

DeDe, G., Parris, D., & Waters, G. (2003). Teaching self-cues: A treatment approach for verbal naming. *Aphasiology, 17,* 465–480.

Demaray, M. K., Elting, J., & Schaefer, K. (2003). Assessment of Attention-Deficit/Hyperactivity Disorder (ADHD): A comparative evaluation of five, commonly used, published rating scales. *Psychology in the Schools, 40,* 341–361.

Devine, D. J., Clayton, L. D., Dunford, B. B., Seying, R., & Pryce, J. (2001). Jury decision making: 45 years of empirical research on deliberating groups. *Psychology, Public Policy, and Law, 7,* 622–727.

Dewey, K. L. (1996). An insider's view into the review process. *Psi Chi Journal of Undergraduate Research, 1,* 51–52.

Diener, E., Emmons, R. A., Larsen, R. J., & Griffin, S. (1985). The Satisfaction With Life Scale. *Journal of Personality Assessment, 49,* 71–75.

Diener, E., Oishi, S., & Lucas, R. E. (2003). Personality, culture, and subjective well-being: Emotional and cognitive evaluations of life. *Annual Review of Psychology, 54,* 403–425.

Diener, E., & Seligman, M. E. P. (2004). Beyond money: Toward an economy of well-being. *Psychological Science in the Public Interest, 5,* 1–31.

Dillon, K. M. (1999). I am 95% confident that the earth is round: An interview about statistics with Chris Spatz. *Teaching of Psychology, 26,* 232–234.

Dukes, W. F. (1965). $N = 1$. *Psychological Bulletin, 64,* 74–79.

Dunston, P., & Ross, S. (1986). Deception in psychological research: A continuing problem. *Perceptual and Motor Skills, 62,* 290.

English, J. B. (2002). *Subjective sleep quality and dream type in perimenopausal women.* Dissertation, University of Arkansas for Medical Sciences. Little Rock, AR.

Eysenck, H. J. (1952). The effects of psychotherapy: An evaluation. *Journal of Consulting Psychology 16,* 319–324.

Fabrega, H. (2004). Culture and formulations of homicide: Two case studies. *Psychiatry: Interpersonal and Biological Processes, 67,* 178–196.

Fallis, R. K., & Opotow, S. (2003). Are students failing school or are schools failing students? Class cutting in high school. *Journal of Social Issues, 59,* 103–120.

Feldman, H. M. (2001). Attention-deficit/hyperactivity disorder. In N. J. Smelser & P. B. Baltes (Eds.), *International encyclopedia of social & behavioral sciences* (Vol. 2, pp. 871–875). Oxford: Elsevier.

Feyerabend, P. (1975). *Against method.* London: New Left Books.

Files, J. (2004, December 19). Defense dept. asks to resume anthrax shots. *The New York Times,* Section 1, p. 36.

Fischer, J., & Corcoran, K. (2000a). *Measures for clinical practice: A sourcebook: Adults.* (3rd ed.). New York: Simon & Schuster.

Fischer, J., & Corcoran, K. (2000b). *Measures for clinical practice: A sourcebook: Couples, families and children.* (3rd ed.). New York: Simon & Schuster.

Fleeson, W., Malanos, A. B., & Achille, N. M. (2002). An intraindividual process approach to the relationship between extraversion and positive affect: Is acting extraverted as "good" as being extraverted? *Journal of Personality and Social Psychology, 83,* 1409–1422.

Folkman, S., Lazarus, R. S., Dunkel-Schetter, C., DeLongis, A., & Gruen, R. (1986). Dynamics of a stressful encounter: Cognitive appraisal, coping, and encounter outcomes. *Journal of Personality and Social Psychology, 50,* 992–1003.

Ford-Martin, P. A. (2006). Fatigue. In J. L. Longe (Ed.) *The Gale encyclopedia of medicine* (3rd ed.). Farmington Hills, MI: Thomson Gale.

Foxhall, K. (2000). Suddenly, a big impact on criminal justice. *Monitor on Psychology, 31.* Retrieved September 8, 2006 from http://www.apa.org/monitor/jan00/pi4.html

Frahm, M. J. (2002). Effects of mental imagery, physical practice, and achievement motivation on sport performance. *Journal of Psychological Inquiry, 7,* 7–12.

Francis, L. J. (1993). Reliability and validity of a short scale of attitude towards Christianity among adults. *Psychological Reports, 72,* 615–618.

Freedman, D., Pisani, R., & Purves, R. K. (2007). *Statistics* (4th ed.). New York: Norton.

Gilligan, C. (1982). *In a different voice.* Cambridge, MA: Harvard University Press.

Glass, G. V. (1976). Primary, secondary, and meta-analysis of research. *Educational Researcher, 5,* 3–8.

Goldstein, M., & Goldstein, I. F. (1978). *How we know: An exploration of the scientific process.* New York: Plenum Press.

Goodall, J. V. (1971). *In the shadow of man.* Boston: Houghton Mifflin.

Gould, S. J. (1989, July 30). Judging the perils of official hostility to scientific error. *The New York Times,* p. E6.

Graham, K., & Wells, S. (2001). Aggression among young adults in the context of the bar. *Addiction Research & Theory, 9,* 193–219.

Gravetter, F. J., & Wallnau, L. B. (2007). *Statistics for the behavioral sciences* (7th ed.). Belmont, CA: Wadsworth/Thomson Learning.

Groner, J. (1992). *Hilary's trial: The Elizabeth Morgan case.* New York: Simon & Schuster.

Hacking, I. (1984). Trial by number. *Science, 84 (5),* 69–70.

Harlow, L. L., Mulaik, S. A., & Steiger, J. H. (1997). *What if there were no significance tests?* Mahwah, NJ: Erlbaum.

Hawking, S. (1988). *A brief history of time.* New York: Bantam.

Hemphill, J. F. (2003). Interpreting the magnitudes of correlation coefficients. *American Psychologist, 58,* 78–79.

Hendricks, M. (1996, April). Do unto yourself. *Johns Hopkins Magazine,* 14–19.

Henman, L. D. (2001). Humor as a coping mechanism: Lessons from POWs. *Humor: The International Journal of Humor Research, 14,* 83–95.

Herek, G. M. (1988). Heterosexuals' attitudes toward lesbians and gay men: Correlates and gender differences. *Journal of Sex Research, 25,* 451–477.

Hogan, T. P., & Evalenko, K. (2006). The elusive definition of outliers in introductory statistics textbooks for behavioral sciences. *Teaching of Psychology,* in press.

Horgan, J. (1996). *The end of science.* New York: Addison-Wesley.

Howell, D. C. (2007). *Statistical methods for psychology* (6th ed.). Pacific Grove, CA: Thomson Wadsworth.

Howell, D. C. (2004). *Fundamental statistics for the behavioral sciences* (5th ed.). Belmont, CA: Brooks/Cole, Thomson Learning.

Jackson, S. M., & Cram, F. (2003). Disrupting the sexual double standard: Young women's talk about heterosexuality. *British Journal of Social Psychology, 42,* 113–128.

Jaffee, S., & Hyde, J. S. (2000). Gender differences in moral orientation: A meta-analysis. *Psychological Bulletin, 126,* 703–726.

Johnson, M. E. (1998). Being restrained: A study of power and powerlessness. *Issues in Mental Health Nursing, 19,* 191–217.

Johnson, R. C., McClearn, G. E., Yuen, S., Nagoshi, C. T., Ahern, F. M., & Cole, R. E. (1985). Galton's data a century later. *American Psychologist, 40,* 875–892.

Judge halts forcing of anthrax shots. (2004, October 28). *The New York Times,* p. A20.

Jurica, B., Alanis, K., & Ogletree, S. (2002). Sex differences related to video arcade game behavior. *Psi Chi Journal of Undergraduate Research, 7,* 145–148.

Kallgren, C. A., & Tauber, R. T. (1996). Undergraduate research and the institutional review board: A mismatch or happy marriage? *Teaching of Psychology, 23,* 518–537.

Kantowitz, B. H., Roediger, H. L., & Elmes, D. G. (2005). *Experimental psychology: Understanding psychological research* (8th ed.). Belmont, CA: Wadsworth.

Keith-Spiegel, P., Aronson, K., & Bowman, M. (1994). *Scientific misconduct: An annotated bibliography.* Retrieved November 8, 2006, from http://www.lemoyne.edu/OTRP/otrpresources/otrp_sci-misc.html

Kennedy, C. H. (2004). Recent innovations in single-case designs. *Journal of Behavioral Education, 13,* 209–211.

Keselman, H. J. (2005). Sphericity test. In B. S. Everitt & D. C. Howell (Eds.), *Encyclopedia of statistics in behavioral science* (pp. 1888–1890). West Sussex UK: Wiley.

Keselman, H. J., Othman, A. R., Wilcox, R. R., & Fradette, K. (2004). The new and improved two-sample *t* test. *Psychological Science, 15,* 47–51.

Killeen, P. R. (2005). An alternative to null-hypothesis significance tests. *Psychological Science, 16,* 345–353.

Kimmel, A. J. (1998). In defense of deception. *American Psychologist, 53,* 803–805.

Kirk, R. E. (1995). *Experimental design: Procedures for the behavioral sciences* (3rd ed.). Pacific Grove, CA: Thompson Wadsworth.

Kirk, R. E. (1999). *Statistics: An introduction* (4th ed.). Fort Worth, TX: Harcourt Brace.

Kirk, R. E. (2001). Promoting good statistical practices: Some suggestions. *Educational and Psychological Measurement, 61,* 213–218.

Kirk, R. E. (2005). Effect size measures. In B. S. Everitt & D. C. Howell (Eds.), *Encyclopedia of statistics in behavioral science* (pp. 532–542). West Sussex UK: Wiley.

Kohlberg, L. (1969). Stage and sequence: The cognitive-developmental approach to socialization. In D. A. Goslin (Ed.), *Handbook of socialization theory and research* (pp. 347–480). Chicago: Rand McNally.

Korn, J. H. (1998). The reality of deception. *American Psychologist, 53,* 805.

Kuhn, T. (1962). *The structure of scientific revolutions.* Chicago: University of Chicago Press.

Landis, C. (1924). Studies of emotional reactions II: General behavior and facial expression. *Journal of Comparative Psychology, 4,* 447–509.

Lê Cook, B. L., Wayne, G. F., Keithly, L., & Connolly, G. (2003). One size does not fit all: How the tobacco industry has altered cigarette design to target consumer groups with specific psychological and social needs. *Addiction, 98,* 1547–1562.

Lifton, R. J. (1986). Reflections on genocide. *Psychohistory Review, 14,* 39–54.

Light, L. L., Kayra-Stuart, F., & Hollander, S. (1979). Recognition memory for typical and unusual faces. *Journal of Experimental Psychology: Human Learning and Memory, 5,* 212–228.

Lipsey, M. W., & Wilson, D. B. (2001). *Practical meta-analysis.* Thousand Oaks, CA: Sage.

Loftus, E. F. (1993). The reality of repressed memories. *American Psychologist, 48,* 518–537.

Loftus, E. F. (1997). Creating childhood memories. *Applied Cognitive Psychology, 2,* S75–S86.

Loftus, E. F. (1999). Lost in the mall: Misrepresentations and misunderstandings. *Ethics & Behavior, 9,* 51–60.

Loftus, E. F., & Pickrell, J. E. (1995). The formation of false memories. *Psychiatric Annals, 25,* 720–725.

Lyubomirsky, S. (1999). A measure of subjective *happiness:* Preliminary reliability and construct validation. *Social Indicators Research, 46,* 137–155.

Mallen, M. J., Day, S. X., & Green, M. A. (2003). Online versus face-to-face conversation: An examination of relational and discourse variables. *Psychotherapy: Theory, Research, Practice, Training, 40,* 155–163.

Martin, B. (1994). Plagiarism: A misplaced emphasis. *Journal of Information Ethics, 3,* 36–47.

Mayo, E. (1946). *The human problems of an industrial civilization.* Boston: Harvard University Press.

McGaha, A. C., & Korn, J. H. (1995). The emergence of interest in the ethics of psychological research with humans. *Ethics & Behavior, 5,* 147–159.

McKelvie, S. J. (1985). Effect of depth of processing on recognition memory for normal and inverted photographs of faces. *Perceptual and Motor Skills, 60,* 503–508.

McKenna, R. J. (1995). *The undergraduate researcher's handbook: Creative experimentation in social psychology.* Boston: Allyn & Bacon.

McNair, D. M., Lorr, M., & Droppleman, L. F. (1992). *Profile of Mood States (POMS) Manual.* San Diego, CA: Educational and Industrial Testing Service.

Mehrabian, A. U. (1968). Male and female scales of the tendency to achieve. *Educational and Psychological Measurement, 28,* 493–502.

Michell, J. (2004). The place of qualitative research in psychology. *Qualitative Research in Psychology, 1,* 307–319.

Milgram, S. (1963). Behavioral study of obedience. *Journal of Abnormal and Social Psychology, 67,* 371–378.

Milgram, S. (1964). Issues in the study of obedience: A reply to Baumrind. *American Psychologist, 19,* 848–852.

Miller, G. A. (1969). Psychology as a means of promoting human welfare. *American Psychologist, 24,* 1063–1075.

Miller, J. M., & Peden. B. F. (2003). Complexity and degree of tempo modulation as factors in productivity. *Psi Chi Journal of Undergraduate Research, 8,* 21–27.

Miller, M. B., Kingstone, A., & Gazzaniga, M. S. (2002). Hemispheric encoding asymmetry is more apparent than real. *Journal of Cognitive Neuroscience, 14,* 702–708.

Mjøset, L. (2001). Theories: Conceptions in the social sciences. In N. J. Smelser & P. B. Baltes, (Eds.), *International encyclopedia of social & behavioral sciences, 23,* 15,641–15,647.

Mook, D. G. (2003). In defense of external invalidity. In A. E. Kazdin (Ed.), *Methodological issues & strategies in clinical research* (3rd ed.) (pp. 109–125). Washington, DC: American Psychological Association.

Morgan, J. E. (1996). Types of dissociative behaviors observed in an urban jail: 25 months of participant observation. *Progress in the Dissociative Disorders, 9,* 89–97.

Morin, L., & Latham, G. P. (2000). The effect of mental practice and goal setting as a transfer of training intervention on supervisors' self-efficacy and communication skills: An exploratory study. *Applied Psychology: An International Review, 49,* 566–578.

Mueller, J. H., Bailis, K. L., & Goldstein, A. G. (1979). Depth of processing and anxiety in facial recognition. *British Journal of Psychology, 70,* 511–515.

Mullen, B. (2001). Ethnophaulisms for ethnic immigrant groups. *Journal of Social Issues, 57,* 457–476.

Mulvey, P. W., Bowles-Sperry, L., & Klein, H. J. (1998). The effects of perceived loafing and defensive impression management on group effectiveness. *Small Group Research, 29,* 394–415.

Murphy, K. R., & Davidshofer, C. O. (2005). *Psychological testing: Principles and applications* (6th ed.). Upper Saddle River, NJ: Prentice Hall.

Murphy, K. R., & Myors, B. (2004). *Statistical power analysis* (2nd ed.). Mahwah, NJ: Lawrence Erlbaum.

Murray, B. (2002a). Keeping plagiarism at bay in the Internet. *Monitor on Psychology, 33.* Retrieved August 18, 2006 from http://www.apa.org/monitor/feb02/plagiarism.html

Murray, B. (2002b). Research fraud needn't happen at all. *Monitor on Psychology, 33.* Retrieved August 18, 2006 from http://www.apa.org/monitor/feb02/fraud.html

Nation, M., Crusto, C., Wandersman, A., Kumpfer, K. L., Seybolt, D., Morrissey-Kane, E., et al. (2003). What works in prevention: Principles of effective prevention programs. *American Psychologist, 58,* 449–456.

Nice, S., Garland, C. H., Hilton, S., Baggett, J., & Mitchell, M. (1996). Long-term outcomes and medical effects of torture among US Navy prisoners of war in Vietnam. *Journal of the American Medical Association, 276,* 375–381.

Nickerson, R. S. (2000). Null hypothesis statistical testing: A review of an old and continuing controversy. *Psychological Methods, 5,* 241–301.

Nicks, S. D., Korn, J. H., & Mainieri, T. (1997). The rise and fall of deception in social psychology and personality research, 1921 to 1994. *Ethics & Behavior, 71,* 69–77.

Nicol, A. A. M., & Pexman, P. M. (2003). *Displaying your findings: A practical guide for creating figures, posters, and presentations.* Washington, DC: American Psychological Association.

Nissen, H. W. (1931). A field study of the chimpanzee. *Comparative Psychology Monographs, 8,* vi–122.

Onghena, P. (2005). Single-case designs. In B. S. Everitt & D. C. Howell (Eds.), *Encyclopedia of statistics in behavioral science* (pp. 1850–1854). West Sussex UK: Wiley.

Ortmann, A., & Hertwig, R. (1998). The question remains: Is deception acceptable? *American Psychologist, 53,* 806–807.

O'Sullivan, C. S., & Durso, F. T. (1984). Effect of schema-incongruent information on memory for stereotypical attributes. *Journal of Personality and Social Psychology, 47,* 55–70.

O'Toole, K. (1997, January 8). The Stanford prison experiment: Still powerful after all of these years. *Stanford News,* p. 30.

Parker, K. C. H., Hanson, R. K., & Hunsley, J. (1988). MMPI, Rorschach, and WAIS: A meta-analytic comparison of reliability, stability, and validity. *Psychological Bulletin, 103,* 367–373.

Pagano, R. R. (2007). *Understanding statistics in the behavioral sciences* (8th ed.). Belmont, CA: Wadsworth/Thomson Learning.

Patton, M. Q. (2005). *Qualitative evaluation and research methods* (3rd ed.). Newbury Park, CA: Sage.

Pavot, W., & Diener, E. (1993). Review of the Satisfaction With Life Scale. *Psychological Assessment, 5,* 164–172.

Peden, B. F., & Hausmann, S. E. (2000). Data graphs in introductory and upper-level psychology textbooks: A content analysis. *Teaching of Psychology, 27,* 93–97.

Pedhazur, E. J., & Schmelkin, L. P. (1991). *Measurement, design, and analysis: An integrated approach.* Hillsdale, NJ: Lawrence Erlbaum.

Pinel, P. (1806). *A treatise on insanity.* London: Messers, Cadell & Davies, Strand.

Pittenger, D. J. (1995). Teaching students about graphs. *Teaching of Psychology, 22,* 125–128.

Quinn, J. F. (1987). Sex roles and hedonism among members of "outlaw" motorcycle clubs. *Deviant Behavior, 8,* 47–63.

Rewey, K. L. (1996). An insider's view into the review process. *Psi Chi Journal of Undergraduate Research, 1*. Retrieved September 8, 2006 from http://www.psichi.org/pubs/articles/article_321.asp

Robinson, J. P., Shaver, P. R., & Wrightsman, L. S. (1991). *Measures of personality and social psychological attitudes.* New York: Academic Press.

Rosenhan, D. L. (1973). On being sane in insane places. *Science, 179,* 250–258.

Rosenthal, R. (1994). Science and ethics in conducting, analyzing, and reporting psychological research. *Psychological Science, 5,* 127–134.

Rosnow, R. L., & Rosenthal, R. (1989). Statistical procedures and the justification of knowledge in psychological science. *American Psychologist, 44,* 1276–1284.

Rosnow, R. L., & Rosenthal, R. (2005). *Beginning behavioral research: A conceptual primer* (5th ed.). Upper Saddle River, NJ: Prentice Hall.

Roszak, T. (1975). *Unfinished animal.* New York: Harper & Row.

Runyon, R. P., Coleman, K. A., & Pittenger, D. J. (2000). *Fundamentals of behavioral statistics* (9th ed.). Boston: McGraw-Hill.

Saville, B. K., & Buskist, W. (2003). Traditional idiographic approaches: Small-*N* research designs. In S. F. Davis (Ed.), *Handbook of research methods in experimental psychology.* Malden, MA: Blackwell.

Schaffer, J., & Pritchard, M. (2003). Impact of stress on health and coping tactics in relation to sex. *Psi Chi Journal of Undergraduate Research, 8,* 12–20.

Scheier, M. F., Carver, C. S., & Bridges, M. W. (1994). Distinguishing optimism from neuroticism (and trait anxiety, self-mastery, and self-esteem): A reevaluation of the Life Orientation Test. *Journal of Personality and Social Psychology, 67,* 1063–1078.

Serbin, L. A., Tonick, I. J., & Sternglanz, S. H. (1977). Shaping cooperative cross-sex play. *Child Development, 48,* 924–929.

Shapiro, P. N., & Penrod, S. (1986). Meta-analysis of facial identification studies. *Psychological Bulletin, 100,* 139–156.

Shore, E. G. (1995). Effectiveness of research guidelines in prevention of scientific misconduct. *Science and Engineering Ethics, 1,* 383–387.

Sidebotham, P. (2001). Culture, stress and the parent–child relationship: A qualitative study of parents' perceptions of parenting. *Child: Care, Health and Development, 27,* 469–486.

Sieber, J. E. (1991). Openness in the social sciences: Sharing data. *Ethics & Behavior, 1,* 69–86.

Sieber, J. E., Iannuzzo, R., & Rodriguez, B. (1995). Deception methods in psychology: Have they changed in 23 years? *Ethics & Behavior, 5,* 67–85.

Silverman, D. (2004). *Qualitative research: Theory, method, practice* (2nd ed.). Thousand Oaks, CA: Sage.

Smith, M. L., & Glass, G. V. (1977). Meta-analysis of psychotherapy outcome studies. *American Psychologist, 32,* 752–760.

Spatz, C. (2000, November–December). Our changing statistical methods: Controversies about the null hypothesis. *Psychology Teacher Network,* 3–4.

Spatz, C. (2005). *Basic statistics: Tales of distributions* (8th ed.). Belmont, CA: Wadsworth/Thomson Learning.

Spatz, C. (2008). *Basic statistics: Tales of distributions* (9th ed.). Belmont, CA: Thomson Wadsworth.

Sporer, S. L. (1991). Deep—deeper—deepest? Encoding strategies and the recognition of human faces. *Journal of Experimental Psychology: Learning, Memory, and Cognition, 17,* 323–333.

Sternberg, R. J. (1997). The concept of intelligence and its role in lifelong learning and success. *American Psychologist, 52,* 1030–1037.

Sternberg, R. J., & Grigorenko, E. L. (2001). Unified psychology. *American Psychologist, 56,* 1069–1079.

Stevens, S. S. (1946). On the theory of scales of measurement. *Science, 103,* 677–680.

Stice, E., & Shaw, H. (2004). Eating disorder prevention programs: A meta-analytic review. *Psychological Bulletin, 130,* 206–227.

Suedfeld, P., Krell, R., Wiebe, R. E., & Steel, G. D. (1997). Coping strategies in the narratives of Holocaust survivors. *Anxiety, Stress, & Coping, 10,* 153–180.

Sun, M. (1988). EPA bars use of Nazi data. *Science, 240*(4848), 21.

Szuchman, L. T. (2005). *Writing with style: APA style made easy* (3rd ed.). Belmont, CA: Thomson/Wadsworth.

Terry, R. L. (1993). How wearing eyeglasses affects facial recognition. *Current Psychology:*

Developmental, Learning, Personality, Social, 12, 151–162.

Thomas, S. B., & Quinn, S. C. (1991). The Tuskegee Syphilis Study, 1932 to 1972: Implications for HIV education and AIDS risk education programs in the Black community. *American Journal of Public Health, 81,* 1498–1505.

Triplett, N. (1898). The dynamogenic factors in pacemaking and competition. *American Journal of Psychology, 9,* 507–533.

Tufte, E. R. (2001). *The visual display of quantitative information* (2nd ed.). Cheshire, CT: Graphics Press.

Tukey, J. W. (1972). Some graphic and semigraphic displays. In T. A. Bancroft (Ed.), *Statistical papers in honor of George W. Snedecor.* Ames: Iowa State University Press.

Tuthill, K. (2003). John Snow and the Broad Street pump. *Cricket Magazine, 31*(3), 23–31.

U.S. Department of Health and Human Services. (2005). *Code of federal regulations: Protection of human subjects, Part 46.* Retrieved September 8, 2006 from http://www.hhs.gov/ohrp/humansubjects/guidance/45cfr46.htm

van Gelder, L. (1996, June 19). Thomas Kuhn, 73; devised science paradigm. *The New York Times,* p. B7.

Vitiello, M. V., Prinz, P. N., & Schwartz R. S. (1994). The slow wave sleep of healthy older men and women is enhanced with improved aerobic fitness. *Journal of Sleep Research, 3* (Suppl. 1), 270.

Voss, David (1999, March). Whatever happened to cold fusion? *Physics World, March.* Retrieved September 8, 2006 from http://physicsweb.org/article/world/12/3/8

Wainer, H., & Velleman, P. F. (2001). Statistical graphics: Mapping the pathways of science. *Annual Review of Psychology, 52,* 305–335.

Walker-Hill, R. (2000). *An analysis of the relationship of human sexuality knowledge, self-esteem, and body image to sexual satisfaction in college and university students.* Dissertation, University of Tennessee, Knoxville.

Watson, J. B., & Rayner, R. (1920). Conditioned emotional reactions. *Journal of Experimental Psychology, 3,* 1–14.

Weissberg, R. P., Kumpfer, K. L., & Seligman, M. E. P. (2003). Prevention that works for children and youth. *American Psychologist, 58,* 425–432.

Welch, B. L. (1938). The significance of the difference between two means when the population variances are unequal. *Biometrika, 29,* 350–362.

Welter, W., Canale, S., Fiola, C., Sweeney, K., & L'Armand, K. (2002). Effects of social loafing on individual satisfaction and individual productivity. *Psi Chi Journal of Undergraduate Research, 7,* 142–144.

Whalen, C. K. (2001). Attention-deficit/hyperactivity disorder, neural basis of. In N. J. Smelser & P. B. Baltes (Eds.), *International encyclopedia of social and behavioral sciences* (Vol. 2, pp. 875–878). Oxford: Elsevier.

Wicherts, J. M., Borboom, D., Kats, J. & Molenaar, D. (2006). The poor availability of psychological research data for reanalysis. *American Psychologist, 61,* 726–728.

Wight, R. D. (1993). The Pavlov-Yerkes connection: What was its origin? *Psychological Record, 43,* 351–360.

Wilkinson, L., & the Task Force on Statistical Inference. (1999). Statistical methods in psychology journals: Guidelines and explanations. *American Psychologist, 54,* 594–604.

Yacker, N., & Weinberg, S. L. (1990). Care and justice moral orientation: A scale for its assessment. *Journal of Personality Assessment, 55,* 18–27.

Yesavage, J. A. (1989). Techniques for cognitive training of memory in age-associated memory impairment. *Archives of Gerontology & Geriatrics,* Suppl. 1, 185–190.

Young, J. R. (2001, July 6). The cat-and-mouse game of plagiarism detection. *Chronicle of Higher Education, 47,* p. A26.

Zimbardo, P. G. (1973). On the ethics of intervention in human psychological research: With special reference to the Stanford prison experiment. *Cognition, 2,* 243–256.

Credits

Index